John Calvin as Teacher, Pastor, and Theologian

John Calvin as Teacher, Pastor, and Theologian

The Shape of His Writings and Thought

Randall C. Zachman

Baker Academic

Grand Rapids, Michigan

Published by Baker Academic
a division of Baker Publishing Group
P.O. Box 6287, Grand Rapids, MI 49516-6287
www.bakeracademic.com

Printed in the United States of America

Library of Congress Cataloging-in-Publication Data

Zachman, Randall C., 1953–
    John Calvin as teacher, pastor, and theologian : the shape of his writings and thought / Randall C. Zachman.
        p.   cm.
    Includes bibliographical references and index.
    ISBN 10: 0-8010-3129-X (pbk.)
    ISBN 978-0-8010-3129-8 (pbk.)
    1. Calvin, Jean, 1509–1564. I. Title.
BX9418.Z33 2006
230'.42092—dc22   2005031955

CONTENTS

PREFACE

This book has arisen out of two insights into the theology of John Calvin that I discovered in the course of teaching his theology for the past two decades. First, I learned that Calvin had as his ultimate objective teaching every single man, woman, and child how to read Scripture for themselves, so that they might apply its genuine meaning to every aspect of their lives. To this end, Calvin dedicated himself in his office as teacher to training orthodox and evangelical pastors who would act as guides to the interpretation of Scripture for their congregations, primarily by means of the *Institutes* and biblical commentaries. Calvin also acted as a pastor in Geneva, teaching the ordinary Christians in his congregation the sum of the doctrine of piety in the *Catechism*, and then guiding their own reading of Scripture by his exposition and application of Scripture in his sermons. Calvin envisioned the church as a school in which all Christians act as both students and teachers, under the instruction of the Holy Spirit, the author of Scripture. In this school, teachers who guide others in their reading must always be willing to be taught themselves, both by other teachers and by their students, whereas students must also be ready to teach as well as to be taught. It has been my delight to discover more of Calvin's vision of the "teachable teacher" with my own students, who became my teachers as well. I would therefore like to dedicate the first part of this book to my students who studied Calvin together with me for the first two decades of my teaching career, as well as to the teacher, Brian A. Gerrish, who above all others taught me what to look for in Calvin's theology.

Second, I discovered that for all his interest in teaching and reading Scripture, Calvin was a deeply contemplative theologian, who claimed that the invisible God becomes somewhat visible to us in what he called "living images of God," which form the self-manifestation of God. Calvin exhorted the godly to contemplate these living images of God for themselves, in conjunction with their hearing and reading of Scripture, so that they might perceive, feel, and enjoy the goodness of God portrayed therein and be drawn upwards to God from the inmost affection of their hearts, being transformed themselves thereby into the image of God. Calvin pointed to two living images in particular in which the fountain and author of every good is manifested to us, the universe and Jesus Christ. As a theologian, therefore, Calvin was especially concerned to follow the analogy and anagoge between the visible self-manifestation of God and the realities manifested therein. I would like to dedicate the second part of this book to my wife Carolyne Call, for she has consistently pointed me to the living image of God in the beauty of creation and especially in the other creatures with whom we share our life on earth, and she has been for me an especially vivid image of the goodness of our Creator and Redeemer.

ABBREVIATIONS

Calvin: Commentaries	*Calvin: Commentaries*, trans. and ed. Joseph Haroutunian (Philadelphia: Westminster, 1958)
Calvin: Theological Treatises	*Calvin: Theological Treatises*, ed. J. K. S. Reid (Philadelphia: Westminster, 1954)
CNTC	*Calvin's New Testament Commentaries*, ed. David W. Torrance and Thomas F. Torrance, 12 vols. (Grand Rapids: Eerdmans, 1959–72)
CO	*Ioannis Calvini opera quae supersunt omnia*, ed. Wilhelm Baum, Edward Cunitz, and Edward Reuss, 59 vols., Corpus reformatorum 29–87 (Brunsvigae: Schwetschke [Bruhn], 1863–1900)
Comm.	Commentary
CR	Corpus reformatorum, vols. 1–28, *Philippi Melanthonis opera* (Halis Saxonum: Schwetschke, 1834–60)
CTS	*The Commentaries of John Calvin on the Old Testament*, 30 vols. (Edinburgh: Calvin Translation Society, 1843–48)
Inst. and LCC	John Calvin, *Institutio christianae religionis* (Geneva: Rob. Stephani, 1559). Cited by book, chapter, and section, from *OS* 3–5, followed by LCC references to Calvin, *Institutes of the Christian Religion*, ed. John T. McNeill and trans. Ford Lewis Battles, 2 vols., Library of Christian Classics (Philadelphia: Westminster, 1960)
Letters	*The Letters of John Calvin*, trans. Jules Bonnet, 4 vols. (New York: Franklin, 1972)
LW	*Luther's Works*, ed. Jaroslav Pelikan and Helmut T. Lehmann, American edition (St. Louis: Concordia; Philadelphia: Fortress, 1955–)

Abbreviations

MWA	*Melanchthons Werke in Auswahl*, ed. Robert Stupperich (Gütersloh: Gerd Mohn, 1961)
OE	*Ioannis Calvini opera omnia*, series 2, *Opera exegetica veteris et novi testamenti* (Geneva: Librairie Droz, 1992–)
OS	*Ioannis Calvini opera selecta*, ed. Peter Barth, Wilhelm Niesel, and Dora Scheuner, 5 vols. (Munich: Kaiser, 1926–52)
Romanos	*Iohannis Calvini commentarius in epistolam Pauli ad Romanos*, ed. T. H. L. Parker, Studies in the History of Christian Thought 22 (Leiden: Brill, 1981)
Tracts and Treatises	John Calvin, *Tracts and Treatises,* trans. Henry Beveridge, 3 vols. (Grand Rapids: Eerdmans, 1958)
WA	*D. Martin Luthers Werke: Kritische Gesamtausgabe* (Weimar: Böhlau, 1883–)

PART 1

Calvin as Teacher and Pastor

John Calvin lived during a time when many Christians, both Roman and evangelical, recognized that the ministry of the church was in crisis. It is difficult for us to imagine what the training of ministers must have been like before seminaries were created precisely to address the lack of adequate ministerial formation during this period. John Calvin was well aware of the dire consequences of this lack of ministerial formation. According to Calvin, neither bishops nor priests were skilled in the interpretation of Scripture or particularly adept at teaching the summary of the doctrine that leads to genuine piety. "Those who were regarded as the leaders of faith neither understood thy Word, nor greatly cared for it. They drove unhappy people to and fro with strange doctrines, and deluded them with I know not what follies."[1] Due to the neglect of Scripture and its teaching by the leaders of the church, Calvin thought that the ordinary people in the church were liable to believe anything that their pastors told them, leading to the superstitious worship of God.

1. John Calvin and Jacopo Sadoleto, *A Reformation Debate: Sadoleto's Letter to the Genevans and Calvin's Reply*, ed. John C. Olin (Grand Rapids: Baker, 1976), 82.

"Among the people themselves, the highest veneration paid to thy Word was to revere it at a distance, as a thing inaccessible, and abstain from all investigation of it. Owing to this supine state of the pastors, and this stupidity of the people, every place was filled with pernicious errors, falsehoods, and superstition."[2] The neglect of Scripture was compounded by the lack of adequate catechesis for ordinary Christians. "Then, the rudiments in which I had been instructed were of a kind which could neither properly train me for the legitimate worship of thy Deity, nor train me aright for the duties of the Christian life."[3] Ordinary Christians were turned away from Scripture to human-made images, statues, and pictures in the churches, which were understood to be the "books of the unlearned." Thus, the neglect of Scripture by the ministers of the church led directly to the superstitious adoration of images, and the confinement of God to those images.

From the time of his "sudden conversion to teachableness" between 1532 and 1535, Calvin dedicated all of his efforts to addressing the neglect of the summary of godly doctrine and the interpretation of Scripture by both the pastors and the ordinary people in the church. The astonishing literary production of Calvin between 1535 and 1564 bears witness to the tremendous energy and dedication he gave to this effort. During this time he produced five different editions of the *Institutes*, as well as commentaries on the entire New Testament, with the exception of 2 and 3 John and Revelation, the "five books of Moses," Joshua, the entire Psalter, and all of the prophets except for Ezek. 21–48. He also produced three editions of his *Catechism*, and preached sermons through entire books of Scripture, including Genesis, Deuteronomy, 1 and 2 Samuel, Job, Galatians, and Ephesians, to name but a few. Calvin dedicated all of these efforts to the restoration of the sum of godly doctrine and the proper interpretation of Scripture to the future pastors of the church, so that they might teach the rudiments of the faith and apply the genuine meaning of Scripture to their congregations.

The work of Calvin scholars over the past decades has drawn attention to the full scope of Calvin's contribution to restoring the ministry of the church. For years, the interpretation of Calvin had been dominated by considerations of the doctrine taught by Calvin in the final edition of the *Institutes*. Ever since T. H. L. Parker called our attention to the importance of the commentaries of Calvin, however, a number of scholars, among them David Steinmetz and his students, have provided detailed analyses of Calvin's work as a biblical interpreter, in light of his predecessors and contemporaries. The further work done on the sermons of Calvin

2. Ibid.
3. Ibid., 87.

in the *Supplementa Calviniana* has greatly enhanced our understanding of Calvin as a preacher, again first highlighted by T. H. L. Parker in his book *The Oracles of God* and developed more fully by the work of Richard Stauffer, Wilhelmus Moehn, and Max Engammare.[4] Our understanding of Calvin's work as a pastor has been further clarified by the research of Robert Kingdon and his students on the Consistory records of Geneva during Calvin's time in that city.[5] Building on the work of these scholars, this book argues that all of these efforts are best understood in light of Calvin's attempt to revive the ministry of the church by restoring the summary of pious doctrine and the genuine interpretation of Scripture to pastors and their congregations.

Calvin understood himself to be called to two distinct offices: the office of teacher, and the office of pastor. The teacher has as his audience future pastors of the church, not only in Geneva but also throughout Christendom, as well as educated and theologically interested laity, especially magistrates. The office of teacher entails both the teaching of the summary of the doctrine of piety, as in Melanchthon's *Loci* or Calvin's *Institutes*, and the exposition of Scripture in commentaries. The office of pastor has as its audience ordinary Christians in a particular congregation, who may know only a vernacular language and may even be unable to read. The pastor teaches the young the rudiments of the doctrine of piety in the Catechism, and then expounds Scripture and applies it to the life of the congregation, not only in public worship, but also in private visitation.

The first part of the book addresses Calvin's understanding of his work as a teacher and pastor, as well as the objectives he had for each aspect of his work. We begin by examining the life of Calvin, with particular emphasis on those figures who most decisively shaped his own work as a teacher and pastor. Since Calvin regarded Philip Melanchthon to be the greatest teacher of the evangelical church, who directly influenced the development of Calvin's *Institutes*, we will highlight the distinctiveness of Calvin's understanding of the office of teacher by comparing him and Melanchthon on the proper method of teaching in the evangelical church. We then turn to the programmatic chapter of this section, which lays out the offices of teacher and pastor, and the works Calvin produced in

4. Richard Stauffer, *Dieu, la création et la Providence dans la prédication de Calvin* (Las Vegas: P. Lang, 1978); Jean Calvin, *Sermons sur la Genèse, chapitres 1,1–11,4*, ed. Max Engammare (Neukirchen-Vluyn: Neukirchener Verlag, 2000); Wilhelmus H. Th. Moehn, *"God Calls Us to His Service": The Relation between God and His Audience in Calvin's Sermons on Acts* (Geneva: Droz, 2001).

5. See especially *Registers of the Consistory of Geneva in the Time of Calvin,* vol. 1, *1542–1544,* ed. Robert M. Kingdon, Thomas A. Lambert, and Isabella M. Watt, trans. M. Wallace McDonald (Grand Rapids: Eerdmans, 1996).

light of each office. The following chapters examine each of these works in greater detail, showing how the *Institutes* and biblical commentaries were meant to train future pastors in the summary of godly doctrine and the genuine interpretation of Scripture. We then turn to Calvin's educational efforts as a pastor, beginning with his efforts to develop a clear and compelling summary of the rudiments of the faith in a catechism. This section ends with a consideration of Calvin's objectives as a preacher, using the sermons on Ephesians as an example. As we shall see, all of these efforts culminate with the restoration of the reading of Scripture by unlearned and ordinary Christians, women and men, children and adults, servants and masters, under the guidance of their pastors, who themselves are guided by their teachers.

1

THE LIFE AND WORK OF JOHN CALVIN

In order to understand Calvin as a teacher, pastor, and theologian, it is necessary first of all to set him in the context of those scholars and theologians who most influenced his own development. John Calvin (1509–64) was deeply committed to two movements that emerged at the beginning of the sixteenth century: the recovery of classical and patristic literature, best exemplified by Guillaume Budé and Desiderius Erasmus; and the recovery of the gospel in the midst of the Roman Church, best exemplified by Martin Luther and Philip Melanchthon. Calvin used the skills and insights gained by the recovery of the liberal arts in his day to teach the gospel and interpret the Scriptures with clarity and integrity.

Calvin was initially educated in Noyon in the home of Charles de Hangest, a local aristocrat, and then at the College de Montaigue at the University of Paris. While at Paris, Calvin had the opportunity of studying with one of the finest Latinists there, Mathurin Cordier, who was himself part of the recovery of classical Latin in the sixteenth century, and who first awakened in Calvin a love for good letters and refined Ciceronian

This essay was originally published in a slightly different form under the title "John Calvin," in *The Reformation Theologians*, ed. Carter Lindberg (Oxford: Blackwell, 2002), 184–97. Reprinted by permission.

Latin. "When my father sent me as a boy to Paris I had done only the rudiments of Latin. For a short time, however, you were an instructor sent to me by God to teach me the true method of learning, so that I might afterwards be a little more proficient."[1] Throughout his life, Calvin sought to write in a refined, clear, and vivid style of Latin. Calvin then pursued the study of law at the request of his father, first at Orleans, and then at Bourges. While at Orleans, Calvin studied classical Greek with the German Hellenist Melchior Wolmar, who reinforced Calvin's love of classical arts and letters, and who taught Calvin Greek. "The first time my father sent me to study civil law, it was at your instigation and under your tuition that I also took up the study of Greek, of which you were at that time a most distinguished teacher." Even though Calvin was not able to complete his studies with Wolmar due to his father's death, he nonetheless acknowledges that he gave him "a good grounding in the rudiments of the language and that was of great help to [him] later on."[2] Indeed, so deeply committed was Calvin to the study of classical Latin and Greek literature that he may have ruined his health studying both law and literature during his time as a law student. Calvin continued to study the writings of classical authors for the rest of his life, especially Plato, whom he deemed to be the most sober and religious of the philosophers, as well as Cicero, Seneca, and Aristotle. Indeed, like Erasmus, Calvin thought that it was impossible to interpret Scripture properly without a thorough knowledge of classical literature.

After his father's death in 1531, Calvin directed the whole of his attention to classical literature, studying at the newly founded College of Royal Readers in Paris. There Calvin came under the influence of the two great philologists of his day, Guillaume Budé and Desiderius Erasmus. Calvin may have come across the work of Budé in his study of law, especially his *Annotationes in Pandectas* (1508), which was intended as a commentary on Roman civil law and contained a tremendous amount of lexical information and learning.[3] He certainly became familiar with Budé's philological work in his massive Greek lexicon, the *Commentarii linguae Graecae* (1529), which he used for the rest of his life with high appreciation for the learning of its author. Calvin also came to appreciate the labors of Erasmus in the recovery of Greek and Latin literature, especially in his critical editions of the classical authors and church fathers, and also in his collections in the *Adagia* (1508).

Calvin learned from Budé and Erasmus the importance of establishing reliable critical editions, and of interpreting texts in light of their

1. Dedication to Comm. (commentary) on 1 Thessalonians, *CNTC* 8:331.
2. Dedication to Comm. on 2 Corinthians, *CNTC* 9:1.
3. T. H. L. Parker, *Calvin's New Testament Commentaries*, 2nd ed. (Louisville: Westminster John Knox, 1993), 187.

literary, linguistic, and cultural contexts, so that their genuine meaning would emerge from that context. He first applied this method to Seneca's treatise *De clementia*, in a work published at his own expense in April 1532. The work itself was an attempt to restore Seneca to his rightful place of honor in the world of the most learned, over against the critical comments of Quintilian about Seneca's inferior Latin style. In the work, Calvin's clear preference for Budé over Erasmus comes to light, a preference that would remain in evidence to the end of his life. Calvin refers to Budé as "the first ornament and pillar in literature, on account of whom our France today claims for itself the palm of learning."[4] Erasmus, on the other hand, is referred to as "the second glory and darling of literature,"[5] who missed certain things in Seneca's treatise even though he published two works on it. This deference to the learning and erudition of Budé and critical independence over against Erasmus are tendencies Calvin will display throughout his life, even after he turns from restoring Seneca to his rightful place in the reading of the most learned in the world of letters, to concentrate on restoring Scripture to its rightful place in the reading of the unlearned in the church.

John Calvin first appears to have come to an appreciation of the writings of Martin Luther in the years 1533–34, during which time he most likely experienced his "sudden conversion to teachableness" detailed in his preface to his Psalms Commentary. "First, when I was too firmly addicted to the papal superstitions to be drawn easily out of such a deep mire, by a sudden conversion He brought my mind (already more rigid than suited my age) to submission."[6] In the only letter written directly to Luther (not actually delivered), Calvin addresses him as "the very excellent pastor of the Christian Church, my much respected father."[7] It is quite likely that Calvin viewed Luther as his father in the faith, as the one who brought him to faith in the gospel, most likely through his own reading of Luther's 1520 treatises *The Freedom of a Christian* and *The Babylonian Captivity of the Christian Church.*[8] Calvin had the highest praise for the role of Luther in restoring the church of his day, viewing him as an apostle raised up miraculously by God to free the

4. *CO* 5:54, cited in Parker, *Calvin's New Testament Commentaries*, 188.

5. John Calvin, *Calvin's Commentary on Seneca's "De clementia,"* trans. Ford Lewis Battles and André Malan Hugo (Leiden: Brill, 1969), 7.

6. *CO* 31:21; *Calvin: Commentaries*, 52. See B. A. Gerrish, "The Pathfinder: Calvin's Image of Martin Luther," in *The Old Protestantism and the New: Essays on the Reformation Heritage* (Edinburgh: Clark, 1982), 27–48.

7. *CO* 12:7; *Letters* 1:440.

8. I say this because the last two sections of the 1536 *Institutes* directly echo these two treatises, whereas the first section directly echoes Luther's *Small Catechism*. See Alexandre Ganoczy, *The Young Calvin*, trans. David Foxgrover and Wade Provo (Philadelphia: Westminster, 1987), 137–45.

church from the papacy. "Concerning Luther there is no reason . . . to be in any doubt when . . . we openly bear witness that we consider him a distinguished apostle of Christ whose labour and ministry have done most in these times to bring back the purity of the gospel."[9] Because of Luther's role in restoring the gospel, Calvin was willing to acknowledge that the evangelical churches were in fact founded on his ministry, as the divine restoration of apostolic doctrine. "God raised up Luther and others, who held forth a torch to light us into the way of salvation, and on whose ministry our churches are founded and built."[10] Calvin was firmly convinced by Luther's claim that justification by faith alone apart from works was the turning point of the controversy with Rome, and that such faith could only be created and sustained by the preaching of the gospel of the free grace and mercy of God in Jesus Christ, through the power of the Holy Spirit. Calvin also agreed with Luther, over against Zwingli, that the sacraments are signs appended to the gospel to aid and strengthen faith.[11]

Calvin began to have a more complicated relationship with Luther after the attack Luther launched on Heinrich Bullinger in 1544. Calvin was quite critical of Luther's temper and pride, exacerbated by the fact that he surrounded himself with flatterers who would not point out his shortcomings. "Would that he had been more observant and careful in the acknowledgment of his own vices. Flatterers have done him much mischief, since he is naturally too prone to be over-indulgent to himself."[12] Calvin realized that it was the very vehemence and tenacity of Luther that made him such an effective opponent of the papacy.

> But of this I do earnestly desire to put you in mind, that you would consider how eminent a man Luther is, and the excellence of the endowments wherewith he is gifted, with what strength of mind and resolute constancy, with how great skill, with what great efficacy and power of doctrinal statement, he hath hitherto devoted his whole energy to overthrow the reign of Antichrist, and at the same time to diffuse far and near the doctrine of salvation.[13]

9. *CO* 6:250; *The Bondage and Liberation of the Will*, trans. A. N. S. Lane (Grand Rapids: Baker, 1996), 28.

10. *CO* 6:459; *The Necessity of Reforming the Church* (1543), in *Calvin: Theological Treatises*, 185.

11. For a detailed comparison of Luther and Calvin on the nature of faith, see Randall C. Zachman, *The Assurance of Faith: Conscience in the Theology of Martin Luther and John Calvin* (Louisville: Westminster John Knox, 2005).

12. Calvin to Heinrich Bullinger, 25 November 1544, *CO* 11:774; *Letters* 1:433.

13. *CO* 11:774; *Letters* 1:433.

However, when Luther's vehemence was directed against his fellow preachers of the gospel, it became a great liability.

Calvin was also critical of Luther's method of interpreting Scripture. As early as 1540, he wrote to Pierre Viret concerning Luther's commentary on Isaiah: "Luther is not so particular as to propriety of expression or the historical accuracy; he is satisfied when he can draw from it some fruitful doctrine."[14] After Luther's death, Calvin made such criticisms of Luther's exegesis more publicly, going out of his way in his Genesis commentary to criticize the "groundless speculations" Luther made in his own lectures on Genesis. When other Lutherans such as Westphal took strong exception to these critical comments, Calvin responded, "If I was not permitted at any point to depart from the opinion of Luther, it was utterly ridiculous of me to undertake the office of interpretation."[15] By demonstrating his own independence from Luther, Calvin was attempting to challenge the subservient attitude to Luther he saw in others, which he thought undermined Luther's own efforts to restore the preaching of the gospel and the interpretation of Scripture in the church of his day. Calvin was willing to give Luther the pride of place in the restoration of the church in his day, but he was not willing to let Luther be the dominant individual in the newly restored church.

> We all of us do acknowledge that we are much indebted to him. Neither shall I submit myself unwillingly, but be quite content, that he may bear the chief sway, provided that he can manage to conduct himself with moderation. Howbeit, in the Church we must always be upon our guard, lest we pay too great a deference to men. For it is all over with her, when a single individual, be he whosoever you please, has more authority than all the rest, especially where this very person does not scruple to try how far he may go.[16]

After his sudden conversion to teachableness, most likely through the writings of Martin Luther, Calvin was led first to internal exile within France, and then to exile in the city of Basel in the years 1535–36. While in Basel, Calvin most likely first studied Hebrew under the tutelage of the great Christian Hebraist Sebastian Münster.[17] Calvin also came into contact with the teaching and exegesis of the Swiss reformers, especially John Oecolampadius and Ulrich Zwingli. Oecolampadius had been the

14. *CO* 11:36; *Letters* 1:188.

15. Calvin to Francis Burkhardt, 27 February 1555, *CO* 15:454.

16. Calvin to Philip Melanchthon, 28 June 1545, *CO* 12:99; *Letters* 1:467.

17. Max Engammare, *"Johannes Calvinus trium linguarum peritus?* La question de l'Hebreu," *Bibliotheque d'Humanisme et Renaissance* 58 (1996); Darryl Phillips, "An Inquiry into the Extent of the Abilities of John Calvin as a Hebraist" (D.Phil. thesis, Oxford University, 1998).

reformer of Basel until his death in 1531, and was deeply admired by Calvin for the depth of his learning and for his skill as a biblical interpreter. In the letter to Viret cited above, Calvin discusses the comments of Oecolampadius on Isaiah: "No one, as I think, has hitherto more diligently applied himself to this pursuit than Oecolampadius, who has not always, however, reached the full scope or meaning."[18] Calvin appreciated the way Oecolampadius recovered for the church of his day the symbolic thinking of the fathers, especially about the sacraments, over against the language of substance that had dominated the papacy after the Fourth Lateran Council. While in Basel, Calvin undoubtedly read Zwingli's *Commentary on True and False Religion* of 1525.[19] Calvin was persuaded by Zwingli's claim that the true body of Christ is in heaven, where it will remain until he comes again in glory. He was also persuaded by Zwingli's criticism of the Roman doctrine of ex opere operato, for that bound the efficacy of the sacraments too much with the ministry of the church and not with the free mercy of God in Christ through the Holy Spirit. Calvin also seems to have been decisively influenced by Zwingli's description of God as the freely self-giving fountain of every good thing, both as Creator and as Redeemer. However, Calvin throughout his life was highly critical of the way Zwingli divorced the sacraments from the self-offer of Christ, making them empty signs. He was also critical of Zwingli's disorderly method of teaching, and of his exegesis, which wandered too far from the text. "Zwingli, although he is not wanting in a fit and ready exposition, yet, because he takes too much liberty, often wanders far from the meaning of the prophet."[20] Throughout his life, Calvin demonstrated more respect for Oecolampadius than for Zwingli, viewing Oecolampadius as the more learned, moderate, sober, and diligent of the two reformers. When Osiander wrote against the Swiss, Calvin made this protest to Melanchthon: "For what good purpose could it serve to assault the Zwinglians every third line, and to attack Zwingli himself in such an unmannerly style; and not even to spare Oecolampadius, that holy servant of God, whom I wish he resembled, even in being half as good, in which case he would certainly stand far higher in my esteem than he does?" Calvin does note, however, that the memory of both Zwingli and Oecolampadius "ought to be held in honorable esteem by all the godly."[21]

Calvin's sudden conversion to the gospel preached by Luther, Zwingli, and Oecolampadius meant that he felt called to teach the same gospel, and to restore the reading of Scripture, for everyone in the church, especially

18. *CO* 11:36; *Letters* 1:188.
19. Ganoczy, *Young Calvin*, 90–102, 151–58.
20. Calvin to Viret, 19 May 1540, *CO* 11:36; *Letters* 1:188.
21. Calvin to Melanchthon, 21 January 1545, *CO* 12:11; *Letters* 1:437–38.

those whom Calvin called "the unlearned" (those with no knowledge of, or training in, Greek, Hebrew, or Latin). It is clear that this meant producing catechetical works for the unlearned, such as the first edition of the *Institutes*, as well as comments on Scripture to guide their reading into its proper meaning. However, Calvin saw neither the office of teacher nor that of interpreter as involving any public work, but rather pursued a life of quiet retirement. We owe it to Guillaume Farel to have presented to Calvin the call of God to the public ministry of teaching and preaching the gospel, when Farel summoned Calvin to help in the restoration of the church in Geneva, under the threat of God's wrath were he to refuse this call. "But William Farel forced me to stay in Geneva not so much by advice or urging as by command, which had the power of God's hand laid violently upon me from heaven."[22] Calvin accepted this call, first as teacher of Scripture, then as pastor, in the newly restored church of Geneva, with absolutely no training either as a public teacher or as a pastor. Calvin was therefore initiated into his public ministry by both Farel and his colleague from the Pays-de-Vaud, Pierre Viret.

Calvin always understood himself as first assisting, and then inheriting, the work of restoring the church first begun in Geneva by Farel and Viret. "For when with great labor and much risk you had set your hands to raise up the church at Geneva, I arrived later first of all as your assistant, and then afterwards I was left behind as your successor, to strive to the best of my ability to carry on the work that you had begun so successfully and well."[23] Calvin was deeply impressed by the prophetic fire and tenacity of Farel, but was also aware that this could lead him to become overardent and vehement, making those already opposed to him into his hardened enemies. Commenting on this aspect of Farel's personality to Bucer, Calvin says, "It becomes us, however, in the case of so eminent an instrument of Christ, in some degree to pass by his over-ardent spirit and vehemency of manner."[24] Calvin was equally impressed by the calm moderation of Pierre Viret, who manifested not only quiet self-control even when angry, but even a sense of humor most appreciated by the citizens of Geneva.[25] Throughout the rest of his ministry, Calvin attempted, with varying degrees of success, to wed the prophetic zeal and tenacity of Farel (reminiscent of Luther)

22. *CO* 31:23; *Calvin: Commentaries*, 53.

23. Dedication to Titus, *CNTC* 10:347.

24. Calvin to Martin Bucer, 15 October 1541, *CO* 11:296; *Letters* 1:290. See David N. Wiley, "Calvin's Friendship with Guillaume Farel," in *Calvin and His Contemporaries: Calvin Studies Society Papers 1995–1997* (Grand Rapids: CRC Product Services, 1998), 187–204.

25. Robert D. Linder, "Brothers in Christ: Pierre Viret and John Calvin as Soul Mates and Co-laborers in the Work of the Reformation," in *Calvin and His Contemporaries*, 134–58.

with the moderation and self-control of Viret (reminiscent of Bucer and Melanchthon). He consistently referred to Farel and Viret as his "most amiable and excellent brothers" and appears to have forged close and lifelong bonds of genuine friendship with each, sharing with them his inmost concerns, hopes, and fears. "I think there has never been in ordinary life a circle of friends so heartily bound to each other as we have been in our ministry."[26]

After the expulsion of Calvin and Farel from Geneva in 1538, Calvin thought he was no longer suited for the ministry and that he should instead pursue the life of quiet retirement from which he had been diverted by Farel in 1536. It was the great Strasbourg reformer Martin Bucer who refused to let Calvin go back into hiding, comparing him to Jonah in his desire to flee from his calling from God to be a teacher and pastor in the church. "Then loosed from my vocation and free [to follow my own desire], I decided to live quietly as a private individual. But that most distinguished minister of Christ, Martin Bucer, dragged me back again to a new post with the same curse which Farel had used against me. Terrified by the example of Jonah, which he had set before me, I continued the work of teaching."[27] Calvin came to Strasbourg deeply conscious of his failings as a pastor and teacher in the church. He therefore sought above all else to learn how to become a more effective teacher and pastor. Above any other in his life, Martin Bucer was the one from whom Calvin learned the most about the office of ministry, reflected in his description of Bucer as "that most distinguished minister of Christ."[28] In one of his letters to Bucer, written as Calvin was leaving Strasbourg to return to Geneva in 1541, Calvin addresses him as "my much honored father in the Lord," and acknowledges himself to be subject to Bucer's authority. "And if in any way I do not answer your expectation, you know I am under your power, and subject to your authority. Admonish, chastise, and exercise all the powers of a father over a son."[29] So far as I know, Bucer is the only person besides Luther to whom Calvin referred as his father, and it may be that Luther was Calvin's father in the doctrine of salvation, whereas Bucer was Calvin's father in the ministry.

Calvin especially learned from Bucer how rightly to order the polity and worship of the church, especially with the fourfold office of teacher, pastor, elder, and deacon, and how to order the community via discipline, which Calvin came to describe as the sinews of the body of Christ. Calvin also developed a deep appreciation for Bucer's skill as an interpreter of

26. Dedication to Titus, *CNTC* 10:347.
27. *CO* 31:25; *Calvin: Commentaries*, 54.
28. *CO* 31:25; *Calvin: Commentaries*, 54.
29. Calvin to Martin Bucer, 15 October 1541, *CO* 11:296; *Letters* 1:294–95.

Scripture, demonstrating his great depth of learning and attention to context. Commending Bucer's abilities to Bullinger, Calvin says,

> For Bucer I will answer, that there is no cause why he ought in anything to be suspected by you. Endowed, as indeed he is, with a singularly acute and remarkably clear judgment, there is at the same time, no one who is more religiously desirous to keep within the simplicity of the word of God, and is less given to hunt after niceties of interpretation that are quite foreign to it, but who actually holds them more in abhorrence, than himself.[30]

In this regard, Calvin called Bucer "that most faithful teacher of the Church" and praised his commentaries on Romans and the Psalms in particular. Speaking of his Romans commentary of 1536, Calvin says, "In addition to his profound learning, abundant knowledge, keenness of intellect, wide reading, and many other various excellencies in which he is surpassed by hardly anyone at the present day, this scholar, as we know, is equaled by few and is superior to many. It is to his special credit that no one in our time has been more precise and diligent in interpreting Scripture than he."[31]

If Bucer was a decisive influence on Calvin's effectiveness as a pastor and interpreter of Scripture, Johann Sturm and Philip Melanchthon were equally influential in terms of Calvin's development as a teacher. Calvin was called to teach Scripture at Sturm's new academy in Strasbourg, which not only refined his abilities as an interpreter of Scripture, beginning with the publication of the Romans commentary in 1539, but also gave him a vision of how to train and educate a new generation of pastors in the newly restored church. Calvin's deep appreciation for Sturm's work at the Academy of Strasbourg was to bear fruit twenty years later in the opening of the Geneva Academy in 1559, which had as its primary task the training of future pastors for ministry in Geneva and in France.[32] Calvin also used his time in Strasbourg to redesign the purpose and method of his *Institutes*, under the influence of Melanchthon's 1535 *Loci communes*. The impact of Melanchthon on Calvin was reinforced by the personal meetings they had at the colloquies of Worms and Ratisbon, which Calvin attended as part of the Strasbourg contingent,

---

30. Calvin to Heinrich Bullinger, 12 March 1539, *Letters* 1:114.

31. "John Calvin to Simon Grynaeus," *Romanos* 5.53–59; *CNTC* 8:2. This assessment of Bucer is echoed many years later, when Calvin praises his singular erudition, diligence, and faithfulness in the preface to his Psalms commentary of 1557 (*CO* 31:16).

32. Karin Maag, *Seminary or University? The Genevan Academy and Reformed Higher Education, 1560–1620*, St. Andrews Studies in Reformation History (Aldershot, UK: Scolar; Brookfield, VT: Ashgate, 1995).

leading to an epistolary friendship that would last until Melanchthon's death in 1560.[33]

If Bucer was to Calvin the most distinguished minister of Christ, Melanchthon was to him the "most illustrious light and distinguished teacher of the Church."[34] Calvin has great respect for Melanchthon's work as an interpreter of Scripture, based as it was on his great learning in both biblical and classical literature. Calvin speaks of Melanchthon in glowing terms as "Master Philip, who excels in genius and learning, and is happily versed in the studies of history."[35] He makes similar comments on him in the dedication to his commentary on Romans: "Philip Melanchthon has given us a great deal of light by reason of the outstanding character of both his learning, industry, and the skill of all kinds of knowledge in which he excels, in comparison with those who had published commentaries before him."[36] Calvin was especially impressed by the clear, orderly, and simple plan of teaching that Melanchthon followed in his major theological handbook, the *Loci communes*. In a dedication written for Melanchthon, Calvin says: "You are pleased by an unembellished and frank clarity which, without any concealment, sets a subject before the eyes and explains it. This quality of yours has often stirred in me great admiration, just because it is so rarely found."[37] From 1539 onward, Calvin sought to bring that same clarity to his own *Institutes*, being finally content with the clarity of the order of its topics in the 1559 edition.[38] Like Melanchthon, Calvin understood the office of the teacher to involve guiding future ministers of the church by setting forth the major topics to be sought in their reading of Scripture, so that they might teach this doctrine to their congregations. However, Calvin thought the teacher of godly doctrine not only led the pious and teachable by the hand to show them what they should seek in Scripture, but also contended in hand-to-hand combat with the ungodly enemies of pious doctrine. He found this combative zeal (reminiscent of Farel and Luther) lacking in Melanchthon, and it led him to become increasingly

33. Timothy Wengert, "'We Will Feast Together in Heaven Forever': The Epistolary Friendship of John Calvin and Philip Melanchthon," in *Melanchthon in Europe*, ed. Karin Maag (Grand Rapids: Baker, 1999), 19–44.

34. Calvin to Philip Melanchthon, 13 December 1558, *CO* 17:384–86; *Letters* 3:484.

35. Comm. on Dan. 9:25, *CO* 41:176.

36. "Calvin to Grynaeus," *Romanos* 2.45–47; *CNTC* 8:2.

37. *CO* 6:229–30; *Bondage and Liberation of the Will*, 3.

38. For the influence of Melanchthon on Calvin's *Institutes*, see Richard A. Muller, *The Unaccommodated Calvin: Studies in the Foundation of a Theological Tradition* (New York: Oxford University Press, 2000).

critical of his friend for having a pliant and weak manner of teaching, a tendency Calvin also saw in his friend Martin Bucer.[39]

Both Martin Bucer and Philip Melanchthon were deeply committed to the efforts undertaken in the sixteenth century to heal the rifts created by the attempt to restore the church by the teaching and preaching of the gospel, both between the evangelicals and the Church of Rome, and among the evangelicals themselves. Calvin was deeply suspicious of the attempt to seek an accord with Rome, since he viewed the papacy as being in principle opposed to reform. However, in spite of this difference, Bucer and Melanchthon made Calvin aware of the need to address the question of the catholicity of evangelical doctrine, and its continuity with the previous tradition, in light of the charges of innovation and schism leveled by Rome against the evangelicals. The 1543 edition of the *Institutes* directly addressed these questions, reflecting the enduring influence of Bucer and Melanchthon. Calvin was more enthusiastic about the efforts of Bucer and Melanchthon to unite the divided evangelicals, especially over the question of the Holy Supper of the Lord.[40] Calvin accepted as legitimate the Wittenberg Concord of 1536—drafted by Melanchthon and signed by Luther, Melanchthon, and Bucer—to unite the churches of Wittenberg and Strasbourg. It is also highly likely that he signed the 1540 Augsburg Confession, which included the terms of this concord in the article on the supper (that the body of Christ is both exhibited and presented in the bread and wine). Calvin was convinced (perhaps wrongly) that he and Melanchthon were of one mind concerning the Supper, and that it was therefore possible to reach a union between Wittenberg, Strasbourg, Geneva, and Zurich. For such an agreement to succeed, however, Calvin would need to bring Heinrich Bullinger and the pastors of Zurich from their adherence to Zwingli's position to one that reflected the Wittenberg Concord and the 1540 Confessio Augustana.[41]

Calvin had deep respect for Heinrich Bullinger as his senior pastor in the evangelical churches of the Swiss regions. He consistently referred to him in his letters as his "respected and learned brother." Bullinger was renowned for his learning, both of Scripture and of the fathers, having

---

39. Calvin to Melanchthon, 10 December 1555, *CO* 16:738; *Letters* 3:337. About both Melanchthon and Bucer, Calvin says, "In their method of proceeding they accommodate themselves too much to the time" (Calvin to Farel, 11 May 1541, *CO* 11:217; *Letters* 1:263).

40. See Randall C. Zachman, "The Conciliating Theology of John Calvin," in *Conciliation and Confession: The Struggle for Unity in the Age of Reform, 1415–1648*, ed. Howard Louthan and Randall Zachman (Notre Dame: University of Notre Dame Press, 2004), 89–105.

41. One can see his interest in reaching such an agreement early during his stay in Strasbourg, when he wrote his *Short Treatise on the Holy Supper of Our Lord and Only Saviour Jesus Christ*, 1539, *CO* 5:429–60; *Calvin: Theological Treatises*, 140–66.

been brought to the evangelical side by comparing the writings of Luther with those of the fathers, and finding Luther to be more catholic than Rome was.[42] Calvin sought the counsel of Bullinger in matters regarding the church of Geneva, beginning with the convulsions in Geneva leading to the expulsion of Calvin and Farel in 1538.[43] However, Calvin was aware that Geneva and Zurich were not of one mind regarding the meaning of the Holy Supper of the Lord. At the urging of Farel, Calvin went to Zurich (itself a sign of deference to the greater authority of the church there) in order to initiate talks designed to reach an agreement on the Supper, which finally came to fruition in the Zurich Consensus of 1549, published in 1551. This ecumenical achievement of Calvin, demonstrating an irenic side of his nature not often noted, was quickly brought under a cloud by the harsh attacks on it, first by Westphal and then by Heshusius, both of whom rejected the claim made by Calvin that the Zurich Consensus reflected the teaching of the Augsburg Confession. Calvin himself describes this period of his life as one of the most bitter, made all the more painful by the utter silence of Philip Melanchthon on the dispute, perhaps indicating his own problems with the Consensus.[44] However, Bullinger never wavered in his adherence to the consensus reached with Calvin, as is reflected in the Second Helvetic Confession, written by Bullinger as a statement of his faith two years after the death of Calvin.

From his association with other reformers of his day, the picture that emerges of Calvin is significantly different from the commonplace picture of Calvin. Calvin was first of all a highly learned person, trained and skilled in the interpretation of Hebrew, Greek, and Latin texts, deeply committed to the recovery of letters brought about by the labors of Guillaume Budé and Desiderius Erasmus. Calvin was also a teacher of the gospel of Jesus Christ, whose teaching was founded on the ministry and teaching of his father in faith, the apostle of Christ, Martin Luther. However, like Zwingli and Oecolampadius, Calvin was not only concerned with the Roman denial of justification by faith alone; he was also dismayed by the superstitious Roman worship of the signs of spiritual realities instead of the spiritual realities themselves, confining our minds

42. Parker, *Calvin's New Testament Commentaries*, 72.

43. Calvin to Bullinger, 21 February 1538, *CO* 10:153–54; *Letters* 1:65–67.

44. "And as though it were not enough for me to suffer the inhumanity of neighbors, a throng of evil-driven men from the frozen sea [Germany] stirred up (*accenderet*) against me a storm I have no words to describe. I am still speaking of internal enemies of the church, proud proclaimers of the gospel of Christ, who, because I do not accept their crass explanations of [the Lord's Supper as] devouring the flesh of Christ, are roused against me more violently than my open enemies. . . . Moreover they all show great ingratitude when they attack on the flank and rear a man who is laboring in defense of the common cause, and deserves their support" (*CO* 31:33; *Calvin: Commentaries*, 56–57).

and hearts to earth rather than lifting them by degrees to heaven. Calvin was called to the public ministry of teacher and pastor by the prophetic Guillaume Farel, in the company of the moderate and self-controlled Pierre Viret. Calvin was called back to the ministry by his father in the ministry, Martin Bucer, who advanced his training both as pastor and as interpreter of Scripture. Calvin was decisively shaped as a teacher by Johann Sturm and especially by Philip Melanchthon, whose method of teaching via *Loci communes* Calvin followed in every edition of the *Institutes* from 1539 to 1559. Finally, in large part under the influence of Bucer and Melanchthon, Calvin was profoundly committed to the cause of ecumenical unity among the evangelicals, even though his hopes in this regard were frustrated. In sum, Calvin saw himself as both a teacher and a pastor, called to restore the preaching of the gospel to the church of Christ, by restoring the right way to read Scripture both to pastors and to unlearned laity, in the company of other learned and godly teachers and pastors, such as Budé, Erasmus, Luther, Oecolampadius, Zwingli, Farel, Viret, Bucer, Sturm, Melanchthon, and Bullinger.

2

CALVIN AND MELANCHTHON ON THE OFFICE OF THE EVANGELICAL TEACHER

John Calvin and Philip Melanchthon first came into personal contact with each other in 1538, and in the ensuing three years they developed a friendship that was to last until the death of Melanchthon in 1560.[1] Their friendship was no doubt founded on their love for each other

1. On the friendship between Calvin and Melanchthon, see Philip Schaff, *History of the Christian Church* (Grand Rapids: Eerdmans, 1910), 8:385–98; A. Lang, "Melanchthon und Calvin," in *Reformierte Kirchen-Zeitung*, 21 February–28 March 1897; Émile Doumergue, *Jean Calvin: Les hommes et les choses de son temps*, vol. 2 (Lausanne: Bridel, 1902), 545–61; Williston Walker, *John Calvin* (New York: Schocken, 1969), 238–44; B. Hagglund, *History of Theology*, trans. G. Lund (St. Louis: Concordia, 1968); J. T. Hickman, "The Friendship of Melanchthon and Calvin," *Westminster Theological Journal* 38 (1975–76): 152–65; Timothy Wengert, "'We Will Feast Together in Heaven Forever': The Epistolary Friendship of John Calvin and Philip Melanchthon," in *Melanchthon in Europe*, ed. Karin Maag (Grand Rapids: Baker, 1999), 19–44.

This essay was originally published in a slightly different form under the title "Restoring Access to the Fountain: Calvin and Melanchthon on the Task of Evangelical Theology," in *Calvin Studies Society Papers, 1995, 1997*, ed. David Foxgrover (Grand Rapids: CRC Product Services, 1998), 205–28. Reprinted by permission.

and their mutual love for piety, but it was above all founded on their genuine respect for each other as highly gifted teachers of the church. Melanchthon and Calvin were learned men who had been trained in the interpretation of Greek, Hebrew, and Latin texts, and who sought to use their learning to build up the piety of Christians and to restore the church after it had fallen into ruin at the hands of the pope, the monks, and the scholastic theologians. Both theologians were convinced that the way to build up piety and restore the church was to open access to the fountains of pious doctrine and learned piety that had been blocked up or polluted by the Roman Church.

However, their understanding of the sources of pious doctrine not only united them, but also was the source of tensions that increasingly tried their friendship. According to Melanchthon, the Roman Church had been led astray above all by the obscure, speculative, and disputatious theology of the scholastics, which distorted both Scripture and philosophy, especially the philosophy of Aristotle, and resulted in a barbarous method of inquiry and an obscure style of presenting doctrine, thus making doctrinal consensus impossible. The way to restore the church, therefore, is to train the future teachers of the church by returning to the sources of genuine doctrine found in true philosophy, Scripture, and the consensus of the early church, so that students might learn the proper way to inquire into and teach true doctrine.

> All sane-minded men admit that disputatious theology has gone so far in vanity that Christian doctrine ought to be called back to its sources. To this effect the study of eloquence will be profitable. If ever our people begin to cultivate it, I hope some Hercules will rise up to free the earth of these monsters and restore the native beauty of philosophy and Christian doctrine.[2]

Only in this way can the next generation of teachers be true guardians of Scripture and catholic dogma, by teaching accurately, clearly, and without contention the weighty articles of Christian doctrine, in consensus with the teachers of the early church.

According to Calvin, the Roman Church had been led into ruin above all by the useless speculations and distorting glosses of the monks and scholastic theologians, which closed access to Scripture for all Christians. The way to restore the church is for godly teachers to use their gifts of learning to open access to the reading of Scripture for the unlearned. The initial path into Scripture is paved by teaching the sum of doctrine to be

---

2. *Responsio Philippi Melanchthon pro Hermolao*, CR 9:689–90; "Reply of Philip Melanchthon in behalf of Ermolao," in *Christianity and Humanism: Studies in the History of Ideas*, by Quirinius Breen (Grand Rapids: Eerdmans, 1968), 67.

sought in Scripture in the *Institutes*, which in turn opens access to the commentaries that set forth with lucid brevity the true, genuine meaning of Scripture, by revealing the mind of the authors of Scripture. The true teacher, therefore, acts as a guide who leads the unlearned by the hand to the goal to be sought in the reading of Scripture: the knowledge of Jesus Christ, who alone opens access to the Father for us.

For Calvin, however, the true teacher not only guides the humble by the hand, but also strives hand to hand with the contentious who would lead the godly astray, according to the biblical precedent of Paul and the prophets. Moreover, the true teacher faithfully teaches whatever God teaches in Scripture, even when others think such teaching is harsh. "For our wisdom ought to be nothing else than to embrace with humble teachableness, and at least without finding fault, whatever is taught in Sacred Scripture."[3] All teaching is to be drawn from Scripture in order to lead Christians further into Scripture, so that they might test for themselves what they are being taught.[4]

As we shall see, the friendship of Calvin and Melanchthon was founded on the passion they shared to restore the church by teaching useful, clear, certain, and solid doctrine, with the sole aim of building up Christian piety and religion. Yet their friendship was severely tried, though never broken, by the tension that developed between them on the basis of their different understandings of the proper form and method of teaching, and of the office of the teacher in the church. We will first examine the initial years of their friendship (1538–46), in which they come to appreciate each other as teachers of the gospel, culminating in Calvin's publication of Melanchthon's *Loci communes 1543* in French. We will then follow their friendship as it passes through the various trials presented by the attack of Luther on the Swiss, the Leipzig Interim, the Bolsec and Trolliet disputes in Geneva over free will and election, and the attacks of Westphal on the Zurich Consensus (1545–60) and see how all of these trials were grounded in their different methods of teaching, which did not, for all that, end their friendship.

Teachers of Pious Doctrine and Learned Piety

When Calvin was pastor of the French congregation in Strasbourg, he first came into personal contact with Melanchthon. At this point, Bucer was energetically attempting to unite Wittenberg and Zurich on the basis of

3. John Calvin, *Inst.* 1.18.4, *OS* 3:227–30; LCC 1:237.

4. John Calvin, *Praefatio in Chrysostomi homilias*, *CO* 9:833; "Calvin's Preface to Chrysostom's Homilies," trans. W. Ian P. Hazlett, in *Humanism and Reform: The Church in Europe, England, and Scotland, 1400–1643: Essays in Honour of James K. Cameron*, ed. James Kirk (Oxford: Blackwell, 1991), 142.

the Wittenberg Concord that he and Melanchthon had worked out in 1536. In a letter Calvin sent with Bucer for Melanchthon, he sought to come to an agreement over the matter of the Holy Supper of the Lord. "I delivered to him a letter for Philip, in which I requested that he would inform me of his opinion in this matter. I appended twelve Articles, which if he can acquiesce in them to me, nothing farther can be required, either from himself or Luther, in this business."[5] Calvin was as hopeful as he ever would be that the division between Zurich, Strasbourg, and Wittenberg could be mended, and he seems intentionally to have formulated his *Short Treatise on the Holy Supper of the Lord* to further this possibility of union among the French evangelicals. It is also clear that Calvin considered Melanchthon, and not Luther, to be the crucial person with whom to seek agreement.

Calvin first met Melanchthon in person at the Diet of Frankfurt, 1539. Calvin was a member of the Strasbourg contingent under the leadership of Martin Bucer. Charles V arranged for this colloquy in order to seek to unify the evangelical and Roman parties. However, it is clear from his correspondence that Calvin was interested not in unity with Rome, but in explicit unity with Wittenberg, via Philip Melanchthon. He and Melanchthon discussed the articles Calvin had sent to Melanchthon via Bucer. "To these, without any controversy, he himself at once assented, but confessed that there were in that party some persons who required something more gross and palpable, and that with so great obstinacy, not to say despotism, that for long he seemed to be in actual jeopardy, because they saw that he differed from them in opinion."[6] Melanchthon indicated to Calvin that he was entirely of the same opinion regarding the sacrament, but he preferred instead to remain with the Wittenberg Concord until further agreement could be attained.[7] However, Melanchthon's adherence to the Wittenberg Concord was of more than strategic importance to him; in his will, drafted on November 12, 1539, Melanchthon stated, "In regard to the Lord's Supper I embrace the Form of Concord [the Wittenberg Concord] which was made here. Therefore, I unite myself with our churches, and I declare that they profess the doctrine of the

5. Calvin to Farel, October 1538, *CO* 10:279C; *Letters* 1:93.

6. Calvin to Farel, March 1539, *CO* 10:331A; *Letters* 1:129–30.

7. Calvin to Farel, March 1539, CO 10:331A; *Letters* 1:129–30. The second article of the Wittenberg Concord is especially significant: "Although they deny that transubstantiation takes place, and do not hold that there occurs a local confinement to the bread or any lasting conjunction apart from the use of the sacrament, yet they grant that by the sacramental union the bread is the body of Christ; that is to say, they hold that when the bread is offered, the body of Christ is at the same time present [*porrecto*] and truly presented [*exhiberi*]. For apart from this sacramental use they maintain that the body of Christ is not present, that is, when the bread is kept in the pyx or displayed in processions as is done by the papists" (*Common Places of Martin Bucer*, trans. and ed. D. F. Wright [Appleford, UK.: Sutton Courtenay, 1972], 362).

Catholic Church of Christ, and that they truly are churches of Christ."[8] Given the fact that Melanchthon drafted the Concord, it is clear that he thought it contained the catholic doctrine of the Supper, in union with the consensus of the apostles and the purer church.

For the rest of their friendship, Calvin was convinced that Melanchthon really agreed with him, and that the Wittenberg Concord was a step on the way to their private agreement becoming public. In light of his will, however, and his refusal publicly to support Calvin's teaching on the Supper, it may well be that Melanchthon agreed with Calvin to the extent that Calvin agreed with the Wittenberg Concord—that the signs of bread and wine truly exhibit and present the body and blood of Christ, which they signify and represent—but would not go along with Calvin regarding the ascended body of Christ and his explicit rejection of the oral eating of the body of Christ.[9] However, at Frankfurt Calvin was convinced that he and Melanchthon were entirely of the same opinion; and this had to increase his confidence that he and Melanchthon could restore the unity of the church.

Calvin also discussed another matter of direct personal concern with Melanchthon: discipline. Calvin and Melanchthon were entirely agreed about the authority pastors should have in their congregations, and they both lamented the lack of such authority in various evangelical churches. "Thus, for the future we may expect that it will form a kind of sport to hunt away pastors from the ministry and drive them into banishment; nor can this evil be remedied, because neither the common people nor the civil magistrate can rightly distinguish between the yoke of Christ and Papal tyranny."[10] Again, Melanchthon was of the opinion that this evil had to be tolerated until a more peaceful time allowed a remedy to be applied. Calvin, on the other hand, was convinced that a remedy had to be sought immediately and tirelessly, given his recent expulsion from Geneva. "If our calling is indeed of the Lord, as we firmly believe that it is, the Lord himself will bestow his blessing, although the whole

8. Clyde Leonard Manschreck, *Melanchthon: The Quiet Reformer* (New York: Abingdon, 1958), 258.

9. This is especially likely given his last word on the subject, a testimony written in his own hand in 1560, a week before he died, on the rear flyleaf of his *Loci praecipui theologici* (1558), which appears to be his interpretation of the Augsburg Confession of 1540: "The true body and the true blood of Christ are presented [*exhibetur*] in the bread and in the cup. Now the question has arisen, How can Christ physically [*corporaliter*] be in the sacrament, since the same body cannot be in different places [*in diversis locis*] at the same time? I respond: Christ said he was the true presence. Therefore, he is truly present in the sacrament, and physically [*corporaliter*]; and no other reason need be sought. The word sounds, therefore it is necessary that it be so" (*Scriptum de sacra coena*, 7 April 1560, CR 9:1087; Ralph Keen, trans., *A Melanchthon Reader* [New York: P. Lang, 1988], 132, with my modifications).

10. Calvin to Farel, March 1539, *CO* 10:331; *Letters* 1:129–30.

universe may be opposed to us. Let us, therefore, try every remedy, while, if such is not to be found, let us, notwithstanding, persevere even to the last gasp."[11] This assessment to Farel indicates a significant difference between Calvin and Melanchthon that would haunt their friendship for the next twenty-one years. Melanchthon was convinced that one must wait to reform the internal order of the church until the external enemies of the church were quiet. Calvin, on the other hand, was certain that the church in his day would be restored the way the temple of Jerusalem was rebuilt, with a trowel in one hand and a sword in the other.

Finally, Calvin spoke with Melanchthon about the abundant Roman ceremonies that remained in use in Wittenberg even until 1539. It is clear from Calvin's letter to Farel that Melanchthon was much less receptive to Calvin's criticism of the ceremonies at use in Wittenberg, which Calvin described as "not far removed from Judaism."[12] When pressed by Calvin on this point, Melanchthon ascribed the abundance of ceremonies to "the Canonists, who are here the stumbling-block in the way."[13] Moreover, Melanchthon indicated to Calvin that Luther did not approve of the abundance of ceremonies any more than of Calvin's sparing use of them, leading Calvin to agree with Bucer, that he should not be separated from Luther "on account of these trifling observances."[14] Calvin must have known that ceremonies were more a matter of indifference to Melanchthon than they were for himself, but he did not see this matter as church divisive. This would, however, later become an issue seriously dividing them.

In sum, Calvin went to Frankfurt anxious to come to agreement with Melanchthon over the matters that he knew possibly divided him from Wittenberg—the Holy Supper, discipline, and ceremonies—and came away convinced not only of his fundamental unity with Luther and Melanchthon, but also of the sincerity of Melanchthon. "I wish that our excellent friend N. could behold how much sincerity there is in Philip. All suspicion of double-dealing would entirely vanish."[15] The communication Calvin received from Wittenberg after Frankfurt only increased his confidence that he and Wittenberg were of one mind and heart, and that they both spoke on behalf of the same church, in spite of their different public teaching on the Supper. In a letter to Bucer, Luther said, "Salute for me reverently Sturm and Calvin, whose books I have read with special delight."[16] Melanchthon also included kind words from Luther to Calvin: "Luther and Pomeranus have desired Calvin to be greeted; Calvin has acquired great

---

11. *CO* 10:331C; *Letters* 1:131.
12. Calvin to Farel, April 1539, *CO* 10:340C; *Letters* 1:136.
13. *CO* 10:340C; *Letters* 1:137.
14. *CO* 10:340C; *Letters* 1:137.
15. *CO* 10:340C; *Letters* 1:137.
16. Calvin to Farel, 20 November 1539, *CO* 10:432A; *Letters* 1:167.

favor in their eyes."[17] Melanchthon further informed Calvin that certain people called Luther's attention to Calvin's criticism of his position on the Supper, but that Luther had responded by saying, "I hope that Calvin will one day think better of us; but in any event it is well that he should even now have a proof of our good feeling towards him."[18] In light of this intelligence from Melanchthon, Calvin exclaimed, "If we are not affected by such moderation, we are certainly of stone. For myself, I am profoundly affected by it."[19] By the end of 1539, Calvin and Wittenberg were filled with good will toward one another, and this situation was directly facilitated by Calvin's growing friendship with Melanchthon.

The next—and final—time Calvin and Melanchthon met was at the Diet of Ratisbon, which continued the dialogue between the evangelical and Roman representatives in an attempt to come to an agreement. However, neither Calvin nor Melanchthon was able to concentrate on the kinds of discussions they had engaged in at Frankfurt. Calvin was distracted by two concerns: the plague in Strasbourg affecting his family, his congregation, and Sturm's Academy in which he was teaching; and discussions with Geneva that eventually led to his return. For his part, Melanchthon was overwhelmed with grief and anxiety over the bigamy of Philip of Hesse, and he was convinced he would die of despair.[20] It could well be, however, that in this meeting the two teachers became the closest ever to each other personally, as they sought to comfort each other in their distress. Calvin's reminiscence about Philip in 1561 refers in particular to this time: "O Philip Melanchthon! . . . A hundred times, when worn out with labors and oppressed with so many troubles, did you repose your head familiarly on my breast and say, 'Would that I could die in this bosom!'"[21] Melanchthon in particular was strengthened by the presence of Calvin and did not want him to leave: "for not only was Bucer very sorrowful at the idea of my going away, but Philip also, . . . when the time drew near, requested that I would remain."[22] Calvin was concerned about the willingness of Melanchthon, and especially Bucer, to reach an accommodation with the Roman theologians; but possibly due to Calvin's firm stand at Ratisbon, Melanchthon held firm, to the apparent surprise of the Roman party.[23]

The Diet was not without its ecumenical significance, however, for Melanchthon had been persuaded, probably by Bucer, to alter the Augsburg

17. *CO* 10:432A; *Letters* 1:167.
18. *CO* 10:432A; *Letters* 1:167.
19. *CO* 10:432A; *Letters* 1:167.
20. Manschreck, *Melanchthon*, 261–76.
21. *Dilucida explicatio sanae doctrinae de vera participatione carnis et sanguinis christi in sacra coena ad discutiendas heshusii nebulas, CO* 9:461.
22. Calvin to Farel, July 1541, *CO* 11:251A; *Letters* 1:271.
23. *CO* 11:251B; *Letters* 1:272.

Confession to more accurately reflect the Wittenberg Concord, and to remove the condemnation of the Swiss.[24] Calvin signed this confession and defended his faithful adherence to it until Melanchthon's death in 1560. Calvin's signing the Augsburg Confession was the public manifestation of the bond of agreement he thought he had attained with Wittenberg, mainly by means of his friendship with Melanchthon; and quite significantly, his adherence to the Augsburg Confession ended when Melanchthon died, furthering the confessional division between the German and Swiss evangelicals.

After Calvin left Ratisbon, he was not in touch with Melanchthon again until 1543. In that year, Calvin wrote *The Bondage and Liberation of the Will: A Defense of the Orthodox Doctrine of Human Choice against Pighius*, and dedicated the work to Philip Melanchthon. The first two reasons that Calvin gives for this dedication are Melanchthon's love for Calvin, and the fact that the book "contains a defense of the godly and sound teaching of which you [Melanchthon] are not only a most zealous supporter, but a distinguished and very brave champion."[25] We will speak later about why Calvin associates Melanchthon with a doctrine of the bound will, which Melanchthon had first taught in his 1521 *Loci*, but from which he had later distanced himself in his comments on Colossians 1:15 (1527) and in his 1535 *Loci communes*. What is significant for our purposes now is the third "unusual" reason Calvin gives: "the fact that the kind of defense which I employ is straightforward and honest."[26] Calvin dedicates the work to Melanchthon in honor of his gifts as a teacher. These include not only the special sharpness of his judgment, and his incredible insight, but also especially his simplicity.

> For as much as you shrink from crafty, sidelong devices in argument which serve to draw darkness over things which are otherwise clear and open, in short from all pretence and sophistry, so you are pleased by an unembellished and frank clarity, which, without any concealment, sets a subject before the eyes and explains it. This quality of yours has often stirred in me great admiration, just because it is so rarely found.[27]

24. "De coena domini docent, quod cum pane et vino vere exhibeantur corpus et sanguis christi vescentibus in coena domini," cited in Schaff, *History of the Christian Church*, 8:665.

25. John Calvin, *Defensio sanae et orthodoxae doctrinae de servitute et liberatione humani arbitrii: Adversus calumnias Alberti Pighii Campensis*, with its dedication: "Ioannes Calvinus clarissimo viro Philippo Melanchthoni," CO 6:229–30; *The Bondage and Liberation of the Will: A Defense of the Orthodox Doctrine of Human Choice against Pighius*, ed. A. N. S. Lane, trans. G. I. Davies (Grand Rapids: Baker, 1996), 3.

26. Calvin, *Defensio*, CO 6:229–30; *Bondage*, 3.

27. Calvin, *Defensio*, CO 6:229–30; *Bondage*, 3.

Calvin praises Melanchthon for those qualities of teaching which Philip strove throughout his life to attain, best summarized by his ideal of eloquence, which he defined as "the faculty for proper and clear explication of mental sense and thought."[28] As in Calvin's description, Melanchthon thought of eloquence as clearly setting before the eyes the subject being discussed. "So the object of the rhetorician, or of eloquence . . . is to paint, as it were, and to represent the mind's thoughts themselves in appropriate and clear language."[29] It is quite revealing that in 1546 Calvin defends the use of eloquence in theological teaching in a way that directly echoes the qualities that he praises in Melanchthon: "Its aim is to call us back to the original simplicity of the Gospel. . . . It follows that the eloquence, which is in keeping with the Spirit of God, is not bombastic and ostentatious, and does not make a lot of noise that amounts to nothing. Rather, it is genuine and efficacious, and has more sincerity than refinement."[30]

The dedication to Melanchthon therefore not only reveals Calvin's respect for Philip as a teacher, but also shows how much Calvin was influenced by the writings of Melanchthon. Alexandre Ganoczy has demonstrated the clear influence of Melanchthon's 1521 *Loci* on Calvin's 1536 *Institutes*.[31] More to the point, Olivier Millet has recently demonstrated the almost certain influence of Melanchthon's treatises on eloquence and rhetoric when Calvin was a student and scholar in Paris.[32] According to Millet, there were twelve editions of Melanchthon's texts on rhetoric published in Paris between 1522 and 1534, including his *Elementorum rhetorices libri duo*. In these texts, Melanchthon seeks to unite the right method of teaching with the proper way of speaking. The first task belongs to dialectics, which Melanchthon defines as the art or way of teaching rightly and perspicuously.[33] Dialectics in particular has the task of selecting and ordering the *loci communes* of a discipline, which are the principal points containing the sources and sum of the art in question (common topics of discussion). Rhetoric, on the other hand, concerns the way or method of speaking rightly and ornately.[34] Rhetoric in particular uses the device

28. *Responsio Philippi Melanchthon pro Hermolao*, CR 9:690; Breen, *Christianity and Humanism*, 55.

29. *Responsio Melanchthon*, CR 9:690; Breen, *Christianity and Humanism*, 55.

30. Comm. on 1 Cor. 1:17, *CO* 49:322; *CNTC* 9:35.

31. Alexandre Ganoczy, *The Young Calvin*, trans. David Foxgrover and Wade Provo (Philadelphia: Westminster, 1987), 146–51.

32. Olivier Millet, *Calvin et la dynamique de la parole: Étude de rhétorique réformée* (Geneva: Slatkine, 1992).

33. Ibid., 127. See also Sachiko Kusukawa, *The Transformation of Natural Philosophy: The Case of Philip Melanchthon* (Cambridge: Cambridge University Press, 1995), 58–60.

34. Millet, *Calvin et la dynamique*, 127.

of *hypotyposis*, in which the object under discussion is set before the eyes in signs and images.[35]

The goal of both dialectics and rhetoric is clarity: "Dogmas should be clear and properly articulated, since 'the clear is good,' as Euripides says [*Iph. aul.* 560], that is, clarity is the sign of a generous mind. Thus let us flee from the hiding places of words and let us love clarity, especially in teaching."[36] Such clarity was intended by Melanchthon to end the fruitless and obscure disputations of the scholastic theologians, which brought the church near ruin, whereas the selection and order of the *loci communes* was meant to teach the necessary and weighty articles of Christian doctrine over against the empty speculations of the scholastics. In his continual effort to discover the right method of teaching and speaking, Melanchthon increasingly turned to the works of Plato, Cicero, and especially Aristotle.

> Plato said that the fire that had been taken by Prometheus from the sky was method. [*Phileb.* 16c5–6]. But if that little fire is lost, men will be transformed back into beasts; for indeed if the true plan of teaching is removed, nothing will separate man from beasts. So then let us hold on to that fire, that type of doctrine that Aristotle handed down, and preserve it with the greatest zeal.[37]

Thus, even though the content of philosophy and theology are as different for Melanchthon as the law and the gospel,[38] no one can be a trustworthy teacher of Christian doctrine if he is not also a student of philosophy. "For nobody can become an artisan in method unless he is well and properly trained in philosophy, and even in the one class of philosophy which is opposed to sophistry, the one that inquires and makes truth known by an orderly and correct path."[39]

There can be no doubt that Melanchthon's understanding of the order of right teaching and the proper way of speaking directly and fundamentally influenced Calvin. The primary aim of the teacher of doctrine for both Calvin and Melanchthon is to teach in a clear and sincere way the solid, certain doctrine of piety. "The theologian's task is not to divert the ears with chatter, but to strengthen consciences by teaching things true, sure, and profitable."[40] Although the content of the 1536 *Institutes*

---

35. Ibid., 130.

36. Melanchthon, *Commentary on Aristotle's Ethics*, book 1 (1546), CR 16:294; in Keen, *Melanchthon Reader*, 190; Millet, *Calvin et la dynamique*, 135.

37. *De vita Aristotelis* (1537), *MWA* 3:104.32–38; Keen, *Melanchthon Reader*, 77.

38. "It may be said that the Gospel is the doctrine of spiritual life and of justification before God; and that philosophy is the doctrine of the bodily life" (Philip Melanchthon, *Paul's Letter to the Colossians*, *MWA* 4:241.30–32, trans. D. C. Parker [Sheffield: Almond, 1989], 56).

39. *MWA* 3:91.16–20; Keen, *Melanchthon Reader*, 67.

40. *Inst.* 1.14.4, *OS* 3:157.11–13; LCC 1:164.

reflects many of Melanchthon's themes in the 1521 *Loci*, the 1539 edition of the *Institutes* directly takes up into its central form of argumentation Melanchthon's dialectical use of *loci communes* and the order of right teaching, as well as a concern for the right way to seek and inquire into the knowledge of God.[41] As is widely acknowledged, Calvin continued to work on the order of right teaching until he had arranged the *loci communes* of the *Institutes* in the order they attained in 1559. The form of teaching that Calvin pursued in the *Institutes* from 1539 to 1559 is therefore fundamentally influenced by Melanchthon's understanding of dialectics and rhetoric, which Calvin may have encountered as early as his years in Paris.

However, Calvin expresses his love for Melanchthon, and his sincere admiration for his clear and sincere teaching, in the dedication to a work defending the orthodox doctrine of the bound and liberated will. The argument that Calvin makes is clearly in line with that pursued by Luther against Erasmus, but that very debate seems to have caused Melanchthon to reconsider his own thinking on the subject. Melanchthon seems in particular to have adopted several of Erasmus's contentions against Luther: that speaking about the bound will seems to make God the author of sin, undermines our confidence in the mercy of God, and undermines civil and ecclesiastical discipline.[42] Melanchthon also seems to have been moved by Erasmus's claim that free choice of the will is the orthodox catholic consensus of the early, and especially Greek, church, over against the dualistic teaching of the Manichaeans and Marcion.[43]

In his 1527 lectures on Colossians, Melanchthon began to distance himself from Luther. According to Melanchthon, "Holy Scripture itself says that the flesh has both a kind of prudence, and a kind of righ-

41. "Yet however the knowledge of God and of ourselves may be mutually connected, the order of right teaching [*ordo recte docendi*] requires that we discuss the former first, then proceed afterward to treat the latter" (*Inst.* 1.1.3, *OS* 3:34.1–3; LCC 1:39). "Consequently, we know that the most perfect way of seeking God [*rectissimam Dei quaerendi viam*] and the most suitable order [*aptissimum ordinem*], is . . . for us to contemplate him in his works" (*Inst.* 1.5.9, *OS* 3:53.18–22; LCC 1:62).

42. "Why, you will say, grant anything to free choice? In order to have something to impute justly to the wicked who have voluntarily come short of the grace of God, in order that the calumny of cruelty and injustice may be excluded from God, that despair may be kept away from us, that complacency may be excluded also, and that we may be incited to endeavor" (*On the Freedom of the Will: A Diatribe or Discourse by Desiderius Erasmus of Rotterdam*, in *Luther and Erasmus: Free Will and Salvation*, trans. E. Gordon Rupp and A. N. Marlow [Philadelphia: Westminster, 1969], 96).

43. "If the reader shall see that my own argument meets the other side with equal weapons, then let him also consider whether more weight ought not to be ascribed to the previous judgments of so many learned men, so many orthodox, so many saints, so many martyrs, so many theologians old and new, so many universities, councils, so many bishops and popes—or to trust instead the private judgment of this or that individual" (ibid., 43).

teousness; in saying this, it bestows on the reason a kind of freedom or power of choice."[44] Without this freedom of will, it would be impossible to explain how Paul claims we can of our own do external works of the law. Yet Melanchthon also thinks free choice of the will is important so that we do not make God the author of sin. "Yet it seems far more absurd to the reason that, if God is at work in nature, he should seem to compel and incite it to sin."[45] Thus Melanchthon concludes that "God does not take away this power to choose," even though this power is hindered by the weakness of the flesh and by the devil.[46] Melanchthon further refines this position and makes it central to his 1532 *Romans* and 1535 *Loci communes*, with its famous statement of the three causes of our conversion: the Word, the Holy Spirit, and the will resisting its own weakness.[47] God commands us to hear his Son in the gospel, and the promise of the gospel is universal. Hence, those who are lost should not blame God for their perdition, but admit the resistance of their own free will. "Since the promise is universal, and there are no contradictory wills in God, the cause must be in *man* that Saul is cast away and David is accepted."[48]

There can be no doubt that Calvin knew of Melanchthon's divergence from Luther on the question of free will and predestination. Calvin explicitly refers to Melanchthon's 1532 *Romans* in the dedication to his Romans commentary in 1539, and in his 1539 *Institutes* Calvin explicitly critiques Melanchthon's claim in the 1535 *Loci* that the election of God coincides with the promise of the gospel.[49] Why then does Calvin dedicate a work on the bound and liberated choice of the will to a teacher who had come to maintain the free choice of the will even in sinners? One reason may be that he underestimated the degree to which Melanchthon had distanced himself from his own position on this question in his 1521 *Loci*, in which he claimed, "Since all things that happen, happen necessarily according to divine predestination, our will has no liberty."[50] Calvin does note in his treatise against Pighius that Melanchthon does

---

44. *MWA* 4:224.4–7; Melanchthon, *Paul's Letter to the Colossians*, 40.

45. *MWA* 4:224.20–22.

46. Ibid., 4:224.32.

47. Manschreck, *Melanchthon*, 296–97.

48. Ibid.

49. "But, you [Melanchthon] will say, if this is so, there will be little faith in the gospel promises, which, in testifying to the will of God, assert that he wills what is contrary to his inviolable decree. Not at all. For however universal the promises of salvation may be, they are still in no respect inconsistent with the predestination of the reprobate, provided we pay attention to their effect" (*Inst.* 3.24.17, *OS* 4:429.32–36; LCC 2:985).

50. Philip Melanchthon, *Loci communes 1521*, ed. Horst Georg Pöhlmann (Gütersloh: Gerd Mohn, 1993), 28.19; Wilhelm Pauck, ed., *Melanchthon and Bucer* (Philadelphia: Westminster, 1969), 24.

not express himself the same way Luther does on this question, but he seems to ascribe this more to rhetorical accommodation to his audience than to a difference of doctrine. "It is also true that Philip Melanchthon, by careful and very adept softening of the outward form of some things that Luther had written in scholastic language, in a style alien to popular taste, accommodated them to the general mass of humanity and to common usage."[51] Calvin clearly reads Melanchthon's own position in light of the 1530 Augsburg Confession, which does not fully reflect Melanchthon's position on this question by 1532.[52] This is all the more likely given the fact that Calvin had just signed the confession three years earlier, and he represents himself as defending Luther and Melanchthon along with himself against the calumnies of Pighius. However, in his letter to Melanchthon informing him of this dedication, Calvin seems to indicate his knowledge that Melanchthon's position was somewhat different from his own, but he expresses his confidence in Melanchthon's affection for him. "But that you may not suppose that I have made an improper use of your name in the Essay which I have lately published, I ask you to recognize or approve of it on the score of my affection for you, or to yield so far to your own kindly disposition as to acquiesce in what I have done."[53]

Melanchthon responded to Calvin's letter and dedication with the longest extant letter that he wrote to his friend. In the letter Melanchthon thanks Calvin for his public testimony of his love for him, and especially for his ingenuous testimony that Melanchthon loves and seeks simplicity above all else, citing again the saying of Euripides that "the clear is the good."[54] Melanchthon affirms that he has sought such simplicity in order to avoid many horrible and intricate disputations, so that he might teach only useful things and lead the church more and more into consensus. He then urges Calvin to turn his eloquence to the principal articles of teaching, basically representing the various *loci* taught by Melanchthon in his *Loci communes* of 1543, both to confirm those of sound judgment and to terrify their adversaries, since Calvin in disputation is gifted with

51. Calvin, *Defensio sanae et orthodoxae doctrinae* . . . , *CO* 6:250; Lane, *Bondage and the Liberation of the Will*, 29.

52. "Of free will they teach that the human will has some liberty in bringing about civil justice and choosing things that are subject to reason. But it does not have force without the Holy Spirit for effecting the justice of God or spiritual justice, since the human animal does not perceive those things which are of the Spirit of God; but this happens in the heart when the Spirit is perceived through the word" (Augsburg Confession, in Keen, *Melanchthon Reader*, 104). The Augsburg Confession ascribes only two causes to faith, the Word of God, and the Holy Spirit, in its seventh article, omitting any mention of free will (ibid., 101).

53. Calvin to Melanchthon, 14 March 1543, *CO* 11:515; *Letters* 1:374.

54. "Gratum mihi et illud tuum testimonius esse ingenue fateor, quod me et amare et quaerere simplicitatem dicis" (Melanchthon to Calvin, 11 May 1543, CR 5:107).

an energetic and luminous style.[55] Melanchthon is especially hopeful that God has inspired Calvin to undertake the explication of the gospel, since to do otherwise would be to quench the gifts of the Spirit. The implication is that the doctrine of the bound and liberated will is not a useful *locus* for a person of Calvin's gifts and eloquence, but is rather a question that leads to horrible disputations and the loss of consensus.

Melanchthon also makes clear his own disagreement with Calvin's treatment of the bound and liberated will:

> I maintain the proposition that God is not the author of sin, and therefore cannot will it. David was by his own will carried into transgression. He might have retained the Holy Spirit. In this conflict there is some margin for free will. . . . Let us accuse our own will if we fall, and not find the cause in God. He will help and aid those who fight in earnest. "Only want to," writes Basil, "and God has helped you." God promises and gives help to those who are willing to receive it. So says the Word of God, and in this let us abide.[56]

Melanchthon reiterates the position he has been developing from 1527 to the edition of the *Loci* coming out in 1543, making it clear to Calvin that he does not agree either with the concept of a bound will, nor with reprobation, since both doctrines appear to make God the author of sin. However, Melanchthon concludes his disagreement with Calvin with a sign of great respect for him as a teacher, confident that their teaching on this matter is not all that different. "I am far from prescribing to you, the most learned and experienced man in all things that belong to piety. I know in general you agree with my view. I only suggest that this mode of expression is better adapted for common use."[57]

Three things become clear in light of Calvin's dedication and Melanchthon's response in 1543. First, both men had the highest regard and respect for each other as eloquent teachers of Christian doctrine. Second, Melanchthon thought that the doctrine of the bound will was not useful or fruitful doctrine, and that Calvin should apply his eloquence to more useful *loci* of Christian doctrine. Third, both Calvin and Melanchthon thought that they nonetheless agreed on this question of doctrine, and that their differences had to do more with their style of teaching than with its substance. Ten years later, their differences on free will and election would be much more clear to them.

55. "Ad harum maximarum rerum doctrinam ornandam transferas velim eloquentiam tuam, quae et confirmare nostros, terrere adversarios et sanabiles iuvare poterit. Cuius est enim oratio hoc tempore in disputando vel nervosior, vel splendidior?" (ibid., CR 5:108).

56. Ibid., CR 5:109; Schaff, *History of the Christian Church*, 8:392.

57. CR 5:109; Schaff, *History of the Christian Church*, 8:392.

The final testimony that Calvin gave of his admiration and respect for Melanchthon as a clear, sincere, simple teacher of Christian doctrine came three years later, when Calvin arranged for the publication of the 1543 edition of Melanchthon's *Loci* in French. As Philip Schaff rightly points out, such an event is not only unique in the Reformation; it also shows the humility and deference that Calvin exhibited toward his fellow teacher of the gospel, especially given the fact that, unlike the Pighius dedication, Calvin never let Melanchthon know he had done this.[58] Calvin wrote a preface to the *Loci* in which he commends the reading of this text for those not familiar with Melanchthon from his Latin writings. In this work, he tells the prospective reader, one will find a brief summary of all that a Christian must know to be guided on the way of salvation.[59] Calvin then summarizes the major *loci* treated by Melanchthon and claims that the book contains the profitable doctrine with which a Christian must be occupied throughout life. As in the Pighius dedication, Calvin above all praises Melanchthon for his simplicity, for he uses his great learning to abase himself to the level of his readers, seeking only their edification.[60] Calvin notes the difference between this style and his own. "It is, certainly, the style and fashion which we would observe, did not our adversaries constrain us by their cavils to turn aside from this course."[61]

The rest of the preface alerts the reader to the differences between Calvin and Melanchthon's teaching about free will, predestination, and absolution. Calvin, as we suspected above, describes Melanchthon's position on free will according to the teaching of the Augsburg Confession—that we have a civil freedom with regard to external things—and claims that Melanchthon ascribes all spiritual good to the grace of God. Calvin accounts for Melanchthon's different teaching about predestination on the grounds that he wants to avoid speculation and disputation. Calvin expresses his sympathy for this concern, but also expresses his opinion that teachers should teach all that God reveals to us in Scripture. "I confess that the whole of what God has been pleased to reveal to us in Scripture ought not to be suppressed, whatsoever happens; but he who seeks to give profitable instruction to his readers, may very well be excused for dwelling upon what he knows to be most essential, passing lightly over or leaving out of sight that which he does not expect to be

58. Schaff, *History of the Christian Church*, 8:392–93.

59. *CO* 9:847: "Et pour en dire en somme ce qui en est, on y trouvera un brief recueil des choses qu'un Chrestien doit savoir pour se guider au chemin de salut."

60. *CO* 9:848: "Et de faict, ce qui est bien à priser, je voy que l'auteur, estant homme de profond savoir, n'a pas voulu entrer en disputes subtiles, ne traiter les matieres d'un artifice tant haut qu'il luy eut esté facile de faire, mais s'est abaissé tant qu'il à peu, n'ayant esgard qu'à la seule edification."

61. *Preface de la Somme de Melanchthon* (1546), *CO* 9:848; *Letters* 2:368.

equally profitable."[62] Finally, Calvin claims that Melanchthon makes absolution one of the sacraments out of accommodation to the common usage, and not as though he would make absolution as necessary as baptism or the Holy Supper of the Lord. We therefore see the ways in which Calvin interpreted Melanchthon so that he could still agree with him: he reads his doctrine of free will via the Augsburg Confession, he thinks he omits predestination out of concern for edification, he claims he teaches absolution out of accommodation, not as a necessity. If readers approach the *Loci* with these things in mind, Calvin claims that Melanchthon will conduct them to the pure truth of God.[63]

A Different Method of Teaching

Given Calvin's presentation of Melanchthon's goals as a teacher, how does Melanchthon himself describe his objectives in his 1543 *Loci*, and how do they relate to the doctrines to which Calvin takes exception? In order to understand the purpose of the *Loci*, it is important to remember that it was written in the twenty-fifth year of Melanchthon's tenure at Wittenberg. When Melanchthon first arrived at Wittenberg, he saw his task to be the revival of humane letters, both classical and biblical, especially Greek literature. "It was not possible, when the Greeks were held in contempt, for a single philosopher to be of any use to humane studies; and concern for sacred things as well slowly died."[64] With Homer in one hand, and Paul in the other, Melanchthon hoped to show "how much a sense of appropriate language contributes to understanding the mystery of sacred things: and also what difference there is between learned and unlearned interpreters of Greek."[65] By his 1521 *Loci communes*, however, Luther had convinced Melanchthon that theology could only be restored by turning to the teaching of the Holy Spirit in Scripture alone, over against the use of Greek philosophy by the scholastics. "But more important, in this book the principal topics of Christian teaching are pointed out so that youth may arrive at a twofold understanding: 1. What one must chiefly look for in Scripture. 2. How corrupt are all the theological hallucinations of those who have offered us the subtle-

---

62. *CO* 9:848; *Letters* 2:368.

63. *CO* 9:850: "Parquoy que celluy qui voudra estre enseigné au present livre se rendre docile, excusant ce qui le pourroyt achopper à passer tousiours plus outre, pour estre conduict droyt à la pure verité de Dieu, à laquelle seule il nous convient tenir, nous servant des hommes pour nous ayder à y parvenir."

64. *De corrigendis adolescentiae studiis* (1518), *MWA* 3:33.16–19; Keen, *Melanchthon Reader*, 50.

65. *MWA* 3:41.35–38; 3:42.1; Keen, *Melanchthon Reader*, 56.

ties of Aristotle instead of the teachings of Christ."[66] Melanchthon also wanted to avoid the previous tradition of scriptural commentaries. "On the whole I do not look very favorably on commentaries, not even those of the ancients."[67]

The Wittenberg disturbances in 1521–22, and Karlstadt's condemnation of university education in particular, made Melanchthon reconsider his 1521 position, and caused him to return to the conjoint teaching of Greek philosophy along with Scripture.[68] The Peasants' War of 1525 and his visitations in Thuringia in 1527 convinced him that the real danger to the church was unlearned teachers, and not the neglect of Scripture for philosophy.[69] "First of all, an uneducated theology is an *Iliad* of ills."[70] Thus, youth need to be trained in all literature and the arts—which Melanchthon termed philosophy—as well as in the literature of Scripture, for "the need of the Church spans the world of all disciplines."[71] Moreover, the controversies over free choice and the Lord's Supper convinced Melanchthon that his earlier rejection of the ancient teachers and commentators was mistaken. He sought instead to be a student of orthodox, catholic, doctrine, represented in particular by the Greek fathers, so that he might avoid novelty, which only leads to dissension, and instead speak according to the consensus of the pure, ancient, catholic, and orthodox church.

> For I do not wish to be either the author or defender of any new doctrine in the Church. . . . I have always, as you know, been a student of Christian doctrine; and for that reason it has been my concern to know it diligently; and not without small effort, when I sought what I might follow safely, I extricated myself from scholastic disputes, of which matter there is quite some evidence.[72]

66. *Loci communes* (1521), 12.4; Pauck, *Melanchthon and Bucer*, 19.

67. *Loci communes* (1521), 12.4; Pauck, *Melanchthon and Bucer*, 19. Peter Fraenkel challenges this interpretation of the development of Melanchthon's theology. "Melanchthon's early activities as a patrologist make it equally difficult to assume, with some modern interpreters, that his career was marked by a 'biblicist' hiatus between two periods of humanist esteem for the ancients. Indeed it will be our contention that this is not so, but that, however strongly his thought evolved on such subjects as predestination, the role that he attributed to theological 'tradition' remained substantially the same throughout his career" (Peter Fraenkel, *Testimonia Patrum: The Function of the Patristic Argument in the Theology of Philip Melanchthon* [Geneva: Droz, 1961], 29). My own reading of the 1521 *Loci* suggests otherwise.

68. For an excellent discussion of these developments, see Kusukawa, *Transformation of Natural Philosophy*, 7–74.

69. Manschreck, *Melanchthon*, 137.

70. Melanchthon, *De philosophia oratio* (1536), *MWA* 3:90.25–26; Keen, *Melanchthon Reader*, 66.

71. *De philosophia oratio* (1536), *MWA* 3:92.13–14; Keen, *Melanchthon Reader*, 68.

72. Melanchthon to Oecolampadius, 8 April 1529, CR 1:1048; Keen, *Melanchthon Reader*, 128. Fraenkel (*Testimonia Patrum*, 46–51) sees three factors behind such a move by Melanchthon: the Antitrinitarians, the eucharistic debates, and the Augsburg Confession.

Hence, by 1539, the year Melanchthon met Calvin, he had as his aim the teaching of the pure philosophy of the Greeks and the teaching of the catholic, orthodox doctrine of the church, especially the Greek fathers, so that the weighty articles of faith revealed in Scripture might be clearly taught, faithfully guarded, and accurately handed down to posterity.

All of these concerns are reflected in the 1543 edition of the *Loci*. In the letter to the pious reader, Melanchthon highlights the *catholicity* of the doctrine taught in the *Loci*. "With great care and concern, I investigated the doctrine of the church and tried to state these great truths as clearly as I could. I am not creating new opinions. . . . This teaching unquestionably is the consensus of the universal church of Christ, that is, of all learned men in the church of Christ."[73] By avoiding novelty and by speaking in consensus with the catholic church of Christ, Melanchthon hopes to train pastors and teachers who would faithfully guard and hand down to posterity Scripture and the dogmas of the church: "We must seek the truth, love it, defend it, and hand it down uncorrupted to our posterity."[74]

In the preface to the *Loci*, Melanchthon immediately introduces the question of method, and the relation of philosophy to theology and revelation: "Human beings are so created by God that they understand numbers and order, and in the learning process they are much aided by both numbers and order. Thus in teaching a subject, the order of the various parts must be demonstrated with singular care, and we must indicate the beginning, the process, and the goal. In philosophy they call this process the 'method.'"[75] The doctrine of the church should follow a definite order, but it does not proceed by demonstration, since the articles it teaches are sure, certain, and immutable by means of revelation, and are confirmed by the sure and clear testimonies of God. The order of the *loci* of catholic doctrine must be sought from the prophetic and apostolic books, for they "have been written in the best possible order, and they set forth the articles of faith in the best possible order."[76] The articles of faith themselves are to be sought in the prophetic and apostolic books *and* in the witness of the purer ancient church, which set forth the "correct explanations of pious men and careful writings and testimonies drawn from pure fountains."[77]

At the heart of the articles of faith is the self-revelation of the Father in the sacrifice of the Son and the gospel he preaches, shown to us by the

73. Philip Melanchthon, *Loci praecipui theologici* (1543), CR 21:602; *Loci communes, 1543*, trans. J. A. O. Preus (St. Louis: Concordia, 1992), 15.

74. CR 21:602; Preus, *Loci communes* (1543), 16.

75. *Loci communes* (1543), CR 21:603; Preus, *Loci communes* (1543), 16.

76. CR 21:603; Preus, *Loci communes* (1543), 16.

77. CR 21:603; Preus, *Loci communes* (1543), 16.

Holy Spirit. Godly teachers must instruct others about the Father, Son, and Spirit in the language of the pure and ancient church. "Care behooves the pious, for the sake of harmony, to speak in line with the church. And it was not without good reason that the ancient church approved some ways of speaking and rejected others."[78] Pious Christians differ from philosophers above all in praying with confidence to the God who has revealed himself in Christ.

> [God] did not wish to be sought by idle and vagrant speculations, but he wills that our eyes be fixed on the Son who has been manifested to us, that our prayers be directed to the eternal Father who has revealed himself in the Son whom He has sent, and in the Gospel which has been given by the God who accepts us and hears our prayers for the sake of his Son our Mediator.[79]

The goal of the self-revelation of God, and therefore of Christian doctrine, is the invocation of God. Hence, Melanchthon includes in many of his *loci* forms of prayer that the godly are to use, so that they might both learn and put to use the doctrine they are taught. "Therefore we must cling to a definite and true form, the very recitation of which admonishes us concerning the true doctrine."[80]

We can now see the bases upon which Melanchthon formulates his doctrines to which Calvin took exception in his preface: free will, predestination, and absolution. The doctrine of free will is established primarily on the basis of speaking in consensus with the purer, ancient, Greek church: "The ancients said that good works arose out of preceding grace and an assenting will."[81] The doctrine of predestination is based on the self-revelation of the Father in the sacrifice of the Son and in the preaching of the gospel, which reveal that God does not will sin but, rather, is wrathful toward sin and wants to have mercy on sinners: "Therefore, we must look for a promise in which God has expressed his will, and we must understand that no other will is to be sought concerning his grace outside of his Word."[82] The doctrine of private confession and absolution is directly linked to the self-revelation of God in the gospel, and for Melanchthon is the most vivid application of the forgiveness of sins to the individual: "Because of private absolution, which must be retained in the churches, the custom of seeking absolution must also be retained."[83] These are not,

---

78. *Loci communes* (1543), CR 21:627; Preus, *Loci communes* (1543), 27.
79. *Loci communes* (1543), CR 21:608; Preus, *Loci communes* (1543), 18.
80. *Loci communes* (1543), CR 21:635; Preus, *Loci communes* (1543), 31.
81. *Loci communes* (1543), CR 21:658; Preus, *Loci communes* (1543), 43.
82. *Loci communes* (1543), CR 21:914; Preus, *Loci communes* (1543), 173.
83. *Loci communes* (1543), CR 21:894; Preus, *Loci communes* (1543), 162.

as Calvin suggests in his preface, tangential concerns for Melanchthon, but are based on the central principles of his theology.

The ensuing years of their friendship would reveal to both men just how much they differed from each other in the form and content of their teaching. Calvin was constantly frustrated by Melanchthon's desire to reach consensus by accommodating as much as possible to his theological adversaries. He could not understand why Melanchthon did not exert his influence to moderate Luther's behavior after he attacked the Swiss in 1544:

> It is indeed most true, as I acknowledge it to be, that which you teach, and also that hitherto, by a kindly method of instruction, you have studiously endeavored to recall the minds of men from strife and contention. I applaud your prudence and moderation. While, however, you dread . . . to meddle with this question from fear of giving offence, you are leaving in perplexity and suspense very many persons who require from you somewhat of a more certain sound, on which they can repose.[84]

Calvin was even more appalled by the concessions that Melanchthon made to the Roman Church after the defeat of the Smalcald League, by the signing of the Leipzig Interim. Calvin claims that Melanchthon extended the distinction of indifferent matters (*adiaphora*) too far, and candidly rebukes him as one teacher of the gospel to another:

> If you are too facile in making concessions, you need not wonder if that is marked as a fault in you by many. Moreover, several of those things which you consider indifferent, are obviously repugnant to the word of God. . . . Truly if I have any understanding in divine things, you ought not to have made such large concessions to the papists; partly because you have loosed what the Lord has bound with his word, and partly because you have afforded occasion for bringing insult upon the Gospel.[85]

Calvin acknowledges that by rebuking Melanchthon this way he is joining his voice with the theologians like Flacius of Magdeburg attacking Philip, but his understanding of the office of teacher compelled him to speak out against his friend and mentor.[86]

84. Calvin to Melanchthon, 28 June 1545, *CO* 12:99; *Letters* 1:467.

85. Calvin to Melanchthon, 18 June 1550, *Letters* 2:272.

86. Ibid. "It is too well known, from their mocking and jests, how much the enemies of Christ were rejoicing over your contests with the theologians of Magdeburg. . . . Yet forgive me if I do not consider you altogether free from blame. . . . In the mean while, let it be well understood that in openly admonishing you, I am discharging the duty of a true friend; and if I employ a little more severity than usual, do not think that it is owing to any diminution of my old affection and esteem for you."

The most painful divisions between Melanchthon and Calvin took place over the questions of free will and election, and the attacks on the Zurich Consensus by Melanchthon's student Joachim Westphal. Calvin's publication of a French translation of Melanchthon's 1543 *Loci* had the unintended result of giving powerful ammunition to those in Geneva who opposed Calvin's teaching of election and reprobation, especially Trolliet, who explicitly cited Melanchthon's *Loci* against Calvin in 1552.[87] In his letter to the Seigneurs of Geneva, responding to Trolliet, Calvin candidly admits that he and Melanchthon pursue a different method of instruction:

> Notwithstanding, I must confess, as I have formerly declared, that the method of instruction which Melanchthon adopts, is different from mine. I have also, honorable Seigneurs, explained to you the cause of this. It is, that Melanchthon, being a timorous man, has accommodated himself too much to the common feeling of mankind, that he might not give occasion to over-curious people to seek to pry into the secret things of God. And thus, as at last appears, he has spoken of the present question rather as a philosopher than a theologian, having no better authority to rest upon than that of Plato.[88]

In spite of this rather harsh indictment of his friend's manner of teaching, Calvin declares his love and respect for Melanchthon: "He who would place Melanchthon and myself in opposition greatly wrongs both the one and the other, as well as the whole Church of God. . . . If I find anything to reprove I do not conceal it from him, as he gives me full liberty not to do so."[89] Nor was this an insincere declaration, for in a letter that Calvin wrote to Melanchthon a month later, he acknowledges his love and respect for Melanchthon in spite of their differences on this question:

> I know and confess, moreover, that we occupy widely different positions; still, because I am not ignorant of the place in his theater to which God has elevated me, there is no reason for my concealing that our friendship could not be interrupted without great injury to the Church. And that we may act independent of the conduct of others, reflect, from your own feeling of the thing, how painful it would be for me to be estranged from that

87. See Walker, *John Calvin*, 320–21.

88. Calvin to the Seigneurs of Geneva, 6 October 1552, *Letters* 2:368.

89. Ibid. Note again how Calvin's love for Melanchthon is rooted in his respect for him as a teacher of the gospel. "I honour Melanchthon as much on account of the excellent knowledge which is in him, as for his virtues; and more than all, because of his having labored faithfully to further the Gospel. . . . As for him, there are witnesses more than enough, who know how much he loves me" (ibid.).

man whom I both love and esteem above all others, and whom God has not only adorned with remarkable gifts in order to make him distinguished in the eyes of the whole Church, but has also employed as his chief minister for conducting matters of the highest importance.[90]

For all of his love and respect for Melanchthon as a teacher, Calvin writes the same criticisms of his friend's method of teaching that he wrote to the Genevans, that in his teaching Melanchthon follows the philosophers and not Scripture:

> Nevertheless . . . the opposition, which is too plainly manifest in our modes of teaching, pains me not a little. I, for my part, am well aware that, if any weight is due to the authority of men, it were far more just that I should subscribe to your opinions than you mine. But that is not the question; nor is it a thing to be desired by the pious ministers of Christ. This, in all truth, we ought both to seek, viz., to come to an agreement on the pure truth of God. But, to speak candidly, religious scruples prevent me from agreeing with you on this point of doctrine, for you appear to discuss the freedom of the will in too philosophical a manner; and in treating of the doctrine of election, you seem to have no other purpose, save that you may suit yourself to the common feeling of mankind.[91]

Calvin was not unaware of how much Melanchthon detested Calvin's own "Stoic" manner of teaching, which Melanchthon was convinced made God the author of sin. Calvin may have heard about how appalled Melanchthon was by Calvin's behavior in the Bolsec affair a year earlier, but he certainly heard of how Melanchthon reacted violently against the inclusion of reprobation in the Zurich Consensus.[92]

With regard to the Zurich Consensus, Calvin since 1539 had been convinced that he and Melanchthon were of one mind concerning the doctrine of the Holy Supper of the Lord. Calvin had clearly hoped that the Zurich Consensus would bring to an end the division between Zurich and Wittenberg fostered by Luther's last attack on Zurich in 1544. Hence, Calvin was deeply pained when one of Melanchthon's students, Joachim Westphal, attacked the Zurich Consensus. Calvin defended the Consensus on the grounds that it faithfully represented

90. Calvin to Melanchthon, 28 November 1552, *CO* 14:416; *Letters* 2:377.

91. *CO* 14:417; *Letters* 2:379.

92. *CO* 14:417; *Letters* 2:379. "It increases my anxiety, and at the same time my grief, to see you in this matter to be almost unlike yourself; for I heard, when the whole formula of the agreement of our Church with that of Zurich was laid out before you, you instantly seized a pen and erased that sentence which cautiously and prudently makes a distinction between the elect and the reprobate."

the teaching of the Augsburg Confession of 1540, but he was pained and troubled by the utter silence of Melanchthon during this entire controversy.[93] He constantly besought a solid, clear, public declaration from Melanchthon of his own teaching on this issue, and even received a pledge from Melanchthon that he would so declare himself.[94] However, such a declaration was never forthcoming, in spite of Calvin's continual incitements, including the possibility of a conference. "But, in one word, you should maturely consider whether your too obstinate a silence may not leave a stain on your reputation in the eyes of posterity."[95]

Once again, Calvin ascribed this silence on the part of his friend to his flexible and pliant manner of teaching:

> What the world deems worthy of its applause or hatred does not escape me. But far more important I hold it to follow the rule prescribed by our Master. Nor have I any doubt that this ingenuousness will in the end prove more agreeable to all pious and rational minds, than a complacent and wavering manner of teaching, which is always swayed by some empty terror.[96]

During the controversy over the Supper, the silence of Melanchthon led to the harshest words Calvin ever wrote against his friend, in light of the failure of the conference at Worms in 1558 to heal this division:[97]

> The unfortunate issue of the conference at Worms does not so much distress me, as the inconstancy of Philip moves both my anger and detestation. For although I had not forgotten how pliant and weak he has always been, and knew that on the present occasion also he is too timid and indolent, nevertheless he has exceeded himself far beyond what I could ever have expected.[98]

93. "In regard to the Confession of Augsburg, my answer is, that, as it was published at Ratisbon [1541], it does not contain a word contrary to our doctrine. If there is any ambiguity to its meaning, there cannot be a more competent interpreter than its author, to whom, as his due, all pious and learned men will readily pay this honor. To him I boldly appeal; and thus Westphal with his vile garrulity lies prostrate. . . . The only thing I said, and, if need be a hundred times repeat, is that in this matter Philip can no more be torn from me than he can from his own bowels" (Calvin, *Ultima admonitio ad Westphalum, CO* 9:148–49; cited in Schaff, *History of the Christian Church*, 8:666).

94. Melanchthon to Calvin, 12 May 1555, CR 8:482–83: ". . . quod si edetur decrevi respondere simpliciter et sine ambiguitate. . . ."

95. Calvin to Melanchthon, 3 August 1557, *CO* 16:557; *Letters* 3:337.

96. Calvin to Melanchthon, 10 September 1555, *CO* 16:738; *Letters* 3:219.

97. See Doumergue, *Jean Calvin*, 2:556–58.

98. Calvin to Bullinger, 23 February 1558, *CO* 17:61A; *Letters* 3:410–11.

However, in his last letter to Melanchthon, Calvin expresses his solidarity with Melanchthon, since Melanchthon's students are attacking both of them. In the process, Calvin once again praises Melanchthon's gifts as a teacher: "Wherefore your lot should appear to you less bitter if disciples, who ought to have repaid to your old age what they owed to you, now hostilely attack you, a man who had discharged with the highest fidelity and diligence the function of a teacher, and also deserved the highest honours from the whole church."[99] Moreover, even in the midst of a frank acknowledgment of his disappointment with Melanchthon's silence, and his clear sense that Melanchthon detests Calvin's doctrine of election and reprobation, Calvin declares his undying love for Melanchthon:

> I shall not for all that cease to press towards the mark at which I had begun to aim; in the controversy respecting the Lord's Supper, not only your enemies traduce what they calumniously style your weakness, but your best friends also, and those who cherish you with the pious feelings which you deserve, would wish that the flame of your zeal burned more brightly, of which we behold but some feeble sparks, and thus it is that these pygmies strut like giants. Whatever happens, let us cultivate with sincerity a fraternal affection towards each other, of which no wiles of Satan shall ever burst asunder the ties.[100]

Given the respect that Calvin always had for Melanchthon as a teacher, despite their clear differences in manner and style of teaching, it was only fitting for Calvin's last salutation to Melanchthon be one of respect for his fellow teacher: "Farewell, most illustrious light and distinguished doctor of the church. . . . My colleagues and an innumerable crowd of pious men respectfully salute you."[101]

The very qualities of Melanchthon's gifts as a teacher that drew Calvin to love and respect him also led to Calvin's disagreements with him. Melanchthon sought for clarity and simplicity by studying the method pursued by Plato, Cicero, and especially Aristotle; but Calvin accused Melanchthon of compromising the gospel with philosophy. Melanchthon focused on holding and praying to God as God reveals himself in the Son, but Calvin criticized him for ignoring the clear scriptural doctrine of election and reprobation. Melanchthon sought to speak in consensus with the orthodox, catholic church, yet Calvin accused him of overly accommodating his teaching to the opponents of the gospel. Above all else, Melanchthon sought to free theology from the disputations and brawls of the scholastics, but

99. Calvin to Melanchthon, 13 December 1558, *CO* 17:385–86; *Letters* 3:484.
100. *CO* 17:385–86; *Letters* 3:484.
101. *CO* 17:385–86; *Letters* 3:484.

Calvin criticized his lack of zeal in failing to enter into the fray of doctrinal controversy. In spite of all their differences, however, Calvin never ceased to love, revere, and admire Melanchthon, and to hope that through him the Swiss and the Germans could be reunited. When Melanchthon died in 1560, so did this hope.[102]

102. Nothing more clearly reveals the change in climate created by the death of Melanchthon than the repeated efforts of Calvin to keep the Augsburg Confession, which he himself had signed, from being introduced into France after 1560: "The Augsburg Confession, as you know, is the torch of our deadliest enemy to kindle a conflagration which will set all France on fire. But it behooves you to inquire for what purpose it should be obtruded on you. The author of it repented of his work when his own faintheartedness had always been displeasing to men of energetic character. In most parts, also, it is adapted to the peculiar use of Germany. I forbear to mention that it is obscure in its conciseness, and mutilated by the omission of some articles of capital importance. Besides, it would be absurd, passing by the Confession of the French, eagerly to adopt that one" (Calvin to Beza, 10 September 1561, *Letters*, 4:220). Two years later, the confessional division between Geneva and Germany could not be more clear: "I am carefully on the watch that Lutheranism [*Lutheranismus*] gain no ground, nor be introduced into France" (Calvin to Bullinger, 2 July 1563, *CO* 20:55A). The ecumenical optimism of 1539 is entirely gone.

3

"DO YOU UNDERSTAND WHAT YOU ARE READING?"

Calvin's Guidance for Reading Scripture

One hot day a eunuch of great authority under Candace, Queen of the Ethiopians, was riding home in his chariot. He had just been to the temple in Jerusalem, yet he was not content to have his faith nourished by the priestly exposition of Scripture alone and thus was studiously reading Scripture for himself, specifically the fifty-third chapter of Isaiah. He found enough clarity in the prophet to strengthen his faith; but then he came across a passage that seemed to block his access to the meaning of the prophet, for it spoke of one who in a contradictory way was humiliated beyond all others, and yet exalted above the earth. As he was puzzling over the meaning of this passage, a man appeared and asked him, "Do you understand what you are reading?" The eunuch could

This essay was originally published in a slightly different form under the title "'Do You Understand What You Are Reading?' Calvin's Guidance for the Reading of Scripture," *Scottish Journal of Theology* 54, no. 1 (2001): 1–20. Reprinted by permission.

have dismissed this question with proud disdain. Instead, he responded with modesty and humility, "How can I, unless someone guide me?" Philip answered the eunuch's most pressing question, "Of whom does the prophet speak?" by pointing him to Jesus Christ. The eunuch responded to Philip's help in interpreting Scripture with such faith that he asked to be baptized right there, and then returned home with much joy, for he now knew the one true God, and Jesus Christ, whom he has sent.

As in a picture, this scene from the book of Acts portrays the kind of situation Calvin tried to restore to the church. The reading of Scripture would be restored to all Christians so that they could confirm for themselves the teaching that they heard from others, and interpreters would be available to all Christians to guide them in reading Scripture when further access to its meaning seemed otherwise closed to them. "And we must keep in mind here, that not only is Scripture given to us, but interpreters and teachers are also added to help us."[1] Only in this way did Calvin think that Christ would again be known by all Christians not only in name, but also in power, to be embraced as he is offered to us through the gospel.

Restoring Scripture Reading to All Christians

From the very beginning of his adherence to the evangelical movement, Calvin above all else sought to restore the proper and fruitful reading of Scripture to every Christian, no matter how unlearned that person might be. Evidence of this concern may be seen as early as 1535, in the Latin and French prefaces he wrote to Olivetan's French translation of the Bible. In the Latin preface, Calvin addresses those who oppose the attempt to place Scripture in the hands of ordinary Christians: "But the ungodly voices of some are heard, shouting that it is a shameful thing to publish these divine mysteries among the simple common people. . . . How then, they ask, can these poor illiterates comprehend such things, untutored as they are in the liberal arts, and (if practice is involved) ignorant of all things?"[2] Calvin replies to this objection by saying that all Christians are to be taught by God, for God teaches all Christians in his school by the text of Scripture. "When, therefore, we see that there are people from all classes making progress in God's school, we acknowledge His truth which promised a pouring forth of his spirit on all flesh [Joel

1. Comm. on Acts 8:31, *CO* 48:192B; *CNTC* 6:247.
2. *Ioannis Calvinus caesaribus, regibus, principibus, gentibusque omnibus christi imperio subditis salutem*, *CO* 9:747–48; *Institutes of the Christian Religion*, 1536 edition, trans. and annotated by Ford Lewis Battles, rev. ed. (1975; repr., Grand Rapids: Eerdmans, 1986), 374.

2:28; Acts 2:17]."[3] Calvin also appeals to the fathers to defend the reading of Scripture by all Christians, even in light of the danger of heresy. "Chrysostom and Augustine—when do they not urge the common people to this study—how frequently [don't] they insist that what they hear in church they should apply in [their] homes? Why is it that Chrysostom contends that the reading of Holy Scripture is more necessary for common people than monks?"[4] In the French preface, Calvin claims that all who exercise care over the church have the duty of restoring the reading of Scripture to all Christians. Rulers are to see to it "that the entire teaching of the gospel is kept in its purity and truth; that the Holy Scriptures are faithfully preached, read, and perused."[5] Bishops and pastors are to make sure that "it is not prohibited to any Christian freely and in his own language to read, handle, and hear his holy gospel, seeing that such is the will of God, and Jesus Christ commands it."[6]

Calvin knew, however, that placing Scripture in the hands of ordinary Christians would not of itself be sufficient. Godly interpreters must also be sent to the church to guide Christians in their reading of the Bible so that they might not get lost in their search for the true knowledge of God.[7] Calvin clearly thought that he had been called to offer such guidance himself, although it was not initially clear to him what shape that assistance should take. The design of Calvin's efforts to offer guidance and instruction to the church underwent considerable development in the first six years of his membership in the evangelical movement (1535–41). Calvin's first attempt to guide the unlearned took the form of the 1536 edition of the *Institutes*, which was clearly intended to be a catechism to instruct all Christians in the rudiments of true doctrine.[8]

---

3. *Institutes* (1536 ed.), 374.

4. Ibid., 375.

5. *A tous amateurs de Iesus Christ, et de son S. Evangile, salut, CO* 9:816; *Calvin: Commentaries*, 72.

6. *CO* 9:816; *Calvin: Commentaries*, 72.

7. Calvin therefore agrees in part with Roman critics of the principle of *sola Scriptura*, for with them he emphasizes the central importance of the interpretation of Scripture by the church. According to Calvin, the church fell into ruin when it lost godly interpreters of Scripture, and will only be restored when both Scripture and godly interpreters are again given to the church. Calvin differed from Rome, however, in his desire to make every Christian a godly interpreter of Scripture. Calvin's focus on the need to interpret Scripture also distinguishes him from the Gnesio-Lutheran understanding of *sola Scriptura*, at least as represented by Westphal. "We are perfectly agreed that we must acquiesce in the words of Christ: the only question is as to their genuine meaning. But when it is inquired into, our masters of the letter admit of no interpretation (*nullam interpretationem*). Away, then, with all this cunning, and leave us at liberty to ask what our Savior meant" (*Ultima admonitio ad Westphalum, CO* 9:184A; *Tracts and Treatises* 2:403).

8. "At this period *Institutio* was the synonym of *Catechismus*" (Nubuo Watanabe, "Calvin's Second Catechism," in *Calvinus Sacrae Scripturae Professor*, ed. Wilhelm H.

"My purpose was solely to transmit certain rudiments by which those who are touched with any zeal for religion might be shaped to true godliness. . . . The book itself witnesses that this was my intention, adapted as it is to a simple and, you may say, elementary form of teaching."[9] As many scholars have noted, the format of Luther's *Small Catechism* is clearly discernable in this edition.[10]

When Calvin was detained in Geneva at Farel's insistence in 1536, he accepted the office of "doctor" or "reader of Holy Scriptures."[11] In this office, Calvin embarked upon his lectures of Scripture, beginning with Romans, which were to bear further fruit in his commentaries. When Calvin was called to the office of pastor at the end of 1536, he quickly realized the importance of catechizing the young in the rudiments of godly doctrine, and of the inadequacy of the *Institutes* as a catechetical text. The *Articles concerning the Organization of the Church* of 1537 clearly mandate that "there be a brief and simple summary of the Christian faith, to be taught to all children."[12] To meet this need, Calvin greatly condensed the 1536 *Institutes* into the 1537 *Instruction in Faith*. The *Institutes* would never again be intended to give rudimentary instruction to ordinary Christians. As a pastor, Calvin also became vividly aware of the alarming lack of well-trained pastors for the evangelical congregations, and of the need to instruct future candidates for the ministry.[13]

After his expulsion from Geneva, Calvin used his time in Strasbourg to redesign the whole of his program of instruction for the church, given the inadequacies of his initial attempts in this direction. While in Sturm's Academy in Strasbourg, Calvin lectured on Scripture to future candidates for the ministry and developed a new program of instruction specifically designed for such candidates. He edited the *Institutes* after the pattern of Melanchthon's 1535 *Loci communes*, which was itself intended for future teachers and preachers of the gospel. Instead of adopting a simple and elementary form of teaching, as in the first edition, Calvin in the second edition claimed to "have so embraced the sum of religion in all its parts, and have arranged it in such an order, that if anyone rightly holds to it,

---

Neuser [Grand Rapids: Eerdmans, 1994], 228–29). In 1557, Calvin described the 1536 edition as a *breve enchiridion* (*CO* 31:23).

9. *Institutes* (1536 ed.), 1; *OS* 3:8.6–8, 11–13. See Ford Lewis Battles, "The First Edition of the *Institutes* (1536)," in *Interpreting John Calvin*, ed. Robert Benedetto (Grand Rapids: Baker, 1996), 91–93.

10. Wulfert de Greef, *The Writings of John Calvin*, trans. Lyle D. Bierma (Grand Rapids: Baker, 1993), 195–97.

11. Alexandre Ganoczy, *The Young Calvin*, trans. David Foxgrover and Wade Provo (Philadelphia: Westminster, 1987), 108.

12. *CO* 10a:12–13; *Calvin: Theological Treatises*, 54.

13. Ganoczy, *Young Calvin*, 111.

it will not be difficult for him to determine what he ought especially to seek in Scripture, and to what end he ought to relate its contents."[14] Once this path was opened into Scripture, Calvin directed such candidates to his commentaries, beginning with Romans, which itself is described as a pathway into the whole of Scripture.[15] While Calvin was in Strasbourg, he also began to distinguish the office of teacher from the office of pastor, with the former as teachers of the latter.[16]

Besides developing a new program of study for future candidates for the ministry, Calvin also used his time in Strasbourg to revise his plan of instruction for ordinary Christians, given the inadequacies of his initial catechetical efforts. He wrote a new catechism in French[17] and planned a translation of Chrysostom's homilies into French, so that unlearned Christians might be aided in their reading of Scripture just as candidates for the ministry were aided by Calvin's commentaries.

> The point is, if it is right that ordinary Christians be not deprived of the Word of their God, neither should they be denied prospective resources, which may be of use for its true understanding. . . . It is obvious, therefore, that they should be assisted by the work of interpreters, who have advanced in the knowledge of God to a level that they can guide others as well. . . . All I have had in mind with this is to facilitate the reading of Holy Scripture for those who are humble and uneducated.[18]

Against those who claimed that Chrysostom aimed to be read only by the learned, Calvin claims that "he plainly adjusts both [his] approach and his language as if he had the instruction of the common people in mind."[19] Thus, by 1540 Calvin had clearly designated the *Institutes*

14. Latin preface to the reader, *Institutio Christianae religionis* (1559), *OS* 3:6; *LCC* 1:4. Serene Jones (*Calvin and the Rhetoric of Piety* [Louisville: Westminster John Knox, 1995], 27) notes the centrality of Scripture for the faithful in Calvin's view, but she has Calvin join the persuasive efforts of Scripture and the Holy Spirit with his own rhetoric. I in contrast note that Calvin seeks in the *Institutes* to open access to the main themes of Scripture by the dialectical method of *loci communes*, which he derives in large part from the prior example of Philip Melanchthon, so that students know which themes to look for as they read Scripture. Such guidance is to my mind distinct from the effort to persuade.

15. "If we have gained a true understanding of this epistle, we have an open door to all the most profound treasures of Scripture" (Comm. on Romans, argumentum, *Romanos* 5.10–11; *CNTC* 8:5).

16. Comm. on Rom. 12:7, *Romanos* 271.70–77; *CNTC* 8:269–70.

17. *L'institution puerile de la doctrine chrestienne faicte par maniere de dyalogue*, *OS* 2:152–56; see De Greef, *Writings*, 132.

18. John Calvin, *Praefatio in Chrysostomi homilias*, *CO* 9:833A; "Calvin's Preface to Chrysostom's Homilies," trans. W. Ian P. Hazlett, in *Humanism and Reform: The Church in Europe, England, and Scotland, 1400–1643: Essays in Honour of James K. Cameron*, ed. James Kirk (Oxford: Blackwell, 1991), 141–42.

19. "Calvin's Preface to Chrysostom's Homilies," 141–42.

and the commentaries as the program of instruction for candidates of sacred theology, and the catechism and homilies of Chrysostom as the curriculum for ordinary Christians.[20]

This change in Calvin's method of instruction is clearly reflected in Calvin's literary output immediately after his return to Geneva. The *Draft Ecclesiological Ordinances* of 1541 clearly distinguish between the office of teacher and the office of pastor. Teachers are responsible for the instruction of pastors, primarily through their lectures on Scripture. Pastors are responsible for teaching their congregations by both the catechism and their sermons, which the people are to attend consistently and attentively, as in a class in school.[21] In 1542, Calvin developed a new edition of his catechism, this time in the form of question and answer, no doubt intended to indicate the duty of all Christians to inquire into the truth of the doctrine they profess. In 1543, Calvin published his third edition of the *Institutes*, with major chapters added on the organization of the church, including the distinction between pastors and doctors seen above. In 1546, the publication of the commentaries on Scripture recommenced, beginning with 1 Corinthians, and continuing unabated until Calvin's death. Finally, in 1549, Calvin's sermons began to be transcribed in French, and their publication eventually accomplished the guidance of ordinary Christians that he had initially sought in Chrysostom's homilies.[22] Thus, by 1549 all elements of Calvin's plan of instruction for the school of Christ were emerging in print: the *Institutes* and commentaries for pastors, and the *Catechism* and sermons for ordinary Christians.[23]

20. It is clear that there is not a watertight distinction between these audiences. In the preface to the French translation of the *Institutes* of 1541, Calvin expresses the hope that ordinary Christians will profit from the guidance he offers in the *Institutes*; and in the preface to the Chrysostom homilies, Calvin indicates that the homilies will be useful to pastors who lack a knowledge of classical languages. However, in both cases, it is clear that these are secondary audiences. Calvin's deletion of the French preface from the 1559/60 *Institutes* may well indicate that by this time he no longer had the ordinary Christian in mind even as a secondary audience for that work. See Richard A. Muller, "Calvin's 'Argument du livre' (1541): An Erratum to the McNeill and Battles *Institutes*," *Sixteenth Century Journal* 29, no. 1 (1998): 37.

21. This aspect of the catechism and sermon is clearly manifested in the 1547 *Ordonnances sur la police des églises de la campagne*, *CO* 10a:51–52; *Calvin: Theological Treatises*, 77.

22. The sermons on whole books of Scripture did not appear in print until 1561; see De Greef, *Writings*, 114.

23. Given the fact that this plan of instruction assumes the literacy of each and every Christian, something that was far from being the case in Calvin's day, one would also have to add the opening of the Geneva Academy in 1559 to the curriculum Calvin designed for the instruction of the unlearned. Calvin's vision of Christian education is much indebted to the labors of Melanchthon and Sturm in this area.

Teachers and Pastors as Guides of the Faithful

By 1541, Calvin had become convinced that Christ willed to guide his church by means of two distinct kinds of scriptural interpreters: teachers (doctors) and pastors. Both are teaching offices, guiding the faithful in the right way to read Scripture to confirm their faith. However, doctors teach the universal church its essential dogmas and doctrines of piety, and defend such doctrines from error by preserving the true, simple, and genuine meaning of Scripture.[24] Doctors have the responsibility for teaching future pastors, and for correcting any damage done to the church by faulty pastors.[25] Pastors differ from teachers in that they do not instruct other pastors and the universal church, but teach only a particular congregation. Pastors are also unique because they not only teach and preach doctrine drawn from the genuine meaning of Scripture, but they also exhort, admonish, warn, and censure their congregation and every individual therein, and administer the sacraments.[26] The ultimate objective of the pastor is to apply the genuine meaning of Scripture to the life of each individual in his congregation, over and above preaching in a general way to the whole congregation.[27]

The relation of doctors to pastors therefore moves from the universal to the general to the particular. Doctors teach the doctrines of piety and the true understanding of Scripture to the universal church and its pastors.

24. Sermon on Eph. 4:11, *CO* 51:556C; *John Calvin's Sermons on Ephesians* (Edinburgh: Banner of Truth, 1973), 365.

25. "As things are disposed today, we always include under this title aids and instructions for maintaining the doctrine of God and defending the Church from injury by the fault of pastors and ministers" (*Les ordonnances ecclésiastiques* [1541], *CO* 10a:21–22; *Calvin: Theological Treatises*, 62). These aids might include making available to ordinary Christians the instruction primarily designed for pastors, as may also be indicated by the translation of the *Institutes* and commentaries into French. "In addition, in many places where Calvin is clearly working from the 1539 Latin, the 1541 French text offers considerable argumentation and explanation, often intended to accommodate the text to an audience . . . less erudite than his Latin readers" (Muller, "Calvin's 'Argument du livre' (1541)," 37).

26. *Les ordonnances ecclésiastiques* (1541), *CO* 10a:21–22; *Calvin: Theological Treatises*, 62.

27. "For Christ did not ordain pastors on the principle that they only teach the Church in a general way on the public platform, but that they also care for the individual sheep, bring back the wandering and scattered to the fold, bind up those broken and crippled, heal the sick, support the frail and weak (Ezek. 34:2–4); for general teaching will often have a cold reception, unless it is helped by advice given in private" (Comm. on Acts 20:20, *CO* 48:462; *CNTC* 7:175). Serene Jones (*Calvin and the Rhetoric of Piety*, 28) quotes Calvin's statement that doctrine generally stated does not move us, but she does not attend to the way Calvin leaves the explicit application of doctrine to life first to the sermons of pastors, and then to their private advice. In the whole of Calvin's program of study, the *Institutes* are at the furthest remove from this concrete application.

Pastors preach such doctrine, and interpret Scripture, both in general to the whole congregation and in particular to each individual therein.[28] Even though both are teaching offices, the gifts necessary for each office are distinct. One may be given the gifts of teaching—skill in Scripture and clarity of teaching—without being given those of a pastor, as in the case of Philip Melanchthon. "Teaching is a duty of all pastors; but there is a particular gift of interpreting Scripture, so that sound doctrine may be kept; and a man may be a doctor who is not fitted to preach."[29] Pastors need distinct gifts not always found in teachers, for they need to be able to exhort and advise congregations and individuals, and "he who teaches is not at once endowed with the gift of exhortation."[30]

Calvin was one of the rare people in the church called to be both a doctor and a pastor in the church.[31] The literary legacy Calvin left to us must therefore be evaluated according to the office Calvin exercises in writing each work, and its intended audience. After 1539, Calvin produced the *Institutes*, along with the commentaries and lectures on Scripture, as a doctor of the catholic church, along with the Latin polemical treatises. In these works Calvin is teaching the universal church the sound doctrines of piety and the true interpretation of Scripture, and defending both from error. The catechisms, sermons, and French treatises, on the other hand, were produced by Calvin in his office as a pastor of the church, teaching the doctrines of piety and preaching the true understanding of Scripture to the members of a specific congregation, and applying it to their individual lives.[32] Calvin's work in both offices was

28. "Pastors, to my mind, are those to whom is committed the charge of a particular flock. I have no objection to their receiving the name of doctors, if we realize that there is another kind of doctor, who superintends both the education of pastors and the instruction of the whole church. Sometimes he can be a pastor who is also a doctor, but the duties [*facultates*] are different" (Comm. on Eph. 4:11, *CO* 51:198A; *CNTC* 11:179).

29. *CO* 51:198A; *CNTC* 11:179

30. Comm. on Rom. 12:7, *Romanos* 271.75–76; *CNTC* 8:270. Since Calvin produces the *Institutes* in his office as teacher, it would be the text most remote from Calvin's concern to exhort and persuade. Jones does not adequately consider the fact that Calvin thinks one can be a very fine teacher without being given great persuasive or exhortative skills, as was clearly the case with Philip Melanchthon, whom Calvin greatly admired as a teacher of the church, but who was not called to be a pastor.

31. "In that Church I have held the office [*munere*] first of Doctor [*Doctoris*], and then of pastor [*pastoris*]. In my own right, I maintain that in undertaking these offices I had a legitimate vocation" (*Responsio ad Sadoleti epistolam, CO* 5:386B; John C. Olin, ed., *A Reformation Debate* [Grand Rapids: Baker, 1976], 50). See John T. McNeill, "John Calvin: Doctor Ecclesiae," in *The Heritage of John Calvin*, ed. John H. Bratt (Grand Rapids: Eerdmans, 1973), 10.

32. Jones (*Calvin and the Rhetoric of Piety*, 53) notes four possible audiences for Calvin's writing in the *Institutes*: students, friends and followers in French parishes, humanists, and enemies. I completely agree that we need to take into account the audiences Calvin had in mind for his writings, but it seems to me that Jones misses the different audiences

directed to the goal of bringing the genuine sense of Scripture, and the doctrine to be drawn from it, to bear on the concrete lives of individual, ordinary Christians, so that their own reading of Scripture might bear fruit. In sum, Calvin envisioned a church in which all Christians would read Scripture for themselves, under the guidance of their pastors, who themselves would be guided by the teachers of the church catholic.

Beginning in 1539, Calvin wrote the *Institutes* in fulfillment of his office as doctor of the catholic church; for in the *Institutes* he teaches the pure doctrine of piety to the universal church and defends such doctrine against the errors of false teachers in the church. "I am also duly clear in my own conscience, and have God and the angels to witness, that since I undertook the office of teacher in the church, I have had no other purpose than to benefit the church by maintaining the pure doctrine of godliness."[33] Calvin claims in the *Institutes* to teach everything God teaches us in Scripture, no more and no less. Hence the doctrine of piety taught in the *Institutes* is drawn from the genuine meaning of Scripture, and its topics are even taught in the order that God uses in Scripture. The purpose of such an orderly presentation of doctrine is to open access to the genuine meaning of Scripture for future pastors, so that Calvin might guide them to the true understanding of Scripture.

> Moreover, it has been my purpose in this labor to prepare and instruct candidates in sacred theology for the reading of the divine Word, in order that they may be able to have easy access to it and to advance in it without stumbling. For I believe that I have so embraced the sum of religion in all its parts, and have arranged it in such an order, that if anyone rightly grasps it, it will not be difficult for him to determine what he ought especially to seek in Scripture, and to what end he ought to relate its contents.[34]

The training of future pastors should therefore lead from the summary of doctrine in the *Institutes* to the reading of Sacred Scripture itself.

Once pastors are equipped with such a summary of doctrine, Calvin with his biblical commentaries offers them further assistance in their

---

based on the different offices. The audience for the *Institutes* and commentaries is pastors and other learned teachers of the universal church, including the church in Switzerland, England, the Netherlands, Denmark, northern Germany, southern Germany, Italy, Poland, and Hungary, as well as France. The *Institutes* are written for the godly—the Latin polemical treatises are written for Calvin's enemies, such as Pighius, Westphal, and Heshusius. Members of French parishes would be the audience for the catechism, the sermons, and the French treatises, and only secondarily the *Institutes* and commentaries. Jones, however, does not mention the primary beneficiaries of all of Calvin's labors: the unlearned, who need to be guided by pastors so that they might read Scripture with profit.

33. "Preface to the Reader," *Inst.* (1559), *OS* 3:6.1–4; LCC 1:4.

34. *OS* 3:6.18–25; LCC 1:4.

reading of Scripture. In these commentaries, Calvin sets forth the true, simple, and genuine meaning of Scripture, by showing how such meaning flows smoothly and naturally from the context, thereby revealing the mind of the author of Scripture with lucid brevity.[35] The teacher as biblical interpreter therefore follows a different method than does the teacher in a summary of doctrine like the *Institutes*. This difference emerges in Calvin's comments on Gen. 17:9, regarding circumcision. "Moreover, although it would, perhaps, be more suitable for the purpose of instruction, were we to give a summary of those things which are to be said concerning circumcision; I will yet follow the order to the context, which I think is more appropriate to the office of an interpreter."[36] When teaching the summary of the doctrine of piety, Calvin follows the order of right teaching, gathering all that can be said in Scripture under distinct doctrinal topics, and ordering those topics according to the order of teaching God follows in the whole of Scripture. When interpreting Scripture, Calvin follows the order of the context of a particular book of Scripture, allowing the meaning to emerge in a natural and unforced way from that context. Once Calvin establishes the true meaning of Scripture in this way, he then proceeds to draw fruitful doctrine from that meaning, which pastors should teach in the universal church and apply to the lives of congregations. However, he does so with lucid brevity, leaving the much lengthier work of concrete application to the pastors in their sermons and private advice.[37] Thus, teachers lead future pastors from the summary of doctrine in commonplaces to the true meaning of Scripture in commentaries, so that pastors might draw fruitful doctrine from the genuine meaning of Scripture and apply it concretely to their congregations through their preaching and private advice.

35. "Both of us felt that lucid brevity constituted the particular virtue of an interpreter. Since it is almost his only task to reveal the mind of the writer whom he has undertaken to expound, he misses the mark, or at least strays outside his limits, by the extent to which he leads his readers away from the meaning of his author" (John Calvin to Simon Grynaeus, *Romanos* 1.3–12; *CNTC* 8:1). With regard to the importance of the context, Calvin says, "I am aware that a widely different meaning is given by some to the words of the prophet; but any one who takes a judicious view of the whole context will have little difficulty, I trust, in assenting to my interpretation" (Comm. on Isa. 18:4, *CO* 36:324C; *CTS* 14:42).

36. Comm. on Gen. 17:9, *CO* 23:239C; *CTS* 1:451. Bucer was one who would gather all that is said in Scripture as a locus, and make it part of his commentary. Calvin delegates all such *loci communes* to the *Institutes*, so that in the commentaries he can exclusively follow the order of the context.

37. Calvin was quite explicit about the programmatic distinction between his commentaries and sermons. Commenting on Eph. 4:5 on the unity of all in the Lord, Calvin says, "All these arguments for unity ought to be pondered more than they can be explained. I have been content to point out the apostle's meaning briefly, and leave the fuller treatment to sermons [*concionibus*]" (Comm. on Eph. 4:5, *CO* 51:191B; *CNTC* 11:173).

In his office as pastor, Calvin follows a similar method of teaching, although this time directed to his congregation, and not to other pastors or the universal church. In his *Catechism* of 1542/45, Calvin sets forth for the young a summary of the rudiments of true doctrine, which all Christians should seek in their reading of Scripture, following the order of right teaching also exhibited in the *Institutes*.[38] In his sermons, Calvin guides the congregation in their reading of Scripture by showing how the genuine meaning of Scripture flows from the order of the context, and by drawing fruitful doctrine from that meaning. The bulk of his work as a preacher, unlike his work as a teacher, consists of applying that doctrine to the lives of the members of his congregation, and exhorting them to be transformed by the power of the doctrine they are hearing, which is none other than the power of Christ working by his Spirit. However, such general preaching to the whole congregation is just the first step of the pastor's application of Scripture; the real work begins when the pastor visits every member of the congregation in private in order to apply scriptural doctrine specifically to them. Yet as we have seen, doctrine drawn from the true meaning of Scripture has the effect of opening access to the fruitful reading of Scripture for the one learning that doctrine. Hence, the doctrine that the preacher draws from the genuine meaning of Scripture, in conjunction with the *Catechism*, plays the same role for the congregation that the commentaries did for the pastor, in conjunction with the *Institutes*. In his sermons, the pastor is to guide each member of his congregation in the right reading of Scripture, just as Calvin guides pastors to the true meaning of Scripture in his commentaries.

Reading Scripture While Hearing Instruction

Calvin worked to create a church in which all Christians—teachers, pastors, and ordinary Christians—would be reading Scripture for themselves and would also be hearing and receiving instruction from others to guide their reading. "But when Paul speaks of the usefulness of Scripture, he concludes not only that everyone should read it, but also that teachers ought to administer it, which is the duty laid upon them."[39] Calvin juxtaposed his vision for the church with that of three other groups: the "enthusiasts," the Church of Rome, and the "fanatics."

38. It is also likely that Calvin translated the *Institutes* into French, beginning with the 1539 edition, so that ordinary Christians would be guided in their reading of Scripture by that more extensive summary of the doctrine of piety and religion. All I am maintaining here is that the primary audience for the *Institutes* was future pastors and teachers.

39. Comm. on 2 Tim. 4:1, *CO* 52:384C; *CNTC* 10:332.

Calvin agreed with the "enthusiasts" that the Holy Spirit was the necessary guide into all truth, but he rejected their claim that the gift of the Holy Spirit made it unnecessary for them to read the Word of God and hear instruction from others. "It is an illusory belief of the Enthusiasts that those who keep reading Scripture or hearing the Word are children, as if no one were spiritual unless he scorned doctrine. In their pride, therefore, they despise the ministry of men, and even Scripture itself, in order to attain the Spirit."[40] Calvin agreed with the Church of Rome that all Christians need to listen teachably to the preaching of their pastors, but he rejected the claim that Christians were simply to listen to what they were told without verifying what they heard by their own reading of Scripture. "I maintain that it is easy to judge the spirit that actuates those who scarcely allow men to touch what the apostle bids them to handle constantly; who pretend that the neglect that is here so severely reproved is in fact praiseworthy; who take away the Word of God, the only true rule of discernment, which is declared here to be necessary for all Christians."[41] Finally, Calvin agreed with the "fanatics" that all Christians should read Scripture for themselves, but he denied their claim that this made seeking guidance from teachers and pastors unnecessary. "Let us remember that the fact that the reading of the Scripture is recommended to all does not annul the ministry of pastors, so that believers should learn to profit both by reading and by hearing, since God has not ordained either in vain."[42] Christians must not only read but also hear, so that they may constantly make progress in the school of Christ under the instruction of their pastors. However, Christians must not only hear but also read, in order to confirm that their pastors are drawing their teaching from the pure fountain of Scripture.[43]

Ordinary Christians are not the only ones who must undertake a life-long discipline of reading Scripture and hearing instruction from others. Calvin claims that even the most skilled and experienced teachers of the church must exercise themselves in the daily reading of Scripture. Even when the apostle Paul was nearing the end of his life, he nonetheless asked Timothy to bring his "books and parchments." "Where are those who think that they have progressed so far that they need do no

40. Comm. on 1 Thess. 5:20, *CO* 52:176; *CNTC* 8:377.
41. Comm. on Heb. 5:14, *OE* 19:86; *CNTC* 12:69.
42. Comm. on 2 Tim. 4:1, *CO* 52:385; *CNTC* 10:332.
43. "C: While everyone ought to exercise himself in daily reading, at the same time also all are to attend with special regularity the gatherings where the doctrine of salvation is expounded in the company of the faithful. M: You deny then that it is enough for each to read privately at home; and affirm that all should meet together to hear the same doctrine? C: They must meet when they can, that is, when opportunity offers" (*Catechismus ecclesiae Genevensis, hoc est, formula erudiendi pueros in doctrina Christi, CO* 6:110; *Calvin: Theological Treatises*, 130).

more, and which of them dare compare himself with Paul? . . . But we should note that this passage commends continual reading to all godly men as a thing from which they can profit."[44] Teachers must also be ready and willing to listen to the instruction of others throughout their lives, because God has not revealed the fullness of his wisdom to any individual. We need to remain in humble communion with others not only as their teachers but also as their students. "For no one will ever be a good teacher, if he does not show himself teachable, and always ready to learn; and the man will never be met who is so self-sufficient in the fullness and completeness of his knowledge that he would gain nothing by listening to other people."[45] Scripture is lowly enough to be read with profit by the most unlearned Christian; yet it contains enough obscurities and difficulties to humble even the most learned Christian, so that he, like Daniel, might seek guidance from others. "Therefore, as Daniel approached the angel who was near him, so we are daily commanded to approach those who have been entrusted with the gift of interpretation, and who can faithfully explain to us things otherwise obscure."[46]

Pastors are also to read Scripture daily, so that they might ensure that what they teach the congregation is drawn from the Word of God in Scripture. Commenting on 1 Tim. 4:13, "Till I come, give heed to reading, to exhortation, to preaching," Calvin says, "For how can pastors teach others unless they themselves are able to learn. . . . We should notice the order, how he mentions reading before teaching and exhortation, for Scripture is the source of all wisdom and pastors ought to draw from it all that they set before the flock."[47] In conjunction with their reading of Scripture, Calvin wanted pastors to hear the interpretation of Scripture set forth by the doctors of the church in their lectures and/or commentaries.[48] Calvin also wanted pastors to meet together regularly to discuss Scripture and doctrine, so that they might continue to learn

44. Comm. on 2 Tim. 4:13, *CO* 52:392–93; *CNTC* 10:340–41; see also Calvin's sermon on the same passage.

45. Comm. on 1 Cor. 14:31, *CO* 49:530; *CNTC* 9:303. Calvin was clearly indebted to the instruction he received from other teachers of doctrine, especially Irenaeus, Augustine, Luther, Melanchthon, Bucer, Zwingli, and Bullinger. He was also indebted to the guidance in the interpretation of Scripture he received from others, especially Chrysostom, Ambrosiaster, Cyril, Oecolampadius, Melanchthon, Bucer, and Bullinger, along with Budé and Erasmus.

46. Comm. on Dan. 7:15–16, *CO* 41:65A; CTS 25:48.

47. Comm. on 1 Tim. 4:13, *CO* 52:302; *CNTC* 10:246–47.

48. "The degree nearest to the ministers and most closely conjoined to the government of the church is the lecturer in theology, of which it will be good to have one in Old Testament and one in New Testament" (*Draft Ecclesiological Ordinances*, *CO* 10a:21; *Calvin: Theological Treatises*, 62–63).

from one another, and preserve unity with one another.[49] Significantly, the congregations of the pastors in Geneva discussed Scripture following the same method of continuous reading practiced by Calvin in his commentaries and sermons.[50]

The church Calvin envisioned is therefore one in which every Christian, from the most learned to the most unlearned, is simultaneously both a teacher and a student.

> Therefore away with this foolish arrogance to think ourselves wise enough (I speak even of those who are able to teach others) and let us continue scholars still. For although Jesus Christ has appointed certain men to be leaders and guides to show other men the way, yet it does not follow that they are so wise that they must not be learners as well as the rest. For he that speaks must take instruction by it himself, and a man will never be fit to declare God's will to other men, unless he himself learns daily.[51]

In such a school of Christ, the unlearned would not be too proud to learn from pastors and teachers more learned than they; nor would learned and eloquent pastors and teachers be too proud to learn from those they might regard as less learned than they. A striking instance of this latter dynamic occurs in Acts 18:26, when the learned and eloquent Apollos is taken aside to be given further instruction by Aquila and Priscilla.

> Aquila and Priscilla are not devoted to themselves, with the result that they are not envious of another man's ability. . . . Again, Apollos was unusually modest, for he allowed himself to be taught and refined, not only by a manual worker, but also by a woman. For he was mighty in Scripture, and far superior to them; but those, who could have given the impression of being hardly suitable ministers, give him the finishing touches about what makes the kingdom of Christ complete. We see also that at that time women were not so unacquainted with the Word of God as the papists wish to have them, since we see that one of the chief teachers of the Church was taught by a woman.[52]

Calvin insisted that in a rightly ordered church women could give private instruction even to the most learned of pastors and teachers (even though he also thought that it was contrary to the order prescribed by God for women to teach publicly in the church); and pastors and teach-

---

49. *CO* 10a:18; *Calvin: Theological Treatises*, 60.

50. De Greef, *Writings*, 117.

51. Sermon on Eph. 4:13, *CO* 51:572B; *Sermons on Ephesians*, 382.

52. Comm. on Acts 18:26, *CO* 48:437–38; *CNTC* 7:144–45. See Jane Dempsey Douglass, *Women, Freedom, and Calvin* (Philadelphia: Westminster, 1985); and John Lee Thompson, *John Calvin and the Daughters of Sarah* (Geneva: Droz, 1992).

ers would be willing to accept such instruction by women. This picture of the church was confirmed by what he read in the fathers. "Jerome did not disdain mere women as partners in his studies. . . . Pamphilius the Martyr, who always had sacred codices ready at home to pass out to men and women, was praised by Eusebius."[53]

Because every Christian is as much a teacher as a student, all Christians must have the right and ability to judge the truth of the doctrine being taught to them by their own investigation of Scripture. "For instance: an unknown teacher will profess that he is bringing true teaching; I shall come to him, ready to listen, and my mind will be disposed to obey the truth; nevertheless at the same time I shall ponder what sort of teaching it is, and I shall embrace what I recognize to be the certain truth."[54] Calvin wanted all Christians to follow this method in order to find their way through the confusion of teachings in his day, which all claimed to come from the Word of God in Scripture. Calvin himself applied this combination of a teachable disposition and a critical inquiry in his treatment of Anabaptist doctrine. Because the Anabaptists claim to be teaching the Word of God, "we grant that everything that appears to have come from God and derives from his holy Word ought to be received by us all, humbly and without any further controversy or difficulty." On the other hand, their claim to teach nothing but what is drawn from Scripture must be verified. "Therefore, whether Anabaptists or others say to us that what they declare they have received from God and taken from his mouth, let us give this glory to God and listen to see if such is the case."[55]

Calvin wanted all Christians to be given the ability to judge the truth of all doctrine by their own reading of Scripture, so that they might decide for themselves that the preaching they hear is true, even as the Jews of Beroea were allowed to inquire into the truth of Paul's preaching. "The Pope wishes all to accept without questioning, whatever he has blabbed out according to his fancy. But will he be regarded as superior to Paul, into whose teaching learners were allowed to make inquiries?"[56] When the church prohibits Christians from making inquiries into the truth of its teaching, it is already on the path to error. Calvin ascribes the source of the corrupt teaching of the Church of Rome to the fact that the laity were prohibited from reading Scripture for themselves,

---

53. *Ioannis Calvinus caesaribus*, *CO* 9:788; *Institutes* (1536), 375.

54. Comm. on Acts 17:11, *CO* 48:401B; *CNTC* 7:101.

55. *Brief Instruction for Arming All the Good and Faithful against the Errors of the Common Sect of the Anabaptists*, *CO* 7:56; *Treatises against the Anabaptists and against the Libertines*, trans. and ed. Benjamin W. Farley (Grand Rapids: Baker, 1982), 42.

56. Comm. on Acts 17:11, *CO* 48:401B; *CNTC* 7:101.

making them unable to detect that what the priests told them was not the Word of God.

> Those who were regarded as the leaders of faith neither understood the Word, nor greatly cared for it. They drove unhappy people to and fro with strange doctrines, and deluded them with I know not what follies. Among the people themselves, the highest veneration paid to the Word was to revere it at a distance, as a thing inaccessible, and abstain from all investigation of it. Owing to this supine state of the pastors, and the stupidity of the people, every place was filled with pernicious errors, falsehoods, and superstition.[57]

By restoring the investigation of Scripture to all Christians, Calvin sought to make it possible for them not only to falsify doctrine not being drawn from Scripture, but also to confirm their faith in the truth of preaching drawn from the fountain of Scripture.

> Therefore, let this firm axiom stand, that no doctrine is worth believing except as we perceive it to be based on the Scriptures, . . . which makes it all the clearer that individuals are called to read Scripture. . . . For instance, I shall hear from the Gospel that I am reconciled to God by the grace of Christ, and that my sins are expiated by his sacred blood; evidence will be produced which makes me believe. If afterwards I examine the Scriptures more thoroughly, other testimonies will repeatedly present themselves, and these will not only help my faith, but increase and establish it, so that greater certitude will come. Similarly, as far as understanding is concerned, faith makes progress from the reading of Scripture.[58]

Christians who read Scripture for themselves are preserved from error, confirmed in the truth by what they read, and equipped to teach others on the basis of what they draw from Scripture themselves, even as they are guided in their reading of Scripture by what they hear from their pastors and teachers. The teachers and pastors of the church succeed most in their office when their students can test the truth of their teach-

---

57. *Responsio ad Sadoletum, CO* 5:408; Olin, *Reformation Debate*, 82. The same observation is made by the member of the evangelical congregation before the judgment seat of God: "I, O Lord, as I had been educated from a boy, always professed the Christian faith. But at first I had no other reason for my faith than that which everywhere prevailed. Thy Word, which ought to have shown on all thy people like a lamp, was taken away, or at least suppressed as to us. And lest anyone should long for a greater light, an idea had been instilled into the minds of all, that the investigation of that hidden celestial philosophy was better delegated to a few, whom the others might consult as oracles—that the highest knowledge befitting plebian minds was to subdue themselves into obedience to the Church" (*CO* 5:411; Olin, *Reformation Debate*, 87).

58. Comm. on Acts 17:11, *CO* 48:401–2; *CNTC* 7:102.

ing for themselves by their own reading of Scripture, and in the process teach others, including their pastors and teachers.

From Doctrine to Scripture: Isaiah 53

The course of instruction Calvin envisioned for the church passes from doctrine (*Institutes*) to Scripture (commentaries and lectures) for pastors, so that pastors might teach doctrine (catechism) and Scripture (sermons) to ordinary Christians. The literary legacy of Calvin consists primarily of these four aspects of his curriculum for the school of Christ. To illustrate the dynamic relationship between doctrine and Scripture more concretely, it is worthwhile to examine the role Scripture plays in each of the four moments of teaching we have before us. I have chosen Isa. 53:4–7, since it is a key text from the Hebrew Scriptures that clearly portrays the work of Christ before his coming. In the *Institutes*, Calvin cites Isa. 53 in many ways, which reflect the varying tasks of doctrine in that text. Calvin first cites Isa. 53 in support of his claim to teach nothing more than what we are taught in Scripture, over against the vain and fruitless speculations of Osiander about whether the Son of God would have become human if we had not fallen into sin. According to Calvin, Scripture clearly and unanimously teaches that the Son became human to redeem sinners.

> Of all the testimonies to this, Isaiah's famous one will be enough: "He was to be smitten by God's hand . . . for the transgression of the people, . . . that the chastisement of peace should be upon him" [Isa. 53:4–5], and he would be the high priest who would offer himself as the victim [Heb. 9:11–12]; "from his stripes there would be healing for others"; because "all . . . have gone astray" and been scattered "like sheep," it pleased God to afflict him that he might bear "the iniquities of all" [Isa. 53:5–6 p.].[59]

We also saw above that for Calvin a summary of all the parts of religion, itself gathered from Scripture, should have the effect of opening access to Scripture. If this is true of the *Institutes*, it should be even truer of the Apostles' Creed, even if the apostles did not write the latter. "We consider to be beyond controversy the only point that ought to concern us: that the whole history of our faith is summed up in it succinctly and in definite order, and that it contains nothing that is not vouched for by genuine testimonies of Scripture."[60] We see the way the summary of doctrine opens access to Scripture when we come to the phrase "suffered

59. *Inst.* 2.12.4, *OS* 3:441.5–12; LCC 1:467.
60. *Inst.* 2.16.18, *OS* 3:506.24–28; LCC 1:527.

under Pontius Pilate," for Calvin turns from this creedal statement to Isa. 53 for its meaning. "For the title 'prefect' is mentioned, not only to affirm the faithfulness of the history, but that we may learn what Isaiah teaches: 'Upon him was the chastisement of our peace, and with his stripes we are healed' [Isa. 53:5]."[61] Calvin turns again to Isa. 53 to understand what it means when the Creed says that Christ was "crucified": "Now it is clear what the prophet's utterance means: 'The LORD has laid on him the iniquity of us all' [Isa. 53:6]. That is, he who was about to cleanse the filth of those iniquities was covered with them by transferred imputation."[62] Finally, Calvin turns to Isa. 53 in order to confirm and validate a controversial teaching of the Creed, which Calvin knows is not found in all versions: that Christ "descended into hell."

> A little while ago we referred to the prophet's statement that "the chastisement of our peace was laid upon him," "he was wounded for our transgressions" by the Father, "he was bruised for our infirmities" [Isa. 53:5 p.]. By these words he means that Christ was put in the place of evildoers as surety and pledge—submitting himself even as the accused—to bear all the punishments that they ought to have sustained.[63]

The teaching of this version of the Creed is therefore shown to be true because Isa. 53 confirms it, even as it opens access to the meaning of Isa. 53. In light of the meaning of Isa. 53, opened up by the Creed and confirmed by Scripture, Calvin appeals to the same text against the false teaching of Rome about penitential satisfactions: If Isaiah says that our sins have been laid upon Christ so that he may expiate them, then we cannot do the same by our works.[64]

The doctrine of the *Institutes* opens up the meaning of Scripture and defends that meaning against false interpretations and teaching. This in turn becomes the necessary instrument pastors must use when reading Calvin's commentaries. In his commentary on Isa. 53, Calvin establishes the genuine, simple, and true meaning of the passage on the basis of the meaning and context of the Hebrew, often in disagreement with other interpreters and doctors of the church. Thus, Calvin takes "the chastisement of our peace" "to denote simply reconciliation" by the transfer of our chastisement to Christ. From the simple meaning of the passage, Calvin then urges his readers "to draw from this a universal doctrine, namely, that we are reconciled to God by free grace, because Christ

61. *Inst.* 2.16.5, *OS* 3:488.6–9; LCC 1:509.
62. *Inst.* 2.16.6, *OS* 3:490.14–18; LCC 1:510.
63. *Inst.* 2.16.10, *OS* 3:495.9–15; LCC 1:515.
64. *Inst.* 3.4.27, *OS* 4:116.1–3; LCC 1:653.

has paid the price of our 'peace.'"[65] This doctrine is then set against the false doctrine of the papists concerning satisfactions, as was done in the *Institutes*. Calvin finds the next phrase, "In his wound we have healing," directing us from ourselves to Christ, so that we who face destruction and death might find life and salvation in Christ. He then notes the difference between his office as teacher and his office as pastor. "Here we might bring forward many things about the blessed consequences of Christ's sufferings, if we had not determined to expound rather than to preach; and therefore let us be satisfied with a plain exposition."[66] From the doctrine drawn from this passage, Calvin wishes the reader to draw consolation, and to apply such consolation not only to all in general, but also to himself in particular, "for these words are spoken to all in general, and to individuals in particular."[67]

The use of Isa. 53 in the 1545 *Geneva Catechism* reflects Calvin's desire to set forth in summary form the rudiments of doctrine intended to build up the piety of the young, so that they might be brought to a full profession of faith before the gathered assembly and know what to seek in their reading of Scripture. Hence, the use of Isa. 53 as a limit on inquiry, and as a refutation of Roman teaching on satisfaction, is not present in the *Catechism*, in contrast to the *Institutes*. Isaiah 53 remains, however, one of the central scriptural references Calvin uses to inquire into the meaning of the Creed's description of the death of Jesus Christ. As in the *Institutes*, Calvin uses Isa. 53 to explain why Christ "suffered under Pontius Pilate," given Pilate's condemnation of Christ in spite of having declared him to be innocent.

> C: Both things must be considered. For the judge bears testimony to his innocence, so that there might be evidence that he suffered not for his own misdeeds but for ours. Nevertheless at the same time he is formally condemned by the same judge to make it plain that he suffered as a surety the judgment which we deserved, that thus he might free us from guilt. M: Well said. For if he were a sinner, he would not be a fit surety to pay the penalty of another's sin. Nevertheless, that his condemnation might secure our acquittal, it was requisite that he be reckoned among the malefactors.[68]

65. Comm. on Isa. 53:5, *CO* 37:258B; CTS 16:116.

66. Comm. on Isa. 53:5, *CO* 37:258C; CTS 16:117. Calvin was aware of the programmatic distinction between commentaries and sermons. Commenting on Eph. 4:5 on the unity of all in the Lord, Calvin says, "All these arguments for unity ought to be pondered more than they can be explained. I have been content to point out the apostle's meaning briefly, and leave the fuller treatment to sermons" (Comm. on Eph. 4:5, *CO* 51:191B; *CNTC* 11:173).

67. Comm. on Isa. 53:5, *CO* 37:258C; CTS 16:117.

68. *Catechismus ecclesiae Genevensis*, *CO* 6:30; *Calvin: Theological Treatises*, 98.

As in the *Institutes*, Calvin also uses Isa. 53 to validate the Creed's controversial claim that Christ "descended into hell." Calvin first of all refers to the cry of abandonment from the cross to show "it was requisite that his conscience be tormented by such agony as if he were forsaken by God, even as if he had God hostile to him." This leads to the following exchange: "M: Was this not an affront to the Father? C: Not at all, but he exercised this severity against him, that he might fulfill what was prophesied by Isaiah: He was smitten by the hand of God for our sins, wounded for our iniquities (Isaiah 53:4; 1 Peter 2:24)."[69] Once again, we see in the *Catechism* that a summary of godly doctrine, as in the Apostles' Creed, opens up access to the right interpretation of Scripture, which in turn verifies the truth of doctrine. Unlike the *Institutes*, however, the *Catechism* stays exclusively with the goal of edification, and does not use Isa. 53 against fruitless speculation or godless doctrine.

In his sermon on this passage, Calvin begins with the natural meaning of the text and then seeks to apply it vigorously, vividly, and personally to the lives of the members of his congregation. When he comes to the passage, "The chastisement of our peace was upon him," he repeats the simple meaning he uncovered in the commentary. "But we see that the natural meaning of the prophet was, that if we are to have peace with God we must be reconciled by some means outside of ourselves."[70] But then, instead of drawing universal doctrine from this passage, Calvin vividly portrays how the consciences of the members of his congregation will be unable to find peace before God apart from the chastisement of Christ. "There can be no question of peace, then, for our consciences will always torment us; and although we try to put them to sleep by flattering ourselves, God never ceases to prick and goad us so that we unwillingly realize that there is nothing but malice and ingratitude in us."[71] Only when we have a vivid sense of the wrath of God against sinners apart from Christ will we be able to appreciate the peace that the chastisement of Christ brings us, so that we who are otherwise enemies of God might boldly call upon God as our Father.

Calvin then distinguishes the sacrifice of Christ from all other forms of expiation; he brings in not only Roman, but also pagan and Jewish rites of expiation, to show how "the devil has always tried to obscure this teaching, since it is the principal article of our salvation."[72] Calvin also describes in greater detail the interior motivation of those practicing Roman satisfactions, as though in an interview. "And if you ask the

---

69. *Catechismus*, CO 6:32; *Calvin: Theological Treatises*, 99.

70. CO 35:624C; *Sermons on Isaiah's Prophecy of the Death and Passion of Christ*, trans. and ed. T. H. L. Parker (London: Clarke, 1956), 71.

71. *CO* 35:625B; *Sermons*, 71–72.

72. CO 35:626C; *Sermons*, 73.

Papists why they traipse about to see some monkey pouting, why they fast on such and such a day, why they pay for a church to be built, or a mass to be sung, they will say: 'It is to redeem us before God. For when we know our sins we must certainly try to make satisfaction for them, so as to be cleared and absolved before God.'"[73] In his sermon, Calvin does not speak only of the teaching of the Roman theologians, as in the *Institutes* and commentary, but also of what Roman laity would say to members of his evangelical congregation. He is equipping his congregation with the true meaning of Scripture so that they might distinguish true from false piety regarding satisfaction. Hence, the congregation is to "put this passage into effect" in their lives by coming boldly to God in prayer, knowing that their only access to God is through the chastisement of Christ, and not their own satisfactions.[74]

When Calvin preaches on the text "in his wounds we have healing," he not only contrasts the maladies we experience in ourselves with the healing of Christ, as he does in the commentary, but he also tries to unmask the spiritual illnesses lurking in the members of the congregation, which they might be hiding through hypocrisy, in order that they might personally feel their infirmity. "Since then there is in us nothing but spiritual infection and leprosy and that we are corrupt in our iniquities, what shall we do? What remedy is there? Shall we go to seek help from the angels in paradise? Alas! They can do nothing for me. No, we must come to our Lord Jesus Christ."[75] Only Christ can comfort us and appease the wrath of God against us. "This, in brief, is what we have to remember from these words of the prophet."[76]

As we can see from this brief survey, Calvin as doctor of the catholic church uses the summary of doctrine in the *Institutes* to open access to the genuine meaning of Scripture and to limit his students to the teaching of Scripture alone. In the commentaries, Calvin as interpreter reveals the genuine meaning of Scripture as it flows from the context, but with lucid brevity, being content to draw general doctrines that should be preached to all, without vigorously applying such doctrine to life. As a pastor, Calvin first instructs the young in the orderly inquiry into the rudimentary doctrines of piety in the *Catechism*, so that they might know what to seek in their reading of Scripture. In his sermons, Calvin begins with the natural meaning of the passage, but then he applies this meaning to his congregation in many personal ways, so that they might feel the power of this doctrine in their lives. But even as he does so, Calvin is guiding their personal reading of Scripture, so that they might

73. *CO* 35:627B; *Sermons*, 74.
74. *CO* 35:628A; *Sermons*, 74.
75. *CO* 35:628A; *Sermons*, 75.
76. *CO* 35:628A; *Sermons*, 75.

be able to judge the truth of what he preaches, thereby confirming their own faith, and not simply accept his teaching on the basis of obedience to authority. In the *Catechism* and the sermons, the teacher of pastors becomes the teacher of the congregation, so that not only pastors, but also every Christian, might have easy access to the reading of Scripture and be able to advance in it without stumbling. "All I have had in mind with this is to facilitate the reading of holy Scripture for those who are humble and uneducated,"[77] so that they might be guided in their reading of Scripture even as the Ethiopian eunuch was guided by Philip.

---

77. *Preface to Chrysostom's Homilies, CO* 9:833A; Hazlett, *Humanism and Reform*, 142.

4

WHAT KIND OF BOOK
IS CALVIN'S *INSTITUTES*?

According to Calvin, the first task of the teacher of the church is to set forth a clear and orderly summary of pious doctrine, so that future pastors might know what they are to seek in the reading of Scripture. There were three such summaries of evangelical doctrine in Calvin's day: the *Loci communes* (1521–55) of Philip Melanchthon, the *Commentary on True and False Religion* (1525) by Ulrich Zwingli, and the *Institutes* (1536–59) of John Calvin. This chapter will examine the nature of Calvin's 1559 *Institutes* by posing a series of questions to the text, attempting to clarify for whom Calvin wrote the book, what his objectives were, and what means he used to meet those objectives. We will be especially interested in the method Calvin uses to teach the central doctrines of Scripture to future pastors of the church.

Previous discussions of the *Institutes* have tended to focus on the theological method pursued by Calvin. Some have argued for a "cen-

This essay was originally published in a slightly different form under the title "What Kind of Book Is Calvin's *Institutes*?" *Calvin Theological Journal* 35, no. 2 (2000): 238–61. Reprinted by permission.

tral dogma" of Calvin's theology, be it sovereignty, predestination, or union with Christ.[1] Others, following the lead of Hermann Bauke, have claimed that there is no central doctrine, but rather a complex of opposites, creating a dialectical field of tension between two extremes.[2] Other scholars have argued that there is a central structure to the *Institutes*, be it the twofold knowledge of God[3] or the fourfold structure of the Apostles' Creed.[4] Unlike these previous studies, this chapter will examine the nature of Calvin's 1559 *Institutes* in terms of its pedagogical structure and purpose, in an attempt to clarify for whom Calvin wrote the book, what his objectives were, and what means he used to meet those objectives. As a consequence, this examination comes closest to the line of inquiry pursued by Serene Jones.[5] However, Jones reads the *Institutes* primarily as a creative work of rhetoric more interested in moving its readers to certain kinds of dispositions than in teaching them the truth.[6] We instead will argue that whereas Calvin does use rhetoric to move his readers, as Jones rightly notes, his use of rhetoric is based on the foundation of a dialectically arranged series of clear definitions; it is oriented toward bringing the reader to an experience of the nature and force of the realities being defined, made possible by the reader's personal contemplation, and not by rhetoric per se.[7] The central thesis of this chapter is that Calvin's *Institutes* is best understood as being

1. See more recently Charles Partee, "Calvin's Central Dogma Again," in *The Organizational Structure of Calvin's Theology*, ed. Richard Gamble (New York: Garland, 1992), 75–84, in which Partee makes a case for "union with Christ" as the central doctrine.

2. See Ford Lewis Battles, "Calculus Fidei," in *Organizational Structure of Calvin's Theology*, ed. Gamble, 195–221; and Brian Armstrong, "*Duplex cognitio Dei*, or The Problem and Relation of Structure, Form, and Purpose in Calvin's Theology," in *Probing the Reformed Tradition: Historical Studies in Honor of Edward A. Dowey Jr.*, ed. Elsie McKee and Brian Armstrong (Louisville: Westminster John Knox, 1989), 135–51.

3. Edward A. Dowey Jr., *The Knowledge of God in Calvin's Theology*, 2nd ed. (New York: Columbia University Press, 1952).

4. T. H. L. Parker, *Calvin: An Introduction to His Thought* (Louisville: Westminster John Knox, 1995).

5. Serene Jones, *Calvin and the Rhetoric of Piety* (Louisville: Westminster John Knox, 1995).

6. "According to Calvin (like Petrarch), when the language of theology is appropriately accommodated to the needs of its audience, it should actually 'make the reader good.' And . . . this process of making the audience good does not consist solely in telling them what they should believe; rather, it requires that the theologian construct a discourse that will transform the disposition of the audience as they read through a given text" (Jones, *Calvin and the Rhetoric of Piety*, 28–29).

7. John Hesselink comes close to the thesis for which we will be arguing, when he says of the *Institutes*, "It is an aid to understanding the Scriptures and the Christian faith, with the ultimate purpose of challenging the whole man to give himself wholly to God and his church" ("The Development and Purpose of Calvin's *Institutes*," in *Influences upon Calvin and Discussion of the 1559 Institutes*, ed. Richard Gamble (New York: Garland,

a combination of dialectical, rhetorical, and contemplative theology, which has as its objective bringing its readers to a fuller experience of the spiritual realities being defined and explained.[8]

We will begin our examination by setting the *Institutes* in its context, in an attempt to discover the audience Calvin had in mind for the *Institutes*, and the relation of the *Institutes* to the work of other ecclesiastical writers. We will then turn to the objective Calvin had in view in writing the *Institutes*: to present a brief summary and clear explanation of godly doctrine, structured around an orderly series of clear definitions, so that his readers might contemplate and experience for themselves the nature and force of the spiritual realities he defines and explains.

The Audience for the *Institutes*

From the second edition of 1539 to the final edition of 1559, Calvin wrote the *Institutes* "to prepare and instruct candidates in sacred theology," which more than likely meant those who were preparing to be pastors in the evangelical churches.[9] Calvin assumes several characteristics of his intended readers. Such readers are expected to be pious, which means for Calvin that they already trust in, obey, pray to, and seek

---

1992), 71. This article will attempt more fully to fill out how Calvin sought to meet these objectives.

8. By "dialectical," I mean Calvin's concern, shared with Melanchthon and likely derived from him, for the centrality of definitions and the arrangement of those definitions in the clearest and most persuasive order. By "rhetorical," I mean Calvin's attempts to bring the force of the realities being defined to bear on the mind, heart, and conscience of the reader, so that he might feel their force for himself. By "contemplative," I mean Calvin's concern to direct the reader to consider, contemplate, and ponder the reality itself, so that the truth of Calvin's teaching might be confirmed by his own experience of piety. Serene Jones focuses exclusively on the rhetorical aspect of the *Institutes* and therefore misses the central role of dialectics, contemplation, and experience, which form the context of Calvin's use of rhetoric. See also B. A. Gerrish, "Theology within the Limits of Piety Alone: Schleiermacher and Calvin's Notion of God," in *The Old Protestantism and the New: Essays on the Reformation Heritage* (Edinburgh: Clark, 1982), 196–207. Brian Armstrong notes the practical and edifying purpose of Calvin's theology. "It is always at once practical and edifying" (Armstrong, *"Duplex cognitio Dei,"* 142). However, Armstrong seems to contrast this purpose with a concern for the order of right teaching, insisting that Calvin is not a dogmatic theologian, echoing a similar claim made by William Bouwsma ("Calvinism as *Theologia Rhetorica*," in *Calvinism as Theologia Rhetorica*, ed. Wilhelm Wuellner [Berkeley: Center for Hermeneutical Studies, 1986], 11). As we hope to demonstrate, Calvin is a teacher of godly doctrine to future pastors and teachers of the church, and thus is concerned with the right order of teaching precisely so that he might strengthen both their piety and their ability to teach the sum of piety to others.

9. John Calvin, *Institutio christianae religionis* (1559), "John Calvin to the Reader," *OS* 3:6.18–19; LCC 1:4.

to glorify the one true God and Jesus Christ, whom he has sent.[10] Such readers would not be seeking to read the *Institutes* in order to ask fruitless speculative questions, but would rather be seeking sound teaching by which to build up their piety.[11] Calvin also expects that his readers will be modest and teachable, not proudly contending with teaching drawn from Scripture, but reading it attentively and reverently. They will willingly submit to and obey teaching drawn from Scripture and not be proud of their own learning.[12] Calvin wants his readers to be sober and moderate, seeking to know no more and no less than what God through the Holy Spirit teaches them in Scripture, being content with the measure of faith that God has given them and not seeking to venture boldly beyond these limits.[13] Calvin expects his readers to be prudent and sane, meaning that they will not hallucinate like people who have lost their minds, but will rather demonstrate the ability to make proper judgments and distinctions and will be able to discern when certain teachings are beyond controversy.[14] Finally, Calvin assumes that his readers have already experienced the power of the realities he is describing and explicating in the *Institutes*. "I speak of nothing other than what each believer experiences within himself—though my words fall far beneath a just explanation of the matter."[15] As we shall see, such experience of the force of what is being taught is the ultimate confirmation and goal of Calvin's plan of teaching in the *Institutes*.

Over and above these essential personal qualities and dispositions, what other learning does Calvin appear to assume on the part of his candidates for sacred theology? In terms of their mental capacity, Calvin appears to be aiming for a reader of average insight and intelligence.

10. See, for instance, *Inst.* 1.13.24; 1.15.2; 1.15.5; 2.14.8; 2.16.12; 3.5.10; 3.25.3; 4.1.1; et passim.

11. "I am only touching on what could be treated more fully and deserves to be set out more brilliantly. Yet I trust that devout readers [*pios lectores*] will find in these few words enough material to build up their faith" (*Inst.* 3.25.3, *OS* 4:436.3–6; LCC 2:991).

12. "Indeed, the modest and teachable reader [*modestus ac docilis lector*] will be content with this one reason: Isaiah promised all the children of the renewed church that 'they would be God's disciples' [Isa. 54:13 p.]" (*Inst.* 1.7.5, *OS* 3:71.17–19; LCC 1:81). "This will suffice for modest and teachable persons [*modestis et docilibus*] (such as I have undertaken to instruct)" (*Inst.* 4.19.33, *OS* 5:467.13–14; LCC 2:1480).

13. "Therefore, let those who dearly love soberness [*sobrietas*], and who will be content with the measure of faith, receive in brief form what is useful to know" (*Inst.* 1.13.20, *OS* 3:133–34; LCC 1:144).

14. "But discerning readers [*sani lectores*] will recognize without my saying anything that this expression means only that we stand, supported by the sacrifice of Christ's death, before God's judgment seat" (*Inst.* 3.11.9, *OS* 4:191.3–5; LCC 1:736). "Thus intelligent readers [*sani lectores*] may judge by comparison the shamelessness of those who claim antiquity to support present monasticism" (*Inst.* 4.13.10, *OS* 5:247.27–29; LCC 2:1264).

15. *Inst.* 1.7.5, *OS* 3:71.12–14; LCC 1:80–81.

He speaks of his readers as being moderately discerning,[16] of average judgment and of slight intelligence.[17] Although he acknowledges that the teaching of the philosophers may at times be useful and true, he also seeks to address himself to the capacity of all.[18] Hence, Calvin seems to be aiming his teaching to the mental capacities of the average reader of Latin texts, assuming that the reader is of sound judgment, but not brilliant.[19]

In terms of educational background, Calvin not only assumes that the reader has learned Latin, but also that he has become acquainted with Latin and Greek (perhaps in Latin translation) classical literature, especially the writings of Plato and Cicero. Calvin will often remind his readers of points which these authors make, and then tell the readers to draw out the rest for themselves.[20] Calvin assumes a wide acquaintance with the writings of secular authors in all the liberal arts and encourages his audience to read these authors and compare them with the power of Scripture.[21] He even encourages his readers to read and study the teaching of Plato on the subject of the faculties of the soul.[22]

Calvin also assumes that the reader is familiar with the teaching of Scripture and is reading Scripture for himself. He does not expect his readers to be expert in the interpretation of Scripture, but he does expect them to be moderately exercised in the writings to be found therein, including the writings of the prophets and Paul.[23] Calvin will also instruct the reader to do further reading in Scripture to confirm a point he is making more briefly.[24] We shall explore the relation of the

16. *Inst*. 2.10.20, *OS* 3:420.17; LCC 1:446–47.

17. *Inst*. 1.13.1, *OS* 3:109.13–14; LCC 1:121.

18. *Inst*. 1.15.6, *OS* 3:184.11; LCC 1:194.

19. "Men of sound judgment [*recte iudicantibus*] will always be sure that a sense of divinity which can never be effaced is engraved upon men's minds" (*Inst*. 1.3.3, *OS* 3:39.21–23; LCC 1:45).

20. This seems to be especially the case with Cicero's *Tusculan Disputations*, with its proofs for the distinct essence of the soul. See in particular *Inst*. 1.5.5; 1.15.2: "I have briefly touched upon these things which secular writers grandly extol and depict in more brilliant language; but among godly readers this simple reminder will be enough" (*Inst*. 1.15.2, *OS* 3:175–76; LCC 1:185).

21. The discussion of the nonregenerating gifts of the Holy Spirit assumes such familiarity (*Inst*. 2.2.14–16), as does the discussion of the power of the writings in Scripture (*Inst*. 1.8.2).

22. "I, indeed, agree that the things they teach are true, not only enjoyable, but also profitable to learn, and skillfully assembled by them. And I do not forbid those who are desirous of learning to study them" (*Inst*. 1.15.6, *OS* 3:183.20–23; LCC 1:193).

23. "Those who are moderately versed [*mediocriter exercitati*] in the Scriptures will see that for the sake of brevity I have put forward only a few of many testimonies" (*Inst*. 1.18.1, *OS* 3:221.17–19; LCC 1:231). See also *Inst*. 2.8.52; 3.23.13.

24. "If anyone should more attentively ponder what I have only briefly touched upon, it will be clear that Moses was a sure witness and herald of the one God, the Creator" (*Inst*.

Institutes to Scripture more fully when we discuss the objectives of the book below.

Along with a familiarity with Scripture, Calvin expects his readers to have some familiarity with the writings of the church fathers, especially Augustine and Chrysostom.[25] He also assumes that his readers will know the *Sentences* of Peter (the) Lombard and the *Decretum* of Gratian, along with the scholastic tradition of commentaries on these texts, including both those whom he calls "the sounder schoolmen" and "the more recent Sophists." Calvin expects the reader to be able to grasp the degree to which he disagrees with these authors. "I choose to note these two points in passing that you, my reader, may see how far I disagree with the sounder Schoolmen. I differ with the more recent Sophists to an even greater degree, as they are farther removed from antiquity."[26] Finally, Calvin assumes that his readers are familiar with many of the writings circulating during the Reformation period, including those of other evangelical teachers such as Luther, Melanchthon, Bucer, Zwingli, Oecolampadius, and Bullinger (even though they are not usually mentioned by name), as well as the writings of radical reformers such as the Anabaptists, Osiander, and Servetus. Calvin is especially at pains to give a clear explanation of doctrines such as the relationship of the Old and New Testaments to remove the confusion he thinks other writers in his time have created for his readers on this issue. "Nevertheless, because writers often argue at length about the difference between the Old and New Testament, thus arousing some misgiving in the simple reader's mind, we shall rightly devote a special section to a fuller and more precise discussion of this matter."[27] But Calvin is also concerned to reveal the difference between his teaching and that of the Wittenberg reformers, as in his disagreement with their definition of repentance, even though he does not mention them by name.[28]

In sum, Calvin writes for a Latin reading audience of average intelligence, which is familiar with the writings of the Greek and Latin classical world, is moderately exercised in Scripture, and has an acquaintance with the major writers of the church, including the fathers, Peter Lombard, the scholastics, and contemporary reformers, both allies and foes. The level of education assumed by Calvin on the part of his readers suggests that he is primarily writing for those who have already been educated

---

1.14.2, *OS* 3:154.20–22; LCC 1:162).

25. This familiarity is best revealed in his discussion of original sin and its effects, as when he cites both authors on the centrality of humility in the Christian life (*Inst.* 2.2.11).

26. *Inst.* 2.2.6, *OS* 3:248–49; LCC 1:263.

27. *Inst.* 2.10.1, *OS* 3:403.15–19; LCC 1:429.

28. *Inst.* 3.3.4–5.

in the arts and in theology in the universities of Europe, but who have now joined the evangelical movement and need a firmer grounding in the sum of evangelical teaching. In other words, the evidence suggests that Calvin intended the *Institutes* primarily as a book that would re-educate those who had already received a theological education in the Roman Church, so that they could now become more effective teachers and preachers of the gospel and more clearly distinguish the teaching of the gospel from that of the Church of Rome, as well as from other false teachers of doctrine in his day.[29]

The *Institutes* and the Works of Other Ecclesiastical Writers

Given the fact that Calvin expects his readers to be familiar with a wide range of ecclesiastical writers, how does he position his book in relation to those written by his predecessors and peers? It is clear that his primary concern is to demonstrate to his readers that everything he teaches in the *Institutes* is drawn from the clear teaching of the Holy Spirit in Scripture and can be confirmed by a reading of Scripture on their part. "But because nothing will be more effective to strengthen the faith of the pious than to have learned that the doctrine which we have put forward has been drawn from the pure Word of God, and rests upon its authority—I shall also make this plain with as much brevity as I can."[30] Calvin repeatedly insists that he teaches nothing more and nothing less than can be drawn from Scripture. "I desire only . . . that we should not investigate what the Lord has left hidden in secret, that we should not neglect what he has brought into the open, so that we may not be convicted of excessive curiosity on the one hand, or of excessive ingratitude on the other."[31] This relationship with Scripture, as we shall see, is directly related to the objective that Calvin sets for the *Institutes*, to show readers of Scripture what to look for as they read it.

At the same time, Calvin is equally concerned to show that what he teaches in his summary of doctrine is nothing new, but is the same sum of doctrine that has always been handed down in the apostolic

---

29. Serene Jones (*Calvin and the Rhetoric of Piety*, 53) identifies the audience of Calvin's *Institutes* as made up of his students, friends and followers in French parishes, humanists, and enemies. Jones does not sufficiently attend to the fact that Calvin wrote the *Institutes* primarily to teach future pastors, whom he assumes to have been already educated in the theological tradition of Rome.

30. *Inst.* 4.17.26, *OS* 5:378.13–16; LCC 2:1393.

31. *Inst.* 3.21.4, *OS* 4:373.18–21; LCC 2:925. "For our wisdom ought to be nothing less than to embrace with humble teachableness, and at least without finding fault, whatever is taught in Sacred Scripture" (*Inst.* 1.18.4, *OS* 3:227.27–30; LCC 1:237).

and catholic church. Against the attempt by Servetus to have Tertullian testify against the Nicene confession of the Trinity, Calvin insists, "Even if he is sometimes rough and thorny in his mode of speech, yet he not ambiguously hands on the sum of doctrine that we defend."[32] Hence, Calvin's usual method of teaching in the *Institutes* is to support his doctrine first from the testimony of Scripture, and then from the testimony of the fathers, to show that his own interpretation of Scripture is not novel. "Let us undertake to summarize the matter for our readers by but a few, and very clear, testimonies of Scripture. Then, lest anyone accuse us of distorting Scripture, let us show that the truth, which we assert has been drawn from Scripture, lacks not the attestation of this holy man—I mean Augustine."[33] In this way, Calvin intentionally places himself and his writing in the company of those he calls the orthodox, sane, upright, and proved ecclesiastical doctors and writers of the church.[34] Calvin defends the conciliar definitions that these teachers formulated in the first five centuries, including the Apostles' Creed and the definitions of Nicea-Constantinople, Ephesus I, and Chalcedon.[35] "In this way, we willingly embrace and reverence as holy the early councils, such as those of Nicea, Constantinople, Ephesus I, Chalcedon, and the like, which were concerned with refuting errors—in so far as they relate to the teachings of faith."[36] Calvin also defends the patristic formulation of the communication of properties (*communicatio idiomata*) as being useful for resolving the difficulties surrounding the scriptural testimony to the work of the Mediator.[37]

Calvin is concerned to trace a trajectory of orthodox teaching as far as he can from the patristic period to his own day, to demonstrate that he teaches the same doctrine that the true church has always taught. This explains his interest in Bernard of Clairvaux in particular, for in him Calvin sees the continuation of the teaching of Augustine right into the medieval period, transmitted not through the schools, but through the monasteries. "Surely my readers will recognize that I am bringing forth nothing new, for it is something that Augustine of old taught with the agreement of all the godly, and it was still retained almost a thousand years later in monastic cloisters."[38] Calvin usually charges Peter Lombard with beginning the corruption of the patristic and Augustinian tradition of true doctrine, and claims that the subsequent scholastic

32. *Inst*. 1.13.28, *OS* 3:148.33–34; LCC 1:157.
33. *Inst*. 2.3.8, *OS* 3:282.7–12; LCC 1:300.
34. For example, *Inst*. 1.13.10, 21; 1.11.12; 1.13.4; 1.13.9.
35. *Inst*. 4.9.13. See also 1.13.3; 2.14.5; 2.16.18.
36. *Inst*. 4.9.8, *OS* 5:156.30–32; LCC 2:1171.
37. *Inst*. 2.14.2, *OS* 3:459.2–12; LCC 1:482–83.
38. *Inst*. 2.3.5, *OS* 3:278.35–38; LCC 1:296.

commentators on Lombard went steadily from bad to worse, until the whole sum of true doctrine was corrupted or lost. "For when Augustine says anything clearly, Lombard obscures it, and if there was anything slightly contaminated in Augustine, he corrupts it. The schools have gone continually from bad to worse until, in headlong ruin, they have plunged into a sort of Pelagianism."[39]

Calvin's view of the loss of the patristic and orthodox tradition by Lombard and the schoolmen should not blind us, however, to the degree to which Calvin makes positive use of definitions and distinctions that he credits to the schoolmen. Calvin's usual way of appropriating scholastic teaching is to say that the schoolmen did not really understand what they were teaching. It is nonetheless quite significant that Calvin found so much from the labors of the scholastics useful in his own teaching. Calvin affirms the definition of sinful human nature that the scholastics formulated on the basis of Augustine, and he uses this definition in his own discussion of the effects of original sin on human nature. "Indeed, that common opinion which they [the scholastics] have taken from Augustine pleases me: that the natural gifts were corrupted in man through sin, but that his supernatural gifts were stripped from him."[40] Calvin turns this scholastic definition against his sixteenth-century Roman opponents like Pighius. "Surely they cannot make out that we are to abandon Augustine's view, *approved by the common consent of the schools*: the free goods upon which salvation depends were taken away from man after the Fall, while the natural endowments were corrupted and defiled."[41] Calvin also affirms the distinction developed in the schools between three kinds of freedom, and he uses it to defend his contention that free will lacks all power in matters of salvation.[42] Calvin approves of the distinction that the schoolmen developed between relative and absolute necessity, a distinction that Luther had rejected.[43] Calvin endorses the position of the saner schoolmen on the beginning of justification and even goes so far as to acknowledge that their position is similar to Augustine's. However, Calvin is critical both of the schoolmen and of Augustine for making the renewal of sinners part of the definition of justification. In the process, Calvin demonstrates that the sounder

39. *Inst.* 3.11.15, *OS* 4:199–200; LCC 1:745–46.

40. *Inst.* 2.2.12, *OS* 3:254.30–32; LCC 1:270.

41. *Inst.* 2.5.19, *OS* 3:319.28–31; LCC 1:340, with my emphasis.

42. "Now in the schools three kinds of freedom are distinguished: first from necessity, second from sin, third from misery. . . . I willingly accept this distinction, except in so far as necessity is falsely confused with compulsion" (*Inst.* 2.2.5, *OS* 3:26–34; LCC 1:262).

43. "Whence we see that distinctions concerning relative necessity and absolute necessity, likewise of consequent and consequence, were not recklessly invented in the schools" (*Inst.* 1.16.9, *OS* 3:201.25–27; LCC 1:210).

schoolmen accurately hand on Augustine's definition of justification, whereas Calvin prefers a different definition, which he claims is based on the teaching of Paul.[44] Finally, Calvin uses the scholastic distinction that the whole Christ is everywhere, but not the whole of that which is in him, against the Lutheran position on the presence of Christ in the Holy Supper of the Lord.[45]

Calvin's endorsement and use of so many scholastic definitions and distinctions not only confirms the impression that he is writing for those who may already have been trained in scholastic theology before joining the evangelical movement. It also indicates the degree to which Calvin sought to trace the orthodox, Augustinian tradition as far as he could to his own day, extending it beyond Bernard of Clairvaux and the monastic cloisters into the schools themselves. Although Calvin does not, like Bucer, expressly name Aquinas and Gerson as being more or less in this tradition, his appeal to the "saner schoolmen" does bring such theologians to mind. It is clear from all this that Calvin, like Melanchthon, sought to be a catholic theologian who maintained his adherence to the patristic tradition and to the heirs of that tradition up into the scholastic period.

The Objectives of the *Institutes*

The Institutes *as a Summary of Doctrine*

Having considered the audience of the *Institutes* and its relation to other writings, we now turn to consider the objectives Calvin hoped to meet with his book. How does Calvin describe those objectives? The clearest description comes in the preface written in 1539, in which Calvin

44. "For on the beginning of justification there is no quarrel between us and the sounder schoolmen: that a sinner freely liberated from condemnation may obtain righteousness, and that through the forgiveness of sins; except that they include under the term 'justification' a renewal, by which through the Spirit of God we are remade to obedience to the law" (*Inst.* 3.14.11, *OS* 4:230.2–6; LCC 1:778). Calvin acknowledges that this position of the saner schoolmen reflects the teaching of Augustine earlier in his discussion. "For that matter, Augustine's view, or at any rate his manner of stating it, we must not entirely accept. For even though he admirably deprives man of all credit for righteousness and transfers it to God's grace, he still subsumes grace under sanctification, by which we are reborn to newness of life through the Spirit" (*Inst.* 3.11.15, *OS* 4:200.2–6; LCC 1:746).

45. "There is a commonplace distinction of the schools to which I am not ashamed to refer: although the whole of Christ is everywhere, still the whole of that which is in him is not everywhere. And would that the schoolmen themselves had honestly weighed the force of this statement" (*Inst.* 4.17.30, *OS* 5:389.12–15; LCC 2:1403).

claims that the work contains a "sum of religion in all its parts."[46] In the *Institutes* itself Calvin calls his book a "summary of doctrine," in particular a "summary of Evangelical doctrine."[47] There are three things in particular that the genre of "summa" raises in Calvin's mind: brevity, comprehensiveness, and order or method.

In his summa, Calvin seeks to set forth his sum of evangelical doctrine with as much brevity as possible. A summa does not allow Calvin to give a full treatment of every doctrine, for he must touch on every doctrine with an eye to moving on to the next, "lest this book which I am anxious to prepare as a short textbook burst all bounds."[48] Throughout the text, from the first edition to the last, Calvin informs the reader that he studies brevity and is incapable of prolixity. "By nature I love brevity, and perhaps if I wished to speak more amply it would not be successful. But though a more extended form of teaching were highly acceptable, I would nevertheless scarcely care to undertake it."[49] Such brevity is for Calvin closely related to a simple form of teaching, which again seems intended for a reader of average intelligence and learning. "Moreover, the plan of the present work demands that we give a simple outline of doctrine as briefly as possible."[50] The study of brevity influences both the nature of Calvin's discussion of a topic, as well as the scriptural and ecclesiastical testimony he will adduce to support his teaching. "But because I am striving for brevity, I shall be content with but one passage; yet it will be like the clearest of mirrors in which we may contemplate the whole image of our nature."[51] Such brevity often indicates the assumption on Calvin's part that the reader is moderately versed and skilled in Scripture. "Those who are moderately versed in Scripture see that for the sake of brevity I have put forward only a few of many testimonies."[52] Brevity for Calvin is directly related to the clarity and simplicity of teaching, which he is convinced is the most effective method of teaching for his desired readers.

The second aspect of a summa should be its comprehensiveness, for Calvin claims to grasp the sum of religion in all its parts. Although he will strive for brevity so that he may touch on all the topics of doctrine in their proper order, he must still make sure that all the topics of doctrine that build up piety are at least touched upon in the *Institutes*. "We must

46. "John Calvin to the Reader," *OS* 3:6.21–22; LCC 1:4.

47. *Inst.* 2.16.8, *OS* 3:492.7; LCC 1:512; 3.19.1, *OS* 4:282.12–13; LCC 1:833.

48. *Inst.* 3.4.1, *OS* 4:85.2; LCC 1:622.

49. *Inst.* 3.6.1, *OS* 4:147.4–8; LCC 1:685.

50. *Inst.* 3.6.1, *OS* 4:147.8–10; LCC 1:685.

51. *Inst.* 2.3.2, *OS* 3:273.8–11; LCC 1:290. Later in this chapter, we will discuss the importance of the role of contemplation in the *Institutes*.

52. *Inst.* 1.18.1, *OS* 3:221.17–19; LCC 1:231.

now discuss Christian freedom. He who proposes to summarize gospel teaching ought by no means to omit an explanation of this topic."[53] Such comprehensiveness also leads Calvin to include topics that are not well attested in traditional summaries of doctrine, either in the Creed or in the church fathers, such as Christ's descent into hell. "Nevertheless, in setting forth a summary of doctrine a place must be given to it, as it contains a useful and not-to-be-despised mystery of a most important matter."[54] However, Calvin's concern to teach nothing other than the sum of doctrine that has always been taught in the church means that he must assert that this locus has in some way always been part of the sum of godly doctrine. "This much is certain: that it reflected the common belief of all the godly; for there is no one of the fathers who does not mention in his writing Christ's descent into hell, though their interpretations vary."[55] The concern to present a comprehensive summa reinforces in Calvin's mind the need for brevity, since he feels the need to proceed to the next locus of doctrine lest the reader become wearied by his prolixity before he can treat all of the essential doctrines. It is significant that one of the charges Calvin brings against the Roman Church of his day is that "the sum of necessary doctrine" was overturned.[56] For Calvin, the setting forth of the sum of all necessary doctrines in the *Institutes* is an essential part of restoring the life of the church in his day. This makes the need for comprehensiveness all the more important, to make sure that he hands on the sum of doctrine that the true church has always handed on.

The third aspect of the genre of summa is the right order and method of teaching.[57] A brief and comprehensive summary of doctrine must carefully attend to the right ordering of the various doctrinal topics, so that the whole progression of teaching might be clear and persuasive. Calvin

53. "Cuius explicatio praetermitti minime ab eo debet cui summam evangelicae doctrinae compendio complecti propositum sit" (*Inst.* 3.19.1, *OS* 4:282.11–13; LCC 1:833).

54. *Inst.* 2.16.8, *OS* 3:492.7–9; LCC 1:513.

55. *Inst.* 2.16.8, *OS* 3:492.12–15; LCC 1:513. Calvin's appeal here to the *communi piorum omnium sensu* has significant similarities with the efforts in the Roman Catholic Church after Vatican II to describe doctrine as an expression and description of the sense of the faithful, and indicates the essential role that the Christian tradition plays in his attempt to set forth a faithful summary of doctrine.

56. "But, as soon as falsehood breaks into the citadel of religion and the sum of necessary doctrine [*summa necessariae doctrinae*] is overturned and the use of the sacraments is destroyed, surely the death of the church follows—just as a man's life is ended when his throat is pierced or his heart mortally wounded" (*Inst.* 4.2.1, *OS* 5:31.5–9; LCC 2:1041).

57. For the influence of Melanchthon on Calvin's understanding of the order or series of right teaching, see Richard Muller, "*Ordo Docendi*: Melanchthon and the Organization of Calvin's Institutes, 1536–1543," in *Melanchthon in Europe*, ed. Karin Maag (Grand Rapids: Baker, 1999), 123–40. I completely agree with Muller's thesis that Melanchthon exerts a decisive influence on Calvin's concern for the *ordo recte docendi* in the 1539 and 1543 *Institutes*.

calls this progression of teaching the *series docendi*, by which he means the way one doctrinal locus will lead to the next, so that the whole series will constitute a comprehensive argument. Calvin constructs the argument of the *Institutes* by beginning with the doctrines that are the most universally acknowledged by all people, inside and outside of the church, and hence which are the least subject to controversy. In this, he appears to follow the method that he sees Paul using both in the letter to the Romans and the sermons in Acts to Greek audiences.

> We know that in teaching[,] the right order requires a beginning to be made from things that are better known. Since Paul and Barnabas were preaching to Gentiles, it would have been useless for them to attempt to bring them to Christ at once. Therefore they had to begin from some other point, not so remote from common understanding, so that, when assent was given to that, they could then pass over to Christ.[58]

The element that is the nearest to the common understanding of all people is the awareness that there is some Deity who created us, who is to be worshipped and honored by us. "If anyone wishes to discuss religion in general this will be the first point, that there is some deity to whom worship is due from men. But because there was no dispute about that, Paul passes on to the second point, that the true God ought to be distinguished from all fabrications."[59]

Calvin follows the same series of teaching in the 1559 *Institutes*: he begins with what is beyond controversy—that there is some God whom all ought to worship[60]—and then proceeds to distinguish the true God from idols, in order to pass from there to Christ. "But here I shall discuss only how we should learn from Scripture that God, the Creator of the universe, can by sure marks be distinguished from all the throng of feigned gods. Then, in due order, that series will lead us to the redemption."[61] The series of teaching extends beyond the redemption, though, to discuss the nature, power, exercise, source, and goal of the faith that unites us to the Redeemer (book 3), and the aids that God provides to strengthen this faith (book 4).[62] Calvin appears to be convinced that the

58. Comm. on Acts 14:15, *CO* 48:326A; *CNTC* 7:10–11. This concern to begin the summa with that which is nearest to the common understanding of all people brings Calvin close to the method and order of teaching followed by Thomas Aquinas, although the material content of their teaching differs.

59. Comm. on Acts 17:24, *CO* 48:410B; *CNTC* 7:112.

60. "There is within the human mind, and indeed by natural instinct, an awareness of divinity. This we take to be beyond controversy" (*Inst.* 1.3.1, *OS* 3:37.16–18; LCC 1:43).

61. *Inst.* 1.6.1, *OS* 3:61.25–29; LCC 1:71.

62. Calvin acknowledges that the final chapter of the *Institutes*, on civil government, does not seem to fit with the sum of spiritual doctrine that he has up till then been teach-

best series and order of teaching begins with what is the most general, in order to proceed from there to the particular.[63] It is also worth noting that Calvin begins his summary of evangelical doctrine with doctrines that not only are taught in the church but also are or should be known by all human beings in any and every place and time.[64]

Calvin is aware that at times his own method of teaching comes quite close to that of the philosophers. This is especially clear when he defines the faculties of the soul, relying as much on the anthropology of philosophers like Plato and Cicero as on Scripture. He expresses his disagreement with the method of teaching of the philosophers only when it comes to their neglect of the effect of original sin on human nature.[65] The method of the philosophers' teaching also appears in view in Calvin's discussion of the right plan of life for the Christian, although here he uses the philosophers more to contrast their plan of teaching with that of the Holy Spirit in Scripture. "As philosophers have fixed limits of the right and the honorable, whence they derive individual duties and the whole company of virtues, so Scripture is not without its own order, but holds to a most beautiful dispensation, and one much more certain than all

---

ing, since it is a different *argumenti ratio*. However, he argues that compelling reasons lead him to include such a discussion in his summa (*Inst.* 4.20.1, *OS* 5:471.17–25; LCC 2:1485–86).

63. One sees this especially in his discussion of faith, which was one of the most controversial of the doctrinal *loci* of his day. To arrive at his definition of faith, Calvin proceeds from the general to the particular. "Yet it will be an easier and more suitable method [*facilior erit et aptior methodus*] if we descend by degrees from general to particular [*si gradatim a genere ad speciem descendimus*]" (*Inst.* 3.2.6, *OS* 4:14.6–7; LCC 1:548).

64. Regarding the sense of Divinity, Calvin says, "From this we conclude that *it is not a doctrine that must first be learned in school*, but one of which each of us is master from his mother's womb, *and which nature itself permits no one to forget*, although many strive with every nerve to this end" (my emphasis, *Inst.* 1.3.3, *OS* 3:10–13; LCC 1:46). With regard to the self-revelation of this God in the universe, Calvin makes the same point: "Now I have only wanted to touch upon the fact that this way of seeking God is common to both strangers and to those of his household, if they trace the outlines that above and below sketch a living likeness of him" (*Inst.* 1.5.6, *OS* 3:51.18–21; LCC 1:59). The difference in the latter instance is that only those of the household of God are rightly directed to the true Creator and Governor of the universe by the testimony of Scripture, for "unless Scripture guides us in our seeking God, we are immediately confused" (*Inst.* 1.14.1, *OS* 3:153.14–16; LCC 1:161).

65. "We are forced to part somewhat from this way of teaching [*docendi ratio*] because the philosophers, ignorant of the corruption of nature that originated from the penalty for man's defection, mistakenly confuse two very diverse states of man" (*Inst.* 1.15.7, *OS* 3:184.26–29; LCC 1:194). Calvin accuses the fathers, especially the Greeks like Chrysostom, of coming far too close to the philosophers in their teaching on the locus of original sin and its effects. "All ecclesiastical writers have recognized both that the soundness of reason in man is gravely wounded through sin, and that the will has been very much enslaved by evil desires. Despite this, many of them have come far too close to the philosophers" (*Inst.* 2.2.4, *OS* 3:244.18–22; LCC 1:258).

the philosophical ones."[66] Calvin is quite aware that he shares with the philosophers a concern for the proper method and order of teaching, but he also realizes the material difference between the teaching of God in Scripture and the teaching of the philosophers.

Calvin shares with Melanchthon the concern for the right order, series, and method of teaching, and like Melanchthon he is not afraid to learn as much of this method as he can from the philosophers. Indeed, it seems to me quite likely that Calvin's interest in order and method is due to the influence of Melanchthon's 1535 *Loci*. However, it is worth noting that Calvin's favorite philosopher is the one he terms the most religious of them all, Plato, whereas Melanchthon thought that Aristotle was second to none when it came to the question of the right method and plan of teaching. As we shall see, the influence of Plato on Calvin's method of teaching may explain the significant contemplative orientation of Calvin's method of teaching.

The Institutes *as an Explanation of Doctrine*

The progression and series of doctrinal topics not only presents a coherent argument within the *Institutes*; it also presents readers with a guide or index concerning which topics should be sought out in their reading of Scripture. "For I believe I have so arranged the sum of religion in all its parts, and have arranged it in such an order, that if anyone rightly holds to it, it will not be difficult for him to determine what he ought especially to seek in Scripture, and to what end he ought to relate its contents."[67] This aspect of the *Institutes* is most clearly revealed when Calvin is striving for brevity. In his comparison of the self-representation of God in the universe and in Scripture, Calvin gives a brief treatment of what in itself could be a long discussion. "Yet I shall be content to have provided godly minds with a sort of index to what they should primarily look for in Scripture concerning God, and to direct their search to a sure goal."[68] When Calvin discusses the creation of the universe in six days, he says he will not give a full narration of the creation. Instead, he directs the reader to Genesis and to the commentaries on Genesis by Basil and Ambrose, and briefly sets forth the two parts of the universal rule concerning the right apprehension by faith of what it means for God to be creator of heaven and earth.[69] He sets down another universal rule for the right ordering of life for the godly person, leaving it to

---

66. *Inst*. 3.6.1, *OS* 4:147.10–14; LCC 1:685.
67. "John Calvin to the Reader," *OS* 3:21–25; LCC 1:4.
68. *Inst*. 1.10.1, *OS* 3:85.13–16; LCC 1:97.
69. *Inst*. 1.14.20–21, *OS* 3:170–72; LCC 1:179–81.

his readers to seek discussion of individual virtues from the writings of others, especially the homilies of the fathers.[70] However, even in his fuller treatment of doctrine in other topics, Calvin is directing his readers to various subjects that they are to seek out and investigate in their reading of Scripture, in concert with the writings of others, especially the fathers.

However, Calvin is aware that obstacles may be placed in our way that hinder our access to the topics to be sought, which must first be removed if we are to be directed properly to the goal we are seeking. Calvin calls this aspect of his teaching "paving the way," by which he means removing any obstacles so that the readers "may have easy access to [Scripture] and advance in it without stumbling."[71] These obstacles may come from the false teaching of others, such as the difficulty created by the false scholastic distinction between formed and unformed faith.[72] But such obstacles may also come from the reading of Scripture itself, as in its description of God as repenting, or in its apparent suggestion that a reward is promised for our good works.[73] Hence, solving difficulties, and answering the objections raised by opponents such as Servetus, Osiander, and the Anabaptists, is essential for leading the reader to the goal sought in the reading of Scripture.

The resolution of difficulties and objections usually follows after Calvin's own definition and discussion of a particular doctrine, as it does in his discussion of the Trinity, or of original sin and its effects.[74] With other doctrines, such as faith or election, Calvin addresses the obstacles and questions at the beginning of his discussion, before he even arrives at his own definition of the doctrine.[75] In order to answer

---

70. "But I do not intend to develop here, the instruction in living that I am now about to offer to the point of describing individual virtues at length, and of digressing into exhortations. Such may be sought from others' writings, especially from the homilies of the fathers. To show the godly man how he may be directed to a rightly ordered life, and briefly to set down some universal rule with which to determine his duties—this will be quite enough for me" (*Inst.* 3.6.1, *OS* 4:146–47; LCC 1:685).

71. "John Calvin to the Reader," *OS* 3:6.18–26; LCC 1:4.

72. "Before we proceed farther, some preliminary remarks will be necessary to explain difficulties [*ad nodos explicandos*] that could otherwise offer a stumbling block [*obstaculum*] to our readers. First, we must refute that worthless distinction between formed and unformed faith which is tossed about in the schools" (*Inst.* 3.2.8, *OS* 4:16–17; LCC 1:551).

73. *Inst.* 1.17.12; 3.17.

74. *Inst.* 1.13.21–29; 2.5.

75. This is especially clear in the discussion of election, for Calvin knew that his doctrine of election raised serious questions even in the minds of his fellow evangelical teachers such as Melanchthon and Bullinger. "If it is plain that it comes to pass by God's bidding that salvation is freely offered to some while others are barred access to it, at once great and difficult questions spring up, explicable only when reverent minds regard as settled what they may suitably hold concerning election and predestination. A baffling question

the objections, Calvin must not only teach true doctrine, but must also explain it, until every doubt is removed from the minds of the pious. Calvin's goal in answering objections is not to remove their force from the minds of those raising them, but rather from the minds of the pious whom he aims to teach. "But now the truth which has been peaceably shown must be maintained against the calumnies of the wicked. And yet I will exert especial effort to the end that they who lend ready and open ears to God's Word may have a firm standing ground."[76] Calvin will not progress to the next doctrinal locus until he feels satisfied that he has fully explained the doctrine in question, has removed all doubts in the minds of the godly, and has given them a firm standing ground. "Now let us examine the individual parts of the definition of faith. After we have diligently examined it, no doubt, I believe, will remain."[77] At times such explanations can be quite extensive. For instance, the explanation of the phrase "diffused into all parts of the soul" in the definition of original sin (*Inst*. 2.1.8) takes up the next four chapters of the *Institutes* and depends on the definition of the faculties of the soul in book 1, chapter 15. What Calvin says at the end of his discussion of the Trinity could apply to the whole of the *Institutes*: "I trust that the whole sum of this doctrine has been faithfully explained."[78]

The need to explain doctrine until all doubt is removed is often at odds with Calvin's desire to study brevity throughout the *Institutes*. For instance, even though the relationship between the Old and the New Testament can be defined in one sentence, Calvin knows he must give a fuller explanation of the definition. "But because no one can gain a clear understanding from such a short statement, a fuller explanation is required if we wish to make any progress."[79] As much as Calvin strives for brevity and feels the need to move on to the next locus, he repeatedly acknowledges that brevity is obscure and requires much more extensive explanation. "For since there is something obscure in . . . brevity, in which many of the less educated are deceived, I have decided to give a fuller statement, using more words to dispel all doubt."[80] Despite his constant desire to write his summa with brevity, Calvin knows that his readers cannot be guided in their reading of

---

[*perplexa . . . quaestio*] this seems to many" (*Inst*. 3.2.1, *OS* 4:368–69; LCC 2:921). The difficulties with regard to faith spring not from the doctrine itself, but from false teaching about the nature and force of faith. "And we must scrutinize and investigate the true character of faith with greater care and zeal because many are dangerously deluded today in this respect" (*Inst*. 3.2.1, *OS* 4:7.14–16; LCC 1:543).

76. *Inst*. 1.13.21, *OS* 3:136.3–9; LCC 1:146.
77. *Inst*. 3.2.14, *OS* 4:24.32–34; LCC 1:559.
78. *Inst*. 1.13.29, *OS* 3:151.10; LCC 1:159.
79. *Inst*. 2.10.2, *OS* 3:404.8–10; LCC 1:429.
80. *Inst*. 4.14.1, *OS* 5:259.14–17; LCC 2:1277.

Scripture until the obscurity of brevity is more fully explained so that all doubts are removed from their minds.

The Role of Definition in the Institutes

From the standpoint of teaching, the greatest clarity and brevity of a given doctrinal locus should be found in the definition.[81] Calvin seems to be influenced here by Cicero in his discussion of definition in *Orator*. Cicero describes definition as "a statement giving the subject of discussion in the briefest possible form." However, Cicero also knows that such brevity is only clear to the most learned audience. Those of more average intelligence need a fuller explanation of the matter being defined if they are to profit from the definition. "The man whom we wish to be eloquent will, then, possess the ability to define the subject, and will not do it so briefly and compactly as is the custom in the learned discussions of philosophers, but with greater clarity and at the same time with greater fullness, and in a way better adapted to the ordinary judgment and popular intelligence."[82] Given the fact that Calvin is intentionally writing for those of average intelligence and education, it seems that he, like Cicero, knows that even the clearest definition will not be sufficiently clear for his readers, and will therefore need extensive explanation, in which the definition is broken down into its component parts and discussed more fully.

Thus, in his discussion of repentance, Calvin says, "But before we go further, it will be useful to explain more clearly the definition that we have laid down. We must examine repentance mainly under three heads."[83] After affirming the consensus of the scholastics that the definition of the effects of sin is that the supernatural gifts were lost, and the natural gifts corrupted, Calvin says, "This is, indeed, a complete definition, but one needing a fuller explanation."[84] The explanation of the definition may also involve the making of subsequent distinctions for the sake of teaching, as in the case of the acknowledgment of a legitimate meaning for "implicit faith."[85] The explanation may also involve subsequent definitions, as in the definition of the sin against the Holy Spirit in the

81. See Robert H. Ayers, "Language, Logic, and Reasons in Calvin's *Institutes*," in *The Organizational Structure of Calvin's Theology*, ed. Richard Gamble (New York: Garland, 1992), 249–63.

82. Cicero, *Orator* 33.116–17, trans. G. L. Hendrickson and H. M. Hubbell, Loeb Classical Library (Cambridge: Harvard University Press, 1988), 393.

83. *Inst.* 3.3.6, *OS* 4:60.21–22; LCC 1:598.

84. *Inst.* 2.2.12, *OS* 3:255.23–24; LCC 1:271.

85. "Although we concede, for the purpose of instruction [*docendi causa*], that there are divers forms of faith" (*Inst.* 3.2.9, *OS* 4:19.15–16; LCC 1:553).

discussion of repentance.[86] Or the explanation may involve explaining a distinction with a further definition, as when Calvin explains Christian freedom by distinguishing between the two forms of government in people—inner and outer—and explains this distinction by setting forth a definition of conscience as the inner form of government.[87] The explanation will only be as clear as the original definition, but the definition will not be clear if left unsupported by an explanation, especially for readers of average intelligence and education.

Definitions are the essential components in the series of teachings that comprise the *Institutes* and are the hinges on which its argument turns. Since definitions direct the readers to what they are to seek in Scripture, they should be expressions of the teaching of Scripture. However, a definition is never simply taken from a verse of Scripture; it rather is an interpretation of the meaning of Scripture, which will set forth that meaning more clearly. In response to the antitrinitarian charge that the definition of the Trinity is not found in Scripture, Calvin says, "But what prevents us from explaining in clearer words those matters in Scripture which perplex and hinder our understanding, yet which conscientiously and faithfully serve the truth of Scripture itself, and are made use of sparingly and modestly and on due occasion?"[88] Even when there is a clear verse of Scripture that appears to be stated as a definition, such as "This is my body," Calvin insists that such a statement must nonetheless still be interpreted. "They [his Lutheran opponents] reply that they have the word by which the will of God has been made plain—that is, if we concede to them the right to banish from the church the gift of interpretation [1 Cor. 12:10], which sheds light upon the word."[89] Calvin does not introduce the definition of faith in Hebrews until he finishes explaining his own definition; he simply states that they mean the same thing, though he seems to think his definition expresses the nature and force of faith more clearly.[90] The need to resolve doctrinal disputes in the church also reveals the need to make definitions that state the truth more clearly: "The churches should first assemble, examine the question put, and finally, after due discussion, bring forth a definition derived from Scripture which would remove all doubt from the people and stop the

---

86. *Inst*. 3.3.22.
87. *Inst*. 3.19.13.
88. *Inst*. 1.13.3, *OS* 3:112.11–15; LCC 1:124.
89. *Inst*. 4.17.25, *OS* 5:376.31–33; LCC 2:1391.
90. "Yet this does not at all differ from the apostle's definition, or rather the description he applies to his discourse, where he teaches that 'faith is the substance of things hoped for, the indication of things not appearing' [Heb. 11:1, cf. Vg.]" (*Inst*. 3.2.41, *OS* 4:51.3–6; LCC 1:588).

mouths of wicked and greedy men from daring to go any farther."[91] In any controversy over doctrine, attention must above all be paid to the definitions at stake, since they are the turning point of the controversy. "Now, for my part, when there is a dispute concerning anything, I . . . refer everything back to the definition itself, which is the hinge and foundation of the whole debate."[92]

Calvin does not always arrive at his definitions by the same path. Sometimes, as in his discussion of original sin, he simply begins with his own definition and then compares it with those that have been given by other teachers before him.[93] At other times, as in his definition of faith, Calvin first examines the definitions of others before him, and then arrives at his definition by carefully working from the genus to the species.[94] Although the route to the definition may differ in light of the doctrine that Calvin is defining, there is one element that never changes for Calvin: the definition should clearly express the nature and force of the reality being defined. "But it is easy to understand all these matters after a clearer definition of faith has been presented, to enable our readers to grasp its force and nature."[95] Calvin is sharply critical of the definition of faith by the schoolmen because it wears down and almost annihilates the whole force of faith by its obscurity.[96] Even when a definition rightly expresses the meaning of something, such as Anselm's definition of original sin as the loss of uprightness, it may still be deficient because it does not clearly express the force of that reality: "Although they have comprehended in this definition the whole meaning of the term, [they] have still not expressed effectively enough its power and energy."[97] Calvin rejects the scholastics' definition of repentance, for "they take certain clichés from the books of the ancient writers, which do not express the force of repentance at all."[98]

Calvin's understanding of the purpose of a definition strongly echoes both Plato and Cicero. Plato insists that a discussion over any disputed point must begin with its definition, for otherwise the disputants will not know what they are talking about. This is clearly echoed in the *Institutes*, as on original sin: "So that these remarks may not be made concerning an unknown and uncertain matter, let us define original

91. *Inst.* 4.9.13, *OS* 5:161.24–29; LCC 2:1176.
92. *Inst.* 3.3.1, *OS* 4:21–24; LCC 1:624.
93. "It is not my intention to investigate the several definitions proposed by various writers, but simply to bring forward the one that appears to me most in accordance with the truth" (*Inst.* 2.1.8, *OS* 3:236.30–33; LCC 1:250–51).
94. *Inst.* 3.2.1–7.
95. *Inst.* 3.2.1, *OS* 4:6.19–20; LCC 1:542.
96. *Inst.* 3.2.2.
97. *Inst.* 2.1.8, *OS* 3:238.3–7; LCC 1:252.
98. *Inst.* 3.4.1, *OS* 4:85.7–8; LCC 1:622.

sin."[99] Moreover, Plato states that the definition should express the nature and effects of the reality being defined,[100] and Cicero agrees: "Let us rather return to our subject and discuss the essence and nature of eloquence itself."[101] Hence, in the tradition of Plato and Cicero, Calvin seeks to arrive at definitions that clearly express the nature and force of the reality being defined.

The expression of the nature of a reality makes it possible clearly to distinguish that reality from all with which it might be confused. A good definition allows the reader easily to grasp the difference between the reality and all else with which it might be mistakenly identified. Thus, the spiritual and infinite nature of God allows readers of the *Institutes* to distinguish the Creator from idols, and the essential relationship between faith and the Word of God allows readers to distinguish between true faith and the hallucination of "implicit faith." However, a definition must express not only the nature of a given reality but also its force or energy. The realities that Calvin defines are not simply objects for our reflection or speculation, but rather are also dynamic and powerful realities that have a profound effect on us when we encounter them in all their force and power. This is why Calvin prefers to speak of practical rather than of speculative knowledge, for the former arises out of our sense or awareness of the force of the reality, whereas the latter simply flits about in our brains.

The purpose of a definition, therefore, is not simply to identify the reality about which Calvin is teaching, but also to bring readers to an encounter with the force and energy of that reality, so that the readers might feel or experience that force or power themselves. When Calvin discusses the way Scripture defines our salvation by the death of Christ, culminating with his descent to hell, he responds to those who say that

---

99. *Inst.* 2.1.8, *OS* 3:236.29–30; LCC 1:250. Plato makes this point in *Phaedrus*: "Now most people fail to realize that they don't know what this or that really is; consequently when they start discussing something, they dispense with any agreed definition, assuming that they know the thing; then later on they naturally find, to their cost, that they agree neither with each other nor with themselves" (*Phaedrus* 237c, in *Plato: The Collected Dialogues*, trans. R. Hackforth, ed. Edith Hamilton and Huntington Cairns [Princeton: Princeton University Press, 1961], 485).

100. "We ought to agree upon a definition of love which shows its nature and its effects" (*Plato: The Collected Dialogues*, 485).

101. Cicero, *Orator* 31.112. Cicero also echoes Plato's statement that the definition is the foundation and turning point of any discussion or dispute. "Furthermore, since in all subjects that are taught by systematic principles, we must first of all determine what each thing is—for unless the disputants are agreed as to what is the subject under debate there can be no proper discussion, nor can they arrive at any result—we must frequently give a verbal explanation of our ideas about each thing, and must make plain by definition the obscure concept of a subject, since definition is a statement giving the subject in the briefest possible form" (*Orator* 33.116).

Christ did not experience the wrath of God by saying, "From this it appears that these quibblers with whom I am contending boldly chatter about things they know nothing of. For they have never earnestly considered what it is or means that we have been redeemed from God's judgment. Yet this is our wisdom: duly to feel how much our salvation cost the Son of God."[102] In order clearly to express the force of a given reality in the definition, so that readers may be led to experience that power themselves, the teacher must first of all have experienced the force of that reality himself; otherwise he will not know what he is talking about. This may explain why Calvin is consistently concerned to make a transition from the words of the definition to a consideration of the thing itself, for only the thing itself can reveal its force to us, no matter how clearly the definition expresses that force in words. "And to avoid contention over a word, if we look upon the thing itself as described to us, no misgiving will remain."[103] This is especially clear in Calvin's discussion of the nature and power of God. Calvin rejects any definition of God that fails to express the way God's nature makes itself known to us with its force. "For the Lord manifests himself by his powers, the force of which we feel within ourselves and the benefits of which we enjoy. We must therefore be much more profoundly affected by this knowledge than if we were to imagine a god of whom no perception came through to us."[104]

The verbal expression of the force of a reality is therefore secondary to the experience and awareness of the force of the reality, since this force transcends our ability to express it in words. "I speak of nothing other than what each believer experiences within himself—though my words fall far beneath a just explanation of the matter."[105] The experience of the force of the reality on the part of the pious reader is the ultimate proof that what Calvin teaches is true. We see this especially in his discussion of the deity of the Son and the Holy Spirit. "This practical knowledge is doubtless more certain and firmer than any idle speculation. There, indeed, does the pious mind perceive the very presence of God, and almost touches him, when it feels itself quickened, illumined, preserved, justified, and sanctified."[106] So also in his discussion of the Holy Supper of the Lord, Calvin seeks to guide the reader to experience a commu-

102. *Inst.* 2.16.12, *OS* 3:408.31–35; LCC 1:519.
103. *Inst.* 3.11.4, *OS* 4:184.30–31; LCC 1:728. See also *Inst.* 1.12.3; 1.13.6.
104. *Inst.* 1.5.9, *OS* 3:53.14–18; LCC 1:62.
105. *Inst.* 1.7.5, *OS* 3:71.12–14; LCC 1:80–81.
106. *Inst.* 1.13.13, *OS* 3:127.8–12; LCC 1:138. So also regarding the deity of the Spirit, Calvin says, "Thus through him we come into communion with God, so that we in a way feel [*sentiamus*] his life-giving power towards us" (*Inst.* 1.13.14, *OS* 3:128.12–13; LCC 1:139).

nion with Christ that transcends his own abilities to explain it. "Now, if anyone should ask me how this takes place, I shall not be ashamed to confess that it is a secret too lofty for either my mind to comprehend or my words to declare. And, to speak more plainly, I rather experience than understand it."[107]

The Role of Contemplation in the Institutes

The ultimate goal of the *Institutes* is to bring its readers to the point where they may encounter, ponder, consider, and contemplate the nature and force of each reality defined and explained by Calvin, so that they might experience and feel that force for themselves. This contemplative orientation is indicated in the much-discussed opening chapter of the *Institutes*, in which Calvin says that our contemplation of ourselves leads us to a consideration of God, even as our contemplation of God leads us to an examination of ourselves.[108] At times, for the sake of brevity, Calvin will instruct his readers how they on their own should ponder, consider, and contemplate the reality he has discussed, perhaps in consultation with the writings of the fathers. In his discussion of the work of creation, Calvin first instructs his readers to read Genesis in light of Ambrose and Basil, and then he turns them to the contemplation of creation itself:

> Therefore, to be brief, let all readers know that they have with true faith apprehended what it is for God to be Creator of heaven and earth, if they first of all follow the universal rule, not to pass over in ungrateful thought-lessness or forgetfulness those conspicuous powers which God shows forth in his creatures, and then learn so to apply it to themselves that their very hearts are touched.[109]

At other times, because of the importance of the matter being discussed, Calvin will pause to ponder, examine, and contemplate the reality with the reader, as in his discussion of salvation by Christ's death: "But here we must earnestly ponder how he accomplishes salvation for us."[110] He will also set the proper context in which the pondering

---

107. *Inst.* 4.17.32, *OS* 5:389–90; LCC 2:1403.

108. "In the first place, no one can look upon himself without immediately turning his thoughts to the contemplation of God, in whom he 'lives and moves' [Acts 17:28]. . . . To this extent we are prompted by our own ills to contemplate the good things of God. . . . Again, it is certain that a man never achieves a clear knowledge of himself unless he has first looked upon God's face, and then descends from contemplating him to scrutinize himself" (*Inst.* 1.1–2, *OS* 3:31–33; LCC 1:35–37).

109. *Inst.* 1.14.21, *OS* 3:171–72; LCC 1:181.

110. *Inst.* 2.16.1, *OS* 3:483.1–2; LCC 1:504. Calvin makes a similar move in his discussion of the nature of sinful humanity. "Meanwhile, the well-known statement flitted from

of the given reality may be the most fruitful, as in his discussion of justification: "To this question, I insist, we must apply our mind if we would profitably inquire concerning true righteousness: How shall we reply to the Heavenly Judge when he calls us to account? Let us envisage for ourselves that Judge, not as our minds naturally imagine him, but as he is depicted for us in Scripture."[111] Guided by the *Institutes*, we are to seek in Scripture spiritual realities that we should ponder and contemplate, so that we might experience the force of them ourselves, thereby confirming the truth taught to us by Scripture. For Calvin, the pious are taught both by Scripture and by the experience of piety itself.[112]

Calvin considers such contemplation to be *essential* to a profitable reading of the *Institutes*, even if he at times leaves such contemplation up to his readers. Calvin's objective as a teacher is to confirm, clarify, and strengthen the experience and awareness of spiritual reality that the pious already have when they pick up the *Institutes*. He leads readers to this objective first by defining a given reality, and then by explaining that definition to remove all doubt. This clears the way for his readers to be brought to a direct consideration and contemplation of the nature and force of the reality on their own, thereby confirming the teaching both of Calvin and of Scripture, and strengthening their own piety. Calvin's theology is therefore best understood as a combination of dialectical, rhetorical, and contemplative theology. The dialectical moment revolves around the definitions set forth in the right order and series. The rhetorical moment consists in Calvin's attempt to bring the force of the reality to bear in the reader's feeling by the forcefulness of his own writing, especially in his explanations. The contemplative moment is when Calvin instructs his readers to consider for themselves the force of the reality he has defined and described. The contemplative goal clearly reveals the limitations of the first two moments, for the spiritual

---

mouth to mouth: that the natural gifts in man were corrupted, but the supernatural taken away. . . . For my part, if I wanted clearly to teach (*dilucide tradere*) what the corruption of nature is like, I would readily be content with these words. But it is more important to weigh carefully [*attente expendi*] what man can do, vitiated as he is in every part of his nature and shorn of supernatural gifts" (*Inst.* 2.2.4, *OS* 3:245–46; LCC 1:260).

111. *Inst.* 3.12.1, *OS* 4:208.12–17; LCC 1:755.

112. One sees this pedagogical approach already in the *Catechism* of 1538. "When we name Father, Son, and Holy Spirit, we are not fashioning three Gods, but in the simplest unity of God, both Scripture and the very experience of piety [*et scriptura, et ipsa pietatis experientia*] reveal to us God the Father, his Son and Spirit" (*Catechismus*, 1538, *CO* 5:337B). Calvin makes the same appeal to the experience of piety in his discussion of the divine nature of the Holy Spirit. "For what Scripture attributes to him and we ourselves learn by the sure experience of piety [*certa pietatis experientia discimus*] is far removed from creatures" (*Inst.* 1.13.14, *OS* 3:127.25–27; LCC 1:138).

realities with which we have to do transcend all our attempts to define and describe them.

> I urge my readers not to confine their mental interest within these too narrow limits, but to strive to rise much higher than I can lead them. For, whenever this matter is discussed, when I have tried to say all, I feel that I have as yet said little in proportion to its worth. And although my mind can think beyond what my tongue can utter, yet even my mind is conquered and overwhelmed by the greatness of the thing. Therefore, nothing remains but to break forth in wonder at this mystery, which plainly neither the mind is able to conceive nor the tongue to express.[113]

Given this goal, it becomes clear that the order and series of teaching of the *Institutes* is not dictated by logic, or even solely by the order of teaching in Scripture, but rather by Calvin's understanding of the way the awareness and experience of God and ourselves develops and grows. Calvin is extremely sensitive to the way the awareness of one reality will open the way to the awareness of another reality, and constructs his series of teaching in light of this dynamic. The entire series of teaching in the *Institutes* may be outlined in light of this order of awareness or experience. Our awareness of divinity, present in every person from birth, should lead us to an awareness of the powers of God portrayed in the universe. These powers clearly portray to us the Creator and Governor of the universe, though only when we are guided by Scripture and the Holy Spirit, so that the true God might be distinguished from all idols (book 1). Our awareness of the good gifts we were given in Adam should awaken in us the awareness that we have lost these gifts, and this awareness should humble us and lead us to seek these gifts elsewhere than in ourselves. Our awareness of our calamity and poverty revealed by the force of the moral law should lead us to the awareness of how much our salvation cost the Son of God in his death, so that we are led to seek all that we lack in him alone (book 2). Our awareness of our participation in Christ by faith through the gospel and the Spirit should lead us simultaneously to feel the repentance and justification such faith makes possible, as well as the expression of such faith in prayer, the source of such faith in eternal election, and the goal of such faith in the resurrection (book 3). Our awareness of the infirmity of our faith should lead us to experience the power of the aids and helps that God has provided for us in the church, and especially in the sacraments, so that our faith might be confirmed and strengthened thereby (book 4). The *Institutes* is ultimately both an expression of, and a guide to, the kind of experience that strengthens and sustains true piety and religion, as that experience

113. *Inst.* 4.17.7, *OS* 5:349.14–23; LCC 2:1367.

is both expressed and made available by the teaching of Scripture, as interpreted by the orthodox teachers of the church.

Calvin's concern for the order of right teaching, and the centrality of proper definitions within that order, reveal the fundamental role that Melanchthonian dialectic plays in the shape of the *Institutes,* and the way Calvin's attention to rhetoric serves that dialectical structure. Moreover, the ultimate objective of contemplative experience reveals the limitations of rhetoric per se: Calvin wishes to bring the reader to a direct encounter with the spiritual realities found in Scripture, as first defined and explained in the *Institutes*. Calvin's *Institutes* is therefore best categorized as a work of dialectical, rhetorical, and contemplative theology, written for the purpose of clarifying the doctrine and strengthening the piety of the future pastors and teachers of the church.

5

GATHERING MEANING
FROM THE CONTEXT

Calvin's Exegetical Method

Once future candidates for the ministry have been taught and confirmed in godly doctrine as summarized in the *Institutes*, Calvin turns them to his expositions of Scripture in his commentaries.

> If, after this road has, as it were, been paved, I shall publish any interpretations of Scripture, I shall always condense them, because I shall have no need to undertake long doctrinal discussions, and to digress into commonplaces. In this way the godly reader will be spared great annoyance

This essay was originally published in a slightly different form under the title "Gathering Meaning from the Context: Calvin's Exegetical Method," *Journal of Religion* 82, no. 1 (2002): 1–26. © 2002 by The University of Chicago. All rights reserved. Reprinted by permission.

and boredom, provided he approach Scripture armed with the knowledge of the present work, as a necessary tool.[1]

Unlike the summary of doctrine, which follows the order of right teaching, Calvin in his commentaries is most concerned to follow the order of the context, which he considered to be the proper office of the interpreter. This chapter will attempt to explicate the contextual exegesis of John Calvin, with particular attention to his commentaries and lectures on the Hebrew Scriptures, in an attempt to understand more clearly his method of gathering meaning from the context of Scripture, so that pastors might learn to do the same for themselves under his guidance.

In order to highlight the importance of the context for Calvin's interpretation of Scripture, we shall examine Calvin's method of contextual interpretation in relation to the historical-critical method of the nineteenth and twentieth centuries. I am particularly interested in engaging the claim made by Hans Frei and George Lindbeck, that whereas the historical-critical method reads Scripture in the context of the world, Calvin and other "precritical" exegetes read the world in the context of the meaning generated by the narrative of Scripture.[2] According to Lindbeck, the critical reading of Scripture is characterized in the following way: "Scripture ceased to function as the lens through which theologians viewed the world and instead became primarily the object of study whose religiously significant or literal meaning was located outside itself."[3] Calvin, on the other hand, would be among those precritical exegetes who read the world in the context of Scripture. "To describe the basic meaning of these books is an intratextual task, a matter of explicating their contents and the perspectives on extratextual reality that they generate."[4]

If this were true, then one would expect Calvin's exegesis to stay completely within the context of Scripture itself and the world of meaning generated by the narrative of Scripture, and to forego any attempt to understand Scripture in light of a world of meaning outside of it, be that world literary, historical, cultural, scientific, philosophical, or religious. As we shall see, this reading of Calvin as an intratextual exegete is simply not an accurate reflection of his actual exegetical practice. Calvin does, it is true, insist on reading a passage of Scripture in light of its literary context in Scripture, both in relation to the book in which it is found and in relation to the rest of Scripture. But Calvin also reads Scripture

1. "John Calvin to the Reader," *OS* 3:6.26–31; LCC 1:4–5.
2. Hans Frei, *The Eclipse of Biblical Narrative* (New Haven: Yale University Press, 1974); George A. Lindbeck, *The Nature of Doctrine* (Philadelphia: Westminster, 1984).
3. Lindbeck, *Nature of Doctrine*, 119.
4. Ibid., 117.

directly in light of a larger world of meaning outside of Scripture, and he does so precisely to understand the meaning of Scripture itself. This larger context outside of Scripture is given to Calvin almost entirely by the Greek and Latin literature that he studied and committed to memory throughout his life, which raised for Calvin questions concerning the relationship of the statements of Scripture to the history, astronomy, zoology, botany, psychology, meteorology, philosophy, poetry, drama, and religion of the Greek and Latin world. So important are these extrabiblical contexts for Calvin's exegesis that he constantly berates, insults, and dismisses Jewish exegetes for what he takes to be their utter ignorance of all the arts and sciences mediated by Greek and Latin literature, and not, as one would expect, for missing the analogical and anagogical references to Christ in Hebrew Scriptures. Calvin, like subsequent critical readers of Scripture, interprets Scripture in light of its original linguistic, cultural historical, and religious context.

If Calvin does read Scripture in light of its extrabiblical context, then why do scholars such as Frei and Lindbeck think that Calvin's exegetical method differs from the historical-critical method developed in the eighteenth and nineteenth centuries? I will argue that Calvin combines his reading of Scripture in light of its biblical and extrabiblical context with a reading of Scripture in light of its theological context. There are four aspects of this theological setting of Scripture that guide Calvin's exegetical method. First, Calvin places the work of the biblical interpreter completely in the context of the church, with the goal of opening access to the meaning of Scripture for unlearned, ordinary Christians, to confirm their faith in the doctrine they are taught. Second, Calvin establishes the unity of the Old and New Testaments by means of a typological reading of the Hebrew Bible, in which the earthly pledges of God's favor are seen to be meaningful in their own right, while also directing the Israelites to the spiritual blessings of Christ, by means of analogy and anagoge. Third, Calvin assumes that the meaning to be gathered from the contextual reading of Scripture is general doctrine that God wants to be taught and applied to the church of every time and place, even though it must be applied analogically, in light of the differences between then and now. Finally, Calvin rejects the use of the law of contradiction to undermine the credibility of the scriptural narrative, based on his conviction that the ultimate author of Scripture is the Holy Spirit. All four of these differences are based on a second context in which Calvin reads Scripture: his understanding of the nature and activity of God, who, as Calvin insists, "always remains like himself."[5] In other words, Calvin addresses two distinct but not opposed questions when he interprets a

5. Comm. on Heb. 1:1, *OE* 19:15.22–24; *CNTC* 12:5.

text of Scripture: first, what does the text mean in light of its relationship to other scriptural and extrascriptural texts? And second, what does the text mean in light of the nature and activity of God?

One finds this combination of questions not only in Calvin but also in theologians who write after the development of historical criticism, such as Friedrich Schleiermacher, Adolph von Harnack, Rudolf Bultmann, Karl Barth, and Hans Urs von Balthasar. For example, according to Barth, two presuppositions guide biblical exegesis. The first is "held in common with all historical-critical research" and is analogous to Calvin's appeal to the context as the locus of meaning of the text: "In order to read and understand the Bible, biblical theology must conscientiously employ all known and available means, all the rules and criteria that are applicable to grammar, linguistics, and style, as well as all the knowledge gathered in the comparative study of the history of the world, of culture, and of literature." The second presupposition for Barth is analogous to what I have called the theological context of the reading of Scripture for Calvin: "There may also be texts that, according to the intention of their authors and according to their actual character, require that they be read and explained as attestation and proclamation of a *divine* action and speech which have reportedly or really taken place in the midst of general history."[6] One sees the presence of both concerns in the exegetical method of Rudolf Bultmann as well:

> Certainly the Bible is an historical document and we must interpret the Bible by the methods of historical research. We must study the language of the Bible, the historical situation of the authors, etc. But what is our true and real interest? . . . I think our interest is really to hear what the Bible has to say for our actual present, to hear what is the truth about our life and about our soul.[7]

If this is the case, then there is much more continuity between Calvin's method of exegesis and the method of interpretation followed by many theologians in the nineteenth and twentieth centuries—much more continuity than either Frei or Lindbeck would seem to allow. Calvin, like these subsequent theologians, reads Scripture in light of two distinct but related concerns: what the passage means in light of its biblical and extrabiblical context and what the same passage means in relation to his understanding of the nature and activity of God. According to Calvin, and to theologians like Bultmann and Barth after him, sound Christian

6. Karl Barth, *Evangelical Theology: An Introduction*, trans. Grover Foley (Grand Rapids: Eerdmans, 1963), 176.

7. Rudolf Bultmann, *Jesus Christ and Mythology* (New York: Scribner's, 1958), 51–52.

exegesis understands both questions to be essential to the task of rightly interpreting Scripture.[8]

This chapter will explicate the exegetical method of John Calvin by first placing it in the setting of his work as a teacher and pastor in the church. I will then examine the way the context reveals the mind of the author for Calvin and will proceed to develop how he gathers the meaning of the author from the linguistic, historical, and scientific contexts of Scripture. I will conclude by examining the way Calvin deals with the law of contradiction in his reading of Scripture, and the way he resolves such contradictions by reading Scripture in light of his understanding of the nature and activity of God. The goal of this chapter is twofold: first, to show that Calvin's method of gathering meaning from the context of Scripture places him in significant continuity with subsequent historical critics, and second, to show that this method did not at all discourage Calvin from reading Scripture in the context of his understanding of the nature and activity of God, which places him in significant continuity with the theological reading of Scripture practiced by theologians of the nineteenth and twentieth centuries who also adopted the historical-critical reading of Scripture.

Calvin's Exegesis in the Context of His Call as Teacher and Pastor

In order to examine Calvin's contextual interpretation of Scripture, we need first to examine the role of scriptural interpretation in the context of Calvin's self-understanding as a teacher and preacher in the church. Over against Gregory the Great and the Roman theologians, Calvin insists that the books of the unlearned (those who have not mastered Hebrew, Greek, and Latin literature) are to be found not in images but in Scripture. In Scripture, God through the Holy Spirit accommodates his teaching to reach the capacities of the unlearned and the ignorant. This conviction led Calvin to seek to restore access to Scripture for all Christians, so that their faith might be confirmed and strengthened by what they read, and so that they might be able to test the truth of the preaching and teaching they hear from others, as well as teach others themselves. The irony is that at the same time Calvin says that God writes Scripture to teach the unlearned, he also insists that only those who are the most learned may rightly interpret Scripture, even though they do so to open access to Scripture for the unlearned. Hence, unless

8. Richard Muller and John Thompson detail four points that distinguish precritical from critical interpretations of Scripture: "The Significance of Precritical Exegesis," in *Biblical Interpretation in the Era of the Reformation*, ed. Richard A. Muller and John L. Thompson (Grand Rapids: Eerdmans, 1996), 339–42.

God provides learned interpreters along with Scripture, the divine self-accommodation to the unlearned will not fully come to fruition. "And we must keep in mind here, that not only is Scripture given to us, but interpreters and teachers are also added to help us."[9]

Access to Scripture is opened both by a summary of the doctrine of piety and religion, which teaches us what to look for in Scripture, and by commentaries following the method of *lectio continua*, which unfold the mind of the author of Scripture. The *Institutes* and the commentaries are intended by Calvin to open access to Scripture for future pastors, whereas the catechism and the weekday sermons are meant to open access to Scripture for members of the congregation. For Calvin, the proper understanding of Scripture depends on familiarity both with the summary of the rudiments of doctrine and with Scripture itself. Those who lack this kind of training, even though they are expert in the Hebrew language, will inevitably misunderstand Scripture. "But it generally happens with men who are not exercised in the Scripture, nor imbued with sound theology, although well acquainted with the Hebrew language, yet hallucinate and fall into mistakes even in first rudiments."[10] As a teacher and preacher, Calvin sought to exercise his students in Scripture and imbue them with sound theology; however, the procedure for each was distinct for him. The summary of doctrine gathers doctrine from the whole of Scripture under dialectically arranged commonplaces, following the order of right teaching, in a way similar to Melanchthon's 1535 *Loci communes*. The interpretation of Scripture, on the other hand, follows the order of the context, in an attempt to reveal the mind of the author, from which one can then draw fruitful doctrine. Thus, in his comments on Gen. 17:9, in dealing with circumcision, Calvin says, "Moreover, although it would, perhaps, be more suitable for the purpose of instruction, were we to give a summary of those things which are to be gathered concerning circumcision; I will yet follow the order of the context, which I think more appropriate to the office of an interpreter."[11] The context, then, is seen to be the decisive guide for the work of the interpreter of Scripture, according to Calvin. However, it is important to recognize that Calvin assumes a complementary relationship between

9. Comm. on Acts 8:31, *CO* 48:192C; *CNTC* 6:247.

10. Comm. on Ps. 73:26, *CO* 31:689A; CTS 10:156.

11. Comm. on Gen. 17:9, *CO* 23:239C; CTS 1:451. This methodological distinction is in contrast to Melanchthon, who followed only the order of *loci communes* in the text of Scripture, and to Bucer, who followed the order of the context but also included in his commentaries extensive *loci communes*, in which he gathered all that Scripture had to say on a given topic. Like Bucer and unlike Melanchthon, Calvin's exegesis follows the *ordinem contextus*; but like Melanchthon and unlike Bucer, Calvin collected the doctrine to be gathered from Scripture in a separate book of *loci communes*, the *Institutes* of 1539 and following.

the teaching of Christian doctrine and the contextual interpretation of Scripture, with the goal of both being the education and edification of the whole church.

The Mind of the Author Revealed by the Context

As is widely acknowledged, Calvin thought that the primary task of the interpreter of Scripture is to reveal the mind of the author.[12] What is not as widely claimed is that Calvin was convinced that the mind, council, meaning, or sense of the author could only be revealed by the interpreter who carefully followed the contextual order of the Scripture being interpreted.[13] Hence, if the mind of the author is to be revealed *by* the interpreter, that mind is first revealed *to* the interpreter by the context.[14] By "context," Calvin means first of all the relation of a given passage to the text immediately preceding and following it. However, as we shall see, he also extends the context of a passage of Scripture to include the rest of Scripture, as well as any pertinent Hebrew, Greek, or Latin texts, and insists that knowledge of such texts is essential to anyone seeking to interpret Scripture.

The role of the context in revealing the mind of the author is best seen when Calvin interprets texts with obscure meaning, as in the case of Jer. 23:22. "The passage may seem obscure, but from the context itself we can gather that the real design of the prophet was to convict the false teachers, that they might no longer boast of God's name, and falsely pretend that they were indued with the prophetic office, and glory in that distinction."[15] In Isa. 65:7, "The word *rishonah* [*ri'šōnâ*] may be explained in various ways, either 'I will measure back with their antiquity,' or 'in the first place,' or 'formerly,' or 'from the beginning.' But we must take into account the circumstances of the passage, from which the prophet's meaning will be clearly seen."[16] Not surprisingly, therefore,

12. "Et sane quum hoc sit prope unicum illius officium, mentem scriptoris, quem explicandum sumpsit, patefacere" (Iohannes Calvinus Simoni Grynaeo, *Romanos* 1.9–10). See T. H. L. Parker, *Calvin's New Testament Commentaries* (Louisville: Westminster John Knox, 1993), 85–108.

13. See David Steinmetz, "The Superiority of Pre-Critical Exegesis," *Theology Today* 37 (April 1980): 27–38.

14. "And from the context it is clear that this was the intention of the apostle [*Atque hoc fuisse Apostoli consilium liquet ex contextu*] where he assigns the cause of fear and trembling to God's good pleasure, whereby He gives to His people the capacity to will aright and to carry through valiantly [Phil. 2:12–13]" (*Inst.* 3.2.23, *OS* 3:33–34; LCC 1:569).

15. Comm. on Jer. 23:22, *CO* 38:434B; CTS 19:182.

16. Comm. on Isa. 65:7; *CO* 37:41–42; CTS 16:386. See also his discussion of the epithet in Ps. 45, where he rejects the interpretation that *yĕdîdōt* ("loves," a plural noun) refers to

one of Calvin's most common defenses of his translation from Hebrew or Greek into Latin is that it "flows better with the context" than does any other alternative.[17]

The most common errors of interpretation are made by those who take a passage of Scripture out of its original context, thereby giving it a distorted meaning. Thus, when he comments on Isa. 14:12, "How you are fallen from heaven," Calvin notes that this passage has been used in the church to refer to Satan.

> The exposition of this passage, which some have given, as if it referred to Satan, has arisen from ignorance; for the context [14:2, 22] plainly shows that these statements must be understood in reference to the king of the Babylonians. But when passages of Scripture are taken up at random, and no attention is paid to the context, we need not wonder that mistakes of this kind frequently arise.[18]

At times, the chapter divisions, inserted to help commit Scripture to memory, may also work against reading a passage in the right context. "They who have divided them have often unknowingly perverted the meaning. The divisions then are not to be heeded, only the number is to be retained as a help to the memory; but as to the context, they are often a hindrance to readers, for it is preposterous to blend things which are separate, and to divide what is connected."[19] At times the very beauty and power of a passage of Scripture leads to its being considered outside of its context, being treated instead as an independently true aphorism. "Sometimes it happens that, when a sentence is beautiful, it attracts us to it, and causes us to steal away from the true meaning, so that we do not adhere closely to the context, or spend much time in investigating the author's meaning. Let us therefore inquire if this be the true mind of the prophet."[20] This dynamic can be seen in Calvin's comments on Jer. 23:28, "Let the prophet who has a dream tell the dream, but let the one who has my word speak my word faithfully." "Unless we attend to this which the prophet had in view, this passage will appear unmeaning. It has often been quoted, but this circumstance has certainly not

---

the fatherly love of God for Solomon. "Thus the words, of loves, are put for a descriptive epithet, and denote, that it is a love-song. Indeed, Solomon was called *Yedidyah*, which means beloved of the Lord, 2 Sam. 12:25. But the context, in my opinion, requires [*contextus . . . postulat*] that the term *yedidoth*, that is to say, 'loves,' be understood as referring to the mutual love which husband and wife ought to cherish towards each other" (Comm. on Ps. 45:1 MT [superscription, ET], *CO* 31:449A; CTS 9:173).

17. Comm. on Ps. 86:14; Isa. 37:21; 41:14; 59:4; Jer. 6:10; 49:19.
18. Comm. on Isa. 14:12; *CO* 36:277C; CTS 13:442.
19. Comm. on Jer. 5:3, *CO* 37:608B; CTS 17:256.
20. Comm. on Isa. 29:7, *CO* 36:489A; CTS 14:316.

been observed. We ought, therefore, to consider why a thing is said. This verse depends on what has gone before."[21] The concern to apply statements of Scripture to the Messiah, exhibited by both Jewish and Christian interpreters, may lead them to take a passage out of context, as in the case of Jer. 30:4–6, which Jews and Christians agree refers to the Messiah. "They all consider this as a prophecy referring to the time of the Messiah; but were any one wisely to view the whole context, he would readily agree with me that the prophet includes here a sum of the doctrine which the people had previously heard from his mouth."[22] The loss of attention to the context can also be due to the rush to draw doctrine from a potent passage of Scripture, such as Jeremiah's statement about the corruption of the human heart, which draws from Calvin an extensive discussion of the importance of the whole context for proper interpretation.

> What is said here depends on what is gone before; and therefore they ought to be read simultaneously in one context. Many lay hold of these words and mutilate them without understanding the design of the prophet. This is very absurd; for we ought first to see what the prophets had in view, and by what necessity or cause they were led to speak, what was their condition, and then the general doctrine may be gathered from their words. If we wish to read the prophets with benefit, we must first consider the reason why a thing is spoken, and then elicit a general doctrine.[23]

As we shall see later in this chapter, this concern for the circumstances that a prophet is addressing will make the historical context of Scripture, discerned as much as possible by extracanonical sources, essential to the right understanding of Scripture itself.

The Linguistic Context of Scripture

Besides the immediate literary context of a passage of Scripture, the meaning of Scripture is further illumined by its relationship to the language in which it was written. According to Calvin, each language has particular forms of speech appropriate to it, but perhaps not appropriate in another language. Commenting on Jer. 24:6, "I will build them up, and not tear them down, I will plant them, and not pluck them up" (NRSV), Calvin observes, "This mode of speaking would not be so significant either in Latin or in Greek; but such repetition, as is well known,

21. Comm. on Jer. 23:28, *CO* 38:433B; CTS 19:196.
22. Comm. on Jer. 30:4–6, *CO* 38:614; CTS 20:8.
23. Comm. on Jer. 17:9–10, *CO* 38:270A; CTS 18:353.

often occurs in Hebrew."[24] Lack of familiarity with the Hebrew way of speaking may lead an interpreter to misunderstand a passage, even if he takes it within its original literary context. Commenting on Isa. 53:9, "And his tomb with the rich" (NRSV), Calvin states, "I consider the singular *gnashir* [*ʿāšîr*], 'the rich men,' to be put for the plural, *gnashirim* [*ʿĕšîrîm*], as is frequently done by Hebrew writers. I see no reason why Oecolampadius rendered it 'high places.'"[25] Not surprisingly, Calvin will often turn to the rabbis, and especially to David Kimchi, for a more complete understanding of Hebrew forms of speech. "The term *debarim* [*dĕbārîm*], in the end of the verse, signifies *words*; but, along with David Kimchi, the most correct expositor among the Rabbis, I take it to mean *affairs*."[26] Given the unique nature of Hebrew forms of expression, an interpreter trained in the use of elegant Latin must learn how to allow Hebraic forms to emerge in translation, so that the force and meaning of the passage might be revealed. "He says, first, 'Behold, I will plead thy cause, and then, I will vindicate or avenge thy vengeance.' These are hard words to Latin ears; yet they contain more force and power than if we were to follow the elegance of the Latin tongue. It is better to retain the genuine terms than to study neatness too much."[27] The meaning of the Hebrew expression may be conveyed to the reader who does not know Hebrew by allowing such expressions to stand in the Latin translation, even though they might strike the Latin reader as improper. Thus, when Calvin discusses the meaning of "righteousness" in the *Institutes*, he says, "Those skilled in the Hebrew language better understand this sense. . . . Yet from the context it readily appears that this word, even when it is read in Latin, cannot otherwise be understood than relatively, but not so as to signify any quality."[28]

A skilled interpreter must therefore be conversant with both Hebrew and Latin forms of expression, since he is bringing the passage from one linguistic context to another in the very act of translating. Ignorance of Latin forms of expression can lead to glaring errors of interpretation, even for an interpreter highly skilled in Hebrew. "He enhances this fear by saying, 'Inquire and see whether a man is in labor [*pariat*].' Some one renders this absurdly, 'Whether a man begets [*generat*]?' by which

24. Comm. on Jer. 24:6, *CO* 38:461A; CTS 19:226.
25. Comm. on Isa. 53:9, *CO* 37:262A; CTS 16:122.
26. Comm. on Ps. 112:5, *CO* 32:174C; CTS 11:326.
27. Comm. on Jer. 51:36, *CO* 39:475B; CTS 21:252. Calvin frequently notes that there are modes of expression proper in Hebrew but improper in Latin. "We find the same words here as before. 'Put now the old tatters, dragged or torn and rotten, under the pit of thy hands underneath the cords.' This is an improper mode of speaking in Latin, but not in Hebrew" (Comm. on Jer. 38:12, *CO* 39:166A; CTS 20:399).
28. *Inst.* 3.11.3, *OS* 4:183.27–35; LCC 1:727.

mistake he has betrayed a defect of judgment as well as ignorance; he was indeed learned in Hebrew, but ignorant in Latin, and also void of judgment."[29] A skilled interpreter must also be highly familiar with Greek forms of expression, not only in order to interpret the Greek New Testament, but also because he must refer to the Greek translation of the Hebrew Scriptures. Calvin will often display his trilingual skill when seeking to arrive at the meaning of a Hebrew term. "As to the word *meshil* [*māšāl*], it is taken, as we know, for a weighty saying, and in the plural, weighty sayings, called by the Latins *sententias* or *dicta*, and by the Greeks *apothegmata*."[30] Calvin thus interprets Scripture in the context of Hebrew, Greek, and Latin literature to try to understand not only the meaning of specific terms but also the larger cultural context out of which such terms emerge.

> He adds, *eidad, eidad* [*hēdād*], shouting, shouting, for there will be no shouting. Some render *eidad* [as] "signal" (*celeuma*), . . . a Greek word, but also used in Latin: *keleuma* is said by the Greeks to be the shouting of sailors, especially when they drive to the shore; they then rouse one another in rowing, and also congratulate one another, because they are nigh to land; for to see the harbor is a cause of special joy to sailors, as though it were a restoration to life and safety. But this word *keleuma* is applied to other things as it may be said that reapers sing a *celeuma* when they finish their work. The vine-dressers also had their songs; and they were sung by the heathen nations, as Virgil says. "Now the worn-out vine-dresser sings at the extreme rows of the vines" (*Georg.* 2.417).[31]

As can be seen in this passage, Calvin is convinced that the skilled interpreter of Scripture must be immersed in the literature of the Greek and Latin world, and will often refer to such literature to help him elucidate the meaning of Scripture. At times, classical writers are used as contrasting examples to the words of the prophets.

> We hence learn that the Prophet did not compose this song to lament the calamity of his own country as heathens were wont to do. An example of heathen lamentation is found in Virgil:
>
> Come is the great day and the unavoidable time
> Of Dardania; we Trojans have been; Ilium has been,
> And the great glory of the Tiberians; cruel Jupiter has to Agor
> transferred all things; the Danai rule in the burnt city. [*Aen.* 2.324–27]

29. Comm. on Jer. 30:6, *CO* 38:615B; CTS 20:10.
30. Comm. on Mic. 2:4, *CO* 43:304A; CTS 27:190.
31. Comm. on Jer. 48:33, *CO* 39:335C; CTS 21:37.

. . . We hence see how the unbelieving, when they lament their own ca-
lamities, vomit forth blasphemies against God, for they are exasperated
by sorrow.[32]

In other passages, Calvin will find confirmation of the prophet's description of the ungodly in the statements of heathen writers. "Ezekiel shows
that it was a complaint commonly prevailing among the people, that
they suffered for the sins of their fathers, as Horace also says, a heathen
and despiser of God (*Ode* 3.6): 'O Roman / Thou dost undeservedly suffer for the faults of thy fathers.'"[33] At other times, Calvin will appeal to
classical authors to confirm the critique of idolatry and superstition
being made by the prophets.

Hardly a Prophet could have inveighed more severely against this gross
superstition than Persius, who compares sacrifices, so much thought of
by all, to puppets, and who shows that other things are required by God,
even 'A well-ordered condition of piety and soul, and an inward purity / Of
mind, and a heart imbued with generous virtue.' . . . And this is what has
been expressed by heathen authors: another poet says—'An impious right
hand does not rightly worship the celestials.' So they spoke according to
the common judgment of natural knowledge.[34]

Calvin not only sets Hebrew Scripture in the context of classical Greek
and Latin literature in order to interpret it; he also uses the categories of
classical rhetoric, especially those of Cicero, to help him identify forms
of expression he comes across in Hebrew, such as hyperbole, hypotyposis, personification, and so on, following the example of Erasmus and
Melanchthon before him.[35]

But there is here what they call a personification [*prosopopoeia*], that is,
an imaginary person is introduced; for the Prophet raises up Rachel from
the grave, and represents her as lamenting. . . . Rhetoricians mention personification among the highest excellencies; and Cicero, when treating of
the highest ornament of oration, says that nothing touches an audience
as much as when the dead are raised from below.[36]

Calvin thinks that the use of striking figurative language is more common among the prophets than in common Latin usage, and must be

32. Comm. on Lam. 1:8, *CO* 39:517A; CTS 21:317.
33. Comm. on Jer. 31:29–30, *CO* 38:686A; CTS 20:123.
34. Comm. on Hag. 2:10–14, *CO* 44:111–12; CTS 29:369–70.
35. See especially Olivier Millet, *Calvin et la dynamique de la parole* (Geneva: Slatkine, 1992).
36. Comm. on Jer. 31:15–16, *CO* 38:664C; CTS 20:88–89.

kept in mind by interpreters.[37] However, Calvin always points out that the prophets use these expressions under the impulse of the Spirit, and not because they were trained by rhetoricians. "The Prophet, then, though not taught in the school of rhetoricians, thus adorned his discourse through the impulse of God's Spirit, that he might more effectually penetrate into the hearts of the people."[38] Calvin also insists that the objective of the prophets differs from orators such as Cicero. "Public speakers [*Rhetores*] affect fine speaking only to catch applause, or to fill men with empty fear or joy; but the Prophets had in view another thing, even to teach, to exhort, to reprove, to threaten, in a way calculated to be effectual."[39] Calvin borrows the literary categories from Cicero to interpret the prophets, even though he thinks the source and objective of those categories is not the same for the prophets as for Cicero.

Calvin does identify one particular form of expression that appears to be unique to the prophets, and that is the way they represent spiritual realities by means of physical types and symbols. "This mode of speaking, common among the prophets, ought especially to be noticed. They describe the kingdom of Christ in a way suited to the comprehension of a rude people, and hence they set before them external images."[40] God does in fact give signs of his favor to the Israelites by promising them land and a temporal kingdom, but these signs must ultimately be seen as referring to the spiritual kingdom of Christ, on the basis of God's spiritual nature. This means, on the one hand, that Calvin will insist on the intrinsic significance of the pledges of God's favor to the Israelites, as in the promise of Isaiah that the Jews would possess the land forever, over against certain Christian interpreters who wish to find only a spiritual meaning in the Old Testament promises.

> Exceedingly unnatural and inconsistent with the style of the prophet is the interpretation of those who explain "the land" to mean heaven and the blessed life; for the land of Canaan was given to the children of God with this intention, that, being separated from the whole world, and having become God's heritage, they might worship him there in a right manner;

37. "Jeremiah now uses a form of speaking very common in the prophet though remote from common use. For the prophets, when they denounced God's judgments and punishments on the ungodly, do not speak in a simple language, as though they were giving a narrative, but they employed figurative expressions, as though they wished to introduce men into the very scene itself" (Comm. on Jer. 46:3–5, *CO* 39:284A; CTS 20:574–75).

38. Comm. on Jer. 31:15–16, *CO* 38:664C; CTS 20:89.

39. Comm. on Jer. 46:14, *CO* 39:292B; CTS 20:586–87.

40. Comm. on Jer. 31:12, *CO* 38:660A; CTS 20:82. See Randall C. Zachman, "Calvin as Analogical Theologian," *Scottish Journal of Theology* 51, no. 2 (1998): 162–87.

and consequently, to dwell in the land by right of inheritance means nothing more than to remain in the family of God.[41]

Similarly, the return of the people of Israel from exile really is a pledge of God's favor in its own right, even though this pledge is ultimately grounded in Christ.

> For it is not necessary nor expedient to introduce an analogical sense, as interpreters are wont to do, by representing the return of the people as symbolical of what was higher, even of the deliverance that was effected by Christ, for it ought to be considered one and the same favor of God, that is, that he brought back his people from exile, that they might at length enjoy quiet and solid happiness when the kingdom of David should at length be established.[42]

The inherent meaningfulness of realities that are also images of spiritual reality is necessitated by the rude and carnal nature of the people to whom God is speaking through the prophets. "Still, there is no defect in the Prophet's expressions, for they depict for us the visible image of Christ's kingdom, and accommodate themselves to our dullness."[43] As we are carnal and earthly, we can only be led to spiritual reality by means of earthly reality.

On the other hand, Calvin is sharply critical of Jewish interpretations that limit the meaning of such symbols to their earthly reality, and do not ascend by analogy and anagoge to the spiritual reality being represented thereby.[44] The need to ascend from earthly to spiritual reality is necessitated by the spiritual nature of God. According to Calvin, since God is Spirit, all temporal blessings given to the Israelites must lead us to the spiritual blessings God promises to all the faithful in Christ. Such analogy and anagoge is the central way Calvin tries to respect the integrity of the history of Israel's relationship with God, while referring the totality of that history to Christ.[45] Frei claims that this typological reading of Scripture preserves the unity of the Old and New Testaments in

41. Comm. on Isa. 60:21, *CO* 37:369A; CTS 16:299.
42. Comm. on Jer. 33:17–18, *CO* 39:71B; CTS 20:260.
43. Comm. on Dan. 7:27, *CO* 41:82B; CTS 25:73.
44. "Here the Rabbi Barbinel, who thinks himself superior to all others, rejects our idea of a spiritual reign of Christ as a foolish imagination. For the kingdom of God, he says, is established under the whole heavens, and is given to the people of the saints. If it is established under heaven, says he, it is earthly, and if earthly, therefore not spiritual" (Comm. on Daniel 7:27, *CO* 41:88C; CTS 25:74–75).
45. See David L. Puckett, *John Calvin's Exegesis of the Old Testament* (Louisville: Westminster John Knox, 1995).

a way not possible for historical-critical exegesis.[46] However, in contrast to Frei, Calvin establishes this unity by appealing to the nature of God, in light of his principle that "God always remains like himself," and not to the unity of the biblical narrative itself. This allows Calvin to see the ultimate reference of all Scripture to be the spiritual blessings God wills to bestow on us in Christ, while also respecting the different ways God has revealed those promises throughout history, in accommodation to the varying capacities of the faithful.[47] Calvin regards the rejection of analogical and anagogical interpretation by some Jews as introducing contradiction into the nature of God, and not as a rejection of a unified biblical narrative. If the kingdom of God is only of this world, then for Calvin "we must infer that God changes his nature. His kingdom, then, will consist in opulence, and military power and parade, and the common luxuries of life, so that God will become unlike himself."[48] Hence, the relationship between earthly sign and spiritual reality can only be preserved by reading Scripture in the context of the nature and activity of God, according to Calvin, especially in light of God's spiritual nature.

The Historical Context of Scripture

Calvin's use of analogy and anagoge does not eradicate the original historical context of prophecy, but rather makes the historical context decisive for determining the meaning of the prophets. One can only elevate to the spiritual meaning after the meaning of the prophet has been determined in the context of the historical circumstances in which the prophet spoke.[49] Calvin's concern to understand what a prophet says in the context of when and why he says it means that the historical context of prophecy, so far as that can be recovered from biblical and extrabiblical sources, will be essential to the interpretation of the prophets, and to

46. "The family resemblance between the literal and figural interpretations, as well as their mutual supplementation, allowed him to view the two testaments as one canon, the unitary subject of which was the story of man's fall and the salvation wrought by Jesus Christ" (Hans Frei, *The Eclipse of Biblical Narrative* [New Haven: Yale University Press, 1974], 31).

47. "But now, after we have grown up in Christ, the figures and external images have ceased; for though godliness has promises respecting the present as well as the future life, as Paul testifies (1 Tim. 4:8), we ought to rise above that doctrine which is elementary" (Comm. on Jer. 31:12, *CO* 20:82–83; CTS 38:660C).

48. Comm. on Dan. 7:27, *CO* 41:88C; CTS 25:74–75.

49. For instance, Calvin states that the "natural meaning" of what we call Second Isaiah is revealed in the context of the return from the Babylonian exile, which itself reveals God's favor. Only then will he ascend from the return from exile to the restoration of all things in Christ (Comm. on Isa. 45:8, *CO* 37:135A; CTS 13:405).

Scripture as a whole.[50] It is true that Calvin does not read the prophets as speaking only to their own time, and not to later times, as some even in Calvin's days were claiming.

> Here it ought to be carefully observed, that the prophecies were not written merely for the men of a single age, but that their children and all posterity ought to be instructed by them. . . . We must therefore reject the fancies of fanatics and wicked men, who say that this doctrine was adapted to those times, but affirm that it is not adapted to our times. Away with such blasphemies from the ears of the godly; for when Isaiah dies, his doctrine must flourish and yield fruit.[51]

On the other hand, without a knowledge of the historical circumstances in which a prophet worked and spoke, it would be next to impossible to read those prophecies today with any benefit. This is why, according to Calvin, each book of the prophets begins with a description of the writer's historical and geographical location, as in the case of Micah.

> And this deserves to be noticed: for at this day his sermons would be use-less, or at least frigid, except his time were known to us, and we might be thereby enabled to compare what is alike and what is different in the men of his age, and those of our own: for when we understand that Micah condemned this or that vice, as we may also learn from other prophets and from sacred history, we are able to apply more easily to ourselves what he said, inasmuch as we can view our own life as it were in a mirror.[52]

According to this statement, the application of prophetic preaching takes place in the direct consciousness of historical difference. The prophet's time, history, and circumstances are not Calvin's own, but what the prophet said to his age may be applied by Calvin to his own circumstances

---

50. Calvin will often be able to infer the historical context of the passage of Scripture he is interpreting from the internal evidence of the text itself. In his attempt to find the historical locus of Ps. 79, Calvin says, "This psalm, like others, contains internal evidence that it was composed long after the death of David. . . . Whoever judiciously reflects upon the context [*iudicio contextum*] of the poem will easily perceive that it was composed either when the Assyrians, after having burnt the temple, and destroyed the city, dragged the people into captivity, or when the temple was defiled by Antiochus, after he had slaughtered a vast number of the inhabitants of Jerusalem. Its subject agrees very well with either of these periods" (Comm. on Ps. 79:1, *CO* 39:746–47; CTS 10:281). This approach indicates that Calvin was not satisfied with the canonical locus of a passage of Scripture, but sought as much as possible to understand it in its original historical context, so that he might draw the general doctrine—to call on God when the ungodly afflict the church—from the meaning discerned in this original context.

51. Comm. on Isa. 30:8, *CO* 36:513; CTS 14:356.

52. Comm. on Mic. 1:1, *CO* 43:281C; CTS 28:151.

on the basis of the similarity amid difference of his circumstances with the prophet's.

Calvin does not confine himself to prophecy and sacred history in his attempt to discover the original circumstances in which and to which a given prophet spoke. In his interpretation of Daniel, Calvin attempts to discover the nature and time of the banquet which Belshazzar gives, and he uses Xenophon—albeit critically—to help determine with historical certainty that the banquet was an annual feast being held at the very time of a siege on Babylon by King Cyrus of Persia.

> Since, then, the king was so keenly opposed [by Cyrus], it is surprising to find him so careless as to celebrate a banquet. . . . For Xenophon—who may be trusted whenever he does not falsify history in favor of Cyrus, because he is then a very grave historian, and entirely worthy of credit; but when he desires to praise Cyrus, he knows no limit—is here historically correct, when he says that the Babylonians were holding a usual annual festival.[53]

Calvin opposes Xenophon's account of both the banquet, and the death of Belshazzar, to the "triflings" and "ignorance" of the Jews, who do not rely on Xenophon, claiming against them, "We must pass by these puerile trifles, and cling to the truth of history."[54]

The truth of history, recovered from Greek and Latin historians, is of crucial importance to Calvin; he insists that secular historians can confirm the truth of the events narrated in Scripture. When the prophet says in Lamentations, "Should women eat their own fruit?" Calvin comments that it seems impossible that mothers could eat their own children. He finds confirmation of this appalling practice in the account in sacred history of events during the siege of Samaria and then turns to secular history for further confirmation. "And Josephus also says, that when the city was besieged by Titus, the state of things was such, that mothers agreed to eat their own children, and that they cast lots who should first slay their child, and that they stole a leg or an arm from one another."[55] Similarly, when Jeremiah prophesies about the fall of Babylon, Calvin finds confirmation of this prophecy first in the sacred

---

53. Comm. on Dan. 5:1, *CO* 40:693–94; CTS 24:307–8.

54. Comm. on Dan. 5:30–31, *CO* 40:721–22; CTS 24:346–47.

55. Comm. on Lam. 2:20, *CO* 39:560C; CTS 21:385. Calvin also uses Josephus to confirm the truth of a prophecy in Zech. 9:16, that God would protect the Jews against their enemies. Calvin sees confirmation of this prophecy in the account Josephus gives of the way Alexander the Great repented of his rage against the Jews when he saw Jadeus the high priest, for God had appeared to him in the garments of the high priest while he was still in Greece. "Thus far Josephus, whose testimony in this instance has never been suspected" (Comm. on Zech. 9:16, *CO* 44:283B; CTS 30:274–75).

history of Daniel, and then in the secular history of Xenophon. "Though Xenophon was not, indeed, by design a witness to Jeremiah, yet that unprincipled writer, whose object was flattery, did, notwithstanding, render service to God, and sealed, by a public testimony, what had been divinely predicted by Jeremiah."[56]

The use of secular historians is of decisive importance for Calvin in his exegesis of the messianic prophecies in Daniel, especially the reckoning of the five ages in Dan. 2. Calvin is convinced that the truth of history, as discovered in Greek and Latin historians, vindicates the Christian claim that Jesus is the Christ who will reign perpetually, and that the Jews can only avoid this necessary conclusion by contradicting the truth of history known from these sources.

> If they grant that the fourth empire or monarchy was accomplished by the Romans, they must necessarily acquiesce in the Gospel, which testifies of the arrival of that Messiah who was promised by the Law. . . . Hence they fly to the miserable refuge that by the fourth monarchy should be understood the Turkish empire, . . . and thus they confound the Roman with the Macedonian empire.[57]

For Calvin, this evasion and distortion of the truth of history, known from secular historians, is quite exasperating, for it flies in the face of conclusions reason itself must draw on the basis of historical testimony. "Reason itself dictates to us to reckon in this way, since unless we confess the fourth monarchy to have succeeded directly on the passing away of the third, how could the rest follow on?"[58]

The clarity of this rational deduction based on the clarity of the historical witness causes Calvin to become exasperated with the anti-Christian Jewish exegesis of Daniel offered by Rabbi Barbinel, leading him to utter one of his most caustic anti-Jewish statements.

> For, he says, the beginning of the fourth and fifth monarchy was the same, which is absurd; for the fourth monarchy ought to endure for some time, and then the fifth should succeed it. But here he not only betrays his own ignorance, but [also] his utter stupidity, since God has so blinded the whole people that they were like impudent dogs. I have had much conversation with many Jews: I have never seen either a drop of piety or a grain of truth or ingenuousness—nay, I have never found common sense in any Jew. But this fellow, who seems so sharp and ingenious, displays his own impudence to his own disgrace.[59]

56. Comm. on Jer. 51:39, *CO* 39:477A; CTS 21:255.
57. Comm. on Dan. 2:44–45, *CO* 40:603B; CTS 24:181–82.
58. Comm. on Dan. 2:44–45, *CO* 40:605B; CTS 24:185.
59. Comm. on Dan. 2:44–45, *CO* 40:605B; CTS 24:185.

Throughout the commentary on Daniel, Calvin singles out Barbinel's utter ignorance of history, which "even boys know . . . by reading the accredited history of those times."[60] When Barbinel claims that more than two hundred years elapsed between the death of Christ and the destruction of the temple, Calvin cries out, "How ignorant he was! Even if we were to withhold all confidence from the evangelists and apostles, yet profane writers would soon convict him of folly."[61] When Barbinel claims that there were only three kings of Persia, instead of the five attested by profane historians, Calvin says, "The Jews are not only very ignorant of everything, but very stupid also—then they have no sense of shame, and are endued with a perverse audacity; for they think there were only three kings of Persia, and they neglect all history, and mingle and confound things perfectly clear and completely distinct."[62]

In light of his disgust with the Jews for their lack of knowledge of history, it is not surprising that Calvin encourages his readers to read the Greek and Latin historians, along with the Maccabean history, in order to profit from the reading of Daniel. "Profane authors inform us accurately of these occurrences, and, besides this, a whole book of Maccabees gives us similar information, and places clearly before us what the angel here predicts. Every one who wishes to read these prophecies with profit, must make himself familiar with these books, and must try to remember the whole history."[63] Calvin even encourages a rather involved method by which the reader might confirm the truth of the term "seventy days" by means of a commonplace approach to the Greek and Latin historians on this question.

> For example, let any studious person, endued with acuteness, experience, and skill, discover what has been written in Greek and Latin and distinguish the testimony of each writer under distinct heads, and afterwards compare each writer together, and determine the credibility of each, and how each is a fit and classical witness; he will find the same result as is given here by the prophet. This ought to be sufficient for us.[64]

Calvin is clearly convinced that the more the interpreter knows secular history, the better his interpretation of Scripture will be, as is revealed in his admiration of Philip Melanchthon. "Master Philip . . . excels in genius and learning, and is happily versed in the studies of history."[65]

---

60. Comm. on Dan. 8:13–14, *CO* 41:107–8; CTS 25:109.
61. Comm. on Dan. 9:26, *CO* 41:186B; CTS 25:223.
62. Comm. on Dan. 11:2, *CO* 41:218; CTS 25:269.
63. Comm. on Dan. 11:29–30, *CO* 41:252C; CTS 25:319.
64. Comm. on Dan. 9:25, *CO* 41:178; CTS 25:211.
65. Comm. on Dan. 9:25, *CO* 41:176B; CTS 25:209.

The meaning of Scripture is both disclosed and confirmed by reading it in the context of extrabiblical historical sources. However, when secular history appears to contradict a historical narrative in Scripture, Calvin always rejects the secular account as being inspired by Satan, and unquestioningly accepts the truth of the biblical account, as may be seen in the contradictory accounts given about the withdrawal of Sennacherib from Jerusalem. "We must indeed reject that invention by which Satan, through profane historians, has attempted to obscure this extraordinary judgment of God, that, in consequence of a part of the army having been destroyed by a plague during the war in Egypt, Sennacherib returned into his own dominions."[66] Calvin will only use secular history to confirm the meaning of a given passage of Scripture, not to falsify it. We will return to this theme below when we consider the law of contradiction in Calvin's interpretation.

Scripture and the Liberal Sciences

Calvin found other liberal sciences besides history to be useful in forming a context for his interpretation of Scripture. In his commentary on Jonah, Calvin decides that the miracle of Jonah's time in the fish was his being preserved in the fish, and not the size of the fish, since recent writings in marine biology reveal to him that there are fish big enough to swallow people whole. "And William Rondolet, who has written a book on the fishes of the sea, concludes that in all probability it must have been the Lamia. He himself saw that fish, and he says that it has a belly so capacious, and a mouth so wide, that it can easily swallow up a man; and he says that a man of armor has sometimes been found inside the Lamia."[67] Calvin also found the zoological writings of Pliny and Aristotle to be helpful in interpreting biblical metaphors about birds, and he contrasts his learning in these areas with the utter ignorance of the Jews. When Isaiah says, "They shall raise their wings as eagles," Calvin says,

> Aristotle and Pliny affirm that [the eagle] never dies of old age, but of hunger; that is, that when the upper part of the beak becomes too large,

---

66. Comm. on Isa. 37:36, *CO* 36:641C; CTS 15:145. It is noteworthy that the reason Calvin rejects secular accounts contradicting scriptural accounts has to do with the way the former obscure the powers of God—in this case the judgment of God—revealed in the works of God. According to Calvin, only Scripture bears witness to the works of God so that they always portray the powers of God, which reveal the nature of God to us. "We must come, I say, to the Word, where God is truly and vividly described to us from his works, while these very works are appraised not by our depraved judgment but by the rule of eternal truth" (*Inst.* 1.6.3, *OS* 3:63.25–28; LCC 1:73).

67. Comm. on Jon. 1:17, *CO* 43:235B; CTS 28:73.

it cannot take food into its mouth, and for a long time subsists entirely on what it drinks. One Zaadias, as all Jews are audacious in constructing fables, pretends that the eagle flies upward into the region that is near the sun, and approaches the sun too closely, that its old wings are burned away, and new ones grow in their place; but this is utterly absurd and fabulous.[68]

Calvin makes a similar move in his exegesis of Jer. 17:11, concerning a metaphor involving partridges.

> The Rabbis, according to their practice, have devised fables; for they imagine that the partridge steals all the eggs of other birds which she can find, and gathers them into one heap. . . . But neither Aristotle nor Pliny say any such thing of partridges. . . . But it is said of partridges with one consent, by Aristotle and Pliny, as well as others, that it is a very lustful bird.[69]

In both instances, Calvin decides the real meaning of the prophet on the basis of the description of eagles and partridges given by Aristotle and Pliny.

Calvin also faults the Jews for their ignorance of astronomy, botany, and all the liberal sciences. In his comments on Amos 5:8, which speaks of "the one who made the Pleiades and Orion," Calvin notes that Amos does not speak as an astronomer, but according to the common notions of his age. Nonetheless, he cannot help but point out the ignorance of astronomy among Jews of his day. "There is no need of laboring about such names; for the Jews, ignorant of the liberal sciences, cannot at this day certainly determine what stars are meant; and they also show their complete ignorance as to herbs."[70] Calvin, by contrast, was a keen student of astronomy, the study of which he considered to be commended by God. "For astronomy is not only pleasant, but also very useful to be known: it cannot be denied that this art unfolds the admirable wisdom of God."[71] However, precisely because of his studies, Calvin was aware that the description of the universe given by astronomers is not the same as the depiction of the universe given in Scripture, as in the creation of the greater and lesser light in Gen. 1:16.

> First, he assigns a place in the expanse of heavens to planets and stars; but astronomers make a distinction of spheres, and at the same time, teach that the fixed stars have their proper place in the firmament. Moses makes two great luminaries; but astronomers prove, by conclusive reasons, that

68. Comm. on Isa. 40:31, *CO* 37:30A; CTS 15:239–40.
69. Comm. on Jer. 17:11, *CO* 38:272B; CTS 18:358.
70. Comm. on Amos 5:8, *CO* 43:77A; CTS 27:261.
71. Comm. on Gen. 1:16, *CO* 23:22B; CTS 1:87.

the star of Saturn, which, on account of its great distance, appears least of all, is greater than the moon.[72]

To avoid an unnecessary conflict between the free investigation of the universe by astronomy and the truth of Scripture, Calvin employs his understanding of the accommodated nature of Scripture, which describes the world from the point of view of a person standing in a field at night, and hence does not claim to be science.

> Here lies the difference; Moses wrote in a popular style things which, without instruction, all ordinary persons endued with common sense are able to understand; but astronomers investigate with great labor whatever the sagacity of the human mind can comprehend. . . . Nor did Moses truly wish to withdraw us from this pursuit in omitting such things as are peculiar to this art; but because he was ordained a teacher as well of the unlearned and rude as of the learned, he could not otherwise fulfill his office than by descending to this grosser method of instruction.[73]

As his discussion of astronomy indicates, Calvin was concerned that the true and genuine meaning of Scripture not conflict with the understanding of the world and of human nature developed by the liberal sciences. Because he was convinced that Scripture was a book for the unlearned, he did not expect to find in Scripture scientific accounts of the nature of the world, for he was convinced that these could be found only in the writings of the learned. Thus, when Scripture states that there are waters above the heavens, Calvin knows that his learned peers will find this contrary to the way they have come to understand the universe.

> For, to my mind, this is a certain principle, that nothing here is treated of but the visible form of the world. He who would learn astronomy, and other recondite arts, let him go elsewhere. Here the Spirit of God would teach all men without exception; and therefore what Gregory declares falsely and in vain respecting statues and pictures is truly applicable to the history of creation, that it is the book of the unlearned.[74]

Beyond reminding his readers that Scripture was written according to the capacities of the unlearned, and so should not be understood as being on the same level as the scientific writings of the learned, Calvin also employs the distinction between proximate and ultimate causality to explain why the investigations of the learned do not conflict with

72. Comm. on Gen. 1:16, *CO* 23:22A; CTS 1:86.
73. Comm. on Gen. 1:16, *CO* 23:22C; CTS 1:86–87.
74. Comm. on Gen. 1:6, *CO* 23:18C; CTS 1:79–80.

Scripture. For instance, when Scripture says that God "brings the winds out of his treasures," Calvin acknowledges that this is not a scientific account of the cause of winds, but insists that the scientific account, based on proximate causes, does not conflict with Scripture's claim that God is the ultimate cause of the wind. "Philosophers indeed mention the causes of these things, but we ought to come to the fountain itself, and the original cause, even this, that things are so arranged in the world, that though there are intermediate and subordinate causes, yet the primary cause appears eminently, even the wisdom and power of God."[75] Calvin applies the same distinction to account for how the same human action may rightly be deemed to be contingent from a philosophical point of view, and yet be deemed to be necessary when viewed from the perspective of the will of God.

> Philosophers think all things are contingent, and why? Because the will of man may turn either way. They, then, conclude, that whatever men do is contingent, because he who wills may change his will. These things are true, when we consider the will of man itself and the exercise of it; but when we raise our eyes to the secret providence of God, who turns and directs the counsels of man according to his own will, it is certain that how much soever men may change in their purposes, yet God never changes.[76]

According to Calvin, the truths taught by philosophy are perfectly compatible with the description of the world in Scripture, because science views events in the world in light of their proximate, mediate causes, whereas Scripture describes the same events from the perspective of their ultimate cause, God.[77]

75. Comm. on Jer. 51:16, *CO* 39:455C; CTS 21:222. See also Comm. on Jer. 10:13, *CO* 38:78A; CTS 18:37. Note again Calvin's concern that the powers of God be manifested in any account of the works of God.

76. Comm. on Lam. 3:37–38, *CO* 39:588C; CTS 21:428.

77. The concern of Calvin to avoid conflicts between Scripture and science has an echo centuries later in Schleiermacher's concern to avoid such conflicts in his own day. "Unless the Reformation from which our church first emerged endeavors to establish an eternal covenant between the living Christian faith and completely free, independent scientific inquiry, so that faith does not hinder science and science does not exclude faith, it fails to meet adequately the needs of our time and we need another one, no matter what it takes to establish it. Yet it is my firm conviction that the basis for such a covenant was already established in the Reformation" (Friedrich Schleiermacher, *On the Glaubenslehre*, trans. James Duke and Francis Fiorenza [Chico, CA: Scholars Press, 1981], 64). See Brian A. Gerrish, "The Reformation and the Rise of Modern Science: Luther, Calvin, and Copernicus," in *The Old Protestantism and the New: Essays on the Reformation Heritage* (Edinburgh: Clark, 1982), 163–78. Gerrish accentuates Calvin's use of accommodation but does not address his use of primary and secondary causality.

Calvin as Teacher and Pastor

Scripture and the Law of Contradiction

We have already seen how Calvin responds to contradictions between biblical and extrabiblical narratives of the same historical event: the former are always seen to be true and the latter false, for the former are inspired by the Holy Spirit, the fount of all truth, while the latter may be inspired by Satan, the father of lies. But how did Calvin respond to the presence of contradiction between various Christian interpretations of Scripture? Calvin was aware that Jews used such contradictory interpretations within the Christian tradition to falsify Christian interpretations of the Hebrew Bible, as Roman opponents used the contradictions between the evangelical interpreters of Scripture to falsify their interpretations. For instance, Rabbi Barbinel wished to use the law of noncontradiction to falsify the Christian interpretation of Daniel, especially among such luminaries as Nicholas of Lyra and Paul of Burgos. "To deprive the Christians of all confidence and authority, [Rabbi Barbinel] objects to their mutual differences; as if differences between men not sufficiently exercised in the Scriptures, could entirely overthrow their truth."[78]

Calvin's first response is to deny the presence of any essential contradiction in the interpretations of the Greek and Latin ecclesiastical writers. He points out that there are discrepancies in the accounts of the secular historians, yet no learned person views these as sufficient to discredit their testimony altogether.[79] Neither should previous interpreters be deprived of credit when they show minor discrepancies, for the consensus among them is much greater.

> Now, if the writers are not self-contradictory, but manifest slight diversities in either years or places, shall we on that account pronounce them entirely destitute of credit? We are well aware of the existence of some differences in all histories, and yet this does not cause them to lose their authority; they are still quoted, and confidence is reposed in them.[80]

This response indicates the catholicity of Calvin's own interpretation of Scripture, in which he sought as much as possible to be in continuity with the previous tradition.

However, Calvin is ultimately willing to let the law of contradiction falsify all prior interpretations of Scripture, including those of Eusebius, Origen, Tertullian, Hippolytus, Jerome, and Augustine; but he refuses to conclude that this therefore falsifies Christian teaching. "I am therefore ready to acknowledge all these interpretations to be false, and yet I do

78. Comm. on Dan. 9:25, *CO* 41:174; CTS 25:206.
79. Comm. on Dan. 9:25, *CO* 41:176–77; CTS 25:209–10.
80. Comm. on Dan. 9:25, *CO* 41:177; CTS 25:210.

not allow the truth of God to fail."[81] Even if contradiction reveals the falsehood of the interpretation of Scripture by ancient and venerable ecclesiastical writers, this does not mean that the truth of God itself, in the Old and New Testaments, will fail. This response indicates the evangelical and reforming nature of Calvin's interpretation of Scripture, based on the normative status of Scripture alone.

But what of the presence of contradictions in Scripture itself? Calvin was aware of contemporaries in his own day who wished to apply the law of contradiction to Scripture itself, in order to reveal the absurdity of the Christian faith.

> Thus we see at this day, that godless men not only in words reject the Law and the Prophets, but also search out pretenses, that they might appear to be doing right in destroying all faith in the oracles of God. For instance, they seek out every sort of contradiction in Scripture, every thing not well received, every thing different from the common opinion—all these absurdities, as they call them, they collect together, and then they draw this conclusion, that all are fools, who submit to any religion, since the word of God, as they say, contains so many absurd things.[82]

Calvin thinks that this attempt to falsify Scripture is utterly futile, for, as Hosea himself says, "The ways of the LORD are right" (Hos. 14:9 NRSV). "However much then the ungodly may vomit forth slanders against the word of God, it is the same as if they threw dust in the air to darken the light of the sun; . . . for perfect rectitude will ever be found in the ways of the Lord; his word will ever be found free from every stain or defect."[83] Human authors like the Greek and Latin fathers may contradict one another, and therefore be revealed to be wrong, but God cannot be so, for God is always true.

For Calvin, therefore, the suggestion that there are contradictions in Scripture which render it uncertain, if not false, reveals a serious problem not in the Scripture being interpreted, but in the interpreter himself. Only the one who actually walks in the ways of the Lord will know by experience that the Word of God is always right and true and can never deceive, no matter how contradictory or absurd it may appear to the ungodly. On the other hand, the ungodly will see any doubt about Scripture, be it ever so insignificant, as being insurmountable, not because it is in fact, but because they wish to find reasons to evade the truth of the word, for they do not walk in its ways.

81. Comm. on Dan. 9:25, *CO* 41:175; CTS 25:207.
82. Comm. on Hosea 14:9, *CO* 42:512B; CTS 26:506. See also *Concerning Scandals*, *OS* 2:199–201.
83. Comm. on Hosea 14:9, *CO* 42:512B; CTS 26:506.

But what of the ungodly? They imagine all doubts, even the least, to be mountains: for as soon as they meet with any thing perplexing or obscure, they are confounded, and say, "I would gladly seek to know the Holy Scriptures, but I meet with so many difficulties." Hence if the least doubt is suggested, they regard it as a mountain; nay, they purposely pretend doubts, that they may have some excuse, when they wish to evade the truth, and turn aside that they may not follow the Lord.[84]

Unless the interpreter is godly and walks in the ways of the Lord, the truth of the Word of God in Scripture will always be open to doubt, and the contradictions in Scripture will show it to be utterly unreliable. Proper scriptural interpretation, therefore, depends not only on the interpreter's knowledge of the wider context of Scripture, but also on the interpreter's relationship with God.

Scripture in the Context of the Nature and Activity of God

The true interpreter of Scripture, according to Calvin, is not only a person skilled in the forms of speech of Greek, Hebrew, and Latin, as well as in the liberal arts of the Greek and Latin world, but is also a person who is guided in his interpretation by the Holy Spirit. "And therefore it is my belief that the Spirit of God is certainly not only the best, but also the sole guide, since without him, there is not even a glimmer of light in our minds enabling us to appreciate heavenly wisdom; yet as soon as the Spirit has shed his light, our minds are more than adequately prepared and equipped to grasp this very wisdom."[85] Without the guidance and illumination of the Spirit, the interpreter will always be subject to doubts about the authority and truth of Scripture. "Thus it is not surprising that many should doubt the authority of Scripture. For although the majesty of God is displayed in it, only those who have been enlightened by the Holy Spirit have eyes to see what should have been obvious to all, but is in fact visible only to the elect."[86] The mind that is ultimately being revealed in Scripture is the mind of the Holy Spirit, but only those who are illumined by the Spirit can see that mind being disclosed in the words of the human authors of Scripture. "The same Spirit who made Moses and the prophets so sure of their vocation

84. Comm. on Hosea 14:9, *CO* 42:514; CTS 26:507.
85. *Praefatio in Chrysostomi homilias*, *CO* 9:832; "Calvin's Preface to Chrysostom's Homilies," trans. W. Ian P. Hazlett, in *Humanism and Reform: The Church in Europe, England, and Scotland, 1400–1643: Essays in Honour of James K. Cameron*, ed. James Kirk (Oxford: Blackwell, 1991), 141.
86. Comm. on 2 Tim. 3:16, *CO* 52:383B; *CNTC* 10:330.

now also bears witness to our hearts that He has made use of them as ministers by whom to teach us."[87]

According to Calvin, the primary author of Scripture is God, and he insists that God through Scripture continues to instruct the church. This is why Calvin as a teacher of the church sees a mutually reinforcing relationship between the teaching of the summary of doctrine and the contextual reading of Scripture. Calvin interprets the historical narratives of Scripture contextually in order to draw fruitful doctrine from them, convinced that God wishes to teach such doctrine to the church today, in spite of the difference in historical circumstances. "If, therefore, we would make a right and proper use of sacred histories, we must remember that we ought to use them in such a way as to draw from them the fruit of sound doctrine. They instruct us how to form our life, how to strengthen our faith, and how we are to arouse the fear of the Lord."[88] The goal of reading Scripture in its literary and historical context is to draw such sound doctrine from its contextual meaning, to instruct the church today. "We ought first to see what the prophets had in view, and by what necessity they were led to speak, what was their condition, and *then a general doctrine may be gathered from their words*. If we wish to read the prophets with benefit, we must first consider the reason why a thing is spoken, *and then elicit a general doctrine*."[89] Moreover, as Scripture is the way by which the treasure of blessings in Christ is disclosed and offered to us by God, all proper interpretation of Scripture will read a passage first in its original linguistic and historical context, and then in the context of God's self-revelation and self-bestowal in Christ.

> This is what we should in short seek in the whole of Scripture: truly to know Jesus Christ, and the infinite riches that are comprised in him and are offered to us by him from God the Father. If one were to sift thoroughly the Law and the Prophets, he would not find a single word which would not draw and bring us to him. . . . Our minds ought to come to a halt at the point where we learn in Scripture to know Jesus Christ and him alone, so that we may be directed by him to the Father, who contains in himself all perfection.[90]

For Calvin, reading Scripture in relation to his understanding of the nature and activity of God, in light of the claim that God is the ultimate author of Scripture, does not eliminate the need to read Scripture in

---

87. Comm. on 2 Tim. 3:16, *CO* 52:383b; *CNTC* 10:330.

88. Comm. on Rom. 4:23, *Romanos* 99.55–59; *CNTC* 8:101.

89. Comm. on Jer. 17:9–10, *CO* 38:270A; *CTS* 18:353 (my emphasis).

90. *Praefatio in N.T. cuius haec summa est: Christum esse legis finem, CO* 9:815B; *Calvin: Commentaries*, 70.

its linguistic and historical context, for God spoke through real human authors in accommodation to the capacities of God's people throughout history. Even when Scripture itself ascribes a prayer of David directly to the Holy Spirit (as in Acts 4:25), Calvin first seeks to understand the meaning of that prayer in the historical context of David's own life and times.

> Why did the Gentiles rage? We must admit that David is speaking about himself. After he was chosen by God to be king and was anointed by Samuel, he had the greatest difficulty in taking possession of his kingdom because of the opposition of enemies in every quarter. . . . Yet because his kingdom was established as an image of the kingdom of Christ, David does not remain in the shadow but grasps the solid form.[91]

However, as Calvin is convinced that Christ is the end or completion of the law, the proper interpretation of Scripture will not stop with the original linguistic and historical context; it will move from that context to God's self-revelation and self-bestowal in Christ, by means of analogy and anagoge. "Indeed, every doctrine of the law, every command, every promise, always points to Christ."[92]

In sum, Calvin did read Scripture in light of its context, but that context for him was twofold. The first context was linguistic and historical, including the whole world mediated to him by Greek and Latin literature, with its history, astronomy, psychology, zoology, poetry, philosophy, meteorology, and rhetoric. The second context was theological, and included the attempt to understand the mind of the Holy Spirit in the words of the human authors of Scripture, so that their teaching might be fruitfully applied to the church today, and the analogical and anagogical application of all signs and promises of God's favor to Christ. Calvin's ability to combine a concern for the historical and linguistic setting of a passage of Scripture with a concern for the relation of that passage to the self-manifestation of God in Christ places him in essential continuity with theologians after him, such as Bultmann, Barth, and von Balthasar, who also took seriously both the historical and linguistic setting of Scripture and what Scripture discloses to us about our relationship with God.

---

91. Comm. on Acts 4:25, *CO* 48:91A; *CNTC* 6:124. One sees the same kind of relationship between the human author and the Holy Spirit in Calvin's interpretation of Jeremiah's lament, "Why is my pain perpetual?" "He was then subject to these feelings, that is, as to himself; yet his doctrine was free from every defect, for the Holy Spirit guided his mind, his thoughts, and his tongue, so that there was in it nothing human" (Comm. on Jer. 15:18, *CO* 8:231B; CTS 17:290).

92. Comm. on Rom. 10:4, *Romanos* 223.66–68; *CNTC* 8:221.

6

BUILDING UP THE FAITH OF CHILDREN

Calvin's Catechisms, 1536–1545

Once pastors are trained by their teachers to seek the topics of piety in their reading of Scripture and to gather general doctrine from the context of Scripture, they are then called to teach the rudiments of piety to their congregations, especially the children, and to apply the genuine meaning of Scripture to their lives in their sermons. Three different times Calvin tried to develop an effective summary of doctrine for children, but he was never satisfied with the results.[1] This is not surprising, especially when one considers Calvin's early training in languages and the liberal arts. Indeed, the literary productions of John Calvin underwent a startling transformation between 1532 and 1545. Calvin's first publication was the 1532 commentary on Seneca's treatise *On Clemency*, in which he sought to restore Seneca to his rightful place of honor in the world of Latin literature. "Add to this, that I simply could not tolerate seeing

---

1. Robert Kingdon, "Catechesis in Calvin's Geneva," in *Educating People of Faith: Exploring the History of Jewish and Christian Communities*, ed. John van Engen (Grand Rapids: Eerdmans, 2004), 294–313.

the best of authors long despised by most, and held in almost no esteem whatsoever; so that I had long since been wishing that some illustrious champion would stand up to vindicate his cause and restore him to his proper place of dignity."[2] Contrary to the denigration of Seneca by Quintilian and others, Calvin seeks to place him just below Cicero. "I do not want to dwell upon this any longer, but allow me to say only this, once and for all: our Seneca was second only to Cicero, a veritable pillar of Roman philosophy and literature," making him "amongst the foremost princes of Latin letters."[3] The commentary itself was to establish Calvin's place among the most learned of his day, revealed by the way that he strives to meet their expectations. "Where such a great variety of tastes and characters exist, it would be difficult, perhaps even wrong, to attempt to satisfy all; wherefore I have resolved upon the only alternative left to me, namely to try to satisfy the best."[4]

Three years later, Calvin wrote a preface to his cousin Olivetan's French translation of the Bible, in which he sought to restore Scripture to its place of honor among unlearned and ordinary Christians, over against the objections of those who would keep the Scriptures out of their hands. "How then, they ask, can these poor illiterates comprehend such things, untutored as they are in all liberal arts, and (if practice is involved) ignorant of all things?"[5] Calvin responds to this objection by pointing out how the authors of the books of Scripture were themselves ignorant and unlearned people, save for the fact that they were taught by God. "Indeed, if for these Rabbis (whose minds are so great and intrepid) learning with common and uneducated people is a shameful fate, how much more disgraceful is it to learn from such teachers who have in no respect surpassed the meanest persons except in that they have been taught by the Lord."[6] Just as God taught the unlearned prophets and apostles, so it is the will of God for all Christians, no matter how unlearned, to read and meditate on the teaching of Scripture, for it is accommodated to their capacities. "It is not prohibited and forbidden to any Christian freely and in his own language to read, handle, and hear this holy gospel, seeing that such is the will of God, and Jesus Christ commands it."[7]

2. *Calvin's Commentary on Seneca's "De Clementia,"* trans. Ford Lewis Battles and Andre Malan Hugo (Leiden: Brill, 1969), 7.

3. Ibid., 11–13, 9.

4. Ibid., 13.

5. "Latin Preface to Olivetan's French Bible (1535)," *CO* 9:787C; *Institutes of the Christian Religion*, 1536 edition, trans. and annotated by Ford Lewis Battles, rev. ed. (1975; repr., Grand Rapids: Eerdmans, 1986), 374.

6. "Latin Preface to Olivetan's French Bible (1535)," *CO* 9:788A; *Institutes*, 1536 edition, 374.

7. "Epistle to the Faithful Showing That Christ Is the End of the Law," *CO* 9:819C; *Calvin: Commentaries*, 72.

Calvin followed the lead of Scripture and sought from this point onward to write no longer in accommodation to "the best," but to the most unlearned, so that they might have access to the teaching of God in Scripture. Not surprisingly, it took the highly trained and learned Calvin a long time, and several efforts, to learn how to reach this new audience. The culmination of this new orientation is revealed by the publication in 1545 of the Latin edition of the *Catechism of the Church of Geneva*, which revealed to the rest of the Latin reading world how Calvin sought to teach the rudiments of pious doctrine to unlearned children. We should note, however, that Calvin never felt that his catechism had succeeded in meeting its objective. In his farewell to the pastors of Geneva, Calvin insists that he taught doctrine faithfully and interpreted the Scriptures according to their simple and natural sense. However, he expresses dissatisfaction with the production of the *Catechism*. "On my return from Strasbourg, I composed the catechism in haste . . . and while I was writing it, they came to fetch bits of paper as big as my hand and carry them to the printing office." As a consequence, Calvin says, "I have sometimes indeed thought of putting a finishing hand to it if I had had leisure."[8]

This chapter will examine Calvin's efforts to teach the rudiments of piety to the children of Geneva, with special attention to the Latin *Catechism or Institution of the Christian Religion* of 1538 and the Latin *Catechism of the Church of Geneva* of 1545. I have chosen these two documents in particular because they were framed by prefaces addressing their purpose and published for the edification of all godly churches emerging from the ruins of the Roman Church. We will be especially interested in discerning the changes in teaching methods and objectives as evidenced in both documents, to discern how Calvin sought to reach the untaught children of his congregations.

From the outset, it must be noted that not much attention has been devoted to Calvin's labors as a teacher of pious doctrine to children. Most attention is devoted to his writings as a teacher of future pastors, initially focusing on the *Institutes* of 1539–59, and now including his commentaries and lectures on Scripture from 1540–64. As important as these writings are for an understanding of Calvin's theology, they do not bring us to the primary target of Calvin's efforts as a teacher and pastor: the unlearned, ordinary Christians and their children, to whom he ministered for almost half of his life. Indeed, many of Calvin's publications between 1534 and 1545 are addressed to this audience, beginning in earnest with the 1536 *Institutes*, in which Calvin adopted a "simple" and "elementary form of teaching" in order to "transmit certain rudiments by which those who are touched with any zeal for

8. *Discours d'adieu aux ministres*, CO 9:894; Calvin, *Letters* 4:376.

religion might be shaped to true godliness."[9] It has often been observed that the first edition of the *Institutes* has the form of a catechism, which is certainly true; however, it is clear that Calvin never intended it to be a form of instruction for children. It is instead directed to adults who have recently left the Roman Church for the evangelical church and need instruction in the godly doctrine taught in these churches. In this sense, the *Institutes* is initially addressed to the same audience for whom Erasmus wrote his *Enchiridion*, ordinary Latin-reading Christians, an impression confirmed by Calvin's later description of the work as a "brief enchiridion."[10]

Calvin apparently did not envision the need to write a catechism for children until he became a teacher and pastor in Geneva in 1536–37. The 1537 *Articles concerning the Organization of the Church* bemoan the "remarkable rudeness and great ignorance which is quite intolerable in the Church of God" in the families of Geneva, and they propose that the practice of catechesis from the ancient church be restored in Geneva to remedy this problem, so that those baptized as infants might make their own profession of faith before the whole church.

> The order which we advise being set up is that there be a brief and simple summary of the Christian faith, to be taught to all children, and that at certain seasons of the year they come before the ministers to be interrogated and examined, and to receive a more ample explanation, according as there is need to the capacity of each of them, until they have been proved sufficiently instructed.[11]

Calvin of course knew that the *Institutes* were not suited for this purpose since they were written for adults already touched with a zeal for religion and piety and could hardly be considered such a "brief and simple summary." Hence, in the same year Calvin produced the *Instruction in Faith* of 1537, which he translated into Latin in 1538 as the *Catechism or Institution of the Christian Religion of the Church of Geneva*. Scholars have repeatedly suggested that this catechism represents a condensation and distillation of Calvin's 1536 *Institutes*, but it is also likely that the work took as its template the 1536 *Confession of Faith*, which Calvin intended to be the confession of faith of all the citizens of Geneva, according to the 1537 *Articles*.

9. *Institutio* (1536), *CO* 1:9B; *Institutes*, 1536 edition, 1.

10. "John Calvin to the Pious and Ingenuous Readers, Greeting," *CO* 31:23B; CTS 8: xlii.

11. *Project d'ordonnances ecclésiastiques*, *CO* 10:13A; *Articles concerning the Organization of the Church and of Worship at Geneva Proposed by the Ministers at the Council, January 16, 1537*, in *Calvin: Theological Treatises*, 54.

At this point, Calvin clearly thinks that the best way to instruct children is to set forth in a clear, brief, and simple way the central topics of pious doctrine, according to the order of law, creed, prayer, and sacraments. Calvin envisioned a situation in which children would be taught these topics by their parents and would then be examined on their grasp of these topics by the pastors. Hence, the 1537 *Articles* ask the Council of Geneva "to command parents to exercise pains and diligence that their children learn this summary and that they present themselves before the ministers at the times appointed."[12] The expectation is that the parents would be the primary teachers of their children, using the topics of the *Catechism* to instruct their children. The pastors would not teach the children, but would rather interrogate and examine the children on the summary of topics they had learned, and would only give greater explanation of those points upon which the children were still unclear.

The *Catechism* adopts a style of teaching in which the teacher identifies with the student as they come to understand things together. Calvin writes in the first-person plural and speaks of the kinds of things "we" need to consider and understand, and that we are taught. This gives the articles of the *Catechism* an objective character; the various doctrines of piety come into view for both teacher and student, as in the discussion of the resurrection in the Creed: "Here we are taught concerning the expectation of the future resurrection."[13] The Creed in turn leads us to be taught more fully by Scripture. "While we are taught to believe in the Holy Spirit, we are also enjoined to await from him whatever is attributed to him in the Scriptures."[14] This feeling of objectivity is increased in the transitional passages in which Calvin speaks of the student in the third person, as in the transition to prayer: "A person duly versed in true faith readily recognizes how needy and empty of all goods he is and how all aids to salvation are lacking to him."[15] The *Catechism* ends with a description of all of us being taught by God in Christ, which is the center and limit of what humans can teach us. "The Lord, therefore, is the King of kings, who, when he has opened his sacred mouth, must alone be heard, before all and above all men."[16] The situation out of which the *Catechism* is written is one in which we are all being taught by God, parents as well as children.

The *Catechism* follows a *loci communes* method of teaching, in which the rudiments of pious doctrine are set forth according to discrete top-

12. *CO* 10:13A; *Calvin: Theological Treatises*, 54.
13. *Catechismus, CO* 5:342B; I. John Hesselink, *Calvin's First Catechism: A Commentary*, trans. Ford Lewis Battles (Louisville: Westminster John Knox, 1997), 26.
14. *Catechismus, CO* 5:340–41; *Catechism*, 25.
15. *Catechismus, CO* 5:343C; *Catechism*, 27.
16. *Catechismus, CO* 5:354B; *Catechism*, 38.

ics ordered into a coherent series, centering around brief expositions of the law, the Creed, the Lord's Prayer, and the sacraments. The order of teaching begins with what is the most universally known by all people, "however barbarous or completely savage," without any human teaching: the sense of religion in all people.[17] This sense should lead all people to acknowledge their Creator and esteem him with "all fear, love, and reverence." Unfortunately, the sense of religion gives birth to hypocrisy and superstition, which worship not God but the dreams of the heart. "Accordingly, with however much care they afterward weary themselves over worshipping God, they get nowhere, since it is not the eternal God but the dreams and ravings of their own heart which they are adoring as God."[18] Calvin then turns the pious to the self-manifestation of God in the universe by the powers of God represented in the works of God. "Accordingly, we are to search out and trace God in his works, which are called in the Scriptures 'the reflection of things invisible,' because they represent to us what otherwise we could not see of the Lord."[19] However, given our blindness and perverse judgment, we need to turn to the Word of God for the proper description of God from God's works, revealing God to be the one from whom all good flows and to whom all praise should return. "Therefore, we must come to God's Word, where God is duly described to us from his works, while the works themselves are reckoned not from the depravity of our judgment but the eternal rule of truth."[20]

After introducing the right way to seek God, Calvin turns to the knowledge of sin, based in the loss of the good things that God gave to Adam when he was created in the image of God, including an article on free choice of the will. Since fallen humanity loathes God's righteousness from the depths of the heart, "it is denied that he is endowed with the free capacity to choose good and evil which men call 'free will.'"[21] The knowledge of sin leads initially to the law, which God sets before us so that we might recognize our sin and thereby have access to the mercy of God in Christ. "When the Lord therefore establishes this first step for those whom he deigns to restore to the inheritance of heavenly life, in order that they, wounded with the consciousness of their own sins and wearied by their weight, may be aroused to fear him, he sets forth his law first of all for us, to exercise us in that knowledge."[22]

17. *Catechismus, CO* 5:323B; *Catechism,* 7.
18. *Catechismus, CO* 5:324B; *Catechism,* 8.
19. *Catechismus, CO* 5:324C; *Catechism,* 8.
20. *Catechismus, CO* 5:325B; *Catechism,* 9.
21. *Catechismus, CO* 5:326A; *Catechism,* 10.
22. *Catechismus, CO* 5:327A; *Catechism,* 11.

God offers his mercy to us in Christ through the gospel, to be grasped by faith. "But in Christ his countenance shines full of grace and kindness even toward poor and unworthy sinners. For he has given this wonderful example of his boundless love, by showing us his own Son, and in him has disclosed all the treasures of his mercy and goodness."[23] However, the fact that not all embrace the gospel by faith reveals the election and predestination of God.

> Now in this difference [between believers and unbelievers] we must consider the sublime secret of the divine plan. For the seed of God's Word takes root and bears fruit only in those whom the Lord has by his eternal election predestined as his children and heirs of the kingdom of heaven; for all the rest, who were condemned by the same plan of God before the foundation of the world, the utterly clear preaching of the truth can be nothing but the stench of death unto death.[24]

Calvin then turns to the definition and effects of faith, especially the twofold grace of justification and regeneration, culminating in an exposition of the Creed, which reveals that all we lost in Adam must be sought anew in Christ. "We spoke above of what we obtain in Christ through faith. Now we must hear what our faith ought to look to in Christ and to ponder how it is to be strengthened. This is explained in what is called 'the Creed.' That is to say, in what way Christ was by the Father for us made wisdom, redemption, life, righteousness, and sanctification."[25] Calvin uses an article on the relation of faith and hope to lead to a discussion of prayer, which itself is based on the knowledge of every good thing in Christ. "It therefore remains for him to seek in [Christ], and in prayers to ask of him, what he has learned to be in him."[26] The sacraments are introduced as exercises and confirmations of our faith. "For because the Lord foresaw it to be expedient for the ignorance of our flesh, he set forth lofty and heavenly mysteries to be contemplated under physical elements."[27] The *Catechism* concludes with a discussion of the office of pastors and the role of human traditions and discipline in the church, including excommunication. The final article is on the magistrate.

The order of the topics in the *Catechism* is reminiscent of both the *Institutes* and the *Confession of Faith* of 1536. The topics follow the order set forth in the opening locus of the *Catechism*, that we are "to seek God, to aspire to him with our whole heart, and to rest nowhere else but in

23. *Catechismus, CO* 5:332B; *Catechism*, 16.
24. *Catechismus, CO* 5:332–33; *Catechism*, 17.
25. *Catechismus, CO* 5:337B; *Catechism*, 21.
26. *Catechismus, CO* 5:343C; *Catechism*, 27.
27. *Catechismus, CO* 5:349B; *Catechism*, 33.

him."[28] The series of teachings seems to follow the opening insight that God manifests Godself as the author and source of every good thing. "From this, therefore, we learn that God is for us the sole and eternal source of all life, righteousness, wisdom, power, goodness, and mercy. As all good flows, without any exception, from him, so ought all praise deservedly to return to him."[29] We lost every good thing in Adam, yet the awareness of our poverty opens access to faith in Christ, in whom God returns to us every good thing we lost in Adam, so that we might seek those good things from God in prayer and have them confirmed in us through the sacraments. However, this order is never really made explicit in the sequence of the articles, although there are key transitional passages from one topic to the next, as in the transition from faith to prayer. Calvin reminds us that we are destitute of all good things, but that God has set forth Christ as the one in whom all good things are offered to us, so that we might rest in and cleave to him alone.

> A man duly versed in true faith first readily recognizes how needy and empty of all goods he is and how all aids to salvation are lacking to him. Therefore, if he seeks resources to succour himself in his need, he must go outside himself and get them elsewhere. On the other hand, he sees that the Lord willingly and freely reveals himself in his Christ, and in him opens all heavenly treasures that his whole faith may contemplate his beloved Son, his whole expectation depend upon him, and his whole hope cleave to and rest in him.[30]

The similarity between the *Catechism* and the *Confession* goes beyond the similar progression of topics, however. In the preface to the Latin edition, Calvin clearly associates the two, so that together they represent the doctrine being taught to the church in Geneva. Calvin is especially concerned to answer the charge of Caroli that he teaches a heretical doctrine of the Trinity. One reading this summary of "the doctrine with which we are instructing the people entrusted to us by the Lord" can clearly see that what is being taught in Geneva is drawn "from God's pure Word" and is in accord with "the orthodox consensus of the church."[31] The preface nowhere mentions the importance of teaching children this doctrine, and the *Catechism* itself nowhere gives evidence that it is being addressed to children. This may be deliberate on Calvin's part—he may have sought in the *Catechism* to teach the parents themselves, so that they could then teach the children the sum of what they themselves

28. *Catechismus, CO* 5:323B; *Catechism*, 7.
29. *Catechismus, CO* 5:325B; *Catechism*, 9.
30. *Catechismus, CO* 5:343C; *Catechism*, 27.
31. *Catechismus, CO* 5:318C; *Catechism*, 2.

had learned. Given the "remarkable rudeness and great ignorance" that Calvin saw in the parents of Geneva, combined with their "neglect of the Word of God," it would be surprising if Calvin did not seek to teach the parents first, so that they might teach their children.

Calvin was expelled from Geneva before he could really set this catechetical program into place. The intervening period in Strasbourg brought Calvin much greater clarity about the different methods of teaching he should use in his two callings as teacher and pastor. While in Strasbourg, Calvin developed the *Institutes* into a manual of instruction for the training of candidates in sacred theology, following the commonplace method initially used in the 1538 *Catechism*. By taking large portions of the 1538 *Catechism* into the 1539 edition of the *Institutes*, Calvin implicitly acknowledged that the *Catechism* is more suited to students of sacred theology than to parents and children. Calvin dropped the objective tone of "what we are taught" in catechesis and adopted the dialogical form of question and answer that he likely derived from Bucer. In Strasbourg, Calvin also became convinced that catechesis was the work of pastors themselves, not of parents.

All of these changes are reflected in the *Draft Ecclesiastical Ordinances* that Calvin submitted on his return to Geneva in 1541. Unlike the 1537 *Articles*, the *Ordinances* institute a midday service on Sunday for "catechism, that is, instruction of little children in all three churches," and clearly set the boundaries of the parishes "for bringing children to catechism."[32] The *Ordinances* explicitly require all citizens and inhabitants of Geneva "to bring or convey their children on Sundays at midday to Catechism," and ask that "a definite formulary" be composed "by which they will be instructed" and on which "they are to be interrogated about what has been said, to see if they have listened and remembered well."[33] Catechesis will henceforth be the task of pastors, who will themselves have been instructed in a topical summary of pious doctrine, the expanded *Institutes*. Moreover, the whole style of catechesis will move from a topical summary of doctrine to an instructional interrogation, based on a dialogical model, so that children might be able to understand and defend the faith they profess before the whole church. "When a child has been well enough instructed to pass the Catechism, he is to recite solemnly the sum of what it contains, and so to make profession of his Christianity in the presence of the Church."[34] Before this time, parents are not to bring their children to the Holy Supper of the Lord, for "it is a very perilous thing, for children as for parents, to introduce them

32. *Project d'ordonnances ecclésiastiques*, *CO* 10:20C; *Calvin: Theological Treatises*, 62.
33. *Project d'ordonnances ecclésiastiques*, *CO* 10:28A; *Calvin: Theological Treatises*, 69.
34. *Project d'ordonnances ecclésiastiques*, *CO* 10:28A; *Calvin: Theological Treatises*, 69.

without good and adequate instruction, for which purpose this order is to be used."[35]

The Registers of the Consistory of Geneva between 1542 and 1544 reveal that the catechism service on Sunday was not only used for the education of children; it was also mandated for those adults who were deemed to have an insufficient grasp of the evangelical faith. For instance, when Jacques Emyni, a packsaddler, reveals insufficient progress in the faith and the Creed, "the Consistory resolves that he be remanded every Sunday to the catechism with the others and examined like the others, and every day at the sermons."[36] As this passage reveals, Calvin saw the catechism as working in conjunction with the sermons to give the godly a greater understanding of their faith, confirmed by their own reading of Scripture. Hence, Claudaz, wife of Jehan Du Nant, and her son Amblard are given remonstrances by the Consistory "to frequent the sermons and the catechism and to buy a Bible in their house and have it read."[37] Moreover, the catechism taught by the pastors was not seen by Calvin as absolving parents of their responsibility to instruct their children and households in the faith. Master Mathieu Gathsiner receives admonitions "to frequent the sermons and instruct his children in religion," whereas Claude de Miribello is admonished "to teach his wife and his children and to frequent the sermons."[38] Thus, parents as well as children were expected to attend the Sunday catechism service, while parents were also to instruct their children in the faith at home, in conjunction with their attendance of the sermons and their reading of Scripture to their households.

The Latin *Catechism* of 1545 gives evidence of all the changes in Calvin's catechetical approach since the first catechism of 1538. The very opening of the preface highlights the responsibility of the church to instruct its children in the faith. "It has always been a practice and diligent care of the Church, that children be rightly brought up in Christian doctrine."[39] While Calvin acknowledges that this includes the role of parents in this instruction, he insists on a primary role for the church, for "it was accepted public custom and practice to examine children in the Churches concerning the specific points which should be common and familiar to all Christians."[40] If children are to be examined and

35. *Project d'ordonnances ecclésiastiques*, *CO* 10:28B; *Calvin: Theological Treatises*, 69.

36. *Registers of the Consistory of Geneva in the Time of Calvin*, vol. 1, *1542–1544*, ed. Robert M. Kingdon, Thomas A. Lambert, and Isabella M. Watt, trans. M. Wallace McDonald (Grand Rapids: Eerdmans, 1996), 70.

37. Ibid., 1:134.

38. Ibid., 1:217, 201

39. *Catechismus Genevensis*, *CO* 6:4B; *Calvin: Theological Treatises*, 88.

40. *Catechismus Genevensis*, *CO* 6:4B; *Calvin: Theological Treatises*, 88.

interrogated by the pastors before the whole church, then this means that they are required to make a serious inquiry into the meaning of the faith they are seeking to profess; they must investigate for themselves its truth by their own reading of Scripture. They cannot simply receive doctrine from a summary, as they did in Calvin's first catechism, in order to hand it back again upon demand; they must make the doctrine of the church their own and defend it on their own terms, having inquired into its meaning and veracity on their own, under the guidance of the pastor. The difference is clear in the opening line of each catechism. The 1538 *Catechism* began with a general observation: "No human being can be found, however barbarous or completely savage, untouched by some awareness of religion." The 1545 *Catechism* begins with a question posed by the Minister to the Child: "What is the chief end of human life?"

The 1545 *Catechism* also has a unifying theme that holds all four major topics together and is explicitly cited throughout the catechism at each major transition. After the child answers that the purpose of knowing God is to honor or worship God, the minister asks what the right way of honoring God would be. The fourfold answer of the child—that God is to be trusted, obeyed, invoked, and acknowledged as the source of every good thing—provides the theological framework in which to understand the four major components of the catechism: the Creed (trust), the law (obey), the Lord's Prayer (invoke), and the sacraments (acknowledge). The child is thereby given the reason why she is being asked to learn the catechism, because it teaches us how to honor and worship God by trusting, obeying, invoking, and thanking God. The pastor will spend the rest of the catechism asking the child "to consider these things in order and explain them more fully." The net effect of these major headings is to simplify the doctrine being taught in the catechism. Even though the second catechism is much longer than the first, it is also much simpler—instead of thirty-three topics arranged in order, there are four major headings examined more methodically and in much greater detail. In particular, Calvin eliminates any discussion of the free choice of the will, the doctrine of election and reprobation, human traditions, and the magistrates; he also greatly attenuates the discussion of the knowledge of sin through the law, the office of pastors, and excommunication. The *Catechism* focuses exclusively on the right worship of God, which is itself described as the chief end of human life. The goal of catechesis is therefore the full and informed participation of the child in the worship of God, rather than a mastery of all the rudiments or topics of pious doctrine, as in 1538.

In order to clarify the consideration of each aspect of the worship of God, the pastor will ask the child to break down each part of the catechism into its constituent parts, in order to consider each in turn. Thus, the Creed has "four principal parts," the law has "two parts," the Lord's Prayer "has six parts," and there are only two sacraments. Even these headings may be more closely considered by examining their parts: baptism itself "has two parts," the word "Christ" has three uses, and so on. The division of the catechism into sets and subsets aids the consideration of each aspect of its teaching and also reveals the order inherent in the whole series; one part organically leads into another, as in this transition to the Sacraments: "The order outlined and adopted by us demands that now we consider the fourth part of divine worship."[41] The discussion of the Creed, prayer, and sacraments is preceded by a general discussion about the meaning of the aspect of the worship of God being addressed, to place the teaching in its larger theological context. For example, before the Creed is introduced, the child is asked about how we know that God loves us and is the author of our salvation. "M: Where will this be apparent to us? C: In his Word, where he reveals his mercy to us in Christ, and testifies of his love towards us."[42] So also before the Lord's Prayer is discussed, the minister asks the child about the nature of the proper invocation of God. "M: Do you think that [God] alone is to be invoked? C: Certainly. For he requires this as the proper worship of his divinity."[43] Before the sacraments are introduced, they have a dialogue about the Word of God both read and preached. "M: Is there no other medium, as they call it, than the Word by which God communicates with us? C: He has joined the sacraments to the preaching of the Word."[44] These introductory sections indicate that Calvin wanted the catechumen not just to know what each part of the catechism meant but also to know why the knowledge of each part is essential to the aspect of the worship of God under consideration.

The central aspect of each of the four sections of the catechism consists of the catechumen reciting one of the parts of the doctrine under consideration, followed by a word-by-word exposition of its meaning. The minister interrogates the catechumen as though the words that were recited—be they from the Creed or the law—are the catechumen's own and asks, "What do you mean when you say this?" Such questions make the catechumen take ownership of the words of the Creed or the law, so that the child can explain and defend what he or she means in speaking this way about or to God. For example, after the catechumen recites the Apostles' Creed, the minister asks her to repeat the first part and then inquires, "M: Why do you call him Father? C: Primarily with regard to Christ, who is his eternal wisdom, begotten of him before all

41. *Catechismus Genevensis, OS* 2:127.20–21; *Calvin: Theological Treatises,* 129.
42. *Catechismus Genevensis, OS* 2:76.4–6; *Calvin: Theological Treatises,* 92.
43. *Catechismus Genevensis, OS* 2:113.7–8; *Calvin: Theological Treatises,* 119.
44. *Catechismus Genevensis, OS* 2:130.14–16; *Calvin: Theological Treatises,* 131.

time, and who, being sent into the world, was declared his Son. From this, however, we infer that, since God is the Father of Jesus Christ, he is also our Father."[45] When the catechumen recites the Lord's Prayer, the minister asks, "Why do you call God in general our Father, and not in particular your Father? C: Each believer may indeed call him his own Father. But our Lord used the common term to accustom us to exercise charity in prayer, not neglecting others in caring only for ourselves."[46]

At times the minister asks not only what a word means but also how the child knows that this meaning is true, as in the threefold office of "Christ." "M: How do you know this? C: Because Scripture applies anointing to these three uses; and also because it attributes these three offices to Christ."[47] The minister may also ask the catechumen to explain her statement more fully, as in the following exchange about the Lord's Prayer. "What is the force of the added phrase, that God is in heaven? C: It is the same as if I were to call him exalted, powerful, and incomprehensible. M: How is this and why? C: By this means we are taught to raise our minds upwards, when we pray to him, lest we should think carnally or materially of him, or measure him by the gauge of our own little standard."[48] At other times, the minister will ask the child for the grounds of the claim being made, or to prove the validity of the point the catechumen has just made. When the child says that prayer does not always need words, but always needs intelligence and affection, the minister asks, "How will you prove this to me?" The child then answers, "Since God is Spirit, and in other cases always requires of men their heart, so especially in prayer by which they communicate with him."[49] When the child states that we must both read Scripture privately and attend the sermons of the pastors, the minister asks, "Can you prove this to me?" The child replies, "The will of God ought to be abundantly sufficient proof for us. But this order which he commends to his church (Eph. 4:11) is not what two or three might observe, but what all should obey in common."[50] It should be noted that not every ground for a position is taken from Scripture. For instance, the catechumen knows that the sacraments are necessary because "we are surrounded by this gross earthly body," and so "need symbols and mirrors, to exhibit to us the appearance of spiritual and heavenly things in a kind of earthly way."[51] When the child is asked how Christ could have been seized with fear on

45. *Catechismus Genevensis, OS* 2:77.9–13; *Calvin: Theological Treatises*, 93.
46. *Catechismus Genevensis, OS* 2:120.14–17; *Calvin: Theological Treatises*, 124.
47. *Catechismus Genevensis, OS* 2:79.18–20; *Calvin: Theological Treatises*, 95.
48. *Catechismus Genevensis, OS* 2:120.19–25; *Calvin: Theological Treatises*, 124.
49. *Catechismus Genevensis, OS* 2:114.19–27; *Calvin: Theological Treatises*, 120.
50. *Catechismus Genevensis, OS* 2:129.19–22; *Calvin: Theological Treatises*, 130.
51. *Catechismus Genevensis, OS* 2:131.12–20; *Calvin: Theological Treatises*, 131.

the cross, he gives an answer indebted more to Irenaeus than to Scripture: "We must hold him to have been reduced to this necessity in respect of the feelings of his human nature. That this might happen, his divinity was for a short time concealed, that is, it did not exercise its power."[52]

It becomes clear that one reason for interrogating the child in this way is to prepare the child to answer those who do not agree with the way she worships God. Thus, after the child provides the right definition of faith on the basis of the Creed, the minister asks a series of questions that clearly reflect objections raised by Roman opponents of evangelical teaching. "What? Are men not justified by good works, when they study to approve themselves before God by holy and righteous living?"[53] When the child states that God forgives sins gratuitously, the minister asks, "It follows then that in no sense do we by our own satisfaction merit the pardon of sins which we obtain from God?"[54] When the child says that God directly cursed death by crucifixion, the minister asks, "What? Is this not to offer an affront to the Son of God to say that he was subject to the curse, even before God?"[55] Other objections sound like the Anabaptists, as when the child gives a defense of infant baptism and the minister asks, "Can you show with reason that there is nothing absurd in this?"[56] In all these ways, the minister is training the child to give an account of the hope that is within her to those who strongly disagree with what she believes. The basis for such answers is almost always from Scripture. Thus, when the child states that Christ's descent into hell was revealed in his cry of dereliction from the cross, the following exchange takes place. "M: Was this not an affront to the Father? C: Not at all. But he exercised his severity against him, that he might fulfill what was prophesied by Isaiah: He was smitten by the hand of God for our sins, wounded for our iniquities (Isa. 53:4; 1 Peter 2:24)."[57] In the same way, the catechumen shows that there is nothing absurd in baptizing infants by pointing to Moses and Paul, and the parallel between circumcision and baptism. "For while Moses and all the prophets taught that circumcision was the sign of repentance (Deut. 10:16; Jer. 4:4), and was even the sign of faith, as Paul witnesses (Rom. 4:11), so we see that it does not exclude infants."[58]

Finally, in order to show the child the usefulness of what she is learning, the minister will frequently ask about the benefit to be derived from

52. *Catechismus Genevensis*, OS 2:84.23–27; *Calvin: Theological Treatises*, 99.
53. *Catechismus Genevensis*, OS 2:93.1–2; *Calvin: Theological Treatises*, 105.
54. *Catechismus Genevensis*, OS 2:90.14–15; *Calvin: Theological Treatises*, 103.
55. *Catechismus Genevensis*, OS 2:83.21–22; *Calvin: Theological Treatises*, 98.
56. *Catechismus Genevensis*, OS 2:136.1–2; *Calvin: Theological Treatises*, 134.
57. *Catechismus Genevensis*, OS 2:84.19–22; *Calvin: Theological Treatises*, 99.
58. *Catechismus Genevensis*, OS 2:136.3–6; *Calvin: Theological Treatises*, 134.

a particular subject under discussion. When the child states that the devil and wicked people are bridled by the power of God so that they are unwillingly ministers of God's will, the minister asks, "What benefit accrues to you from the knowledge of this? C: Very much. For it would go ill with us, if anything were permitted wicked men and devils without the will of God; then our minds could never be tranquil, for thinking ourselves exposed to their pleasure."[59] In the midst of the catechumen's discussion of the threefold office of Christ, made possible by the anointing of the Holy Spirit, the minister asks, "But do you reap any benefit from this? C: Indeed, all these things have no other purpose than our good. For Christ is vouchsafed these things by the Father, in order that he may share them with us, and out of this fulness of his we all draw (John 1:16)."[60] After the child claims that God forgives sin by gratuitous mercy, the minister asks, "What advantage accrues to us from this remission? C: We are accepted as if we were just and innocent; and at the same time our conscience is confirmed in trust in his fatherly goodness, in which our salvation is assured."[61] Since the worship of God is directed to the one who is the author and fountain of every good thing, the catechumen is reminded that the goodness of God, and our enjoyment of it, stands behind every aspect of our relationship with God.

The overall direction of the line of questioning pursued by the minister in the catechism is to see if the child knows why she worships God the way that she does. What are her grounds for doing so? What do the words that she uses to speak of or address God mean to her? How does she know? Why are the details of the Creed important? What of the objections of those who object to the way we worship God? What benefit comes to us from believing these things about God? It is true that the catechism provides the answers to all these questions, but it seems that the overall effect was rather to teach the child to inquire into and investigate the meaning and truth of what he believed, so that he might be able to give his own account of its truth to those who ask this of him. The public profession of faith made before the church by the catechumen reinforces this dynamic, for it takes place by a series of questions posed to the catechumen by the pastor. "The Father, Son, and the Holy Spirit, are they more than one God?" "Can you accomplish the commandments of God by yourself?" "By what means then are you saved and delivered from the condemnation of God?" "Where then must we seek Jesus Christ to have fruition of him?" "How can we have true

---

59. *Catechismus Genevensis, OS* 2:78.23–28; *Calvin: Theological Treatises*, 94.
60. *Catechismus Genevensis, OS* 2:80.5–8; *Calvin: Theological Treatises*, 95.
61. *Catechismus Genevensis, OS* 2:125.1–4; *Calvin: Theological Treatises*, 127.

faith?"[62] Even though the answers are clearly provided in this rite, the interrogation nonetheless accustoms the believer to make such questions her own, so that she might continue to inquire more deeply into the meaning and integrity of the faith she professes before the church. This formed for Calvin one of the most important differences between the restored evangelical church and the Church of Rome: in the former, the godly are encouraged, even required, to investigate and inquire into the truth of their faith, so that they might be able to know both what they believe and why they believe it.

62. "The Way of Questioning the Children Whom You Wish to Receive at the Supper of Our Lord Jesus Christ," *CO* 6:147–60; *John Calvin: Writings on Pastoral Piety*, ed. and trans. Elsie Anne McKee (New York: Paulist Press, 2001), 101–4.

7

EXPOUNDING SCRIPTURE AND APPLYING IT TO OUR USE

Calvin's Sermons on Ephesians

As we have seen, Calvin believed that he was called to be both a teacher and a pastor of the catholic church. As a teacher, Calvin sought to prepare future pastors to preach and teach doctrine drawn from Scripture and defend such doctrine from error, first by having them read a summary of godly doctrine drawn from all of Scripture (in the *Institutes*), and then by having them read contextual commentaries on each book of Scripture. In recent years, the interpretation of Calvin has shifted from the almost exclusive emphasis on the 1559 *Institutes* in the first half of this century to his work as an interpreter of Scripture in his biblical commentaries.[1] Even studies that focus on Calvin's *Institutes* have sought

1. See especially T. H. L. Parker, *Calvin's New Testament Commentaries*, 2nd ed. (Louisville: Westminster John Knox, 1993); David Steinmetz, *Calvin in Context* (New York: Oxford University Press, 1995); and David Puckett, *John Calvin's Exegesis of the Old Testament* (Louisville: Westminster John Knox, 1995).

This essay was originally published in a slightly different form under the title "Expounding Scripture and Applying It to Our Use: Calvin's Sermons on Ephesians," *Scottish Journal of Theology* 56, no. 4 (2003): 481–507. Reprinted by permission.

to understand it in light of the development of Calvin's theology in his work as an exegete manifested in his commentaries.[2] Calvin's sermons have also received increasing attention, although they have at times been treated as though they were no different than his commentaries, as manifestations of the way he interpreted Scripture.[3] Although it is a welcome development to have attention brought to bear on a major component of Calvin's labor as a teacher of the catholic church, the recent focus on the commentaries is in danger of creating the same distortions in our perceptions of Calvin's work as the previous focus on the *Institutes*. After all, the goal Calvin had in view was to train pastors who would teach their congregations, and every individual therein, the doctrine drawn from Scripture, first in summary form (the Catechism), and then contextually (the sermons), so that they might profitably apply this doctrine to their lives. Calvin was convinced that the church would only be restored when Scripture was rightly expounded and skillfully applied to the use of ordinary Christians, so that they might profit by their own reading of Scripture.

Hence, the sermons differ from the commentaries in both their audience and their objective.[4] The commentaries have as their audience future pastors of the catholic church, with the goal of revealing the mind of the author with lucid brevity. The sermons have as their audience ordinary Christians within a specific congregation, with the goal of expounding the intention or meaning of the author and of applying that meaning to their use, so that they might retain that meaning in their minds and hearts and put it into practice in their lives. In order better to understand the specific objectives Calvin had in mind in his sermons, this chapter will examine the sermons on Ephesians that he preached in 1558–59. I will first compare them to the commentary on Ephesians that Calvin first published in 1548, in order to disclose the different audience and objectives of the two works. I shall then examine in detail the structure,

2. Elsie A. McKee, "Exegesis, Theology, and Development in Calvin's *Institutio*: A Methodological Suggestion," in *Probing the Reformed Tradition: Historical Studies in Honor of Edward A. Dowey Jr.*, ed. Brian Armstrong and Elsie A. McKee (Louisville: Westminster John Knox, 1989), 154–72; Richard Muller, *The Unaccommodated Calvin: Studies in the Foundation of a Theological Tradition* (New York: Oxford University Press, 2000); Barbara Pitkin, *What Pure Eyes Could See: Calvin's Doctrine of Faith in Its Exegetical Context* (New York: Oxford University Press, 1999).

3. Susan Schreiner, *Where Shall Wisdom Be Found? Calvin's Exegesis of Job from Medieval and Modern Perspectives* (Chicago: University of Chicago Press, 1994).

4. See especially T. H. L. Parker, *Calvin's Preaching* (Louisville: Westminster John Knox, 1992); Dawn de Vries, *Jesus Christ in the Preaching of Calvin and Schleiermacher* (Louisville: Westminster John Knox, 1996); and Wilhelmus H. Th. Moehn, *"God Calls Us to His Service": The Relation between God and His Audience in Calvin's Sermons on Acts* (Geneva: Droz, 2001).

methods, and objectives of the sermons themselves, in order better to understand what Calvin hoped to accomplish in his preaching and how he sought to accomplish it.

I shall argue that there are three steps Calvin consistently followed in each of his sermons, though this order is clearer in some sermons than in others.[5] First, he sought to show the meaning and intention of Paul contained in the words of the epistle. Next, he pointed out that the meaning revealed in his exposition should be kept in mind, retained in memory, and imprinted on the hearts of the congregation. Third, Calvin sought to apply the doctrine of Paul to the use, edification, and instruction of the congregation, so that they might profit from the doctrine by putting it in practice in their lives. Such practice has not so much to do with their actions as with the thoughts and affections of their hearts. The sermon only reaches its objective when the exposition and application of Scripture makes an impact on the thoughts and affections of the hearts of the members of the congregation, so that they feel the power of the realties being set forth by Paul and expounded and applied by Calvin.

The Exposition of Scripture in the Commentaries

In order to disclose the unique audience and objectives for Calvin's sermons, it is useful to compare the sermons on Ephesians with the commentary on Ephesians written a decade earlier and published in final form in 1555. The objective in this commentary is the same as in all Calvin's commentaries: to reveal the mind of the author with lucid brevity. Calvin was convinced that the mind of the author was best revealed by the context of the text being interpreted. This context was comprised of many layers: the immediate linguistic context, including the use of any rhetorical or dialectical techniques by the author; the relationship of the author to his original audience; the relationship to other works by the same author; the relationship to the rest of Scripture; the relationship to other Hebrew, Greek, and Latin literature; and finally, the relationship to previous and contemporary interpreters of the same text. Calvin also assumed that the commentary on Ephesians would be read within the

---

5. Parker points out that Calvin's sermons always move from exposition to application, and that the application often includes exhortations, rebukes, and the like (Parker, *Calvin's Preaching*, chap. 11). However, he is wary of attributing any method to Calvin's sermons; he sees them as having their own unpredictable dynamic. "The sermons are like rivers, moving strongly in one direction, alive with eddies and cross-currents, now thundering in cataracts, now a calm mirror of the banks and the sky; but never still, never stagnant" (ibid., 132). I agree that the method Calvin follows is not always explicitly clear, but I argue nonetheless that Calvin does follow such a method quite consistently in his sermons.

context of his other writings for the instruction of future pastors: the *Institutes* and the previous commentaries on Romans, 1 and 2 Corinthians, and Galatians.

One sees all of these aspects of the context of Ephesians addressed in the commentary. Calvin treats the epistle as though its primary audience was the church at Ephesus at the time of Paul, although there are many places where he clearly brings the statements of Paul into his present day without any hesitation.[6] Calvin makes several references to the problems created by the multiple codices of the epistle extant in his day, thereby showing the need to establish a reliable primary text.[7] He is critical of the way the division of chapters breaks up the context of Paul's line of thinking.[8] He even considers the possibility that a verse may have been added by someone other than Paul, though "as it is perfectly agreeable to the context," he is willing to accept it as written by Paul.[9] He also refers to other letters Paul most likely wrote but that have subsequently been lost.[10] Calvin makes repeated reference to issues of translation from Greek to Latin, usually taking exception to the translation of the Vulgate and Erasmus by insisting that his translation "fits the context better."[11] Even when the word itself can be translated following Erasmus, Calvin will prefer another translation because "the context induces us to prefer another view."[12] Calvin also notes the places where Paul's Greek betrays the presence of a Hebraic way of speaking.[13]

Calvin assumes a familiarity with classical authors on the part of his readers. He twice seeks help from the writings of Plato to determine the

6. For example, at the beginning of chap. 3, Calvin makes it very clear that Paul is speaking to the Ephesians in their own context. Whereas, at the beginning of chap. 4, Calvin makes Paul sound like he is intentionally opposing the Roman Church in the sixteenth century.

7. "Most Greek copies omit the word *all*; but I was unwilling to strike it out, because it must at least be understood" (Comm. on Eph. 1:1, *CO* 51:145C; *CNTC* 11:123). See also Comm. on Eph. 1:16; 5:9, 14, 21.

8. "We see that the division of chapters is particularly unhappy, as it has separated statements which are closely related" (Comm. on Eph. 5:1, *CO* 51:213C; *CNTC* 11:196).

9. "I do not know whether this has been inserted by another hand, but, as it is perfectly agreeable to the context, I am satisfied to receive it as written by Paul" (Comm. on Eph. 2:5, *CO* 51:164A; *CNTC* 11:142–43).

10. "If we adopt the almost universal view, that the apostle had formerly written to the Ephesians, this is not the only epistle which we have lost" (Comm. on Eph. 3:3, *CO* 51:178C; *CNTC* 11:159).

11. Comm. on Eph. 1:10, *CO* 51:151A; *CNTC* 11:129; see also Comm. on Eph. 2:6, 16, 22; 3:9; 4:6; 5:13–14; 6:23.

12. Comm. on Eph. 4:32, *CO* 51:213B; *CNTC* 11:195.

13. "'The Father of glory' is a well-known Hebrew idiom [*ex usu linguae hebraicae dici*] for 'the glorious Father'" (Comm. on Eph. 1:16, *CO* 51:156A; *CNTC* 11:134). See also Comm. on Eph. 1:21; 2:2; 3:16; 4:15, 26.

meaning of Greek terms.[14] He also refers to Cicero, most likely his treatise *De officiis*.[15] Calvin highlights the use of rhetorical techniques by Paul, such as periphrasis, amplification, *epexergasia, hyperbaton, epinikion,* apposition, metaphor, *emphatikoteron,* and synecdoche.[16] He also notes the presence of dialectical arguments in Paul, such as fourfold causality, syllogisms, arguments from effect, arguments from contraries, and the distinction between genus and species.[17]

Calvin sets his own interpretation in the context of the work of other interpreters before him, especially Chrysostom, Augustine, Ambrose, Ambrosiaster, Cyprian, and Jerome.[18] He also makes implicit reference to other sixteenth-century interpreters, such as Zwingli and Luther.[19] He contrasts his interpretation with the distortions of the same passages by previous heretical groups such as the Manichaeans, the Pelagians, the Marcionites, the Arians, and the Sabellians.[20] He also contrasts his "simple and natural interpretation" with the "distortions" of his con-

14. One time he cites Plato's *Republic* (Comm. on Eph. 4:17, *CO* 51:204B; *CNTC* 11:186), and another time he paraphrases Plato without citation: "Plato also teaches correctly that *hosiotēs* lies in the worship of God, and that the other part, righteousness, relates to men" (Comm. on Eph. 4:24, *CO* 51:209A; *CNTC* 11:191).

15. "We need not wonder at this, for if those voluptuous sorts of trades which can only bring corruption were denounced by the heathens, Cicero among them, as shameful, would an apostle of Christ reckon them among the lawful callings of God?" (Comm. on Eph. 4:28, *CO* 51:211A; *CNTC* 11:193).

16. "*And you when you were dead*. An *epexergasia* of the former statements—that is, an exposition and clarification. . . . But by struggling to heighten each of these parts, he makes a break in his argument by a *hyperbaton*" (Comm. on Eph. 2:1, *CO* 51:160B; *CNTC* 11:139). See also Comm. on Eph. 1:12, 19; 4:8, 13; 5:30; 6:1.

17. "Three causes of our salvation are mentioned in this clause, and a fourth is shortly afterwards added. The efficient cause is the good pleasure of the will of God; the material cause is Christ; and the final cause is the praise of his grace" (Comm. on Eph. 1:5, *CO* 51:148C; *CNTC* 11:126). See also Comm. on Eph. 2:14, 18; 4:17; 5:28; 6:1, 18.

18. "Some think that *pastors and doctors* denote one office, because there is no disjunctive particle, as in other parts of the verse, to distinguish them. Chrysostom and Augustine are of this opinion. For what we read in the Ambrosian commentaries is too childish and unworthy of Ambrose" (Comm. on Eph. 4:11, *CO* 51:197C; *CNTC* 11:179). See also Comm. on Eph. 1:3, 10; 3:3, 10, 18; 4:9, 19, 30; 5:3, 23, 27; 6:15.

19. Zwingli seems to be in view in his discussion of baptism: "Some try to weaken this eulogy of baptism, in case too much is attributed to the sign if it is called the washing of the soul" (Comm. on Eph. 5:26, *CO* 51:223B). Lutheran exegesis seems to be referenced in the discussion of being made members of Christ: "Some assert that it is a twisting of this passage to refer it to the Lord's Supper, when no mention is made of the Supper; but they are very much mistaken" (Comm. on Eph. 5:30, *CO* 51:225–26; *CNTC* 11:209).

20. "At present, we shall only notice the foolish nonsense of the Manichees in endeavoring to form from this passage two principles, as if Satan could do anything against God's will" (Comm. on Eph. 2:2, *CO* 51:161C; *CNTC* 11:140). See also Comm. on Eph. 2:10, 20; 3:14; 4:5; 5:27; 6:12.

temporary Roman opponents, whom he usually calls "the Sophists of the Sorbonne."[21]

Calvin also gives abundant evidence that he expects his readers to be familiar with his own writings for future pastors: the *Institutes* and the previous commentaries on the Pauline epistles. He explicitly directs his readers to the *Institutes* for fuller discussions of the certainty of faith and the blessings of God in this temporal life.[22] He also refers his readers to his discussions of issues in other commentaries, making explicit mention of the previous commentaries on Romans, 1 Corinthians, and Galatians, and telling the reader that other issues will be discussed in the forthcoming Colossians commentary.[23]

Finally, Calvin gives evidence of the programmatic distinction he made between the method pursued in his commentaries and the method pursued in sermons, saying that in his comments he is content to indicate the mind of the apostle briefly, leaving the fuller treatment to the sermons.[24] He also makes an explicit distinction between the office and responsibilities of teachers and pastors, again reflecting the difference between commentaries written by teachers and sermons delivered by pastors. "Teaching is the duty of all pastors; but there is a particular gift of interpreting Scripture so that sound doctrine may be kept, and a man may be a doctor who is not fitted to preach." Calvin goes on to note that pastors are given charge of a specific flock, whereas teachers educate pastors and are responsible for the instruction of the entire church.[25]

21. *"Christ himself being the chief corner-stone.* Those who transfer this honour to Peter, and maintain that the Church is founded on him, are so shameless as to pervert this text to support their error" (Comm. on Eph. 2:20, *CO* 51:175C; *CNTC* 11:155). See also Comm. on Eph. 1:4–5; 3:12; 4:11, 17; 5:26, 32.

22. "Let us remember, therefore, that the certainty of faith is knowledge [*scientia*], but it is acquired by the teaching of the Holy Spirit, and not by the acuteness of our own intellect. If readers desire more on this, let them consult the *Institutio*" (Comm. on Eph. 3:19, *CO* 51:188C; *CNTC* 11:169). "The promise is of a long life; from which we may understand that the present life is not to be despised among the gifts of God. Of this and other subjects readers may learn in the *Institutio*" (Comm. on Eph. 6:2, *CO* 51:229A; *CNTC* 11:213).

23. "He therefore tells the Ephesians how eagerly the Gospel should be embraced, how highly esteemed. On this we have spoken in the Epistle to the Galatians, Chapter 2:15" (Comm. on Eph. 3:8, *CO* 51:181C; *CNTC* 11:162). "We have already spoken in 1 Cor. 12 about the offices which he here reviews" (Comm. on Eph. 4:11, *CO* 51:197A; *CNTC* 178). *"The old man,* as we have taught in the sixth chapter of Romans and other passages, means the natural disposition which we bring from our mother's womb" (Comm. on Eph. 4:22, *CO* 51:207C; *CNTC* 11:189–90). "The difference between hymns and psalms, or between psalms and songs, is not easy to determine. But I will say something about it in Colossians Chapter 3" (Comm. on Eph. 5:19, *CO* 51:221A; *CNTC* 11:203–4).

24. *"Ideo breviter apostoli mentem indicare mihi sufficit: plenam tractationem concionibus relinquo"* (Comm. on Eph. 4:5, *CO* 51:191B; *CNTC* 11:173).

25. Comm. on Eph. 4:11, *CO* 51:198A; *CNTC* 11:179.

It is clear from Calvin's method in the commentary that he is seeking to reveal the mind of the author with lucid brevity, a mind that is itself revealed by the context of the language he uses. Calvin clearly assumes that his reader is skilled in Latin, Greek, and Hebrew, and is familiar with classical philosophy and rhetoric. He also assumes that his reader knows the major figures of the Christian tradition, both orthodox (Cyprian, Jerome, Ambrose, Augustine, and Chrysostom) and heretical (Marcion, Sabellius, Arius, Mani, and Pelagius). He assumes that his readers are acquainted with the sixteenth-century interpretations of Luther, Zwingli, and his Roman opponents. Finally, he clearly sets his commentary on Ephesians in the context of his other commentaries and the *Institutes*, making it clear that in these texts he is exercising his office as a teacher, teaching the true, genuine, natural, and simple sense of Scripture to present and future pastors, so that they might preach the doctrine of Scripture to their congregations.

The Exposition and Application of Scripture in the Sermons

When one comes to the sermons on Ephesians, one is immediately made aware that Calvin is speaking to a very different audience, one comprised not of learned future pastors but of unlearned ordinary Christians. In his exposition of the text in his sermons, Calvin makes no reference to variant readings in other codices, nor does he discuss issues of translation in light of the efforts of the Vulgate and Erasmus. He does note variant meanings of words Paul uses, but simply gives his own preferences in French without referring to the Greek.[26] Only twice does he refer to the difficulty of translating certain words Paul uses into French.[27] He cites not one word from Greek, Latin, or Hebrew, and only once, in the last sermon, refers to the Hebraic way of speaking familiar

26. "Now before we come to the rest, let us note that this word 'blessing' is taken in different senses when Paul applies it either to God or to ourselves" (sermon 1 on Ephesians, *CO* 51:255A; *Sermons on the Epistle to the Ephesians*, trans. Leslie Rawlinson and S. M. Houghton (Edinburgh: Banner of Truth, 1973), 17 (henceforth *Sermons*, 17). Calvin also notes how the word "love" can refer to either God's love for us or our love for one another (sermon 2 on Ephesians, *CO* 51:269B; *Sermons*, 33; sermon 20 on Ephesians, *CO* 51:493C; *Sermons*, 293). Parker makes the same point: "Occasionally, he will explain the meaning of a word more carefully, but without ever (so far as I have noticed) giving the Hebrew or Greek original" (Parker, *Calvin's Preaching*, 86).

27. He notes that the terms for inner and outer person are not yet common in French (sermon 19 on Ephesians, *CO* 51:482B; *Sermons*, 279) and also remarks that "person" does not mean the same in Scripture that it does in French (sermon 45 on Ephesians, *CO* 51:811C; *Sermons*, 650).

to the apostles.[28] Calvin does refer to the writings of the heathen and the books of the philosophers, including one paraphrase from Plato, but never cites any by name.[29] He does not point out any dialectical devices in the epistle and names only one rhetorical category, the similitude.[30] Calvin mentions other Christian interpreters five times, all anonymously, and opposes their suggestions with the simple and natural meaning of Paul and his intention that clearly emerges from the words he uses.[31] Three times he flags the interpretations of the heretics, only once mentioning the Manichaeans, and again shows how easily they are refuted from the intention of Paul.[32] He only refers twice to Roman theologians, calling them friars, monks, school divines, and doctors, but not specifying that they are working in the Sorbonne.[33] In almost every sermon he refers to what the "papists" say, however.

28. The apostles, "being accustomed to the Hebrew tongue," use the word "peace" to mean both prosperity and concord (sermon 48 on Ephesians, *CO* 51:856B; *Sermons*, 700).

29. Calvin paraphrases Plato without citing him when he speaks of how we are to resemble God: "Even the poor heathen had some understanding of it. For they said that man's life is to tend to God, and to be conformed to his image, and that the same is also the full perfection of happiness" (sermon 33 on Ephesians, *CO* 51:667B; *Sermons*, 488). He otherwise makes general references to the writings of the heathens or books of the philosophers (sermon 28 on Ephesians, *CO* 51:600C; *Sermons*, 414).

30. See, for instance, his discussion of the breaking down of the wall between Jews and Gentiles: "He uses that figure of speech [*similitude*] to declare that the ceremonies and types are abolished" (sermon 13 on Ephesians, *CO* 51:405C; *Sermons*, 191).

31. Typical in this regard is his discussion of the role of angels in the mystery of salvation: "There are others who, not being able to dispose [*despescher*] of this passage of St. Paul's, have thought that the angels are here among us to be like scholars and to hear the preaching of God's Word. But that is too stupid and childish a speculation" (sermon 18 on Ephesians, *CO* 51:467–68; *Sermons*, 263). So also in his discussion of not giving place to the devil, he says, "Some indeed have expounded it as being spoken of the enemies of faith, who seek occasion to slander it. But it is easy to see from the words themselves [*mais on voit facilement par ces mots*] that he intended to warn us against something we ought to be more afraid of" (sermon 31 on Ephesians, *CO* 51:633A; *Sermons*, 450).

32. Calvin is especially at pains to refute Manichaean ways of interpreting Paul's discussion of opposing principalities and powers: "Now although some heretics in old time have abused this passage, intending to have made, as it were, two principles, as if God were hindered from making provision to maintain himself against Satan and from making arrangements to defend those whom he has taken into his protection. Nevertheless, if we pay attention to Paul's meaning [*l'intention*], this question will be easily resolved" (sermon 46 on Ephesians, *CO* 51:823B; *Sermons*, 663).

33. It is clear from the way Calvin describes the scholastics that he does not expect his congregation to be familiar with their positions or their office. "The papists (at least such of them as have excelled others in their walk, and I speak even of the monks and friars who are called school divines [*qu'on nomme docteurs scholastiques*]) grant even more—that this election of God's is free and that he did not choose any man for any other reason than that it pleased him" (sermon 2 on Ephesians, *CO* 51:267C; *Sermons*, 31).

Calvin never refers to the *Institutes* but does refer twice to articles of faith in the Apostles' Creed.[34] He does not refer to any other commentaries, but he does remind the congregation several times of the sermons he preached on Galatians, which immediately preceded the sermons on Ephesians, and also refers repeatedly to their own reading of Scripture in conjunction with their going to hear sermons.[35] Moreover, Calvin consistently employs French idioms, with the refrain "as one says," to make his presentation more down to earth and accessible to his congregation, and he uses a very plain and simple style of French throughout his sermons.[36] Finally, far from studying lucid brevity, the sermons are long expositions of short passages of Scripture. There are forty-eight sermons on Ephesians, compared to thirty-five sections of the Ephesians commentary, with approximately seven thousand words per sermon, compared to approximately two thousand words per section of commentary. As we shall see, the much greater length of the sermons is directly related to the need to apply Scripture to all aspects of the congregation's life.

In sum, from the evidence internal to the sermons, it is clear that Calvin is intentionally preaching to an audience that he assumes is familiar only with the French language, the Apostles' Creed, and the Scriptures in French translation, as well as the previous sermons of Calvin himself. In other words, Calvin is preaching to the very audience he had in mind from the beginning of his work as a teacher of godly doctrine: ordinary, unlearned Christians. He assumes that they have been through the first part of their education, the Catechism, and that they have been attending the second lifelong part, the sermons, in tandem with their own reading

34. In one instance he refers to "the communion of saints" (sermon 8 on Ephesians, *CO* 51:338C; *Sermons*, 114), and in another to the confession that God is the Creator, in contrast to free choice of the will (sermon 11 on Ephesians, *CO* 51:381A; *Sermons*, 163).

35. Calvin frequently reminds his congregation of what he has told them in his exposition of Galatians: for instance, "Also we have seen before in the Epistle to the Galatians how St. Paul said to Peter, 'We are Jews by nature' [Gal. 2:15]" (sermon 5 on Ephesians, *CO* 51:298; *Sermons*, 67).

36. Calvin listened carefully to the expressions and idioms used by his congregation in everyday life, and he acknowledges that such forms of expression come from them, by introducing each idiomatic saying with the phrase, "As one says [*comme on dit*]." There are idiomatic expressions in almost every sermon on Ephesians, such as the following: "Now then, what audacity is it to open our mouths to reply against God. Is it not a perverting of the whole order of nature? Is it in our power to pluck the sun out of the sky, or to take the moon between our teeth, as they say?" (sermon 2, *CO* 51:261C; *Sermons*, 25). Parker rightly notes of such expressions, "But here, in the sermons, he deliberately adapts his style to the grasp of the common people of his congregation" (Parker, *Calvin's Preaching*, 148). See also Erwin Mülhaupt, *Die Predigt Calvins: Ihre Geschichte, ihre Form und ihre religiösen Grundlagen* (Berlin: de Gruyter, 1931), 39–63, and his attempt to catalog Calvin's sayings and images by category.

of Scripture in French translation. However, it was Calvin's conviction that Scripture was written precisely for this audience, for the Holy Spirit had accommodated the teaching of God in Scripture to the capacities of the unlearned, those untrained and unskilled in the liberal arts, sciences, and languages of Latin, Greek, and Hebrew literature. Thus, it is only in the sermons, and not in the commentaries, that Scripture finds its intended audience.

Even though his congregation is by Calvin's own admission "unlearned," he nonetheless treats all of them as students and scholars in the school of Christ. He assumes that all of them have been attending sermons and reading Scripture for themselves, as good scholars would both attend lectures and read the primary text for themselves. He contrasts such students with the deluded fanatics who reject both preaching and reading, preferring instead to await direct revelations of God from heaven.

> Let us not be carried away with such foolish conceit, but let all of us both great and small submit ourselves soberly to the order that our Lord Jesus Christ has set, which is that such as have great skill and are well versed in the holy Scriptures, and have the gift of teaching, should strive to serve the whole Church as they are bound to do, for to that end God has advanced them above others [John 15:8].[37]

It is clear from this passage that Calvin sees pastors as those who have great skill and are well versed in Scriptures, and who have the gift of teaching. Hence, others who are not so gifted should submit themselves humbly and patiently to be taught by the pastors who have these gifts, for this is the will of God in Jesus Christ: "The preaching of the gospel and the meeting of men together to hear the holy Scripture expounded, is not something invented by men, but . . . God has so ordained it and our Lord Jesus Christ has set it down for a law, and we must keep it as a thing inviolable."[38]

On the other hand, Calvin did not want his congregation simply to listen to the teaching of pastors without inquiring into the truth of what they heard for themselves by their own reading of Scripture, in contrast to the customary practice of the Roman Church.

> Since this is so, we ought to come together so much the more soberly and advisedly, as to God's school and not as to man's school, to hear the preaching. It is true that we ought to examine the doctrine, and that we must not receive all things that are preached indifferently, even like brute

37. Sermon 25 on Ephesians, *CO* 51:554B; *Sermons*, 362.
38. Sermon 25 on Ephesians, *CO* 51:554B; *Sermons*, 362.

beasts (after the manner of the papists, who call it simplicity, to be without any understanding at all) but we must bear such honor to God's name that when the doctrine of the holy Scripture is expounded to us, each one of us must withdraw himself from the world and forsake his own reason, so that we may submit ourselves with true obedience and humility to the things which we know have come from God.[39]

However, even with the guidance of pastors and our own reading of Scripture, the ultimate guide to the meaning of Scripture is the Holy Spirit. "For there we have a warning to hold ourselves in check, that we, being God's true scholars, and distrusting ourselves, may not go for five feet on one sheep (as they say) but handle the holy Scripture with such reverence that God may guide us to the true understanding of it by his Holy Spirit."[40] Calvin was convinced that neither hearing the doctrine of Scripture preached, nor reading it for ourselves, would be sufficient to lead us into the truth, without the enlightenment of the Holy Spirit guiding all of our studies. "Therefore, let us not think that it is enough for us to come to a sermon, or for each to read God's Word in private, but we must have recourse to God that he may give us increase."[41] The true students of God not only hear sermons and read in private, but above all pray to God for the guidance of the Holy Spirit, especially when they come across something that they do not understand.[42]

Since Calvin assumes that his listeners are reading Scripture for themselves, he makes several suggestions in his sermons regarding how they might read with the most profit. Without such guidance, one might read Scripture for a very long time without ever really benefiting from it. "You will see a number of people who labor very hard indeed at reading the holy Scriptures—they do nothing else but turn over the leaves of it, and yet after ten years they have as much knowledge of it as if they had never read a single line. And why? Because they do not have a particular aim in view, they only wander about."[43] The target at which we must aim is the grace of God in Jesus Christ, for it is to him that all Scripture bears witness. "So much the more therefore it behooves us to go to him, and when we read the holy Scripture, let the object we aim at always to be

39. Sermon 25 on Ephesians, *CO* 51:442B; *Sermons*, 233.
40. Sermon 42 on Ephesians, *CO* 51:773C; *Sermons*, 607.
41. Sermon 19 on Ephesians, *CO* 51:478–79; *Sermons*, 275. "Therefore when we come to be taught God's Word, or when any one of us reads it in private, let us not imagine our minds to be so discerning that we are able sufficiently to understand whatever the Scripture tells us, but let us acknowledge our own lack of understanding and pray God to make his doctrine prevail with us in such a way that it may not slip from us" (sermon 6 on Ephesians, *CO* 51:310C; *Sermons*, 82).
42. Sermon 16 on Ephesians, *CO* 51:445–46; *Sermons*, 237–38.
43. Sermon 15 on Ephesians, *CO* 51:427C; *Sermons*, 217.

to know what is the grace of God which he has shown us in the person of his only Son, and when once we know it, we shall have profited very well in God's school, and we may well cast away all other things as filth and poison."[44] Calvin cautions his congregation not to listen to the "fanatical people" who in their day are telling them they do not need to read the Law and the Prophets any more, but only the New Testament, for the Law and the Prophets also point to the Lord Jesus Christ. "So let us study the law and the prophets, knowing well that they lead us to our Lord Jesus Christ."[45]

The knowledge to which Calvin directs his readers, however, is one that is ultimately rooted in the awareness of the grace and goodness of God in the heart, leading us to cleave to God in Christ from the inmost affection of the heart. "For the purpose of the Scripture is not to feed us with vain and superfluous things, but to edify us for our salvation, that is to say, to make us perceive God's goodness that we might be joined to him, and that this might be our happiness."[46] Once the goodness of God is felt in the heart, it leads us to praise God for all God's benefits, and to pray to God with confidence.

> For there are two things at which we must chiefly aim and to which it is fitting for us to apply all our studies and endeavors, and they are the very sum of all the things that God teaches us by the holy Scripture. The one is the magnifying of God as he deserves, and the other is the assurance of salvation, so that we may call on him as our Father with full liberty [Rom. 8:15]. If we do not have these two things, woe to us, for there is neither faith nor religion in us.[47]

Ultimately, the goal to be sought in reading Scripture is so to experience and feel the grace of God in Christ that it ravishes us completely in love.[48] "To be brief, we must be sure of the infinite good that is done to us by our Lord Jesus Christ, in order that we may be ravished in love with our God and inflamed with a right affection to obey him, and keep ourselves strictly in awe of him, to honor him with all our thoughts, with all our affections, and with all our hearts."[49]

Calvin therefore addresses his congregation as fellow scholars of God in the school of Christ, studying to learn the meaning of Scripture under the guidance of a pastor skilled in the exposition of Scripture, and pray-

44. Sermon 20 on Ephesians, *CO* 51:499B; *Sermons*, 299.
45. Sermon 15 on Ephesians, *CO* 51:427B; *Sermons*, 216.
46. Sermon 7 on Ephesians, *CO* 51:326A; *Sermons*, 99.
47. Sermon 26 on Ephesians, *CO* 51:262C; *Sermons*, 26.
48. Sermon 1 on Ephesians, *CO* 51:253C; *Sermons*, 16.
49. Sermon 20 on Ephesians, *CO* 51:496A; *Sermons*, 295.

ing for the guidance of the Holy Spirit. They have been delivered from the false teachers and superstitious teaching of the Roman Church in a way no less remarkable than the original inclusion of the Gentiles into the covenant made with Israel. They know what the "papists" still say about free will, merits, saints, and the Mass, but they know now that such matters should be treated as "rubbish" compared to the surpassing worth of knowing God in Christ Jesus. They should know that the fact that they are now students in the school of Christ is a sign that the Holy Spirit is at work among them. "Now then when we see the holy Scripture truly expounded and applied rightly to our use, we know that the Spirit of God bears us testimony that he dwells among us, provided that we learn to receive so excellent a gift and that we realize that such is the homage that our Lord Jesus demands from us."[50] They have heard Scripture truly expounded and rightly applied for decades now, and have been encouraged to read Scripture for themselves.

And yet for all this, Calvin still wonders whether they have profited from the teaching of God, or rather have been made even worse by the preaching of the gospel. People may have the gospel on their tongues more than they did before, but their lives betray what they confess. "But we see even among all that bear the name of Christians that their whole life is disordered and loose, inasmuch that they mock God to the full and despise all religion, and yet nevertheless in the meanwhile think . . . that they are greatly wronged if they are not taken as good and catholic Christians."[51] Many use the freedom of the gospel to make as much profit as they possibly can, often at their neighbors' expense. "A man will find that they who are converted to the gospel often take most liberty to do evil. . . . But they have so profited in reverse from God's school that they are far more wily than they were before in looking after their own interest and advantage, and in taking more liberty, and in making themselves believe that all things are lawful for them."[52] Even pagans knew of the proper way to order marriage by the law of nature, but those who have benefited from clear doctrine and exhortations concerning marriage appear to be no better than beasts to Calvin. "But now we have teaching and we have exhortations added to spur us further forward, in order that we should not flatter ourselves in our vices; but how much have we profited? It is to be seen daily that men storm at their wives, and wives are pert with their husbands."[53]

The problem, according to Calvin, is that everyone is resistant to the message of the gospel and is a very reluctant student of God in the

50. Sermon 25 on Ephesians, *CO* 51:555B; *Sermons*, 363.
51. Sermon 1 on Ephesians, *CO* 51:251C; *Sermons*, 14.
52. Sermon 31 on Ephesians, *CO* 51:636B; *Sermons*, 453.
53. Sermon 42 on Ephesians, *CO* 51:778C; *Sermons*, 612.

church. Both preaching and the Scriptures are clear enough and are accommodated to our capacities, but for all that, Calvin thinks that we make up endless excuses in trying to explain why the gospel does not pertain to us. Some use the fact that they are ordinary, unlearned Christians as an excuse not to know what is required of them. "Now therefore let us not plead that we are ignorant and thickheaded, nor the biggest idiots in the world who think they escape by subterfuges, saying, I am no scholar, I never went to school. For God has stooped in such a way that all of us from the greatest to the least may be taught in a familiar fashion by his Word."[54] Others use the excuse of the alleged novelty of the preaching of the gospel to remain with what they had always been taught, presumably under the Roman Church.

> Some having heard sermons, or having been taught at some lecture, or by some other means, will perhaps say, It is possible that this may be true, and as for me, I will not oppose it, but since I am no cleric or divine, it is all the same to me, I will leave it to take its ordinary course. Some other will say, Ho! I will keep the faith of my forefathers, for it is too dangerous a matter to change. Some again may say thus, How so? It is a new doctrine that we have never heard before.[55]

Still others claim to be incapable of comprehending the truth, all the while hiding the fact that they think they are wiser than God in his Word.

> And for proof of this, men will always judge according to their own ideas, so that if anything is propounded to them out of God's Word, they say, Is it so? And how is that possible? They reason, they call it into question: Is it so? . . . We see, then, that they simply lie in saying they are dull and slow-minded, for they think quite the opposite. The starkest idiots, I say, and the biggest dolts of them all consider themselves to have a wisdom exceeding that of God.[56]

Calvin thinks that all people have a strong affinity for empty doctrines, no matter how complex, but once they are presented with the simple and true wisdom of God in the school of Christ, they claim they are too ignorant to understand. "We are insatiable when anybody feeds us with vanities and falsehoods, but if God calls us to his school, we shrink back as much as we possibly can, and we even set this before us as a shield, that we are simple, and that we have but a small and dull understanding,

54. Sermon 37 on Ephesians, *CO* 51:715A; *Sermons*, 542.
55. Sermon 14 on Ephesians, *CO* 51:414–15; *Sermons*, 202.
56. Sermon 7 on Ephesians, *CO* 51:326–27; *Sermons*, 100.

and that the secrets of God's Word are too deep and incomprehensible for us."[57]

Because of the deep and persistent resistance the scholars of God have to the lessons God wishes to teach them in God's school, it is necessary for pastors to do much more than expound Scripture and teach doctrine in their sermons. As we have already seen above, Calvin thought that pastors were like teachers in that both teach doctrine and expound Scripture; but pastors, unlike teachers, not only expound Scripture, but also apply it to the use of their congregation. "Now then when we see the holy Scripture truly expounded *and applied rightly to our use*, we know that the Spirit of God bears us testimony that he dwells among us."[58] Ultimately, Calvin thinks our resistance to the gospel comes from our refusal to apply the gospel to our own use, so that we might profit from it, because our affections are all contrary to it. We would much prefer to preach the gospel to others than apply it to our own use. "This teaching would be easy enough to understand, if we were not utterly perverted by our wicked affections. And indeed every man is a great teacher when it is a question of preaching to others, but yet, clear and well known as these things are, no one can apply them to their own use."[59] When it comes to preaching, doctrine, and the ability to read Scripture for themselves, Calvin thinks his congregation is in far better shape than it was under the Roman Church. But when it comes to putting the doctrine of God into practice in their lives, those who belong to the "reformation" are no better than the papists from whom they fled.

> As for us, although we have the light of the gospel and can say that the superstitions of the papacy are but trifles, yet we are nevertheless far off from God's teaching. . . . As for the gospel, most men take what they like of it and tread God's truth under their feet as often as they please. In short, you will find that they who boast most often of the reformation nowadays, are unholy and unclean people, yes and for the most part even dogs that bark against God, despise his truth, and blaspheme against his Word, unless it is that they let it slip because they think it is neither here nor there.[60]

57. Ibid.

58. Sermon 25 on Ephesians, *CO* 51:555B; *Sermons*, 363, my emphasis.

59. Sermon 30 on Ephesians, *CO* 51:623B; *Sermons*, 439. In an interesting discussion of what spiritual age his congregation is, Calvin draws an example from a student of the liberal arts and sciences. "At the same time, it may well come to pass that a child of twenty years shall have all the branches of knowledge, in which he has been trained and instructed; but yet he may still be superficial [*volage*] for all that, he may not have the skill to apply them to his use [*appliquer cela en usage*], because he is not yet mature" (sermon 26 on Ephesians, *CO* 51:571C; *Sermons*, 381–82). One wonders if Calvin is drawing from his initial years in Geneva, when he was very well instructed and formed in all knowledge, but did not know how to put such knowledge to profitable use.

60. Sermon 30 on Ephesians, *CO* 51:623C; *Sermons*, 439.

In order rightly to apply the meaning of Scripture to the use of his congregation, Calvin thinks that the preacher must do much more than simply instruct the congregation in what they do not know, for in large part the truth is clear enough to all. Rather, the preacher has to bring the meaning of Scripture to bear on every aspect of the lives of the congregation, so that they feel the force of its teaching, and so that it bears fruit in their lives. "Our resorting to sermons must not be only to hear things we do not know, but also to be stirred up to do our duty and to be wakened when we are slack and slothful by good and holy warnings, and to be rebuked if there be any stubbornness and malice in us."[61] Sermons must include not only teaching, but also exhortations, warnings, incitements, and rebukes, not only in general but in particular. Because we are resistant to the doctrine we hear from God, general teaching is simply not enough, because it does not come to grips with our lives in the concrete, and does not expose the secret recesses in which we hide from what we learn from God. For example, if we were truly teachable, it would be enough for us to hear that we must be reformed according to the image of God in Christ. But because we are resistant to this teaching and want it to go away, God must spell this out in detail so that it comes to grips with us.

> Now if he had gone no further than this, that teaching would have been received without contradiction, but in the meantime no one would have profited from it as by a living instruction. But now he will speak of lewdness, of theft, of deceitfulness, of drunkenness, of hatred, of spite, and of the sly practices that take place among neighbors. When matters are thus explained in detail, men are the more awakened.[62]

In order for us to profit from the instruction we receive in God's school, the exposition of Scripture in sermons must ultimately lead to the exposure of the inmost thoughts and affections of each member of the congregation.

> But we are so entangled in our vanities that if God only says generally that we must be reformed according to his image, and utterly deny ourselves, it does not touch us at all, but we let it pass by. Therefore he has to spell it out in detail, as if he made an anatomy of our affections and thoughts, and brings to light the vices which we want to harbor secretly.[63]

61. Sermon 43 on Ephesians, *CO* 51:783B; *Sermons*, 618.
62. Sermon 30 on Ephesians, *CO* 51:624–25; *Sermons*, 440.
63. Sermon 30 on Ephesians, *CO* 51:624–25; *Sermons*, 440.

The sermon only attains its objective if it brings the meaning contained in every word of Scripture to bear on the lives of the members of the congregation. This is what Calvin has in mind when he speaks of "Holy Scripture truly expounded and rightly applied to our use."[64] Every word written in the letter to the Ephesians contains a meaning that must be brought to bear on the lives of the congregation in Geneva. This is why Calvin repeatedly tells his congregation that nothing that Paul wrote is superfluous; nothing was written or added by him without cause.[65] On the contrary, Calvin can tell the Genevans in his congregation why Paul wrote every single word that he set down in his letter to the Ephesians, because Calvin is convinced that Paul was addressing the same resistant students in Ephesus that Calvin is preaching to in Geneva. Calvin wants the Genevans to see what Paul had in mind as he wrote his letter, what he intended or wished to say when he set each word down on the parchment, in light of the impact Paul wanted his words to have on those who read his letter. Hence, his exposition of the letter focuses on the intention of Paul, and what Paul wanted his words to do in the Ephesians, and by extension, in the Genevans. In other words, the method taken by Calvin in the sermons is inductive: Calvin re-creates the process and context in the Ephesians that led Paul to write what he did, in order to show the Genevans why Paul added every sentence, every phrase, and every word; for the entire letter contains meaning that must be applied to our lives so that we might profit from it.

Calvin's Method of Preaching: Exposition, Retention, and Application to Use and Practice

Exposition

In order to reach his objective of having the meaning of Scripture bear fruit in the lives of his congregation, Calvin followed a very deliberate method with regard to the exposition and application of Scripture. The first step consisted of the exposition of the passage in Scripture on which he was preaching, so that he might reveal the meaning contained in the words Paul used. Calvin used many different terms for this aspect of his work, saying that what he intended to do was to expound (*exposer*), to explain (*deduire*), to deal with (*depescher*), to explicate (*expliquer*), or

64. "*Vraye exposition de l'Escriture saincte, et qu'elle est appliquee droitment à nostre usage*" (sermon 25 on Ephesians, *CO* 51:555B; *Sermons*, 363).

65. A constant refrain in the sermons is the statement, "*Ce n'est point sans cause que sainct Paul dit*," or "*Ce n'est point superflue que sainct Paul dit*," or "*C'est pourquoy sainct Paul dit ici*." For Calvin, the smallest of words may contain the greatest of meanings.

to resolve (*resoudre*) the passage in question.[66] Unlike the commentary on Ephesians, Calvin does not explicate the meaning of the letter in his sermons by means of the original historical and linguistic context of the epistle, but rather in light of the meaning contained in the words Paul uses, always referenced in French translation. In his sermons, Calvin of course assumes the work of the commentaries, but he builds on the revelation of the author's mind, guided by the context in seeking to show the congregation the meaning of the words they hear and read in French. At times this will involve pointing out to them that a word Paul uses has at least two meanings.[67] At other times, Calvin will explain how Paul's words may sound unusual to French ears.[68] But this is the exception and not the rule, as in the commentary. Calvin usually proceeds to show the congregation the meaning that is contained in the words of Paul (*ce qui est ici contenu en ces mots de sainct Paul*).[69] And he usually takes only one or two words at a time in doing this, out of his conviction that each passage contains a great meaning in a few words.[70]

The goal for exposing the meaning of the words is to arrive at the intention of Paul expressed in the passage, for Calvin is convinced that the words Paul uses are all meant to show his intention. Hence, when Paul adds a few words to a phrase, Calvin says that he does this to show his intention better.[71] Indeed, where the meaning of the words is under dispute, the meaning can be attained by following the intention of Paul in the passage, as in the abuse of Eph. 6:12, used by "some heretics in old time" to show two principal powers, God and the devil. "Nevertheless, if we pay attention to the intention of Paul, this question will be easily resolved."[72] The intention of Paul therefore seems to function in the sermons in the same way that the mind of Paul functions in the commentary,

66. Sermon 1 on Ephesians, *CO* 51:245B; *Sermons*, 7. Sermon 2 on Ephesians, *CO* 51:269C; *Sermons*, 33. Sermon 39 on Ephesians, *CO* 51:744C; *Sermons*, 575. Sermon 23 on Ephesians, *CO* 51:529C; *Sermons*, 334. Sermon 1 on Ephesians, *CO* 51:255C; *Sermons*, 18.

67. Calvin indicates that the words "blessing" and "love" can be taken in at least two senses. Sometimes he expounds on both senses, as in his discussion of blessing, and at other times he simply goes with what he calls the genuinely true and natural sense of Paul's words. See sermons 1, 2, and 20 on Ephesians, *CO* 51:255A, 269B, 493C; *Sermons*, 17, 33, 293.

68. Sermon 19 on Ephesians, *CO* 51:482B; *Sermons*, 279. Sermon 45 on Ephesians, *CO* 51:811C; *Sermons*, 650. Sermon 48 on Ephesians, *CO* 51:586B; *Sermons*, 700.

69. Sermon 5 on Ephesians, *CO* 51:306B; *Sermons*, 76.

70. "*Or voici un passage qui est bien digne d'estre noté, et laquel aussi contient une grande sentence en peu de mots*" (sermon 45 on Ephesians, *CO* 51:814B; *Sermons*, 653).

71. "And St. Paul shows his meaning even better [*monstre encores mieux son intention*] when he adds that 'we should walk as children of light'" (sermon 35 on Ephesians, *CO* 51:685B; *Sermons*, 509).

72. Sermon 46 on Ephesians, *CO* 51:823B; *Sermons*, 663.

for Calvin uses the mind of Paul to resolve conflicts of interpretation as well.[73] Although in the commentary Calvin will speak interchangeably of the mind and intention of Paul, in the sermons Calvin speaks only of the intention of Paul. Calvin repeatedly speaks of what Paul wanted to say (*a voulu dire*), what intention (*esgard*) he had, what he intended (*a pretendu, a entendu*) to say, what he had in mind (*a regardé*), what he wanted to show us (*a voulu monstrer*), as well as the line of argument Paul was pursuing (*l'argument qu'il trait*), or the theme (*propos*) he was continuing; for Calvin wants the Genevans to be aware of the deliberate intent behind every word set down by Paul in the letter.[74] When he expounds upon Eph. 1:10, "to gather all things together both in heaven and in earth, by Jesus Christ, in himself," Calvin says, "As for the word 'gather,' St. Paul meant to show (*a voulu monstrer*) us thereby how we are all of us in a state of dreadful dissipation, till such time as our Lord Jesus Christ restores us."[75] The exposition of each passage of Paul's letter is concerned above all else to show *why* Paul says what he does, why he uses each and every word, and what difference each word was intended to make in the church, both in Ephesus and in Geneva. So, for instance, when Calvin expounds the meaning of the phrase, "if you have heard him" from Ephesians 4:21, he says, "That then, in sum, is the reason why St. Paul adds that it is not so with us, for we have learned Jesus Christ. And how? 'You have heard him,' he says. And his setting down of those words is in order to cut off all opportunity of making a shield of ignorance."[76]

To show the intention of Paul in a passage, Calvin will go on to describe, often at length and in great detail, the circumstances in us and in our lives that make the words of Paul both necessary and significant. Thus, after showing that Paul added the words, "You have heard him," to cut off the excuse of ignorance, Calvin proceeds to show how some plead the excuse of ignorance in divine matters, saying, "I am a poor idiot. I am not able to busy myself in such matters; it is impossible for

---

73. "They stray far from Paul's thought [*a Pauli mente*], who twist this text for the purpose of injuring the righteousness of faith. . . . We must look to Paul's design [*Pauli intentio*] . . . ; what has this to do with Paul's intention [*ad Pauli mentem*]?" (Comm. on Eph. 2:10, *CO* 51:167A; *CNTC* 11:146). This passage indicates that for Calvin the mind of Paul is synonymous with the intention of Paul. However, in the sermons, Calvin speaks only of the intention of Paul, never of the mind of Paul.

74. Sermon 1 on Ephesians, *CO* 51:254B; *Sermons*, 7. Sermon 2 on Ephesians, *CO* 51:260B; *Sermons*, 23. Sermon 24 on Ephesians, *CO* 51:546A; *Sermons*, 352. Sermon 2 on Ephesians, *CO* 51:269C; *Sermons*, 33. Sermon 1 on Ephesians, *CO* 51:251A; *Sermons*, 12. Sermon 25 on Ephesians, *CO* 51:561C; *Sermons*, 370. Sermon 27 on Ephesians, *CO* 51:589C; *Sermons*, 401.

75. Sermon 4 on Ephesians, *CO* 51:294A; *Sermons*, 62.

76. Sermon 29 on Ephesians, *CO* 51:607A; *Sermons*, 421.

me to put my mind to that study."[77] So also, in order to show how all is disordered until it is gathered into Christ, Calvin asks his congregation to examine themselves in light of these words of Paul, asking, "Who are you, O wretched creature? For you see that you are separated from God even from your birth. . . . You ought not only to feel this disorder in your own person, but also perceive that everything else is out of order throughout the whole world because of your perverseness."[78] The meaning and intention of Paul can only be rightly seen if the congregation has in mind the circumstances within the Ephesians, and within themselves, that gave rise to Paul writing these words in the first place.

The context that ultimately reveals the meaning and intention of Paul lies not in the world out of which the epistle came but, rather, in the experience, thoughts, perceptions, and affections of the congregation in Geneva. If Calvin is careful to interpret the epistle in his commentary in its original linguistic and historical context, he is insistent from the beginning of his sermons that what Saint Paul taught the Ephesians is to be taught to the church at all times and places. "When we read the epistles which St. Paul wrote to a variety of places, we must always consider that God meant they should serve not only for one time alone, or for certain people only, but for ever, and in general for the whole church."[79] In the sermons, Calvin brings the general doctrine of God in the epistle to bear on the lives of the people of Geneva in his own day. "We see that the doctrine which is contained in this epistle is directed and dedicated to us at this present day."[80] Paul's intention can be fully known only when the congregation has a vivid sense of the nature of their own lives, for it is these lives that the words of Paul are meant to address.

Retention

Once the intention of Paul is made clear from the words he used in the passage, Calvin is confident that he and his congregation have arrived at the natural sense of Paul's words, of what Paul gives them to understand.[81] He usually indicates his satisfaction with the clarity and faithfulness of his exposition by saying, "We see, then, St. Paul's intention

77. *CO* 51:607A; *Sermons*, 421.

78. Sermon 4 on Ephesians, *CO* 51:294C; *Sermons*, 62.

79. Sermon 1 on Ephesians, *CO* 51:245B; *Sermons*, 7: "Now these things serve not only for the city of Ephesus, nor for any one country, nor for any one age or time, but we have need to be urged on more and more, seeing that the devil strives ceaselessly to turn us to evil."

80. Sermon 1 on Ephesians, *CO* 51:246B; *Sermons*, 8.

81. Sermon 24 on Ephesians, *CO* 51:546B; *Sermons*, 353. Sermon 1 on Ephesians, *CO* 51:257A; *Sermons*, 20.

(*nous voyons donc maintenant l'intention de sainct Paul*)."[82] This leads Calvin to his next objective in the sermons—appealing to the congregation to keep the intention and meaning of Paul's words in mind, lest they forget them or no longer think about them. Again, Calvin uses a variety of expressions that all convey the necessity of keeping the meaning of Paul in mind and not forgetting or ignoring it. He will say that this is what we have to gather (*recueillir*) from Paul's words, or what we have to observe (*a observer*), to retain (*a retenir*), to note (*noter*), and to have in memory (*ayons memoire, reduire en memoire*).[83] He also advises his congregation to weigh carefully (*peser*) the words of Paul, to meditate and ruminate on the words, so that they might become imprinted (*imprimé*) on their hearts and spirits.[84] As in his exposition of Paul's words and intention, Calvin will describe at length the circumstances that make it necessary for us to keep the meaning of Paul in mind. One of the most persistent dangers he cites has to do with the superstitious teaching and practice of the "papists," meaning not the official theologians of the Roman Church, but the friends, relatives, and neighbors of the Genevans.[85] Calvin often contrasts the meaning of Paul they are to keep in mind with the sayings of the papists regarding free will, merits, and especially the patronage of the saints and the sacrifice of the Mass. Thus, after speaking of the intention of Paul to make us fall in love with the gospel that brings true peace with God, Calvin contrasts this with the foolish self-confidence of the "papists," who treat God like a baby who can be pacified with trifles.

> And in fact what are the things with which they would try to content God but trifles and petty rubbish, as if they were trying to quiet a baby? The papists must take a sprinkling of holy water; also they cross themselves endlessly; they must keep this and that vigil; they must gad about on pilgrimage; they must forbear eating flesh on such a day; they must babble so many paternosters; they must light a candle to such a saint; they must hear so many masses; they must say so many mea culpas. In short, when a man

---

82. Thus, for example, sermon 7 on Ephesians, *CO* 51:332C; *Sermons*, 101; and sermon 5 on Ephesians, *CO* 51:300A; *Sermons*, 70. He will also use all of his synonyms for Paul's intention, as we have given above.

83. Sermon 3 on Ephesians, *CO* 51:282B; *Sermons*, 48. Sermon 6 on Ephesians, *CO* 51:317B; *Sermons*, 89. Sermon 1 on Ephesians, *CO* 51:249A; *Sermons*, 11. Sermon 1 on Ephesians, *CO* 51:249C; *Sermons*, 12. Sermon 45 on Ephesians, *CO* 51:810C; *Sermons*, 649.

84. Sermon 41 on Ephesians, *CO* 51:766A; *Sermons*, 598. Sermon 47 on Ephesians, *CO* 51:843A; *Sermons*, 685.

85. Parker (*Calvin's Preaching*, 127) makes the same point: "The exodus of priests, monks and nuns in 1535–6 certainly did not mean that there were no Romanists left in Geneva. The *Registres* show how some of the old habits and practices lingered on in a usually quiet sort of way. Calvin had to win people over to become Bible Christians."

has raked them all into a heap, it is certain that they are but scrapings of all that stinks. And yet, it seems to them that God is well paid with them, as though he were being treated like an idol or a babe, as I said before.[86]

On the other hand, he warns them of the danger of trying to find peace with God by blotting all remembrance of God from their minds and consciences, as do the scoffers "who simply nod their heads when men speak to them of their salvation, saying, It is enough if we give only one good sigh, but let us alone in the meantime to have a good time; for what a thing it would be to pass the whole of our life in such melancholy? That would do us no good, and therefore let us enjoy ourselves together."[87]

Keeping the words of Paul in their minds and memories and engraved in their hearts will keep his congregation from being led astray by the folly of the papists, who treat God like a baby, and the scoffers, who want to forget God altogether. In a rare reference to a specific recent event in Geneva, Calvin speaks of how prominent members of his congregation did not keep in mind Paul's injunction to use our gifts to build up the body of Christ, using their gifts instead to make and sell liturgical vestments for the Mass.

> If a silversmith should make a cross on a chalice, he should be punished as he deserves. If some other man makes this or that, useful for popish superstitions, it shall not be countenanced. If a merchantman sells rosary-beads, he shall have his punishment as he deserves. But if a man sells chasubles, albs, and all such other trinkets of the mass, that is to be allowed and borne with! Nevertheless this has been done.[88]

So also, forgetting the words of Paul that we are not to have among us any wantonness or foolish talk, Calvin thinks the women of Geneva have gone from bad to worse in their talk and clothing.

> For women have been allowed for a long time to become increasingly audacious. And besides, speech apart, there are also very provocative clothes, so that it is very hard to discern whether they are men or women. They appear in new dresses and trinkets, so that every day some new disguise is seen. . . . Then too ribald songs are a part of their behavior.[89]

Husbands who forget the words of Paul—that they are to love their wives as their own bodies—think to themselves about their wives, "I cannot live with her, she is a mad beast, there is nothing in her but pride and

86. Sermon 14 on Ephesians, *CO* 51:416C; *Sermons*, 202.
87. Sermon 14 on Ephesians, *CO* 51:417A; *Sermons*, 202.
88. Sermon 23 on Ephesians, *CO* 51:537B; *Sermons*, 341–42.
89. Sermon 34 on Ephesians, *CO* 51:674–75; *Sermons*, 497.

haughtiness and rebellion. I cannot say a word to her without her paying me back with four." On the other hand, one who does keep these words of Paul in mind will think to himself, even when he does not have all that might be desired in his wife, "Yet I am bound to her; yes, and I am not only bound to my wife but also to God, who presides over marriage, and to our Lord Jesus Christ, who is like a mirror and living image of it to us. Therefore I am bound to do my duty toward my wife, and both to love her and support her, even though there may be vices in her."[90]

Application to Use and Practice

As these examples make clear, retaining the intention and meaning of Paul in our minds, hearts, and memories is meant to have a direct impact on the way we think about everything we do, from the least to the greatest act, for it is our interior thoughts that lead to our external actions. Calvin's method in his sermons is to bring Paul's meaning and intention to light, so that the congregation might always have that meaning in mind, in order to transform the way they think and the way they live. So, for instance, if we kept Paul's injunction and example in mind, to pray at all times for the whole church of Christ, our prayer life would be different. "Now if this were well printed in our hearts (as I said before) we should be very alert to pray to our God without end and without ceasing."[91] One can see, therefore, that appealing to the congregation to keep Paul's meaning in mind is but the first step as Calvin applies Scripture to the use, profit, and practice of the congregation. The much greater length of the sermons, noted above, is directly related to Calvin's concern that his congregation profit from the doctrine of Paul. "But this needs to be explained at greater length, that we may understand it and fare the better (*facions nostre profit*) by it."[92] This dynamic is revealed by a transitional expression that frequently recurs throughout the sermons: "That, therefore, is what we have to bear in mind (*à retenir*) from the words St. Paul speaks here. But every one of us ought to apply it generally to his own use (*appliquer cela à son usage*)."[93] So, for instance, when Paul speaks of those who were far off being brought near, he says that Paul intended to show us that everything we invent to distinguish ourselves from others is nothing before God, because what unites us before God is that we were saved by God's mercy from our common miserable plight.

90. Sermon 41 on Ephesians, *CO* 51:763–64; *Sermons*, 596–97.
91. Sermon 47 on Ephesians, *CO* 51:843A; *Sermons*, 685.
92. Sermon 38 on Ephesians, *CO* 51:462B; *Sermons*, 257.
93. Sermon 6 on Ephesians, *CO* 51:310C; *Sermons*, 82.

Now we must apply this well to our own use (*appliquer ceci à nostre usage*). . . . Every man searches and seeks as much as possible to bring forward something for which God has accepted him rather than his neighbors. But let us learn that although we were near God in outward appearance, yet nevertheless the only way to be in his favor and to be able to call on him . . . is that Jesus Christ is our Head.[94]

The application to our use is directly related to the way we are to profit from what we learn in Scripture. Thus, after Calvin comments on the meaning of Paul's description of God as the Father of our Lord Jesus Christ, noting that God gives himself to us in Christ, he says: "And so you see in sum what we have to bear in mind. Yet, that we may the better profit from this passage, let us take note that we must check ourselves lest we wander into many speculations when we know God, the Father of our Lord Jesus Christ." Calvin goes on to contrast seeking to know God in Christ with the invented idols of the "papists" and the Turks, so that we might seek access to God in Jesus Christ alone, God's living image, who is adapted to our finite capacities.[95]

Finally, the application to use and profit is directly related to putting the lesson learned from Paul into practice. Thus, after he expounds the meaning of Paul's exhortation "Be angry and sin not," Calvin says, "Now we see St. Paul's intention. And therefore let us put this teaching into practice, the first point of which is carefully to examine the evil that is in us, that we may be angry with ourselves."[96] So also, when Paul exhorts us to labor to the benefit of those in need, Calvin asks us to consider whether our vocations genuinely profit others. "That is what we have to remember from this doctrine of St. Paul. And it behooves us to put this teaching so much the more in practice, when we consider that theft is more rife nowadays in the world than it ever was."[97]

As these transitions make clear, Calvin assumes that there is an important distinction that must be kept in mind at all times between the meaning and intention of Paul, best summarized as the teaching or doctrine of Paul, and the way we apply that doctrine to use and put that doctrine into practice. For instance, Calvin assumes that the doctrine of Paul concerning marriage is very clear and familiar to his congregation. However, he also knows that everyone has an excuse as to why he or she cannot put this doctrine into practice. "This teaching is clear and familiar enough of itself, but yet for all that, how is it practiced in the world? People would gladly plead the excuse of ignorance to get out of

94. Sermon 13 on Ephesians, *CO* 51:402–3; *Sermons*, 188–89.
95. Sermon 1 on Ephesians, *CO* 51:256B; *Sermons*, 19.
96. Sermon 31 on Ephesians, *CO* 51:632B; *Sermons*, 449.
97. Sermon 31 on Ephesians, *CO* 638A; *Sermons*, 455.

the performance of their duty by saying this is too high and hard to understand."[98] As indicated previously, Calvin was confident that there had been great improvement in the truth of the doctrine preached, taught, and read in the church of Geneva since it had been freed from the papacy. He repeatedly shows his congregation that the doctrine of Scripture should give rise to very different practice than the doctrine of the Roman Church. For instance, Roman doctrine teaches us to trust in our own strength, and thus causes us to falter in uncertainty, whereas Paul teaches us to despair of ourselves and rely only on the Lord for our strength. "Thus you see how we ought to put this teaching of St. Paul into practice."[99] But he was not at all convinced that there had been any improvement in the way the doctrine of God was being applied to use and put into practice by his own congregation, in spite of decades of preaching. "But now we have teaching and we have exhortations added to spur us further forward, in order that we should not flatter ourselves in our vices; but how much have we profited?"[100] Thus, when Calvin expounds the teaching of Paul that the one who steals should do so no more, he asks, "But let us see how this teaching is put into practice." His conclusion is rather striking: "But they have so profited in reverse in God's school that they are far more wily than they were before in looking after their own interest and advantage, and in taking more liberty, and in making themselves believe that all things are lawful for them."[101]

Above all else, Calvin is concerned in his sermons to expound the doctrine of Paul so clearly, so thoroughly, and so forcefully that it might actually be practiced by his congregation; for he realizes that the most difficult transition to make is from instruction in doctrine to practice in life. For example, in spite of the repeated teaching of Scripture that our God is merciful, true, and powerful, our hearts waver at the slightest threats. "So much the more therefore does it behoove us to put this doctrine into practice, and to exercise ourselves in it night and day that we may taste it thoroughly." When we seem to be overwhelmed by adversity, with no way to escape and no help in sight, we ought to recall the promises of God and think thus within ourselves: "Who is it that has spoken? Who is it that has promised to be our defender? Is it not he that is almighty? Could he not with one puff blow away all that the devil contrives? Though all the world were against us, what could it do, provided that our Lord vouchsafed to maintain our cause?"[102]

98. Sermon 42 on Ephesians, *CO* 51:778; *Sermons*, 612.
99. Sermon 45 on Ephesians, *CO* 51:817–18; *Sermons*, 656–57.
100. Sermon 42 on Ephesians, *CO* 51:778C; *Sermons*, 612.
101. Sermon 31 on Ephesians, *CO* 51:636A; *Sermons*, 453.
102. Sermon 21 on Ephesians, *CO* 51:507B; *Sermons*, 308.

The best way to apply Scripture to our use and profit is to bring it into our inmost thoughts, where we deliberate within ourselves concerning all that we hide from others, and even seek to hide from God. This is why Calvin's favorite device in his sermons is the imagined interior monologue, used first to show the way we think when we forget what God teaches us in his school, and then to show what difference it makes to keep the doctrine of God in our inmost thoughts. Only when the meaning and intention of Paul changes the way we actually think in our hearts about God, others, and ourselves will Scripture profit us the way it is intended to do. The message of Paul's gospel is addressed directly to the heart, for it bears witness to the self-giving goodness and grace of God revealed in Jesus Christ through the gospel. "So then, seeing that God has given himself to us in the person of our Lord Jesus Christ, and that the whole fulness of the Godhead dwells in that great sanctuary . . . , ought we not to be fully satisfied when we have that, and to rest ourselves wholly there?"[103] We will only profit from this message if we are brought to a real awareness of the self-giving goodness of God, so that we might be ravished and inflamed in love for God and dedicate our lives to God from the inmost affection of our hearts. "To be brief, we must be sure of the infinite good that is done to us by our Lord Jesus Christ, in order that we may be ravished in love with our God and inflamed with a right affection to obey him, and keep ourselves strictly in awe of him, to honor him with all our thoughts, with all our affections, and with all our hearts."[104]

103. Sermon 18 on Ephesians, *CO* 51:471–72; *Sermons*, 267–68. For similar descriptions of the central message of Scripture, see also Parker, *Calvin's Preaching*, chap. 10.

104. Sermon 20 on Ephesians, *CO* 51:496A; *Sermons*, 295. Calvin sees Paul as having been ravished with the same astonishment himself. "And (as I told you) the only thing that is treated here is the expressing of God's inestimable goodness, insomuch that, instead of executing the office of teacher, to show and declare how we are joined to our Lord Jesus Christ, St. Paul himself is also astonished, and like a man ravished with wonder, confessing that he lacks sufficient and fit words to express adequately God's grace in vouchsafing to join and unite us to his only Son. . . . St. Paul was not able to express that grace, but rather showed us that it ought to ravish our minds in astonishment [*nous doit ravir in estonnement*]" (Sermon 42 on Ephesians, *CO* 51:780A, 781C; *Sermons*, 614, 615).

PART 2

CALVIN AS THEOLOGIAN

Calvin's tireless attempt to give guidance for both pastors and ordinary Christians in their reading of Scripture underscores the impression that in his theological thinking Calvin focuses exclusively on hearing over against seeing. The removal of images, statues, pictures, stained glass, and altars from the churches in Geneva reinforces this impression, as does the replacement of the daily Mass with the daily sermon. In other words, the first section of the book seems to confirm Carlos Eire's description of the transformation that Calvin created from the symbolic and visual world of the Roman Catholic Church to the verbal and exegetical world of the learned clergy.

> It was a cerebral, learned sort of religion, one that only allowed for the Word to stand as an image of the invisible reality of the spiritual dimension. In practical terms, this meant a very concrete shift from a world brimming over with physical, visible symbols that were open to a wider range of interpretations—some intentionally ambiguous—to one charged principally with verbal symbols that were subject to the interpretation of a carefully trained and ostensibly learned ministry.[1]

1. Carlos N. M. Eire, *War against the Idols: The Reformation of Worship from Erasmus to Calvin* (Cambridge: Cambridge University Press, 1986), 316.

However, as we shall see in the second section of the book, Calvin does not focus exclusively on hearing and reading the Word in his theological thinking, but always combines hearing the Word of God with seeing the living images of God, especially in creation and Christ.[2] Stated another way, Calvin does not merely focus on the truth of God, as that truth is revealed in Scripture, but also focuses on the beauty of God, as that beauty is revealed in God's works. Both the beauty and the truth of God combine together to reveal God as the author and source of every good thing. We only know God as the fountain of every good thing when we see with our eyes the beauty and glory of the goodness of God that is proclaimed to our ears.

To highlight the centrality of visual self-manifestation for Calvin, we begin by comparing Calvin's method of interpreting various passages of Scripture with Luther's, in order to discern the way Luther emphasizes hearing the Word and the way Calvin emphasizes seeing the image. We then turn to the programmatic chapter of the second section of the book, which shows how Calvin consistently combines visual manifestation with verbal proclamation in his theology. In his understanding of creation, Calvin begins with the visual self-manifestation of God, then moves on to the proclamation of the Creator in Scripture. In his understanding of Christ, on the other hand, Calvin begins with the proclamation of Christ crucified, then passes on to the self-manifestation of Christ in his glory. Given the centrality of visual self-manifestation for Calvin, the theologian needs to be especially skilled at holding to the analogy and anagoge between the visible symbol of God and the hidden reality that it represents. Calvin therefore is not an "either/or" theologian, as is often claimed, but rather is an analogical and anagogical theologian. This section of the book concludes with a consideration of the two most important living images of God for Calvin: the universe and Jesus Christ. Calvin wanted the godly to contemplate these images of God throughout their lives, so that they might come to know God as the author and fountain of every good thing, and so that they might increasingly express the image of God in their own lives.

2. This theme is explored in much greater detail and depth in my book *Image and Word in the Theology of John Calvin* (Notre Dame: University of Notre Dame Press, forthcoming).

8

Image and Word in the Theology of Martin Luther and John Calvin

One way to begin to discern the distinctive way Calvin thinks theologically is to compare him with the theologian whom he called his "father in the faith," Martin Luther. After all, it is highly likely that Calvin's reading of *The Freedom of a Christian* and *The Babylonian Captivity of the Christian Church* contributed decisively to his sudden conversion to teachableness. Moreover, I have elsewhere argued that Luther and Calvin are in fundamental agreement with regard to the foundation and confirmation of the assurance of faith, contrary to the received view that contrasts the two theologians on this issue.[1] Both base the assurance of faith on the forgiveness of sins freely offered to us by Christ in the gospel; and both insist that such assurance needs to be confirmed by the secondary support of the testimony of a good conscience, so that we know our faith is sincere and not feigned. This is not to deny that genuine differences exist between Luther and Calvin on this issue, such as their understanding of the law of Moses, the definition of repentance, and the role of images in

1. Randall C. Zachman, *The Assurance of Faith: Conscience in the Theology of Martin Luther and John Calvin* (Louisville: Westminster John Knox, 2005).

worship. I attempted to account for their differences by means of their central theological motifs: the theology of the cross for Luther, and God as the triune fountain of every good thing in Calvin.

On closer examination, however, it becomes clear that Luther and Calvin differ with regard to the relationship between seeing and hearing, and hence with regard to the relation of image to word. As a theologian of the cross, Luther consistently contrasts what we see with what we believe, and he claims that the truth is hidden under an appearance that contradicts it. Hence, we must listen to the Word that we hear, in spite of any appearance we see that contradicts it. On the other hand, Calvin always seeks to combine what we hear in the Word with what we see in what he calls "the living images of God," especially in creation and in Christ. According to Calvin, our knowledge is not certain until we see with our eyes the reality about which we are told in the Word, so that our eyes and ears consent together in the truth. Calvin's concern to combine the Word of God that we hear with the living images of God that we see stands in dramatic contrast to Luther's concern to highlight the opposition between the Word that we hear and what we see with our eyes. In other words, the differences between Luther and Calvin cannot be fully understood without taking into account the fundamentally different ways each of them understands the self-revelation of God and the way one appropriates that revelation.

One can see their different ways of thinking theologically in the way they understand the meaning of the Sabbath. Luther interprets the Sabbath solely in terms of the Word that God speaks to us and the words we address to God. "This is what the Sabbath, or the rest of God, means, on which God speaks with us through his Word and we, in turn, speak with him through prayer and faith."[2] Calvin, on the other hand, interprets the Sabbath as affording us the time to contemplate the living image of God in creation. "This is, indeed, the proper business of the whole life, in which men should daily exercise themselves, to consider the infinite goodness, justice, power, and wisdom of God, in this magnificent theater of heaven and earth."[3] Ironically, scholars have missed this difference by reading Calvin as being too much like Luther on this issue, as though he highlighted the Word that is heard in contrast to the image that is seen. This is understandable, given Calvin's rejection of human images in places of worship, along with his emphasis on the sermon, and his description of the church as "the school of Christ."[4] However,

2. *Vorlesung über 1. Mose von 1535–1545*, WA 43:462.18–21; *Lectures on Genesis*, LW 1:81.

3. Comm. on Gen. 2:3, *CO* 23:33A.

4. Carlos N. M. Eire, *War against the Idols: The Reformation of Worship from Erasmus to Calvin* (Cambridge: Cambridge University Press, 1986).

Calvin rejects images created by the human imagination so we can fix our undivided attention on the living images of God, in which the invisible God becomes somewhat visible before our eyes. We cannot fully appreciate the differences between Luther and Calvin unless we attend to the way Luther consistently *contrasts* what we hear with what we see and feel, whereas Calvin consistently *combines* what we hear with what we see and feel.

Luther bases our knowledge of God on the truth of the Word of God, which he understands in light of the power or omnipotence of God. What God declares to us in the Word, God will do, no matter how impossible or foolish it appears to human reason. "Therefore we must take note of God's power, that we may be completely without doubt about the things which God promises in his Word. Here full assurance is given concerning all his promises, nothing is either so difficult or so impossible that he could not bring it about by his Word."[5] Faith clings to the truth of the Word that is *heard* in opposition to what reason and conscience *see* and *feel*. Luther therefore emphasizes what God *declares* to us—the Word of absolution declaring the forgiveness of sins—and understands the sacraments as signs added to the Word of God, in which the power of God performs what the Word declares. Christ in the Supper declares that our sins are forgiven and that he is giving to us his body and blood. We are to trust in the truth of the Word of Christ, not in what we see or feel, so that we might comfort our terrified consciences with the word of absolution and confirm our faith with the body and blood of Christ given to us to eat and drink. This is not to deny that Luther does speak of visible signs and symbols in a positive way, as being an important component of the "clothing" that God wears in order to reveal Godself to us. "Nor does he confirm [his truth] with spiritual proofs; he confirms it with tangible proofs. For I see the water, I see bread and wine, and I see the minister. All this is physical, and in these material forms he reveals himself."[6] Such material signs are especially needed for the weak in faith. "For as I have often said, the signs and visions that God gives in addition to the Word are needed to strengthen all the more the faith of weak or saddened souls who cannot cling to the mere Word as well as to a picture or sign."[7] However, Luther does not consistently speak of God becoming somewhat visible to us in living images, as does Calvin; the direction of Luther's theology leads him to emphasize the Word of God over and above the visible signs of God, along the lines of the theology of the cross, which contrasts what we see and feel with what we hear.

5. *Vorlesung über 1. Mose von 1535–1545*, WA 42:37; *LW* 1:49.
6. *Vorlesung über 1. Mose von 1535–1545*, WA 43:462.18–21; *LW* 5:49.
7. *Praelectiones in prophetas minores: Sacharja* (1525), WA 23:558.13–16; *LW* 20:222–23.

Calvin, on the other hand, speaks of the self-revelation of God in terms of living images of God, in which God renders Godself in a manner visible to us by representing Godself to us in images, mirrors, and pictures painted from life. According to Calvin, the universe is a living image of God, in which the powers of God—goodness, wisdom, power, and so on—are portrayed as in a painting. God created humanity in the image of God so that we might contemplate the powers portrayed to us in the world, and feel the force of these powers in ourselves to the point of enjoying them, so that piety and religion might take root in the inmost affection of our hearts, thereby lifting us up to God. Hence, the original self-representation of God in the universe was first to be *seen* by humanity and then *felt* and *enjoyed* within, for the self-representation of God truly presents and offers the goodness of God that it portrays and represents. Given human blindness and ingratitude, the image of God in the universe cannot be seen clearly without hearing the Word of God in Scripture through the Holy Spirit. Such hearing clarifies our seeing, so that we can be led to feel and enjoy the powers of God presented to us in the self-representation of God in the universe.

However, human sin has defaced the image of God within us and has transformed the image of God in the universe, so that we now see the curse of God against us in the universe, and feel the reason for it within our consciences, due to our poverty, sin, and blindness. God therefore represents Godself as the fountain of every good for sinners in Jesus Christ, the image of the invisible God, in whom God presents to sinners every good thing that they lost in Adam. Christ, in turn, offers himself to us in two distinct yet inseparable forms of self-manifestation. First, as in the manner of painters, Christ sketches a shadow-outline of himself in the shadows and types of the law, and then, after his manifestation in the flesh, he portrays the full and living image of his presence in the gospel and in the sacraments.[8] Faith unites us to the living image of God in Christ so that we participate in him with all his blessings. Faith also contemplates the image of Christ in the gospel, so that we are transformed into the image of God from one degree of glory to another (2 Cor. 3:18). Calvin thus understands the Supper as the way by which Christ both represents and presents himself to believers, through the Word they hear in conjunction with the signs that they see, so that they might be fed by his body and blood in order to be united with him in eternal life.

If this is true, then there appears to be a significant reversal at work in Luther and Calvin's theology regarding the relationship of word and image in Christian worship and in the self-revelation of God. Luther, unlike Calvin, insists on the freedom of Christians to use images as tes-

8. Comm. on Heb. 10:1, *OE* 19:153–54; *CNTC* 12:132.

timonies and memorials in their worship. "But images for memorial and witness, such as crucifixes and images of saints, are to be tolerated."[9] Yet when it comes to his understanding of the self-revelation of God, Luther makes a decided shift away from images to the Word of God, which we are to hear in contrast to what we see and feel. "I must not see, feel, know, or recognize anything. I must only listen and cling to the Word, basing everything on the Word of God alone."[10] Calvin, on the other hand, insists on the categorical prohibition of images in Christian worship, because they directly contradict the infinite, spiritual essence of God. "From this it is clear that every statue man erects, or every image he paints to represent God, simply displeases God as something dishonorable to his majesty."[11] Yet when it comes to the self-revelation of God, Calvin makes a decided shift toward the images of God that we see over and above the Word of God that we hear. "For God would have remained hidden afar off if Christ's splendor had not beamed upon us. For this purpose the Father laid up with his only-begotten Son all he had to reveal himself in Christ so that Christ, by communicating his Father's benefits, might express the true image of his Father."[12]

The distinctive way that Calvin highlights the image of God that we see, in contrast to Luther's emphasis on the Word of God that we hear, can be seen in the way they interpret different passages of Scripture. I have chosen a variety of texts that discuss the self-disclosure of God in the universe and in Christ, as well as the self-manifestation of Christ in the gospel and the sacraments. In what follows, we shall see how Luther interprets the visual elements of the texts in the direction of the Word that is heard, whereas Calvin will interpret the visual elements of the texts in the direction of the living images of God that are to be beheld and contemplated. By comparing the different ways they interpret the same texts, the different ways they think theologically can be more clearly illumined.

In Ps. 104:1, God is described as being "clothed with honor and majesty." Luther appeals to this passage in *De servo arbitrio* in order to make his claim that we only have to do with God as God is clothed, not with God's naked majesty. Although clothing is a visual metaphor, Luther interprets it in terms of the Word of God. "But we have something to do with him insofar as he is clothed and set forth in his Word, through which he offers himself to us and which is the beauty and glory with which

9. *Wider die himmlischen Propheten* (1525), WA 18:74.16–19; LW 40:91.

10. *Auslegung des ersten und zweiten Kapitels Johannis in Predigten* (1537–38), WA 46.664.20–23; LW 22:146.

11. *Inst*. 1.11.2, OS 3:89.22–25; LCC 1:101.

12. *Inst*. 3.2.1, OS 4:8.10–15; LCC 1:544.

the psalmist celebrates him as being clothed."[13] The clothed God is the preached God, in contrast to the hidden God. Hence, Luther interprets the visual image of clothing as referring to the verbal preaching of the gospel, in which God is clothed.

Calvin also makes a distinction between the essence of God that is hidden and the clothing in which God appears to us in his interpretation of Ps. 104:1. However, unlike Luther, Calvin interprets the clothing of God in terms of the universe as the living image of God, in which the invisible God appears in a manner visible to us. "In respect of his essence, God undoubtedly dwells in light that is inaccessible; but as he irradiates the whole world by his splendor, this is the garment in which he, who is hidden in himself, appears in a manner visible to us."[14] Calvin contrasts the hiddenness of God with the beautiful clothing of the world that we see and accentuates the beauty of that clothing: "That we may enjoy the sight of him, he must come forth to view in his clothing; that is to say, we must cast our eyes upon the very beautiful fabric of the world in which he wishes to be seen by us, and not be too curious and rash in searching into his secret essence."[15] Whereas Luther describes God as clothed in the Word of God we are to hear, Calvin interprets the clothing of God in terms of the beautiful form of the world we are to see.

The primacy of the verbal over the visual for Luther is further illustrated by the way he interprets Rom. 1:19, which speaks of the world as the visual manifestation of God. "For what can be known about God is plain to them, because God has shown it to them" (NRSV). Luther refers to this text in his lectures on Genesis, in the midst of his discussion of the self-revelation of God. "God . . . manifests and reveals himself to us in order that we might learn to know him. . . . First of all, it is God's Word itself, just as the creature is the oral Word of God by which all nations should know God, as Romans 1:19 says."[16] Once again, Luther interprets the language of self-manifestation in a decidedly verbal way, by speaking of the creature that is seen as the "oral Word of God" that is heard.

Calvin, on the other hand, interprets Rom. 1:19 in terms of his understanding of the universe as the appearance or representation of the invisible God. "By saying God manifested it he means that man was formed to be a spectator of the created world, and that he was endowed with eyes for the purpose of being led to God himself, the Author of the world, by contemplating so magnificent an image."[17] Calvin maintains his concentration on the visual self-representation of God in the universe

13. *De servo arbitrio* (1525), WA 18:685.16–17; *LW* 33:139.
14. Comm. on Ps. 104:1, *CO* 32:85A; CTS 11:145.
15. *CO* 32:85A; CTS 11:145.
16. *Vorlesung über 1. Mose von 1535–1545*, WA 43:606.34–35; *LW* 5:258.
17. Comm. on Rom. 1:19, *Romanos* 29.33–35; *CNTC* 8:31.

even when he insists that the Word of God is necessary to clarify our contemplation of the world, acting like spectacles. "For by the Scripture as our guide and teacher, he not only makes those things plain which would otherwise escape our notice, but almost compels us to behold them; as if he had assisted our dull sight with spectacles."[18] Calvin will even describe the way God is represented in Scripture itself in a visual way, in light of his insistence that God portrays Godself in Scripture the same way that God manifests Godself to us in the universe. "Indeed, in certain passages clearer descriptions are set forth for us, wherein his true appearance is exhibited, to be seen as in an image."[19]

The same dynamic can be seen in the different ways Luther and Calvin interpret texts that speak of the self-manifestation of God in Christ. For instance, John 1:18 speaks of Christ as the one who makes the invisible God known. "No one has ever seen God; the only Son, who is in the bosom of the Father, . . . has made him known" (RSV). Luther uses this text to distinguish between the "legal knowledge" of God based in reason and conscience, which worships the Creator on the basis of works of the law, with the "evangelical knowledge" of God, which comes through the preaching of Christ. "The knowledge of the Gospel is the face of Christ, the message that we have grace and truth through the death of Christ."[20] The evangelical knowledge of God comes from a message that is "proclaimed from above" by Christ, and not from anything that we see; and Christ himself is understood primarily as the one who teaches and preaches this gospel. "There is no other doctor, teacher or preacher who resides in the Godhead and is in the bosom of the Father but the one Doctor, Christ."[21]

Calvin, on the other hand, interprets John 1:18 by means of the contrast between the hiddenness of God and the visual self-manifestation of God in Christ, who is the living image of God. "Since God dwells in inaccessible light, he cannot be known except by Christ, his lively image."[22] The self-disclosure of God in Christ is now more vivid and visible than it was in Israel, for God "has now in a sense made himself visible. For certainly, when Christ is called 'the express image of God,' it refers to the special blessing of the New Testament."[23] However, even the fathers in Israel were allowed to see God in Christ, though at a distance and not as vividly as in the gospel. "We must also note that, when even the fathers wanted to behold God, they always turned their eyes to Christ."[24]

18. Comm. on Genesis, argumentum, *CO* 23:9–10; CTS 1:62.
19. *Inst*. 1.10.2, *OS* 3:86.6–8; LCC 1:97.
20. *WA* 46:6; *LW* 22:158.
21. *WA* 46:6; *LW* 22:156.
22. Comm. on John 1:18, *OE* 11/1:37.18–19; *CNTC* 4:25.
23. Comm. on John 1:18, *OE* 11/1:25–28; *CNTC* 4:25.
24. Comm. on John 1:18, *OE* 11/1:38.18–20; *CNTC* 4:26.

Hence, Calvin interprets John 1:18 as referring to the living image of God we see in Jesus Christ, even in the shadows of the law, whereas Luther interprets John 1:18 as referring to the preaching of Christ that we are to hear. "This, therefore, is certain—that God, who was formerly invisible, has now appeared in Christ."[25]

The same difference of approach can be seen in their interpretation of Matt. 11:27: "No one knows the Father except the Son and anyone to whom the Son chooses to reveal him" (NRSV). In the last sermon that he preached, Luther says that the Son reveals the Father only to "the childlike and simple, who consider themselves neither wise nor understanding, but rather hear and accept his Word," thereby locating the revealing work of the Son in the Word that he preaches.[26] Calvin, on the other hand, interprets the self-revelation of the Father in the Son in terms of the Son being the living image of God, which must be illumined by the Holy Spirit if we are to see it aright.

> It all comes back to this: It is the Father's gift that the Son is known, for by his Spirit he opens the eyes of our mind and we perceive the glory of Christ which would otherwise be hidden from us. But the Father, who dwells in light incomprehensible, is revealed to us by the Son, his lively image, and in vain do we seek him elsewhere.[27]

Luther does at times speak of Christ as the "image" or "mirror" in whom we behold God. "Therefore Christ alone is the means, the life, and the mirror through which we see God and know his will," for Christ "portrays God himself in a specific form, apart from which there is no God."[28] Luther also speaks of faith as "a constant gaze that looks at nothing except Christ," as the Israelites looked at the bronze serpent lifted up before them by Moses.[29] "We must look at this image and take hold of it with a firm faith."[30] This does not, however, change the overall dynamic of Luther's way of thinking about the self-manifestation of God, which, as we have seen, is in terms of the truth of the Word of God that we hear. "And this is why our theology is certain: it snatches us away from ourselves and places us outside ourselves, so that we do not depend on our own strength, conscience, experience, person, or works, but depend

25. Comm. on John 1:18, *OE* 11/1:38.24–25; *CNTC* 4:26.

26. *Predigt über Matth. 11:25ff. zu Eisleben gehalten* (15 February 1546), *WA* 51:192.9–10; *LW* 51:389.

27. Comm. on Matt. 11:27, *CO* 45:319–20; *CNTC* 2:24.

28. *In epistolam S. Pauli ad Galatas Commentarius*, *WA* 40/1:602–3; *LW* 26:396.

29. *WA* 40/1:545; *LW* 26:356.

30. *WA* 40/1:443.35; *LW* 26:284.

on that which is outside ourselves, that is, on the promise and truth of God, which cannot deceive."[31]

In Gal. 3:1, Paul speaks of the verbal preaching of the gospel in terms of the visual representation of Christ. "O foolish Galatians! Who has bewitched you, before whose eyes Jesus Christ was publicly portrayed as crucified?" (RSV). In explaining this passage, Luther interprets the visual image of painting in terms of the "earlier arguments" that Paul had with the Galatians regarding justification by works of the law. "Earlier he had said that those who seek righteousness on the basis of the law nullify the grace of God, and that for them Christ died to no purpose. Now he adds that such people even crucify Christ, Who had been living and reigning in them."[32] According to Luther, Christ is crucified anew by the teaching of justification by works, and Paul appeals to this image to shame the Galatians, along the lines of Heb. 6:6. "Because you want to be justified through the Law, you have crucified Christ again. And I am showing and depicting this before your eyes so clearly you can see it and touch it."[33] The depiction of Christ crucified is therefore not used to describe the preaching of the gospel in a visual way, but rather becomes a rebuke of the Galatians' sin for rejecting the preaching of the gospel. Elsewhere in these lectures, Luther does speak of the need to "depict Christ correctly," over against the false portrayal of Christ as lawgiver and judge.[34] However, even with this qualification, Luther understands the depiction of Christ in terms of the true "definition," "idea," or "opinion" about Christ, thereby giving it a decidedly verbal meaning. "The highest art among Christians is to be able to define Christ this way [as a merciful Savior]; it is also the most difficult of arts."[35]

Calvin, on the other hand, interprets the verbal elements of Gal. 3:1 in terms of the visual representation of Christ in the gospel. "Therefore he tells them that his teaching was so clear that it was not so much mere teaching as the living and express image of Christ."[36] If all preachers would paint the living image of Christ in their sermons "so that men may see Christ crucified and that his blood may flow," Christians would no longer seek to make dead images of Christ in paintings and sculptures. "Where the Church has such painters as these she no longer needs wood and stone, that is, dead images, she no longer needs any pictures."[37] Calvin thought that "dead images" of Christ were introduced into the

31. *WA* 40/1:589.25–28; *LW* 26:387.
32. *WA* 40/1:324–25; *LW* 26:199.
33. *WA* 40/1:326; *LW* 26:201.
34. *WA* 40/1:563.12–26; *LW* 26:178.
35. *WA* 40/1:298.22–24; *LW* 26:178.
36. Comm. on Gal. 3:1, *OE* 16:59.27–29; *CNTC* 11:46.
37. Comm. on Gal. 3:1, *OE* 16:60–61; *CNTC* 11:47.

church when preaching grew cold and no longer set forth Christ in the vivid and express image of the gospel. "And certainly images and pictures were first admitted to Christian temples when, partly, the pastors had become dumb and were mere shadows, partly, when they uttered a few words from the pulpit so coldly and superficially that the power and efficacy of the ministry were utterly extinguished."[38] The express image of Christ in the gospel should therefore make it unnecessary to seek to depict Christ in images devised by the human imagination. Over against Luther, who interpreted the visual depiction of Christ as the result of the rejection of the gospel, Calvin describes the proper preaching of the gospel as setting before the eyes of the congregation the living and express image of Christ crucified.

As important as the preaching of the gospel is for Luther and Calvin, the most compelling self-attestation of Christ for both of them is found in the Lord's Supper, as attested in 1 Cor. 11:24: "When he had given thanks, he broke it, and said, 'This is my body which is given for you. Do this in remembrance of me'" (cf. Vg.). Luther interprets the statement, "This is my body," in light of Rom. 4:21, "God was able to do what he had promised" (NRSV), thereby locating the meaning of the passage in the truth of the Word of Christ. "What God says, he can do, Romans 4[:21], and with God no word is impossible, Luke 1[:37]. Since he says here, then, 'This is my body,' he certainly can and does make it so."[39] The importance of this exegetical move is reinforced by its appearance in Luther's final statement on the meaning of this passage in 1544. "I want to take my stand with the holy Abraham and all Christians on the passage in Romans 4[:21], 'What God says, he can do,' and again in Psalm 51[:4], 'So that thou art justified in thy sentence and blameless in thy judgment.'"[40] Luther contrasts what one hears in the Word of Christ with what one sees with one's eyes. "The bread we see with our eyes, but we hear with our ears that Christ's body is present."[41] Errors arise with regard to the Supper when one attends to the bread that one sees instead of the truth of the Word that one hears, as happened with Karlstadt, according to Luther. "Always he turns his ears away from the Word of God and sees with single vision the bread and wine. For his spirit will not believe what the Word of God says, but only what he sees and feels. What a fine faith!"[42] When this happens, one cannot but deny that the body of Christ is present, as happened as well with Oecolam-

---

38. Comm. on Gal. 3:1, *OE* 16:61.1–5; *CNTC* 11:47.

39. *Das diese Wort Christi "Das ist mein leib" noch fest stehen widder die Schwermgeister* (1527), *WA* 23:117.26–27; *LW* 37:47.

40. *Kurzes Bekenntnis von heiligen Sakrament* (1544), *WA* 54:157.8–11; *LW* 37:306.

41. *WA* 23:87.34–35; *LW* 37:29.

42. *Wider die himmlischen Propheten* (1525), *WA* 18:212.11–13; *LW* 40:221.

padius and Zwingli, for all that one can see is the bread and wine, and not the body and blood.

Luther therefore interprets the statement, "This is my body," by means of his appeal to the truth of the Word of God over against all that we can see and feel, for the appearance of the bread and wine conceals from our view the presence of the body and blood of Christ hidden therein. "We teach not that the body and blood of Christ are visibly present in external things, but that they are hidden in the sacrament."[43] Given the disjunction between the bread that is seen and the truth of the Word telling us it is the body of Christ, it is no wonder that Luther rejects the possibility that the bread and wine are visible symbols of the body and blood of Christ, as Zwingli had insisted. According to Luther, there is no analogy between bread and wine and body and blood, which would be the case if they were signs or symbols of those realities. "For it is called a natural simile when everyone naturally perceives the object of reference, without any instruction, as is the case with pictures. . . . But bread is by no means similar to the body of Christ in this respect, to say nothing of resembling the body as it was given for us."[44]

Luther claims that the reality being conveyed to us in the Supper is the word of absolution, and its confirming sign is not the bread and wine that we see, but the body and blood of Christ we eat and drink, which are hidden in and under the bread and wine. Paraphrasing the words of Christ, Luther says, "I promise you in these words the forgiveness of all your sins and life everlasting. And that you may be absolutely certain of this irrevocable promise of mine, I shall give my body and pour out my blood, confirming this promise by my very death, and leaving you my body and blood as a sign and memorial of this same promise."[45] The body and blood of Christ offered to each member of the congregation is a sign confirming to each of them that the truth of the promise of forgiveness applies personally to them. "But when I distribute the sacrament, I designate it for the individual receiving it; I give him Christ's body and blood that he may have forgiveness of sins, obtained through his death and preached to the congregation."[46] Since this sign cannot be seen in the bread and wine, it can only be apprehended if we ignore what we see and cling to the truth of the Word of God alone.

Calvin, on the other hand, interprets 1 Cor. 11:24 directly in light of his understanding of the self-manifestation of God in living images, in which the invisible God renders Godself somewhat visible to us. When

43. *WA* 18:212.11–13; *LW* 40:221.
44. *Von Abendmahl Christi, Bekenntnis* (1528), *WA* 26:399.20–22, 23–25; *LW* 37:268.
45. *De captivitate babylonica ecclesiae Praeludium* (1520), *WA* 6:515; *LW* 36:40.
46. *Sermon von dem Sacrament des Leibs und Bluts Christi, wider die Schwarmgeister* (1526), *WA* 19:504–5; *LW* 36:348.

Christ says, "This is my body," he is employing "a sacramental way of speaking," by which "the Lord applies to the sign the name of the reality signified."[47] However, unlike human representations, which take their name from absent realities they portray, the signs used by Christ actually offer the reality they represent. "The name of the reality signified is not given to the sign simply because it stands for it; but rather because it is a symbol by which the reality is held out to us."[48] The sacraments are therefore seen to be visible self-representations or living images of Christ, in which Christ both represents and offers himself to us. "Augustine calls a sacrament 'a visible word' for the reason that it represents God's promises as portrayed in a picture and sets them before our sight, portrayed graphically and in the manner of images."[49] Because sacraments portray the promises of God more vividly than the preaching of the gospel alone, the sacraments give greater confirmation to faith. "For the clearer anything is, the fitter it is to support faith. But the sacraments bring the clearest promises; and they have this characteristic over and above the word because they represent them to us as painted in a picture from life."[50]

Calvin thus interprets, "This is my body," by means of the visual self-representation of Christ in living images, and describes the Supper as setting before our eyes the image of our union with Christ by faith. "Since, however, this mystery of Christ's secret union with the devout is by nature incomprehensible, he shows its image and figure in visible signs best adapted to our small capacity. Indeed, by giving guarantees and tokens he makes it as certain for us as if we had seen it with our own eyes."[51] In particular, Christ sets before our eyes the visible symbol of the way he feeds the souls of the faithful with his body and blood, by means of the analogy created by the bread and wine that they eat and drink. "For this very familiar comparison penetrates even into the dullest minds: just as bread and wine sustain physical life, so souls are fed by Christ."[52] Indeed, Calvin could not imagine what the Supper might mean if there were no analogy between the bread and wine and the body and blood of Christ. "For what will the signification of the Supper be, if there is no analogy between the visible sign and the spiritual reality?"[53] Calvin therefore claims that the Supper strengthens faith because of the self-offer of Christ that we see in the bread and wine, over and

47. Comm. on 1 Cor. 11:24, *CO* 49:486C; *CNTC* 9:245.
48. *CO* 49:486C; *CNTC* 9:245.
49. *Inst.* 4.14.6, *OS* 5:263.13–17; LCC 2:1281.
50. *Inst.* 4.14.5, *OS* 5:262.20–24; LCC 2:1280.
51. *Inst.* 4.17.1, *OS* 5:342–43; LCC 2:1361.
52. *Inst.* 4.17.1, *OS* 5:343.2–5; LCC 2:1361.
53. Comm. on 1 Cor. 11:24, *CO* 49:487A; *CNTC* 9:246.

above the word of the gospel that we only hear. "It remains for all this to be applied to us. That is done through the gospel, but more clearly through the Sacred Supper, where he offers himself with all his benefits to us, and we receive him by faith."[54] Luther, on the other hand, sees no analogy between the bread and wine and the body and blood of Christ. "In all figures and types there must be some similarity which underlies them and brings the two objects into correspondence. But here in the bread and cup there is nothing to which Christ's body and blood could bear a similarity."[55] Luther also insists that the Supper strengthens faith primarily by means of the Word that we hear, offering to us the forgiveness of sins won on the cross. "But I will find in the sacrament or the gospel the word which distributes, presents, offers, and gives to me that forgiveness which was won on the cross."[56]

All of this suggests that scholars have read Calvin as being too much like Luther with regard to the way he understands the self-disclosure of God to humanity and the way we appropriate that self-revelation, thereby missing the distinctive way in which Calvin thinks theologically. According to Luther, the self-revelation of God takes place primarily in the Word that God speaks to us. "This, then, is the true knowledge of God: to know his nature and will, which he reveals in the Word, where he promises that he will be my Lord and God and orders me to take hold of his will in faith."[57] Faith, in turn, is the art of clinging to the truth of the Word of God that is heard, over against all that we see and feel that contradicts the truth of the Word. "For human wisdom and reason cannot progress beyond judging and concluding in accordance with what it sees and feels or with what it comprehends with the senses. But faith must transcend such feeling and understanding and make its decision contrary to these and cling to whatever the Word submits."[58]

Calvin, on the other hand, understands the self-manifestation of God in terms of living images, in which the invisible God renders Godself somewhat visible to us. The Word of God works in conjunction with these living images, so that the knowledge of God comes about by what we see and by what we hear. The Word of God does not eliminate our contemplation of the living image of God in creation, but rather makes it fruitful for us. "Therefore, however fitting it may be for man seriously to turn his eyes to contemplate God's works, since he has been placed in this most glorious theater to be a spectator of them, it is fitting that

54. *Inst.* 4.17.5, *OS* 5:346.1–4; LCC 2:1364.
55. *Von Abendmahl Christi, Bekenntnis* (1528), *WA* 26:392.25–28; *LW* 37:263.
56. *Wider die himmlischen Propheten* (1525), *WA* 18:204.2–4; *LW* 40:214.
57. *Vorlesung über 1. Mose von 1535–1545*, *WA* 44:592.6–8; *LW* 8:17.
58. *Das 15. Kapitel S. Pauli an die Korinther* (1532), *WA* 36:493.4–7; *LW* 28:69.

he should prick up his ear to the Word, the better to profit."[59] Nor does the preaching of the gospel eliminate our contemplation of the living image of God in Christ, for the preaching of the gospel is understood as such a visible and living image, representing Christ crucified before our eyes, so that we might behold Christ in the mirror of the gospel and be transformed by our contemplation of him.

> He uses the similitude of the image in the mirror to make three points: first, that we need not fear obscurity when we approach the Gospel, for in it God shows his unveiled face; second, that this should not be a dead and fruitless contemplation, for through it we should be transformed into God's image; third, that neither of these things happen all at once, but by continual progress we increase both in the knowledge of God and in conformity to his image.[60]

Calvin can even speak of the Word of God itself as a living image in which God appears to us, distinguishing Godself from all other "gods." "In order to know God, therefore, we must not frame a likeness of him according to our own fancy, but we must betake ourselves to the Word, in which his lively image is exhibited to us."[61]

Calvin removes all images forged by human ingenuity from places of worship so that our eyes may concentrate on the living images of God in Christian temples, even as we hear the preaching of the gospel.

> When I ponder the intended use of churches, somehow or other it seems to me unworthy of their holiness for them to take on images other than those living and symbolical ones which the Lord has consecrated by his Word. I mean Baptism and the Supper, together with other rites by which our eyes must be too intensely gripped and too sharply affected to seek other images forged by human ingenuity.[62]

The Supper itself is the most vivid of the living symbols in the church, since it clearly portrays our union with Christ before our eyes and offers us the reality it represents. "In this Sacrament we have such full witness of all these things that we must certainly consider them as if Christ here present were himself set before our eyes and touched by our hands."[63] For Calvin, we only come to the true knowledge of God when we not only hear the truth of the Word of God, but also see the living image of God, so that we come to feel and enjoy the good things that

59. *Inst.* 1.6.2, *OS* 3:62–63; LCC 1:72.
60. Comm. on 2 Cor. 3:18, *OE* 15:66.9–16; *CNTC* 10:50.
61. Comm. on Isa. 40:18, *CO* 37:19B; CTS 15:223.
62. *Inst.* 1.11.13, *OS* 3:102.18–25; LCC 1:113–14.
63. *Inst.* 4.17.3, *OS* 5:344.7–10; LCC 2:1362.

God both represents and offers to us. "This herald therefore approaches, who excites our attention, in order that we may perceive ourselves to be placed in this scene, for the purpose of beholding the glory of God; not indeed to observe them as mere witnesses, but to enjoy all the riches which are here exhibited to us, as the Lord has ordained and subjected them to our use."[64]

64. Comm. on Genesis, argumentum, *CO* 23:9–10; CTS 1:62.

9

MANIFESTATION AND PROCLAMATION IN CALVIN'S THEOLOGY

"So faith comes from what is heard, and what is heard comes by the preaching of Christ" (Rom. 10:17 RSV). These words of Paul became the rallying cry of the evangelical reformers of the sixteenth century and have shaped the understanding of the nature of faith in Protestant traditions to this day, including the Reformed tradition. The focus on the preaching of Christ received its decisive impetus in the sixteenth century from the theology of Martin Luther; it was revived in earnest in the twentieth century by the theology of Karl Barth. According to this vision of faith, the most important aspect of our knowledge of God is the words we use to speak about God. The words of the preacher must be based in and related to the words of Scripture about Christ. Faith is only possible if the language we use to proclaim Christ truly represents the language of Scripture about Christ. This leads to a vision of the church

This essay was originally published in a slightly different form under the title "Believing Is Seeing: Proclamation and Manifestation in the Reformed Tradition," at http://reformedtheology.org/SiteFiles/ZachmanPL.html. Reprinted by permission of The Institute for Reformed Theology, Richmond, VA.

in which teaching and doctrine become primary. The office of the pastor is to teach doctrine drawn from the genuine meaning of Scripture. The congregation is to hear this preaching teachably, while at the same time they are to read Scripture for themselves in order to verify that what they are hearing truly reflects the teaching of Scripture. The goal of both the pastor and the congregation, by means of such preaching, hearing, and reading, is to apply the doctrine drawn from Scripture to their lives, both collectively and individually.

There can be no doubt that John Calvin contributed to this vision of the church as a preaching and teaching community. One of Calvin's favorite metaphors for the church was "the school of Christ," whose primary textbook was Scripture. He thought that the ruin of the church by the Roman hierarchy was rooted in the way they took Scripture away from preachers and ordinary Christians. In order to restore the church, Calvin wanted all Christians to read Scripture and hear it expounded. Pastors were to hear the expositions of Scripture by teachers of the church, to guide their interpretation of Scripture, and ordinary Christians were to hear the expositions of Scripture by their pastors, to guide their own reading of Scripture. The emphasis on teaching, hearing, and reading was reinforced by the liturgical changes made by Calvin and his fellow pastors and teachers. All images, paintings, statues, and stained glass were removed from church, so that nothing would distract the congregation from hearing the exposition and application of Scripture in the sermons. Even the sacraments could be seen as secondary in this construction of the church: Calvin could describe them as "secondary appendages" to the word of promise. In this understanding of faith, the true knowledge of God comes from hearing, reading, and applying the doctrine of Scripture. Such application frequently culminates in exhortation and even in rebuke, as Calvin tries to bring the recalcitrant congregation to obey the teaching and preaching of Christ.

However, it must be said that Calvin has a distinctive interest not only in proclamation, but also in manifestation, guided in large part by another saying of Paul in Romans. "For what can be known about God is plain to them, because God has shown [or manifested] it to them. Ever since the creation of the world his invisible nature, namely, his eternal power and deity, has been clearly perceived in the things that have been made" (Rom. 1:19–20 RSV). According to Calvin's reading of this passage, we were originally created to come to know the one true God not by hearing, reading, and applying the Word of God in Scripture, but rather by beholding and contemplating the self-manifestation of God in the universe. "By saying God manifested it he means that man was formed to be a spectator of the fabric of the world, and that he was endowed with eyes for the purpose of being led to God himself, the Author of the world, by contemplating so magnificent an image."[1] The original way we were to be led to God was by means of our visual contemplation of the image of God in the universe, an image in which the invisible God becomes somewhat visible, in order to lead us to Godself. "God is invisible in himself, but since his majesty shines forth in all his works and in all his creatures, men ought to have acknowledged him in these, for they clearly demonstrate their Creator. For this reason the apostle, in his Epistle to the Hebrews, calls the world a mirror or representation of invisible things (Heb. 11:3)."[2]

In particular, the works of God we are to contemplate in the universe set forth what Calvin calls the "powers" of God, such as wisdom, mercy, righteousness, and goodness. Since these powers are all good things, expressing in a visible way the invisible nature of God, our contemplation of them should lead to our feeling them within ourselves, and ultimately to our enjoyment of them. "For the Lord manifests himself by his powers, the force of which we feel within ourselves and the benefits of which we enjoy."[3] In light of the self-manifestation of God in God's works, Calvin can say, "The most perfect way of seeking God, and the most suitable order, is . . . for us to contemplate him in his works whereby he renders himself near and familiar to us, and in some manner communicates himself."[4] If the understanding of faith related to proclamation emphasizes hearing, reading, and applying the true doctrine drawn from Scripture, the understanding of the knowledge of God related to manifestation emphasizes seeing, contemplating, feeling, and enjoying the powers of God portrayed before our eyes, in the realization that by such means God gently invites and sweetly attracts us to Godself.

Calvin of course does not think that beholding the self-manifestation of God in the works of God is of itself sufficient to lead us to the true knowledge of God. Human blindness and ingratitude keep the image of God in the universe from directing us to the one true God manifested in that image. On the one hand, Calvin will say that we must turn to the Word of God in Scripture in order to be led to the Creator. "Despite this, it is needful that another and better help be added to direct us aright to the very Creator of the universe. It was not in vain, then, that he added the light of his Word by which to become known."[5] This turn to the Word appears to replace seeing and contemplation with teaching and hearing. "Now, in order that true religion may shine upon us, we ought to hold that it must take its beginning from heavenly doctrine and that no one

---

1. Comm. on Rom. 1:19, *Romanos* 29.33–35; *CNTC* 8:31.
2. Comm. on Rom. 1:20, *Romanos* 29.36–40; *CNTC* 8:31.
3. *Inst.* 1.5.9, *OS* 3:53.14–16; *LCC* 1:62.
4. *Inst.* 1.5.9, *OS* 3:53.18–23; *LCC* 1:62.
5. *Inst.* 1.6.1, *OS* 3:60.17–19; *LCC* 1:69–70.

can get even the slightest taste of right and sound doctrine unless he be a pupil of Scripture."[6] On the other hand, Calvin will turn to 1 Cor. 1:21 to show that the self-manifestation of God in the universe profits no one who has not first heard the proclamation of Christ crucified.

> It is vain for any to reason as philosophers on the workmanship of the world, except those who, having been first humbled by the preaching of the gospel, have learned to submit the whole of their intellectual wisdom (as Paul expresses it) to the foolishness of the cross (1 Cor. 1:21). Nothing shall we find, I say, above or below, which can raise us up to God, until Christ shall have instructed us in his own school.[7]

It would seem, then, that the language of manifestation, contemplation, feeling, and enjoyment describes a way of seeking God that only Adam and Eve could have enjoyed before the fall into sin. After the fall into sin, and the ensuing ingratitude and blindness that resulted from sin, we can only seek God in the doctrine we are taught by Scripture in the school of Christ, and by hearing through faith the proclamation of the cross of Christ. "For since, in the wisdom of God, the world did not know God through wisdom, it pleased God through the folly of what we preach to save those who believe" (1 Cor. 1:21 RSV). Commenting on this verse, Calvin suggests that the teaching and preaching of Christ have replaced the contemplation of the self-manifestation of God. "If men were led to true knowledge of God by observation of his works, they would come to know God in a way that is wise, or by way of acquiring wisdom that is natural and appropriate to them. But because the whole world learnt nothing at all from what God revealed of His wisdom in created things, he then set about teaching men in another way."[8] The new way of teaching by preaching and doctrine seems to have replaced the original way of teaching by manifestation and contemplation. This is precisely the claim made by many interpreters of Calvin, especially those who follow the lead of Karl Barth. For such theologians, all right knowledge of God comes only from the proclamation of Christ, drawn from the teaching of Scripture. Seeing and contemplating the self-manifestation of God is entirely replaced by hearing the proclamation of Christ.

This reading of Calvin has been further reinforced by the recovery of Luther's theology of the cross in our own day. Language of self-manifestation and contemplation emphasizes the themes of beauty and glory, by which God draws and attracts us to Godself and ravishes us with admiration. "That we may enjoy the sight of God, he must come

6. *Inst*. 1.6.2, *OS* 3:63.5–9; LCC 1:72.
7. Comm. on Genesis, argumentum, *CO* 23:9–10; CTS 1:63.
8. Comm. on 1 Cor. 1:21, *CO* 49:326B; *CNTC* 9:39.

forth to view with his clothing; that is to say, we must first cast our eyes upon the very beautiful fabric of the world in which he wishes to be seen by us."[9] The proclamation of Christ crucified, on the other hand, presents us with the contradiction between what we see and what we hear, following the words of Isaiah: "He had no form or comeliness that we should look at him, and no beauty that we should desire him" (Isa. 53:2 RSV). Calvin takes this to mean that nothing at all about Christ crucified could attract us to him, in contrast to the beautiful fabric of the universe.

> If men see him, they will not condescend to look upon him; everyone turns his face away from him and thinks him abhorrent. How few men will believe in the Gospel! For we always like to have some fine show before our eyes; we want everything to be bright. But God went to work another way when he wished to redeem us; for, as St. Paul says, since the world profited little from the wisdom of God in declaring himself the Creator in such a way that men could come to him by beholding the sky and the earth, he has changed his method and used, as it were, a kind of foolishness to teach us.[10]

The critique of the theology of glory and beauty by the theology of the cross would therefore reinforce Calvin's turn to the Word of God in Scripture, and the proclamation of Christ crucified, giving one the clear sense that doctrine, preaching, reading, and teaching have replaced manifestation, contemplation, feeling, and enjoying in the theology of John Calvin, and in the subsequent Reformed tradition.

I suggest, however, that the theme of manifestation, contemplation, feeling, and enjoyment never departs from the theology of John Calvin, or from the subsequent Reformed tradition, as seen especially in the theology of Jonathan Edwards. With regard to the manifestation of God in creation, Calvin does, it is true, insist that such manifestation profits us nothing without the Word of God in Scripture; yet he turns to Scripture not to replace contemplation with teaching, but rather to lead us toward the true and fruitful contemplation of the works of God in the universe. With regard to the proclamation of Christ crucified being necessary to lead us to the true God, Calvin insists that we must move from the scandal of the cross of Christ to the glory of the resurrection and ascension of Christ, especially as manifested in the gospel, so that the glory and beauty of Christ begin to appear in the image of the gospel for our contemplation. The manifestation of God in the universe needs the

9. Comm. on Ps. 104:1, *CO* 32:85A; CTS 11:145.
10. Sermon on Isa. 53:2, *CO* 35:610C; *Sermons on Isaiah's Prophecy of the Death and Passion of Christ*, trans. and ed. T. H. L. Parker (London: Clarke, 1956), 51.

proclamation of the Word to be fruitful, and the proclamation of Christ crucified needs the manifestation of the glory of Christ to be fruitful. Both manifestation and proclamation lead us to the true knowledge of God, both in creation and in Christ. The loss of manifestation and contemplation in our understanding of the Reformed tradition today has deprived us of an essential element of the knowledge of God according to Calvin and those who followed him, and has led to an unfortunate impoverishment of the life of piety, the experience of worship, and our relationship with the natural world. In what follows, I will show how the self-manifestation of God in the universe is made fruitful by the teaching of God in the Word, and how the proclamation of Christ crucified is made fruitful by the manifestation of God in Christ, who is "God manifested in the flesh" (1 Tim. 3:16, cf. some MSS).

The Spectacles of Scripture

As discussed above, Calvin thought that the right way to seek God was to contemplate God in the beautiful image of God in the universe.

> Consequently, the most perfect way of seeking God, and the most suitable order, is not for us with bold curiosity to penetrate to the investigation of his essence, which we ought to adore than meticulously to search out, but for us to contemplate him in his works whereby he renders himself near and familiar to us, and in some manner communicates himself.[11]

Calvin claims that human blindness and ingratitude have blinded us to the self-manifestation of God in the universe, making the self-testimony of God the Creator necessary if we would be led to the knowledge of the Creator. However, Calvin calls the Scriptures "spectacles," indicating that they are needed precisely to help us to see better. "For by the Scripture as our guide and teacher, he not only makes those things plain which would otherwise escape our notice, but almost compels us to behold them; as if he had assisted our dull sight with spectacles."[12] If this is true, then the doctrine of Scripture does not replace contemplation, but rather makes it possible for us. We can only rightly behold the beauty of the self-manifestation of God in the universe when we not only see with our eyes, but also hear with our ears. "Therefore, however fitting it may be for man seriously to turn his eyes to contemplate God's works, since he has been placed in this most beautiful theater to be a spectator of them, it is fitting that he prick up his ears to the Word, the better

11. *Inst.* 1.5.9, *OS* 3:53.18–23; LCC 1:62.
12. Comm. on Genesis, argumentum, *CO* 23:9–10; CTS 1:62.

to profit."[13] In particular, hearing the Word makes it possible for us to contemplate the powers of God manifested in the works of God. "Hence, we must strive onward by this straight path if we seriously aspire to the pure contemplation of God. We must, I say, come to the Word, where God is truly and vividly described to us from his works, while these very works are appraised not by our depraved judgment but by the rule of eternal truth."[14]

Calvin wanted the godly to spend their whole lives contemplating the works of God in creation. He thought that God described the work of creation in six days to facilitate this kind of contemplation. "For by this circumstance we are drawn away from all fictions to the one God who distributed his work into six days that we might not find it irksome to occupy our whole life in contemplating it."[15] However, Calvin wanted to extend our contemplation from the creation accounts of Scripture to the image of God in the universe itself.

> There is no doubt that the Lord would have us uninterruptedly occupied in this holy meditation; that, while we contemplate in all his creatures, as in mirrors, those immense riches of his wisdom, justice, goodness, and power, we should not run over them cursorily, and, so to speak, with a fleeting glance; but we should ponder them at length, turn them over in our minds seriously and faithfully, and recollect them repeatedly.[16]

Calvin claimed that this was one of the chief purposes of Sabbath rest, one that had not been abrogated by the coming of Christ.

> This is, indeed, the proper business of the whole life, in which men should daily exercise themselves, to consider the infinite goodness, justice, power, and wisdom of God, in this magnificent theater of heaven and earth. But, lest men should prove less sedulously attentive to it than they ought, every seventh day has been especially selected for this purpose of supplying what was wanting in daily meditation, . . . that they, being released from all other business, might the more readily apply their minds to the Creator of the world.[17]

Calvin offers his readers a great deal of advice about the most fruitful way to pursue such contemplation of God's works in the beautiful fabric of the universe. He advised beginning with the contemplation of the order of the stars in the heavens, and then descending from there

13. *Inst.* 1.6.2, *OS* 3:62–63; LCC 1:72.
14. *Inst.* 1.6.3, *OS* 3:63.24–28; LCC 1:72–73.
15. *Inst.* 1.14.2, *OS* 3:154.1–4; LCC 1:161.
16. *Inst.* 1.14.21, *OS* 3:171.25–32; LCC 1:180.
17. Comm. on Gen. 2:3, *CO* 23:33A; CTS 1:105–6.

to the earth, and finally to the smallest creatures on the earth. "When a person, from beholding and contemplating the heavens, has been brought to acknowledge God, he will learn also to reflect upon and admire his wisdom and power displayed on the face of the earth, not only in general, but even in the minutest plants."[18] We should then descend into ourselves, so that we might feel the force of the powers we behold in God's works, and might enjoy their benefits within us, so that we might be drawn to God thereby. "There comes now the second part of the rule, more closely related to faith. It is to recognize that God has destined all things for our good and salvation but at the same time to feel his power and grace in ourselves and in the great benefits he has conferred upon us, and so bestir ourselves to trust, invoke, praise, and love him."[19]

Under the tutelage of the Word, with the Scriptures as our spectacles, we are able to contemplate God in the beauty of the universe, in order that we might be sweetly allured to God by our enjoyment of his benefits. "So, invited by the sweetness of his beneficence and goodness, let us study to love and serve him with our whole heart."[20] Indeed, beyond our enjoyment of the benefits of God, our contemplation of the universe should lead us to be ravished in astonishment by its beauty and glory. "As soon as we acknowledge God to be the supreme architect, who has erected the beauteous fabric of the universe, our minds must necessarily be ravished with wonder at his infinite goodness, wisdom, and power."[21] In sum, the teaching and instruction of the Word of God does not replace our contemplation of the self-manifestation of God in the universe, but rather makes such contemplation both possible and fruitful.

> For if the mute instruction of the heaven and the earth were sufficient, the teaching of Moses would have been superfluous. This herald therefore approaches, who excites our attention, in order that we may perceive ourselves to be placed in this scene, for the purpose of beholding the glory of God; not indeed to observe as mere witnesses, but to enjoy all the riches which are here exhibited, as the Lord has ordained and subjected them to our use.[22]

According to Calvin, the godly should spend every day, or at least every Sunday, contemplating the beauty and glory of God in heaven and on earth, in stars and in plants, so that they might be ravished in astonish-

18. Comm. on Ps. 19:1, *CO* 31:194C; CTS 8:808–9.
19. *Inst.* 1.14.22, *OS* 3:172.22–27; LCC 1:181.
20. *Inst.* 1.14.22, *OS* 3:173.21–23; LCC 1:182.
21. Comm. on Ps. 19:1, *CO* 31:194C; CTS 8:808.
22. Comm. on Genesis, argumentum, *CO* 23:9–10; CTS 1:62.

ment and sweetly allured to God by the overwhelming display of God's goodness that they contemplate.

The Portrayal of Christ in the Gospel

Calvin's discussion of the knowledge of God the Creator begins with manifestation and contemplation, and then adds teaching and hearing in order that such contemplation might be fruitful. When Calvin turns to his discussion of Christ, he begins with the language of proclamation, following the statement of Paul in 1 Cor. 1:21, "For since, in the wisdom of God, the world did not know God through wisdom, it pleased God through the folly of what we preach to save those who believe" (RSV). Calvin has two distinct ways of relating the preaching of the cross of Christ to the self-manifestation of God in the universe. In the Genesis commentary, Calvin insists that we must first believe the preaching of the cross of Christ before we can profit from the contemplation of the works of God in the universe. "Nothing shall we find, I say, above or below, which can raise us up to God, until Christ shall have instructed us in his school. Yet this does not prevent us from applying our senses to the consideration of heaven and earth, that we may thence seek confirmation of the true knowledge of God."[23] On the other hand, in the *Institutes*, Calvin begins with the proper contemplation of God in the works of God in the universe, clarified by the spectacles of Scripture, and then passes on to the preaching of Christ crucified, without which there can be no saving knowledge of God.

> We must, for this reason, come to Paul's statement: "Since in the wisdom of God the world did not know God through wisdom, it pleased God through the folly of preaching to save those who believe" [1 Cor. 1:21]. This magnificent theater of heaven and earth, crammed with innumerable miracles, Paul calls "the wisdom of God." Contemplating it, we ought in wisdom to have known God. But because we have profited so little by it, he calls us to the faith of Christ, which, because it appears foolish, the unbelievers despise.[24]

As this quote makes clear, the preaching of the cross of Christ lacks all the appearance of glory and beauty that Calvin finds in the self-manifestation of God in the universe. Precisely because Calvin is so attuned to the theme of manifestation and contemplation, he is sensitive to the

23. Comm. on Genesis, argumentum, *CO* 23:9–10; CTS 1:63.
24. *Inst*. 2.6.1, *OS* 3:320.26–33; LCC 1:341.

repulsive and offensive appearance of Christ, both in his life, and in his death.

> And so God has made use, as it were, of something foolish, sending his only Son, subjecting him to all our weaknesses, so that he was rejected by the world, being born in a stable, all his life he was like a poor working man; and at the end we see that every one was against him, and with such fury that he was detested and was every man's enemy; and finally, he was crucified. Now that death was accursed by God; for he was not only disfigured by the buffeting, the spitting and the crown of thorns, but he became a curse when he hung between two thieves, as if he were the most detestable man who had ever lived or could be known. And that sort of death was appalling because it was accursed in the Law. Look how disfigured he was; for this mode of execution has become a scandal to men.[25]

The appearance of Christ in the preaching of the cross, far from sweetly alluring people to God by the glory and beauty of what they behold, rather has the effect of repelling them from Christ. "So we must always come back to what the Prophet says, that every man has turned his back on him and shut his eyes as if he were something hateful. What! Shall I seek for life in death? Shall I hope in him who cannot help himself? Shall I go for strength to him who was so weak? Why should I do that?"[26] The gospel proclaims to us truths about Christ that contradict what we see in the life and death of Christ. To seek for righteousness in a condemned sinner, life in a dead man, and the blessing of God in a cursed man—this seems to all appearances to be the height of folly.

Calvin offers us several steps whereby we might surmount the scandal created by the dreadful appearance of Christ. The first step is to awaken our consciences with the awareness of the sin, death, and curse of God that justly lie upon all of us. When we do so, our proud rejection of Christ will cease, and we will begin to see that there was no other way for God to save us other than to place on Christ all that weighs so heavily upon us, so that he might thereby reconcile us with God.

> The way to begin to glorify the infinite goodness of God is to hate our sins and be utterly confounded. This is how the scandal that we imagine and that each of us weaves around the death and passion of our Lord Jesus Christ will soon be taken away—namely, when we enter into ourselves and make a thorough examination of our sins, and recognize that we are so detestable to God that he had to come in the person of his Son to make

25. Sermon on Isa. 53:2, *CO* 35:610–11; *Sermons on Isaiah's Prophecy*, 51–52.
26. Sermon on Isa. 53:3, *CO* 35:617C; *Sermons on Isaiah's Prophecy*, 59.

satisfaction and reparation for our sins so that by this means we might be reconciled to him.[27]

Once we come to acknowledge that Christ was thus horribly afflicted for our sins, the preaching of the cross will no longer be offensive to us, but will rather be seen as the way God reconciled us to Godself. One believes in spite of what one sees, for what one sees is due to our sins, which have thus disfigured him.

However, Calvin is not content to leave matters thus, as Luther might have done. If faith believes that it was God who was in Christ reconciling the world to Godself, then faith must await the manifestation of God in the flesh of Christ, so that it has a more solid ground on which to stand. We must, it is true, begin with the cross of Christ, so that we might be humbled by the awareness of our sins, and by the realization that he was stricken for our transgressions; but we must pass on to the resurrection of Christ, for that alone begins to remove the scandal of the cross, by manifesting God in Christ. "That dreadful appearance of ignominy and malediction which is seen in the death of Christ, not only obscures his glory, but removes it altogether from our sight. We must not, then, hold to his death alone, but must also consider the fruit that his resurrection bears. In this way nothing will prevent his glory from shining everywhere."[28] The glory that is completely hidden from view in the cross begins to appear to those who patiently move from the cross to the resurrection. "It is true that at first sight God in Christ seems to be low and abject, but his glory appears to those who have the patience to pass on from the cross to the resurrection."[29] The preaching of the cross alone is not enough to support our faith, according to Calvin; we must pass on to the resurrection, in which we begin to see the truth that the gospel proclaims to us. "Therefore, Paul states that 'Christ was declared the Son of God . . . in the resurrection itself' [Rom. 1:4 p.], because then at last he displayed his heavenly power, which is both the clear mirror of his divinity and the firm support of our faith."[30]

When we pass from the cross to the resurrection, Christ appears before our eyes as "God manifested in the flesh." The language of manifestation, which is utterly lacking in Calvin's discussions of the preaching of the cross, begins to emerge again when he speaks of the resurrection, leading Calvin to state that due to the glory that appears in Christ, Christ is the image of the invisible God, who manifests God to us.

27. Sermon on Isa. 53:3, *CO* 35:619A; *Sermons on Isaiah's Prophecy*, 60.
28. Comm. on John 12:24, *OE* 11/2:92.15–19; *CNTC* 5:37.
29. Comm. on 2 Cor. 4:6, *OE* 15:76.3–5; *CNTC* 10:58.
30. *Inst.* 1.16.13, *OS* 3:500.16–19; *LCC* 1:521.

> When Christ is called the image of the invisible God the reference is not merely to his essence, because he is, as they say, co-essential with the Father, but rather to his relationship to us because he represents the Father to us. The Father is called invisible because he himself is not apprehended by the human mind but he shows himself to us by his Son and thus makes himself in a manner visible.[31]

In particular, we behold in Christ every good thing that we have lost due to our sins. Christ is the image of God because in him we behold every good thing that the Father wishes to bestow upon us. "For God would have remained hidden afar off if Christ's splendor had not beamed upon us. For this purpose the Father laid up with his only-begotten Son all that he had to reveal himself in Christ so that Christ, by communicating his Father's benefits, might express the true image of his glory [cf. Heb. 1:3]."[32] The proclamation of the cross of Christ needs the addition of the manifestation of God in Christ, if faith is to be guided to seek the knowledge of God in the face of Christ, and if faith is to behold, feel, and enjoy every good thing that God reveals to us in the flesh of Christ.

Once believers begin to see the glory of God manifested in Christ, they also begin to see in the cross of Christ itself the glory of God's goodness and love that was initially hidden from them by the appearance of shame and malediction.

> Therefore he promises that when the ignominy which he shall endure for a time has been wiped out, a sublime glory will shine in his death. And this was accomplished: for the death of the cross which Christ suffered, so far from obscuring his honor, there shines brightest, since there his incredible love to mankind, his infinite righteousness in atoning for sin and appeasing the wrath of God, his wonderful power in overcoming death, subduing Satan, and, indeed, opening up heaven, put forth its full brightness.[33]

Once we begin to see the glory of God manifested not only in the resurrection, but also in the death of Christ, we will see a manifestation of the goodness of God far more glorious and beautiful than what is manifested in the works of God in the universe.

> For in the cross of Christ, as in a splendid theater, the incomparable goodness of God is set forth before the whole world. The glory of God shines, indeed, in all creatures on high and below, but never more brightly than in the cross, in which there was a wonderful change of things—the condemnation of all men was manifested, sin blotted out, salvation restored

31. Comm. on 2 Cor. 4:4, *OE* 15:73.10–15; *CNTC* 10:55–56.
32. *Inst.* 3.2.1, *OS* 4:8.10–15; *LCC* 1:544.
33. Comm. on John 13:32, *OE* 11/2:130–31; *CNTC* 5:69.

to men; in short, the whole world was renewed and all things restored to order.[34]

The godly will not cease to contemplate the image of God manifested in the universe; but they will add to their contemplation the more glorious image of God in the cross of Christ, so that God might be rightly glorified for all of God's works.

> When we consider the works of God throughout the world, they tell us that he ought to be praised for his majesty and greatness; but when we come to the person of our Lord Jesus Christ, we must learn to glorify God in his abasement. So there is a twofold way of praising God. On the one hand, we must exalt him because he shows us his goodness, righteousness, and infinite power in all that he has created and done, and by ordaining and disposing everything. . . . And on the other hand, since our Lord Jesus Christ, in whom dwells the fullness of Godhead, was not only degraded for our salvation but was willing to be brought to the lowest depths—more, he did not refuse to suffer the pangs of death, as if he had entered into hell—God deserves to be glorified more than for his greatness apparent throughout the world.[35]

We must recognize, however, that we do not behold Christ directly before us as the image of God we contemplate, as is the case with the works of God in the universe. Christ can only be beheld when he appears before us as clothed in the gospel. "This then is the true knowledge of Christ, if we perceive him as he is offered to us by the Father: namely, clothed with his gospel. . . . [For] we say that the Word itself, however it be imparted to us, is like a mirror in which faith may contemplate God."[36] The gospel is therefore the mirror in which we behold Christ, who is himself the image of God. "For the Apostle truly declares that by the mirror of the gospel we clearly behold God in the person of Christ (2 Cor. 3:18)."[37] For this reason, Calvin likes the description of preaching set forth in Gal. 3:1: it is the public portrayal of Christ crucified, which vividly sets before our eyes his death on our behalf. "Therefore we will keep to this meaning, that Paul's doctrine had taught them about Christ in such a manner that it was as if he had been shown to them in a picture, even crucified among them."[38]

However, the gospel declares to us spiritual truths that we cannot in fact see with our earthly eyes, so that if we were left with the gospel

---

34. Comm. on John 13:31, *OE* 11/2:130.16–22; *CNTC* 5:68.
35. Sermon on Isa. 53:4, *CO* 35:622A; *Sermons on Isaiah's Prophecy*, 68.
36. *Inst.* 3.2.6, *OS* 4:13.15–16, 14–15; *LCC* 1:548–49.
37. Comm. on John 8:19, *OE* 11/1:269.17–23; *CNTC* 4:213.
38. Comm. on Gal. 3:1, *OE* 19:60.13–15; *CNTC* 11:47.

alone, our contemplation of Christ in the gospel would engage only our ears, and not our eyes. For this reason, Christ has accommodated himself to our condition and offers himself for our contemplation, not only in the gospel but also in the sacraments, which together form the mirror in which we may contemplate Christ. Commenting on Paul's claim that we now see in a mirror, Calvin says,

> I say that the ministry of the word is like a mirror. For the angels do not need preaching, or other inferior aids, or sacraments. They have the advantage of another way of seeing God, for God does not show them his face merely in a mirror, but he presents himself openly before them. But we, who have not yet scaled such heights, look upon the image of God in the Word, in the sacraments, and, in short, in the whole ministry of the Church.[39]

Not only preaching but also the sacraments and ceremonies of the church form the mirror in which faith contemplates Christ, who himself is the image of the invisible God.

Calvin thought that the medieval church was led to install more and more visible images of God and of Christ—such as crucifixes, pictures, stained glass, and statues—because the people could no longer see and contemplate Christ crucified in the preaching, sacraments, and ceremonies of the Roman Church. "And certainly images and pictures were first admitted to Christian temples when, partly, the pastors had become dumb and were mere shadows, partly, when they uttered a few words from the pulpit so coldly and superficially that the power and efficacy of the ministry were utterly extinguished."[40] Calvin wanted such man-made images removed from all places of worship, not to remove all visual contemplation from the faithful, but to focus their contemplation on the images that truly and vividly portray Christ to us: preaching, the sacraments, and the other rites of the church.

> When I ponder the intended use of churches, somehow or other it seems to me unworthy of their holiness for them to take on images other than those living and symbolical ones which the Lord has consecrated by his Word. I mean Baptism and the Lord's Supper, together with other ceremonies by which our eyes must be too intensely gripped and too sharply affected to seek other images forged by human ingenuity.[41]

One can ask how well Calvin designed and implemented a form of worship that would so intensely grip and sharply affect the eyes of the

39. Comm. on 1 Cor. 13:12, *CO* 49.514B; *CNTC* 9:281.
40. Comm. on Gal. 3:1, *OE* 16:61.1–5; *CNTC* 11:47.
41. *Inst.* 1.11.13, *OS* 3:102.18–25; LCC 1:113–14.

congregation. Calvin's practice of worship may have reinforced the understanding of the church as a school, as the center of worship became the line-by-line exposition and application of Scripture in the sermon. However, his theology points us in another direction, one in which sermon, sacrament, and ceremony set forth Christ himself for our contemplation, so that we might behold him as in a mirror, and be led by him to the invisible God who sent him.

Our contemplation of Christ in the mirror of the gospel and the sacraments has one other objective, one that distinguishes it from our contemplation of God in the universe. When we contemplate Christ in the mirror of the gospel, we not only contemplate an image of the goodness of God that is greater than what we contemplate in the universe, but we also behold an image that has the power to transform us into itself. Calvin develops this theme on the basis of the statement of Paul in 2 Cor. 3:18, which I give in Calvin's rendering of the passage: "But we all, with unveiled face reflecting as in a mirror the glory of the Lord, are transformed into the same image from glory to glory, even as from the Lord the Spirit." On this verse, Calvin comments:

> At the same time he points out both the force of revelation and our daily progress in it. He uses this similitude of the image in the mirror to make three points: first, that we need not fear obscurity when we approach the Gospel, for in it God shows us his unveiled face; second, that this should not be dead and fruitless contemplation, for through it we should be transformed into God's image; third, that neither of these things happen all at once, but by continual progress we increase both in the knowledge of God and in conformity to his image.[42]

Our contemplation of Christ in the mirror of the gospel and the sacraments transforms us into the image of Christ, and thereby renews the image of God within us. If such contemplation would bear fruit in the congregation, we would not only be able to behold Christ in the mirror of the gospel, sacraments, and ceremonies of the church, but would also see the image of Christ in the worshipping community itself. "For we have been adopted as sons by the Lord with this one condition: that our lives express Christ, the bond of our adoption."[43] We are transformed into the image of God not only by applying godly doctrine concretely to our lives, but also by contemplating the image of Christ in the gospel; for such contemplation transforms us into the image of Christ, from one degree of glory to another. When the church does not attend to the vivid representation of Christ in its preaching, sacraments, and ceremonies,

42. Comm. on 2 Cor. 3:18, *OE* 15:66.9–16; *CNTC* 10:50.
43. *Inst*. 3.6.3, *OS* 4:148.25–26; LCC 1:687.

it is hindering genuine Christian transformation, no matter how much it may be preaching and teaching sound doctrine.

Conclusion: From Calvin to Edwards

As we have seen, Calvin never replaces the language of manifestation and contemplation with the language of proclamation and hearing, but rather combines the two together in an inseparable relationship. On the one hand, speaking about God the Creator, Calvin begins with manifestation, and then adds proclamation to it, so that the manifestation of God might be fruitful for us. We cannot rightly contemplate God in the image of the universe without the Word of God; but once we have the spectacles of Scripture, and are guided in our seeing by what we hear, we can and must truly contemplate God in all that God does, from the loftiest stars to the tiniest plants. Calvin insists that the godly should practice such contemplation every day of their lives, or at least every Sunday, when God gives us rest so that we might engage in such contemplation. On the other hand, when speaking about God the Redeemer, Calvin begins with the proclamation of Christ crucified, in which the manifestation of God in Christ is hidden under an appearance that directly contradicts it. However, once we come to faith in the preaching of the cross, we pass on from the cross to the resurrection, and begin to see the manifestation of God in the flesh of Christ, making Christ the image of the invisible God. In acknowledgment of our infirmity, Christ gives us a mirror of himself in the ministry of the church, so that we might contemplate him in the preaching, sacraments, and ceremonies of the church, in order to be transformed more and more into the image we are contemplating. Manifestation leads on to proclamation in the knowledge of God the Creator, yet without eliminating manifestation; and proclamation leads on to manifestation in the knowledge of God the Redeemer, yet without eliminating proclamation.

I conclude this chapter with a brief reference forward, to the theology of Jonathan Edwards, in order to present a promising trajectory to follow out of Calvin, one that antedates the trajectory set by either Schleiermacher or Barth. Like Calvin, Edwards preached sermons that were expositions and applications of Scripture, leading one to think that he, like Calvin, saw the church more as a school than as the mirror in which to behold Christ. However, in those sermons and in other writings, Edwards leads his congregations to an understanding of faith in which faith is the new perception or contemplation of the glory and beauty of God in all of God's works, and not only the knowledge of doctrine drawn from Scripture. For Edwards knows that one may know and memorize the whole of Scripture, and even use it in discussion to convince others of the correctness of one's faith, without ever beholding or contemplating the beauty and glory of the truths spoken of in Scripture. The true and spiritual knowledge of Scripture is therefore to be given eyes to see the beauty and glory in all the works of God attested in Scripture.

> Spiritually to understand the Scripture is to have the eyes of the mind opened, to behold the wonderful spiritual excellency of the glorious things contained in the true meaning of it, and that always were contained in it, ever since it was written; to behold the amiable and bright manifestations of the divine perfections, and of the excellency and sufficiency of Christ, and the excellency and suitableness of the way of salvation by Christ, and the spiritual glory of the precepts and promises of the Scripture, etc., which things are, and always were, in the Bible, and would have been seen before if it had not been for blindness, without having any new sense added, by the words sent by God to a particular person, and spoken anew to him, with a new meaning.[44]

The saints who are given the ability to behold the beauty of God's holiness in all of God's works will, for Edwards as for Calvin, be gently invited and sweetly allured to God by the object of their contemplation. "But the saints and angels behold that glory of God which consists in the beauty of his holiness; and it is this sight only that will melt and humble human hearts, wean them from the world, draw them to God, and effectually change them."[45] As in Calvin, Edwards describes the godly as ravished by the beauty of the one they behold and contemplate, so that they forget all about themselves for the sake of the one they behold by faith.

> A true saint, when in the enjoyment of true discoveries of the sweet glory of God and Christ, has his mind too much captivated and engaged by what he views outside himself, to stand at that time to view himself, and his own attainments. It would be a diversion and loss which he could not bear, to take his eye off from the ravishing object of his contemplation, to survey his own experience.[46]

The new perception of God's glory that is given to the saints at last frees them from the self-love and self-interest that poison all of our dealings with God, for the saints delight in contemplating the beauty of God's goodness and holiness as it is in itself, and not as it benefits them. "And as

---

44. Jonathan Edwards, *The Religious Affections* (Edinburgh: Banner of Truth, 1961), 206.
45. Ibid., 190.
46. Ibid., 178.

it is with the love of the saints, so it is with their joy and spiritual delight and pleasure: the first foundation of it is not any consideration or conception of their interest in divine things; but it primarily consists in the sweet entertainment their minds have in the view or contemplation of the divine and holy beauty of these things, as they are in themselves."[47]

Thus, we find in Edwards the same combination of manifestation and contemplation that we found in Calvin's theology. As necessary as preaching the Word in accord with right doctrine might be for both of them, it needs to be combined with an equal attention to the contemplation of the manifestation of God's beauty and glory in all of God's works, both in creation and in Christ. For Edwards, such contemplation focuses us on the beauty and splendor of God and Christ; it frees us from being captivated by our own self-interested concerns, with which a doctrinal Christianity can all too easily be combined.

> A proposition concerning the will of God is as properly a doctrine of religion as a proposition concerning the nature of God or a work of God, and a having either of these kinds of propositions, or any other proposition, declared to a person, either by speech or inward suggestion, differs vastly from a having the holy beauty of divine things manifested to the soul, wherein spiritual knowledge does most essentially consist.[48]

47. Ibid., 175.
48. Ibid., 204.

10

CALVIN AS ANALOGICAL THEOLOGIAN

Calvin's concern to combine what we hear with what we see, or manifestation with proclamation, means that he must attend to the relationship between the image or symbol that we see, and the invisible reality that is representing itself therein. The visibility of the invisible God in living images is understood by Calvin to be central to God's accommodation to our own earthly capacities. The theme of accommodation has been recognized by previous Calvin scholars, most notably Ford Lewis Battles. In his oft-cited article "God Was Accommodating Himself to Human Capacity," Battles makes the following claim:

> It may be that we have succumbed to the temptation of putting the concept of accommodation too much at the center of Calvin's thought and of trying to organize everything around this notion. Yet, if this be a faithful interpretation, accommodation would seem (even when Calvin does not explicitly advert to it) his fundamental way of explaining how the secret, hidden God reveals himself to us.[1]

1. Ford Lewis Battles, "God Was Accommodating Himself to Human Capacity," in *Calvin and Hermeneutics*, ed. Richard C. Gamble, Articles on Calvin and Calvinism 6 (New York: Garland, 1992), 27. See also Edward A. Dowey Jr., *The Knowledge of God in Calvin's*

This essay was originally published in a slightly different form under the title "Calvin as Analogical Theologian," *Scottish Journal of Theology* 51, no. 2 (1998): 162–87. Reprinted by permission.

While there is nearly universal agreement that this description of the role of accommodation in Calvin's theology is accurate, it still leaves unaddressed two major questions: *How* does such accommodation on the part of God take place? *Why* does it take the form that it does? This chapter will argue that the method of divine self-accommodation, and hence of divine self-revelation, is understood by Calvin in terms of the analogy and anagoge between the sign and the reality signified, and that Calvin is therefore best understood when he is seen as an analogical and anagogical theologian. Analogy stresses the similarity amid difference between the sign and the reality signified, whereas anagoge stresses the elevation from the temporal sign to the spiritual reality it represents. While Luther can be said to base his theology on making the right distinction at the right time, Calvin can arguably be described as basing his theology on drawing the right analogy and following the proper anagoge from the visible sign to the invisible reality it signifies.

The invisible God reveals Godself to us by creating visible images of God in the world that can be perceived by the human senses. Human beings come to know God by following the intended analogy between the visible images and the invisible reality that they represent and by holding to the proper anagoge, or elevation, from the temporal, earthly images to the eternal, heavenly reality they depict. Conversely, all idolatry comes about by seeking to know the invisible God apart from the visible self-portraits of God, or by seeking God in the images themselves and binding God to them, rather than being led to God by the analogy of the sign to the thing signified and elevating one's mind and heart to heaven.

One sees this characteristic combination of analogy and anagoge in Calvin's critique of the Roman doctrine of transubstantiation. On the one hand, this doctrine destroys the analogy between the sign and the thing signified by denying the reality of the sign. "Where is the analogy or similitude of a visible sign in the Supper to correspond to the body and blood of our Lord, if there is neither bread to eat, nor wine to drink, but only some empty phantom to mock the eye?"[2] On the other hand, transubstantiation eliminates the intended anagoge from the earthly sign to the heavenly reality by binding God to the symbol, thereby fixing the minds and hearts of Christians on earth rather than lifting them to heaven. "While the sacrament ought to have been a means of elevating pious minds to heaven, the sacred symbols of the Supper were abused for an entirely different purpose, and men, content with gazing upon

---

Theology, 2nd ed. (New York: Columbia University Press, 1952), 1–18, 243–44; William J. Bouwsma, *John Calvin: A Sixteenth-Century Portrait* (New York: Oxford University Press, 1988), 124.

2. "The Necessity of Reforming the Church," *Calvin: Theological Treatises*, 204.

them and worshipping them, never once raised their minds to Christ."[3] Calvin saw himself as one in spirit with the Lutherans on the first critique, for he thought they also wished to preserve the analogy between the bread and wine and the body and blood of Christ by maintaining the reality of the former. However, Calvin rejected the Lutheran claim that the humanity of Christ is everywhere that his divinity is, and is hence in the bread and cup, because it abolishes the anagoge between the earthly signs and the body of Christ in heaven.

> We only insist on the distinction, that an anagogy is drawn between the sign and visible action and the spiritual reality. For to what end does Christ hold forth a pledge of his flesh and blood under earthly elements unless it be to raise us upwards? If they are helps to our weakness, no one will ever attain to the reality, but the one who first thus assisted shall climb, as it were, step by step from earth to heaven.[4]

This combination of analogy and anagoge, which emerges so clearly in Calvin's discussion of the Holy Supper, is not unique to the Supper, but rather reveals the way Calvin thinks theologically. In order to substantiate this claim, this chapter will explore Calvin's use of analogy and anagoge in his understanding of the self-revelation of God the Creator in the universe and in Scripture, the self-revelation of God in Jesus Christ, and the self-revelation of Christ in the law and the gospel.

The Revelation of God the Creator

According to Calvin, human beings were created in the image of God and were given reason and intellect in order that they might come to know God. "Why are men endowed with reason and intellect except for the purpose of recognizing their Creator?"[5] The proper use of reason and intellect, therefore, is to seek after and inquire into God. Since God is the summum bonum, and all people are drawn by nature to seek the good, the quest for God also involves the human heart.[6] Calvin explicitly notes his agreement with Plato on this point: "Granted that Plato was groping in the darkness; but he denied that the beautiful which he imagined could be known without ravishing a person with the admiration of itself—this in *Phaedrus* and elsewhere. How then is it possible for you to

3. Ibid., 204–5.
4. *Secunda defensio contra Westphali, CO* 9:48C–49A; *Tracts and Treatises* 2:250.
5. Comm. on Heb. 11:3, *CO* 55:145; *CNTC* 12:159.
6. Comm. on Matt. 6:21, *CO* 45:205B; *CNTC* 1:216.

know God and yet be touched by no feeling?"[7] The more human reason and intellect come to know God, the more the human heart will be drawn and allured to God out of an increasingly ardent love for the goodness of God that it perceives. "Now it must be the case that the grace of God draws us all to himself and inflames us with the love of him by whom we obtain a real perception of it. If Plato affirms this of his Beautiful, of which he saw only a shadowy idea from afar off, this is much more true with regard to God."[8]

The ultimate goal of the quest for God is union with God in eternal life and blessedness. Such union is only possible when human beings are brought into full conformity and correspondence with God in the image of God.[9] "This teaching was not unfamiliar to Plato, because he defines the highest human good in various passages as being completely conformed to God."[10] In sum, inquiry into the knowledge of God should inevitably bring about affections in the heart corresponding to such knowledge, and should create an increasing correspondence of the person as a whole with God, which will elevate the person to union with God. "Plato meant nothing but this when he often taught that the highest good of the soul is likeness to God, where, when the soul has grasped the knowledge of God, it is wholly transformed into his likeness."[11] Already in his discussion of the purpose of human life, Calvin thinks in terms of analogy and anagoge: there should be an analogy and correspondence between the image of God in human beings and the reality of God, which should elevate us to union with God.[12] Calvin also makes his agreement with Plato on these matters explicitly clear.[13]

Since human beings are created to know God, what is the right way to seek after and inquire into the knowledge of God? Indeed, how is it even possible for human beings to come to know God? God is invisible, infinite, and spiritual, whereas human reason and intelligence come to know everything through what is visible, finite, and earthly. According to Calvin, we cannot even begin to seek after God unless God descends to our world and renders Godself somewhat visible, so that God can be

7. Comm. on 1 John 2:3, *CO* 55:311A; *CNTC* 5:245.

8. Comm. on 1 Pet. 2:3, *CO* 55:233B; *CNTC* 12:257–58.

9. "The highest human good is therefore simply union with God. We attain it when we are brought into conformity with His likeness" (Comm. on Heb. 4:10, *CO* 55:48B; *CNTC* 12:48).

10. Comm. on 2 Pet. 1:4, *CO* 55:446–47; *CNTC* 12:330.

11. *Inst.* 1.3.3; *OS* 3:40.18–22; LCC 1:46–47.

12. Comm. on Col. 3:10, *OE* 16:448–49; *CNTC* 11:349–50. Comm. on Gen. 17:22, *CO* 23:247B; CTS 1:463.

13. For the influence of Plato on the thought of Calvin, see Jean Boisset, *Sagesse et sainteté dans la pensée de Jean Calvin* (Paris: Presses Universitaires de France, 1959), 253–314.

perceived by the human senses; "for God cannot reveal himself to us in any other way than by a comparison with things which we know."[14] The right way to inquire into the knowledge of God is therefore to attend to the analogy between the visible image of God and the spiritual reality it represents, and to elevate oneself from the visible sign to the heavenly reality.

The way in which God initially becomes somewhat visible is by clothing Godself with the fabric of the world, thereby making the universe the living image of God. "God is invisible in Himself, but since His majesty shines forth in all his works and in all his creatures, men ought to have acknowledged him in these, for they clearly demonstrate their Creator. For this reason the apostle, in his Epistle to the Hebrews, calls the world a mirror or representation of invisible things (Heb. 11:3)."[15] The image of God in the universe ought to direct us to the God being represented therein by analogy and similitude, just as human portraits direct us to the person being portrayed: "for the likeness of a man ought so to compare with the man himself that by looking at it our minds are immediately directed to the man."[16] Thus, in his interpretation of Rom. 1:19, Calvin says, "By saying *God manifested it* he means that man was formed to be a spectator of the fabric of the world, and that he was endowed with eyes for the purpose of being led to God himself, the Author of the world, by contemplating so magnificent an image."[17] In particular, the works of God that we see in the world portray as in a painting the powers of God.[18] Wherever we turn our eyes, we look upon countless living images of the powers of God: his power, wisdom, and goodness.[19] These powers, in turn, make somewhat visible to us the invisible nature of God. "In the whole architecture of this world God has given us clear evidence of his eternal wisdom, goodness, and power, and though he is invisible in himself he shows himself to us in some measure in his work. The world is therefore rightly called the mirror of divinity."[20] We are directed to the knowledge of God by means of a double analogy and anagoge: the works of God correspond with and elevate us to the eternal powers of God, and the powers of God in the world correspond with and elevate us to their source in the divinity and nature of God.[21] Because we not only contemplate these powers, but also feel and enjoy them, we are to

14. Comm. on Isa. 40:18, *CO* 37:19C; CTS 15:223.

15. Comm. on Rom. 1:20, *Romanos* 29–30; CNTC 8:31.

16. Comm. on Heb. 9:9, *CO* 55:108A; CNTC 12:118.

17. Comm. on Rom. 1:19, *Romanos* 29; CNTC 8:31.

18. *Inst*. 1.5.10, *OS* 3:54.19–21; LCC 1:63.

19. Comm. on Acts 17:27, *CO* 48:412; CNTC 7:118.

20. Comm. on Heb. 11:3, *CO* 55:146A; CNTC 12:159–60.

21. Comm. on Rom. 1:20, *Romanos* 29–30; CNTC 8:31.

be ravished with admiration by our awareness of these powers, and are to be drawn by the taste of the goodness of God that they give us to love the summum bonum itself.[22]

Given human blindness and ingratitude, the image of God in the universe does not lead us to the knowledge of our Creator without the spectacles of Scripture and the inner witness of the Holy Spirit. However, Calvin insists that God represents Godself in Scripture in the same way that God delineates Godself in God's works.[23] This means that Scripture sets forth a living image of God, in which the nature of God is represented by the powers of God, which are portrayed in the works of God. Just such an image was revealed to Moses and handed on to us in Exod. 34:6–7. "The LORD passed before him, and proclaimed, 'The LORD, the LORD, a God merciful and gracious, slow to anger, and abounding in steadfast love and faithfulness'" (NRSV). According to Calvin, the name twice repeated announces the eternity of God. "Thereupon his powers are mentioned, by which he is shown to us not as he is in himself, but as he is towards us: so that this recognition of him consists more in living experience than in vain and high-flown speculation."[24] For Calvin, this passage records a living image of God, "and there is no passage in the law which expresses God's nature more to the life."[25]

Through the image of God in Scripture, the pious can ascend from the works of God to the powers of God portrayed therein, and from the powers of God to the nature of God. This ascent is made possible by the correspondence between the works of God, the powers of God, and the nature of God. From this ascent, the pious gain the certain assurance that God will always act in correspondence to God's nature, and that God will always remain like Godself. A constant refrain in Calvin's commentaries is the observation that "God cannot be unlike himself" and that God "always continues to be like himself."[26] The pious are able to trust in the similitude of God to God's nature even when God appears to be acting contrary to that nature. Thus, when the psalmist asks, "Will the Lord spurn forever, and never again be favorable?" (Ps. 77:7 NRSV), Calvin interprets this to mean, "He does not properly complain or find fault with God, but rather reasoning with himself, concludes, from the nature of God, that it is impossible for him not to continue his free favor towards his people, to whom he has once shown himself to be a father."[27]

22. *Inst.* 1.5.9, *OS* 3:53; LCC 1:62; *Inst.* 1.2.1, *OS* 3:34–35; LCC 1:40–41.

23. *Inst.* 1.10.1, *OS* 3:85.7–16; LCC 1:96.

24. *Inst.* 1.10.2, *OS* 3:86.6–22; LCC 1:97–98.

25. Comm. on Jon. 4:2, *CO* 43:265C; CTS 28:122.

26. Comm. on Jon. 4:2, *CO* 43:266B; CTS 28:123. Comm. on Isa. 33:3, *CO* 36:56A; CTS 15:12.

27. Comm. on Ps. 77:7–8, *CO* 31:714A; CTS 10:211.

The correspondence of the works of God with the nature of God also undergirds Calvin's claim that the end of God's works corresponds with the beginning; hence, the faithful are rightly confident that God will complete what God has begun.

One could ask Calvin whether the same kind of analogy obtains between the nature of God revealed to us in God's works and Word, and the essence of God hidden from us in light inaccessible.[28] Even though Calvin is often at pains to distinguish between the revealed nature of God and the hidden essence of God, there are frequent places where Calvin inseparably links the nature of God with the essence of God, particularly with regard to the powers found in the nature of God. Thus, when the same psalmist asks, "Has God forgotten to be gracious?" (Ps. 77:9 NRSV), Calvin interprets this to mean that "the more violently he was assailed, the more firmly did he lean upon the truth, that the goodness of God is so inseparably connected with his essence as to render it impossible for him not to be merciful."[29] Calvin elsewhere claims that the loving-kindness and mercy of God are also inseparable from the eternal essence of God, as is the readiness of God to hear prayer.[30] The powers that represent the nature of God to us are thus inseparable from the essence of God, even though they are also distinct from it.[31] However, Calvin does not use the language of analogy or similitude to express this relationship.

Language Is the Image of the Mind

Another way in which the Word of God reveals the nature of God to us is by the analogy that Calvin discerns between divine and human self-expression in language. In his interpretation of John 1:1, Calvin agrees with Erasmus that *ho logos* should be translated *Sermo*, because

28. "He does not speak of the hidden and mysterious essence [*abscondita Dei essentia*] which fills heaven and earth, but of the manifestations of his power, wisdom, goodness, and righteousness, which are clearly exhibited, although they are too vast for our limited intelligence to understand" (Comm. on Ps. 77:14, *CO* 31:718B; CTS 10:219).

29. Comm. on Ps. 77:9, *CO* 31:715A; CTS 10:213.

30. Comm. on Lam. 3:32, *CO* 39:584B; CTS 21:421. Comm. on Dan. 9:9, *CO* 41:142B; CTS 25:159. Comm. on Lam. 3:8, *CO* 39:566A; CTS 21:394.

31. In a particularly striking statement, Calvin says, "The majesty, or the authority, or the glory of God does not consist in some imaginary brightness, but in those works [*officiis*] which so necessarily belong to him that they cannot be separated from his very essence [*non possunt ab eius essentia avelli*]. It is what particularly belongs to God, to govern the world, and to exercise care over mankind, and also to make a difference between good and evil, to help the miserable, to punish all wickedness, to check injustice and violence" (Comm. on Zeph. 1:12, *CO* 44:22B; CTS 29:217).

the Word of God functions analogously to human language. "For just as in men speech is called the expression of the thoughts, so it is not inappropriate to apply this to God and say that he expresses himself to us by his Speech or Word."[32] Calvin often cited the proverb "Language is the image of the mind" because both our thoughts and affections are hidden from others until they are revealed by what we say.[33] There ought always to be a correspondence between our inward thoughts and affections, and their image in our language, but Calvin was painfully aware how often this is not the case. Thus, the similarity between God and us is that we both express our hidden thoughts and affections in the image of our language. The difference is that God never uses language to deceive, whereas humans often do. "For while by pretence and lies men often obscure, rather than reveal, their real state of mind, that is not the way with God, whose Word is absolute truth and his own living image."[34] Humans also have the capacity to understand one another's thoughts and affections, whereas God's thoughts and affections are too sublime for the human mind to reach without the illumination of the Holy Spirit.[35]

How then is God to express the thoughts of God's heart to humans? God reveals the inmost thoughts and affections of God's heart to the prophets, who in turn reveal them to us. "And it is no small commendation to prophetic doctrine that God as it were connected his heart with his mouth. The mouth of God is the doctrine itself; and he says now that it had proceeded from the depths of his heart."[36] However, the language that God uses to express the affections of the heart is language that is directly suited to express *human*, not divine, affections. Hence, the only way God can express God's affections toward us is by creating analogies or similitudes from human affections, which can only be properly understood if we carefully attend to the similarity and difference between human and divine affections. Calvin's most illuminating observations in this regard occur in his comments on Isaiah, where God frequently compares Godself to a mother.[37] In one instance, God expresses the warmth and tenderness of affection God has for Israel

32. Comm. on John 1:1, *CO* 47:1C; *CNTC* 4:7.

33. Comm. on Jer. 5:15, *CO* 37:626C; CTS 17:286. Comm. on Ps. 15:2, *CO* 31:144B; CTS 8:206. Comm. on Jer. 9:5, *CO* 38:30C; CTS 17:466. Comm. on Ps. 34:13, *CO* 31:341–42; CTS 8:567.

34. Comm. on 1 Cor. 2:11, *CO* 49:341C; *CNTC* 9:58.

35. *CO* 49:341C; *CNTC* 9:58.

36. Comm. on Jer. 23:20, *CO* 38:429C; CTS 19:175.

37. See Jane Dempsey Douglass, "Calvin's Use of Metaphorical Language for God: God as Enemy and God as Mother," in *Calvin and Hermeneutics*, 89–102. Douglass notes Calvin's interest in metaphors, but does not examine the role of analogy and anagoge. The same holds true of Roland M. Frye, "Calvin's Theological Use of Figurative Language,"

by saying that God is "like a woman in labor." Over against those who think that such comparisons are not suitable for God, Calvin insists that "in no other way than by such figures of speech can his ardent love toward us be expressed. He must therefore borrow comparisons from known objects, in order to enable us to understand those which are unknown to us."[38]

For others who think that the similitude best suited to express the affection God has for us is God as Father, Calvin says:

> If it be objected, that God is everywhere called "a Father," (Jer. 31:9; Mal. 1:6), and that this title is more appropriate to him, I reply, that no figures of speech can describe God's extraordinary affection for us; for it is infinite and various; so that, if all that can be said or imagined about love were brought together into one, yet it would be surpassed by the greatness of the love of God. By no metaphor, therefore, can his incomparable goodness be described.[39]

The one rule governing the use of all such figures and similitudes is that they express God's love and goodness toward us, for "whatever tends to this end—to convince us of God's ineffable love towards us, so that we may rest in it . . .—doubtless illustrates the glory of God and derogates nothing from his nature."[40] We must always bear in mind, however, that God's love differs from and far transcends all human love; "for God loves very differently from men, that is, more fully and perfectly, and, although he surpasses all human affections, yet nothing that is disorderly belongs to him."[41]

Calvin does not mean to say, however, that all similitudes drawn from human relationships of love are equally capable of expressing God's love for us. Even though the customary way God expresses affection toward us in Scripture is by analogy with fathers, Calvin claims that a mother's "love toward her offspring is so strong and ardent, as to leave far behind it a father's love,"[42] thereby making the analogy between the love of mothers and the love of God even more fitting. Thus, when God says through Isaiah, "Can a woman forget her sucking child?" (RSV), Calvin comments:

---

in *John Calvin and the Church*, ed. Timothy George (Louisville: Westminster/John Knox, 1990), 172–89.

38. Comm. on Isa. 42:14, *CO* 37:69C; CTS 15:302. See also Comm. on Isa. 40:18: "For God cannot reveal himself to us in any other way than by a comparison with things which we know" (*CO* 37:19C; CTS 15:223).

39. Comm. on Isa. 46:3, *CO* 37:154C; CTS 15:436.

40. Comm. on Zeph. 3:16–17, *CO* 44:72C; CTS 29:305.

41. Comm. on Isa. 42:14, *CO* 37:69C; CTS 15:302.

42. Comm. on Isa. 49:15, *CO* 37:204C; CTS 16:30–31.

Thus he did not satisfy himself with proposing the example of a father (which on other occasions he very frequently employs), but in order to express his very strong affection he chose to liken himself to a mother. . . . What amazing affection does a mother feel toward the fruit of her womb, which she cherishes in her bosom, suckles on her breast, and watches over with tender care, so that she passes sleepless nights, wears herself out by continued anxiety, and forgets herself![43]

However, no matter how much a mother's love may surpass in ardor and affection a father's love, no analogy drawn from human affection can ignore the great dissimilarity between a mother's love and God's love. For it indeed happens that "mothers degenerate into such monsters as to excel in cruelty the wild beasts" and forget their children, whereas God will never act contrary to God's love. "The affection which he bears toward us is far stronger and warmer than the love of all mothers."[44]

Calvin's interpretation of the similitude of God as mother reveals the characteristic way he interprets all analogies. First, he demonstrates the basis of the analogy, then he highlights the difference between the sign and the reality signified, and finally he indicates the transcendence of God over all comparisons. The paradigm for such interpretation for Calvin is found in Matt. 7:11: "If you then, who are evil [difference], know how to give good things to your children [similarity], how much more your heavenly Father [transcendence]?" (cf. RSV). The language that God uses to express Godself thus shares the two characteristics Calvin detects in all images that God uses both to represent Godself to us and to direct us to God: the analogy and anagoge between the sign and the thing signified.

The Revelation of God the Redeemer in the Law

Due to the entrance of human sin in the person of Adam, the image of God the Creator in the universe and in Scripture no longer suffices to lead us to God. The image of God that made possible our ascent to and union with God has been defaced by sin, which creates a contradiction between humanity and God where formerly there had been an analogy and correspondence. The powers of God in humanity have been replaced by their opposites, and the image of God in the universe reveals God's curse against sin over and above God's favor.[45] If humanity is to have access to God again, God must represent Godself to humanity in

43. *CO* 37:204C; CTS 16:30–31.
44. *CO* 37:204C; CTS 16:30–31
45. *Inst*. 2.1.5; *OS* 3:232–33; LCC 1:246.

the image of the Redeemer and Mediator. Over and above making the invisible God somewhat visible to humanity, such an image would have to remove the contradiction between humanity and God, and would also have to restore the correspondence, analogy, and anagoge between humanity and God. "It is evident from this that we cannot believe in God except through Christ, in whom God in a manner makes himself little, in order to accommodate himself to our comprehension, and it is Christ alone who can make our consciences at peace, so that we may dare to come in confidence to God."[46] After the fall of humanity into sin, God can only rightly be sought in the person of Jesus Christ, who is the image of the invisible Father. "God is made known to us when we believe in Christ. It is then that we begin to see the invisible God as in a mirror or a lively and express image."[47]

In keeping with the principle that the unknown can only be revealed through analogy and similitude with what is known, God initially revealed Jesus Christ to the people of Israel by means of earthly signs and figures that correspond to the reality of the person of Christ and raised the people of Israel from the earthly to the spiritual realm by anagoge. The only way to read the Hebrew Scriptures, therefore, is constantly to attend to the analogy and anagoge between the images of Christ in the history of Israel and the reality of Christ in the gospel. Thus, when the prophets describe the kingdom of Christ, they do so by means of earthly images of happiness and blessedness.[48] "Still, there is no defect in the Prophet's expressions, for they depict for us the visible image of Christ's kingdom, and accommodate themselves to our dullness. They enable us to perceive the anagogy between things earthly and visible, and the spiritual blessedness which Christ has afforded us, and which we now possess through hope in him."[49]

Although Calvin often maintains that such earthly images were necessary because of the rudeness or crassness of the people of Israel, who were like children (Gal. 4:1–3), he will frequently ascribe the necessity of such images to the general infirmity of human beings, who can only comprehend invisible, spiritual reality by similitudes drawn from the visible, earthly world.

> We know that what is beyond and above the world cannot be immediately comprehended by the human mind. We are enclosed, as it were, in prisons—I speak not of our bodies; but while we sojourn on earth, we cannot raise our minds upwards so as to penetrate as far as the celestial glory of

46. Comm. on 1 Pet. 1:21, *CO* 55:227A; *CNTC* 12:250.
47. Comm. on John 6:47, *CO* 47:151A; *CNTC* 4:166.
48. Comm. on Isa. 30:25, *CO* 36:524C; *CTS* 14:375.
49. Comm. on Dan. 7:27, *CO* 41:82B; *CTS* 25:73.

God. As, then, the kingdom of Christ is spiritual and celestial, it cannot be comprehended by human minds, except he raises up our thoughts, as he does, by degrees.[50]

Christians can never do without a consideration of the earthly types and images of Christ in the Hebrew Scriptures, for they teach us what we are to seek in Christ according to our earthly capacity. "From this we are to learn what benefit the reading of the Law brings us in this respect. . . . It greatly assists our faith to compare the reality with the types, so that we may seek in the one what the other contains."[51]

The key to reading the law, therefore, is always to keep in mind the analogy and anagoge between the earthly types and the spiritual reality. The analogy between the types and Christ leads Calvin to attend to the similarity and difference between the two, whereas the anagoge between the sign and reality leads Calvin to attend to the transcendence of Christ over all such comparisons. Thus, in his discussion of why Christ is often set forth in the law in the image of earthly kings, Calvin says: "We now then understand the design of what I said, that we ought to mark the transcendency of Christ over earthly kings, and also the analogy; for there is some likeness and some difference; the difference between Christ and other kings is very great, and yet there is a likeness in some things; and earthly kings are set forth to us as figures and images of him."[52] Moreover, Calvin wants readers and interpreters of the law to be sober and moderate in the way they develop the analogy and anagoge between the earthly images of Christ and Christ himself. Following Chrysostom's interpretation of Heb. 10:1, Calvin describes the images of Christ in the law as shadow outlines, tracing the outline of the image of Christ, not the full image itself, which is found only in the gospel. "The apostle has established this difference between the Law and the Gospel, that the former has foreshadowed in elementary and sketchy outline what today has been expressed in living and graphically printed color."[53] One should not, therefore, be overly anxious to develop analogies out of every aspect of the image, but only out of the main lines by which it delineates Christ. Thus, speaking against those who invented stories about Melchizedek descending from heaven in order to bring him into greater correspondence with Christ, Calvin says: "It is enough that we can see the lineaments of Christ in him, just as the form of a living man can be seen in a painting, and yet the man himself is dif-

50. Comm. on Jer. 31:12, *CO* 38:660B; CTS 20:82.
51. Comm. on 1 Pet. 1:19, *CO* 55:225B; *CNTC* 12:248.
52. Comm. on Jer. 23:5–6, *CO* 38:410C; CTS 19:142.
53. Comm. on Heb. 10:1, *CO* 55:121B; *CNTC* 12:132.

ferent from his picture."[54] The danger of such analogies is that they go beyond the express statements of Scripture about the analogy between the sign and the thing signified, as in the case of those interpreters who saw the main similitude between Christ and Melchizedek in the latter's offering of bread and wine to Abraham, even though this similitude is not mentioned by the Holy Spirit in Scripture.[55] Calvin's criticism of the allegorical interpretation of Scripture is not that it draws analogies between earthly signs and spiritual realities—this, after all, is the way Calvin thinks theologically—but rather because its analogies are speculative and excessive, whereas analogies ought to be grounded in the genuine sense of Scripture and developed with moderation. On the other hand, Calvin never comes across a sign or image without inquiring into its analogy with the reality signified, even when Scripture is silent about the nature of the analogy. "An analogy is always to be sought for between the signs, and the things signified, that there may be a mutual correspondence between them."[56]

The analogical function of the signs and images under the law becomes especially prominent in Calvin's discussion of the worship of Israel. Calvin focuses his attention on Exod. 25:40, echoed in Acts 7:44 and Heb. 8:5, in which Moses is commanded to make all of the elements of the worship of the tabernacle after the pattern shown to him on the mountain. According to Calvin, the pattern is Christ, and therefore "the whole of the legal worship was nothing more than a picture which adumbrated the spiritual in Christ."[57] Although Calvin clearly sought the analogies between the tabernacle/temple and Christ, particularly regarding the priests and sacrifices, he was especially concerned to view the temple as a ladder or vehicle by which the minds of the Israelites might ascend from earth to heaven. Thus, when the psalmist expresses his longing "for the courts of the LORD" (Ps. 84:2 NRSV), Calvin explains this longing in terms of the anagoge between the temple and the heavenly exemplar.

> The reason why he longed so intensely to have access to the tabernacle was, to enjoy the living God; not that he conceived of God as shut up in so narrow a place as was the tent of the ark, but he was convinced of the need he had for steps, by which to rise up to heaven, and knew that the visible sanctuary served the purpose of a ladder, because, by it the minds of the godly were directed and conducted to the heavenly model.[58]

54. Comm. on Heb. 7:3, *CO* 55:84A; *CNTC* 12:90.
55. Comm. on Heb. 7:9, *CO* 55:87–88; *CNTC* 12:94.
56. Comm. on Gen. 15:17, *CO* 23:221A; CTS 1:420.
57. Comm. on Heb. 8:5, *CO* 55:98C; *CNTC* 12:107.
58. Comm. on Ps. 84:2, *CO* 31:780C; CTS 10:355.

The ascent is possible because of the correspondence between the visible sanctuary and the heavenly pattern, to which the words of Moses directed the Israelites. Thus, it is necessary to seek God in the visible image of the temple and its forms of worship, so long as one does not bind God to the image, but rather ascends from the image to God.

> The ladders and vehicles, then, were the sanctuary, the ark of the covenant, the altar, the table, and its furniture. Moreover, I call them vehicles and ladders, because symbols of this kind were by no means ordained that the faithful might shut up God in a tabernacle as in a prison, or might attach him to earthly elements, but that, being assisted by congruous and apt means, they might themselves rise to heaven.[59]

Calvin frequently ascribes the need for such ladders and vehicles to the childlike character of the Israelites; yet he also acknowledges that Christians suffer from the same kind of infirmity and have need of their own earthly ladders and vehicles by which to raise their minds to Christ in heaven. "Nor in the present day, when bidding pious minds rise up to heaven, do we turn them away from Baptism and the Holy Supper. Nay, rather, we carefully admonish them to take heed that they do not rush upon a precipice, or lose themselves in vague speculations, if they fail to climb to heaven by those ladders which were not without cause set up for us by God."[60]

The anagogical element of Calvin's theology seems to be decisively shaped by Exod. 25:40 as interpreted by Heb. 8:5 and 9:24. God descends to us by representing to us visible images and signs of Christ and his grace, so that we might seek God in Christ by ascending as on the steps of a ladder from the visible signs to the reality they represent. "And assuredly, when we consider that the sluggishness of our flesh hinders us from elevating our minds to the height of the divine majesty, in vain would God call us to himself, did he not, at the same time, on his part, come down to us; or, did he not at least, by the interposition of means, stretch out his hand to us, so to speak, in order to lift us up to himself."[61]

The Revelation of God the Redeemer in the Gospel

The images and signs by which God descends to us so that we might ascend to God all correspond to the person of the Mediator, Jesus Christ. Christ is above all the one in whom God descends to us so that we

59. Comm. on Gen. 3:23, *CO* 23:186C; CTS 1:186.
60. *Secunda defensio contra Westphalum*, *CO* 9:84B; *Tracts and Treatises* 2:296.
61. Comm. on Ps. 84:2, *CO* 31:780B; CTS 10:355.

might ascend to God. Thus, when Jacob has a vision at Bethel of a ladder set up on earth whose top reaches to heaven (Gen. 28:12), Calvin relates this sign by analogy to Christ. "It is Christ alone, therefore, who connects heaven and earth: he is the only Mediator who reaches from heaven down to earth; he is the medium through which the fullness of all celestial blessings flows down to us, and through whom we, in turn, ascend to God."[62] Christ is also the one who is signified by the image of the temple, the footstool of the God who is seated in heaven. "Christ is he not only on whom the feet of God rest, but in whom the whole fullness of God's essence and glory resides, and in him, therefore, should we seek the Father. With this in view he descended, that we might rise heavenward."[63] Christ is therefore the image of the invisible God, in whom God becomes somewhat visible to us, so that we might come to know the unknown God by analogy with what we know, and so that we might ascend to God by means of the anagoge between Christ and God.

In order to know God in Christ, we must begin with what we know and what is closest to hand, and work by analogy and anagoge to what we do not know and is more remote from us. We simply cannot begin with the divinity of Christ, according to Calvin, but must rather begin with his humanity, and proceed throughout the whole history of Christ until we gradually ascend to his divinity.

> Therefore, that our faith may arrive at the eternal divinity of Christ, we must start off from that knowledge which is nearer and easier. Thus some have justly said that by Christ-human we are led to Christ-God, because our faith progresses gradually; apprehending Christ on earth, born in a stable and hanging on a cross, it goes on to the glory of his resurrection and then at length to His eternal life and power, in which shines His divine majesty.[64]

One must begin, therefore, with the works that Christ does in the flesh, in order to perceive the analogy between his earthly works and his spiritual power. Calvin sees Matthew in particular as especially concerned to develop this analogy by means of Isa. 53 (Matt. 8:17). "He gave light to the blind in order to show himself to them as the light of the world. He gave life back to the dead, that he might prove himself to be the resurrection and the life; and similarly with the lame and the paralyzed. This is the analogy we must follow."[65] Once one discerns the analogy between the physical and the spiritual healing power of Jesus, one is then to rise

62. Comm. on Gen. 28:12, *CO* 23:391A; CTS 2:112–13.
63. Comm. on Ps. 132:7, *CO* 32:345C; CTS 12:150.
64. Comm. on John 20:28, *CO* 47:444B; *CNTC* 5:211.
65. Comm. on Matt. 8:17, *CO* 45:156A; *CNTC* 1:163.

by anagoge from his human to his divine nature, which is concealed under the visible sign of his flesh. "The Jews saw nothing higher than the human nature in him. And so he insists that it was not his humanity which healed the sick man but his divine power hidden under his visible flesh. The issue revolved around this: they fixed on the sight of the flesh and despised Christ; and so he commands them to rise higher and look at God."[66] Moreover, since the eternal Son of God is the express and living image of God the Father, the ascent to the deity of Christ is followed by an ascent to God the Father.[67]

However, the ascent by analogy and anagoge from the humanity of Christ to his divinity, and from his divinity to the Father, is not nearly as straightforward as this scheme seems to suggest. In order to reconcile and reunite sinners with God, Christ must not only have a clear similarity to God, but must also have an unmistakable similitude with sinful humanity, which exists in contradiction to God. The analogy between the humanity and divinity of Christ will be deeply concealed under the appearance of its opposite, due to the likeness of Christ with sinners under the curse of God. This constitutes for Calvin the scandal of the cross, to which he was especially sensitive.

Calvin develops the likeness of Christ to sinful humanity out of Heb. 4:15, which he translated, "For we have not a high priest that cannot be touched with the feeling of our infirmities; but one that has been in all points tempted like as we are, yet without sin."[68] Calvin understands the similitude between Christ and ourselves to have to do especially with the affections that Christ had in common with us. According to Calvin, this analogy of affections serves at least three purposes. First, over against Marcion, it proves the genuine humanity of Christ and shows "that when the Son of God put on our flesh He also of his own accord put on human feelings, so that he differed in nothing from his brethren, sin only excepted."[69] The qualification "without sin" indicates the difference between the affections of Christ and ours, for our affections are disordered whereas the affections of Christ were always rightly ordered according to the true rule of justice and reason.[70] Second, if the affections of Christ are analogous to ours, this analogy proves over against the Stoics that the affections per se are not evil, but are part of our nature as created by God. "Christ's example alone should be sufficient for rejecting the unbending hardness of the Stoics; for where should we seek for the rule

66. Comm. on John 5:19, *CO* 47:112C; *CNTC* 4:125–26.
67. Comm. on John 17:25, *CO* 47:390C; *CNTC* 5:151.
68. Comm. on Heb. 4:15, *CO* 55:53A; *CNTC* 12:54.
69. Comm. on John 11:33, *CO* 47:265B; *CNTC* 5:12.
70. Comm. on Heb. 4:15, *CO* 55:55A; *CNTC* 12:56. Comm. on John 11:33, *CO* 47:266A; *CNTC* 5:12.

of supreme perfection but in him?"[71] The sympathy of Christ is more in keeping with the image of God than the apathy of the Stoics. Third, the analogy of affections reveals that Christ not only sympathized with our plight as sinners under the wrath of God, but that he also took our place, and suffered in his own person the death, curse, and damnation to which we have subjected ourselves.

> Christ, he says, came in the likeness of sinful flesh. Although the flesh of Christ was unpolluted by any stain, it had the appearance of being sinful, since it sustained the punishment due to our sins, and certainly death exerted every part of its power on the flesh of Christ as though it were subject to it. . . . In this respect too there appeared in him a certain resemblance to our sinful nature.[72]

Christ must have this likeness with sinful human flesh in order to take on himself the contradiction between humanity and God due to sin and remove it, thereby opening access to God and restoring us to the image and likeness of God.

However, this means that the obedience of Christ unto death will manifest not an analogy between Christ and God but rather an apparent contradiction. "That dreadful appearance of ignominy and malediction which is seen in the death of Christ, not only obscures his glory, but removes it altogether from our sight."[73] Moreover, Christ must suffer this contradiction in the inmost affections of his soul if he is really to take our place before God. "It is no fiction or play-acting that prompts his complaint, that he is forsaken by the Father. . . . It is an inner sadness of the soul, with violent fire, that drives him to break out in a cry."[74] At the same time, there is no disorder in the affections of Christ, for he knows in this obedience unto death that he is doing the will of the Father.[75]

How is this apparent lack of correspondence between Christ and God even possible, given the fact, which Calvin strenuously maintains, that Christ is God manifested in the flesh? Calvin interprets Phil. 2:5–8, concerning the self-emptying and self-humbling of Christ, along the lines laid down by Irenaeus of Lyons. "The words of Irenaeus, that he suffered, while his godhead remained at rest, I may interpret not only of his bodily death, but of his incredible grief and torment of mind, as is expressed in his complaining cry, 'My God, why hast thou forsaken

---

71. Comm. on John 11:33, *CO* 47:266B; *CNTC* 5:13.
72. Comm. on Rom. 8:3, *Romanos* 159.22–29; *CNTC* 8:159.
73. Comm. on John 12:23, *CO* 47:288C; *CNTC* 5:37.
74. Comm. on Matt. 27:46, *CO* 45:779B; *CNTC* 3:208.
75. *CO* 45:779B; *CNTC* 3:208.

me?'"[76] Because the divinity of Christ is quiescent throughout much of his life, and especially in his passion and death, there is no apparent analogy between the suffering of Christ and God, but only between the suffering of Christ and sinners, whose place Christ is willingly taking.

> The chief thing to consider in His death is His expiation, by which He appeased the wrath and curse of God. But He could not have done that without transferring to Himself our guilt. Therefore, the death which He underwent had to be full of horror, since He could not perform the satisfaction for us without apprehending the dreadful judgment of God with His senses. . . . Nor was it absurd that the Son of God should be troubled like this. For His divinity was hidden, did not put forth its power and, in a sense, rested, that an opportunity might be given for making expiation.[77]

The faith of the thief on the cross is for Calvin the highest example of faith, since he penetrates through to the divinity of Christ when it is completely concealed and quiescent. "What marks, what tokens adorned Christ as he saw him, that should raise his mind to kingship? Indeed it was to step from the depths of hell to the heights of heaven."[78]

For us, on the other hand, the analogy and anagoge between the humanity and divinity of Christ, and between Christ and the Father, is progressively restored, beginning with his resurrection from the dead.

> For since only weakness appears in the cross, death, and burial of Christ, faith must leap over all these things to attain its full strength. . . . Therefore, Paul states that "Christ was declared the Son of God . . . in the resurrection itself" [Rom. 1:4], because then at last he displayed his heavenly power, which is both the clear mirror of his divinity and the firm support of our faith.[79]

However, an even fuller manifestation of God in the humanity of Christ comes with his ascent into heaven and session at the right hand of the Father. "Now having laid aside the mean and lowly state of the cross, Christ by rising again began to show forth his glory and power more fully. Yet he truly inaugurated his Kingdom only at his ascension into heaven."[80] Calvin associates this fuller manifestation of the glory of Christ with the sending forth of the gospel and Holy Spirit, by which Christ came to establish his kingdom over all nations.[81] However, given the

76. Comm. on Luke 2:40, *CO* 45:104B; *CNTC* 1:107.
77. Comm. on John 12:27, *CO* 47:291A; *CNTC* 5:39.
78. Comm. on Luke 23:42, *CO* 45:774B; *CNTC* 3:203.
79. *Inst.* 2.16.13, *OS* 3:499.29–31, 500.16–19; *LCC* 1:520–21.
80. *Inst.* 2.16.14, *OS* 3:501.22–25; *LCC* 1:522.
81. Comm. on John 12:23, *CO* 47:288B; *CNTC* 5:36–37.

apparent infirmity and weakness of the kingdom of Christ on earth, the ultimate display of God in the human Jesus will come on the last day, when the entire world will see his immortality and divine glory.[82] Without the resurrection, ascension, and return of Christ in glory, faith would not be able to follow the analogy and anagoge between the humanity of Christ and his divinity, and rise from Christ to the Father.

However, the resurrection and the sending of the gospel cast a retrospective light on the cross itself. For the resurrection and the gospel reveal that the ignominy and malediction appearing in the cross are due to the incomparable love of Christ for us, by which he was willing to take on our contradiction with God in order once again to open access to the Father. Seen in the context of the goodness of God, the cross is the brightest image of God in the world.

> For in the cross of Christ, as in a splendid theater, the incomparable goodness of God is set before the whole world. The glory of God shines, indeed, in all creatures on high and below, but never more brightly than in the cross, in which there is a wonderful change of things—the condemnation of all men was manifested, sin blotted out, salvation restored to all men; in short, the whole world was renewed and all things restored to order.[83]

In light of the resurrection and the gospel, the very powers that seemed to be quiescent in the cross are seen to have been most fully displayed, "since there his incredible love to mankind, his infinite righteousness in atoning for sin and appeasing the wrath of God, his wonderful power in overcoming death, subduing Satan, and, indeed, opening up heaven, put forth its full brightness."[84] The resurrection and ascension of Christ do not therefore mean that we may now ascend directly to the divinity of Christ and bypass his crucifixion. Rather, the proper analogy and anagoge between Christ and God is only followed when we first submit our attention to Christ crucified, and then rise to the resurrection.[85]

> We can see how he leads his disciples by the hand to the cross, and thence raises them to the hope of the resurrection. They had to be guided to Christ's death that they might use it as a ladder to ascend to heaven, so now, because Christ died and was received into heaven, by looking on the

82. *Inst.* 2.16.17, *OS* 3:504.27–35; LCC 1:525.

83. Comm. on John 13:31, *CO* 47:316–17; *CNTC* 5:68.

84. Comm. on John 13:32, *CO* 47:317B; *CNTC* 5:69.

85. "Proud men are ashamed of Christ's humiliation and therefore fly to God's incomprehensible divinity. But faith will never reach heaven unless it submits to Christ, who appears as [a] God lowly in aspect; nor will it be firm unless it seeks a foundation in the weakness of Christ" (Comm. on John 14:1, *CO* 47:322A; *CNTC* 5:74).

cross we should be led up to heaven, that his dying and his life restored should hold together.[86]

Moreover, such is our infirmity that we cannot rise from the cross of Christ to his session with the Father in heaven unless Christ sets his death and resurrection before us in the living images of the gospel and the sacraments. The Holy Supper of the Lord in particular sets forth the death and resurrection of Christ for us in a mirror, so that we might rise from contemplating the sign to the thing signified in heaven. The accommodation of God to us by means of the analogy and anagoge between the humanity of Christ and God is further supplemented by the accommodation of Christ to us by means of the analogy and anagoge between the signs of the gospel—baptism and the Holy Supper—and his crucified and risen humanity in heaven.

> Nor in the present day, when bidding pious minds rise up to heaven, do we turn them away from Baptism and the Holy Supper. Nay, rather, we carefully admonish them to take heed that they do not rush upon a precipice, or lose themselves in vague speculations, if they fail to climb to heaven by those ladders which were not without cause set up for us by God. We teach, therefore, that if believers would find Christ in heaven they must begin with the word and sacraments.[87]

Even in our present infirmity, we now have access to God the Father by following the analogy and anagoge between the gospel and the sacraments and Christ's humanity in heaven, and then by following the analogy and anagoge between Christ's human and divine natures, in order finally to rise from the Son to the Father, the author and fountain of all good things.

Finally, the humanity of Christ is not only the living image of God that leads us by analogy and anagoge to God the Father, but it is also the image that progressively transforms us into the image and likeness of God, so that we might be united with God in eternal life. "Our happiness lies in having God's image, which was blotted out by sin, restored and reformed in us. Christ is not only, as the eternal Word of God, his lively image, but even on his human nature, which he has in common with us, the imprint of the Father's glory has been engraved, that he might transform his members to it."[88] Calvin also sees the same dynamic in the living image of Christ in the gospel. Commenting on 2 Cor. 3:18, one of his favorite texts, Calvin says,

86. Comm. on Matt. 26:29, *CO* 45:709A; *CNTC* 3:137.
87. *Secunda defensio contra Westphalum, CO* 9:84; *Tracts and Treatises* 2:296.
88. Comm. on John 17:22, *CO* 47:388A; *CNTC* 5:149.

He uses the similitude of the image in the mirror to make three points: first, that we need not fear obscurity when we approach the Gospel, for it is there God shows his unveiled face; second, that this should not be a dead and fruitless contemplation, for through it we should be transformed into God's image; third, that neither of these things happen all at once, but by continual progress we increase both in the knowledge of God and in conformity to his image.[89]

Since the gospel sets forth the living image of the goodness of God in Christ crucified, the image to which we are conformed in this life is the image of the cross. However, since the cross is the brightest image of the goodness and love of God in the universe, our contemplation of it will not only transform us into its image, but will also ignite in our hearts the fire of love, which will raise us up to God. "Let us remember that it is the true fruit of heavenly teaching, whoever may be its minister, to light the fire of the Spirit in men's hearts, to refine and purify, yes, to consume, and to whip up a true fever of love for God and snatch all men to heaven in its flames."[90] Thus, the gospel not only leads us to Christ, and from him to God, by analogy and anagoge, but it also restores the image of God in us and raises our hearts on high to God in the fire of love.

89. Comm. on 2 Cor. 3:18, *OE* 15:66; *CNTC* 10:50.
90. Comm. on Luke 24:32, *CO* 45:810A; *CNTC* 3:239.

11

THE UNIVERSE
AS THE LIVING IMAGE OF GOD

According to Calvin, the primary self-manifestation of God takes place in the universe that God created, sustains, and governs. Even though this image of God cannot be properly contemplated without the spectacles of Scripture and the testimony of the Holy Spirit, Calvin insists that the self-manifestation of God in the world should be carefully contemplated daily by the pious, or at least once a week on the Sabbath. In order to highlight the significance of such contemplation for Calvin, I place his discussion in the context of the contemporary controversy over the role of Christianity in the degradation of the environment. Did Calvin's understanding of the living image of God in the universe lead those who followed his teaching to exploit the world for their own benefit and

This essay was originally published in a slightly different form under the title "The Universe as the Living Image of God: Calvin's Doctrine of Creation Reconsidered," *Concordia Theological Quarterly* 61, no. 4 (1997): 299–312. Reprinted by permission.

enjoyment? Or would Calvin have restrained such exploitation by his emphasis on the most beautiful image of God in the universe?

I remember standing in the mountains of North Carolina several years ago, in a beautiful gorge that opened out onto the low hills of South Carolina. In this gorge was a magnificent waterfall, cascading in the sunlight over the smooth granite rocks into the shadows of the pine trees below. As I stood there gazing at this scene, I overheard two gentlemen speaking next to me. The man nearest me turned to his friend and observed, "Just think of all of the kilowatts of hydroelectricity being wasted in this falls!"

How should we regard the world in which we live? Should we contemplate it as full of marvels, wonders, and miracles, which fill our minds with awe and ravish our hearts with astonishment and admiration? Or should we look upon the earth as a treasure trove of resources bequeathed to us, to be used for our own advantage and profit, to be exploited for the fulfillment of our desires? We are becoming well aware of the blindness, cruelty, and folly of the latter attitude, given the alarmingly rapid degradation of the environment since the scientific and industrial revolutions, creating our current ecological crisis. Many today accuse the Christian tradition of helping to create this crisis by its teaching about the purpose of the natural world, that God created it for the good and enjoyment of humankind. This Christian teaching has been blamed for fostering an attitude toward the world that encourages the exploitation of nature to satisfy human needs and desires, at the expense of the welfare of the world. Christians are said to teach, on the basis of Gen. 1:26, that humankind has been given dominion over every living creature and may therefore use all creatures for the fulfillment of human aims and objectives. Such teaching is said to be anthropocentric: it places the interests of human beings at the center of the world. In his landmark article on the historical roots of the ecological crisis, Lynn White Jr. claimed, "Especially in its Western form, Christianity is the most anthropocentric religion the world has seen," since it insists "that it is God's will that man exploit nature for his proper ends."[1] According to White, the consequence of Western Christian teaching is to make it "possible to exploit nature in a mood of indifference to the feelings of natural objects."[2] Hence, White claims that "we shall continue to have a worsening ecological crisis until we reject the Christian axiom that nature has no reason for existence save to serve man."[3] David Kinsley has recently reiterated White's charge and has identified John Calvin

1. Lynn White Jr., "The Historical Roots of Our Ecological Crisis," in *Western Man and Environmental Ethics*, ed. Ian Barbour (Englewood, NJ: Addison-Wesley, 1973), 25.
2. Ibid., 25.
3. Ibid., 29.

as a theologian who taught an ecologically harmful view of creation. Kinsley describes Calvin's teaching in this manner: "God controls and directs nature; as God's agent or special creation, human beings are to imitate this relationship in their dealings with nature."[4] So self-evident is this claim to Kinsley that he does not cite one text from the writings of Calvin to warrant it.

Kinsley's claim, if true, would do much to substantiate the claims made by White, for Calvin has a highly developed doctrine of the creative and providential works of God. More ominously still, Calvin is arguably the most influential theologian of the English-speaking world, in which the scientific and industrial revolutions developed. Is it true that Calvin taught that it is God's will that humanity exploit nature for its own ends, with indifference for the natural world per se? At first sight, White and Kinsley would seem to have support for their claims in Calvin's writings. In his comments on Gen. 1:26, the key text about human dominion over all creatures, Calvin appears to confirm their worst suspicions in saying, "We must infer [from this text] what was the end for which all things were created; namely, that none of the conveniences and necessities of life might be wanting to men."[5] Lest we think this to be an isolated statement, Calvin repeats this thought in his exposition of Ps. 24:1. "To what purpose are there produced so many kinds of fruit, and in so great abundance, and why are there so many pleasant and delightful countries, if it is not for the use and comfort of men?"[6] Calvin also makes this one of the major points for the reader to contemplate in the narration of the six days of creation. "God himself has shown by the order of creation that he created all things for man's sake."[7]

It is therefore undeniable that Calvin consistently and repeatedly taught that the world was created for the use and comfort of humanity, and that the abundance of good things found in the world were given to us by God for our necessities as well as for our enjoyment. However, this leaves the most important question unanswered: Why did God will to give us all the good things of the world, even before we were created? And how does God want us to regard the good things of the world that God has bequeathed to us? We assume that when Calvin teaches that God created all things for the use and comfort of humans, this means that we are free to treat the created world as we see fit, like spoiled children in a toy store. But what did Calvin mean by this teaching? How did Calvin teach Christians to regard the created order? In order to answer these

4. David Kinsley, *Ecology and Religion: Ecological Spirituality in Cross-Cultural Perspective* (Englewood, NJ: Prentice Hall, 1995), 111.

5. Comm. on Gen. 1:26, *CO* 23:27C; CTS 1:96.

6. Comm. on Ps. 24:1, *CO* 31:244A; CTS 8:402.

7. *Inst.* 1.14.22, *OS* 3:172.27–28; LCC 1:181–82.

questions, we will examine the meaning of the three central metaphors that Calvin used to describe the created order: the theater of God's glory, the living image of God, and the beautiful garment of God.

The Theater of God's Glory

It is a commonplace that Calvin taught that the created world is the theater of God's glory; indeed, Susan Schreiner used this phrase from Calvin as the title of her book on nature in the thought of Calvin.[8] Oddly enough, however, Schreiner did not directly examine what this phrase might mean, although it would seem to deserve greater attention than it has hitherto received. Schreiner does note that for Calvin nature is "a mirror, a painting, and a theater of the divine glory" that reveals God, but this is not the focus of her work.[9] If the world is a theater, then humans have been created as spectators in the audience to behold the drama enacted before them on the stage. The performance itself must be the works of God that reveal the glory of God to us. As in any good theater, the actions of God on the stage are not meant to leave us coldly indifferent but rather are designed to move our minds and affections in a particular way. More important, by attentively beholding the actions of God on the stage, we are meant to arrive at a greater recognition and acknowledgment of the nature and character of the actor.

How might all this take place? According to Calvin, the actions of God in the world set forth the powers of God; and these powers of God in turn reveal to us who God is and what God is like. As spectators of the divine performance in the world, we are to contemplate the works of God in order to discern the powers of God that shine forth in these works. "We must admit that in God's individual works—but especially in them as a whole—that God's powers are actually represented as in a painting. Thereby the whole of mankind is invited and attracted to recognition of him, and from this to true and complete happiness."[10] Since the powers of God that we see also invite and allure us to seek our happiness in the source of these powers, they must be good things that both individually and as a whole manifest to us the goodness of God. "It is no small honor that God for our sake so magnificently adorned the world, in order that we may not only be spectators of this bounteous theater, but also enjoy the multiplied abundance and variety of good things which are presented

8. Susan E. Schreiner, *The Theater of His Glory: Nature and the Natural Order in the Thought of John Calvin*, Studies in Historical Theology 3 (Durham, NC: Labyrinth, 1991).

9. Ibid., 121; see also 65, 107.

10. *Inst.* 1.5.10, *OS* 3:54.19–24; LCC 1:63.

to us in it."[11] According to Calvin, the powers that especially reveal the nature of God are eternity, wisdom, power, goodness, justice, mercy, and truth.[12] When we behold these powers in the works of God, we are led to feel the force of these powers within ourselves; and since these powers are all good things, our feeling of these powers will lead to our enjoyment of them. "For the Lord manifests himself by his powers, the force of which we feel within ourselves and the benefits of which we enjoy."[13] More important, by our contemplation, feeling, and enjoyment of the powers of God that we behold in the theater of the world, we are invited, allured, and attracted to seek the God who is the source and author of all these powers, in whom alone is found human happiness and blessedness. Both the beauty of creation, and the enjoyment of good things revealed and offered therein, should ravish us outside of ourselves so that we seek God from the inmost affection of the heart.

The creation of all good things in the world for the benefit and enjoyment of humans is not, therefore, an end in itself, but is rather the way God initially reveals to humankind that God is the author and fountain of every good thing. Our use and enjoyment of the good things of creation is not intended by God to be an end in itself, but is rather the way God allures and invites us to seek God as the source of every good thing. It would be a perversion of the theater of God's glory and a sign of manifest ingratitude for us to feel and enjoy the good things of creation, and yet to ignore the one who invites and allures us to Godself by means of these benefits.

The Living Image of God

Calvin uses other visual metaphors besides the theater in order to describe the self-manifestation of God in the universe. On the basis of Heb. 11:3, Calvin develops the metaphor of the universe as the living image of the invisible God. The text itself reads, "By faith we understand that the worlds have been framed by the word of God, so that what is seen has not been made out of things that appear." Calvin translates the latter phrase, "so that they become the visibles of things not seen, that is, the spectacles." He combines this passage with Rom. 1:20 in order to develop his metaphor of the universe as the living image of God. "These words contain the very important teaching that in this world we have a clear image of God, and in this passage our apostle is saying the

11. Comm. on Ps. 104:31, *CO* 32:96C; CTS 11:169.
12. Comm. on Rom. 1:20, *Romanos* 30–31; *CNTC* 8:32.
13. *Inst.* 1.5.9, *OS* 3:53.14–16; LCC 1:62.

same thing as Paul in Rom. 1:20, where he says that the invisible things of God are made known to us by the creation of the world, since they are seen in his works."[14] In particular, the universe is the image of God because of the powers of God that are manifested in the works of God. "In the whole architecture of his world God has given us clear evidence of his eternal wisdom, goodness, and power, and though he is invisible in himself he shows himself to us in some measure in his work. The world is therefore rightly called the mirror of divinity."[15]

The invisible God appears to us as in a mirror or image in the works that God does in the world. This means that we must, on the one hand, distinguish between the world that we see and the God who is represented therein. On the other hand, there must be a similarity or analogy between the image of God in the world and the God who is manifested therein. Inasmuch as God is the invisible, spiritual Creator of the visible and earthly image, the analogy must be one that elevates us from the world to God by means of anagoge. In other words, when we see the image of God in the universe, we are to lift the eyes of our minds to God, just as we turn our mind to the person whose portrait we behold. "By saying 'God manifested it' he means that man was formed to be a spectator of the created world, and that he was endowed with eyes for the purpose of his being led to God himself, the Author of the world, by contemplating so magnificent an image."[16] The image must also incite us to lift our hearts to seek the God representing Godself in the image, which happens when we feel and enjoy within ourselves the force and benefit of the powers of God that we behold in the image. By these powers, we are sweetly invited to seek God from the inmost affection of our hearts.

According to Calvin, there is an ascending order of the good things set forth in the image of God in the universe, which are to lead us gradually to God like steps on a ladder. At the bottom of the ladder are the temporal benefits of this life, such as food, housing, spouses, children, and wealth, among others. From our enjoyment of these benefits we should be led to the spiritual powers of God that these temporal blessings reveal, especially God's goodness, wisdom, and power. "For in this world God blesses us in such a way as to give us a mere foretaste of his kindness, and by that taste to entice us to desire heavenly blessings with which we may be satisfied."[17] Finally, we should be led from these spiritual benefits to the love and care of God for us, so that we might cling to God alone. "But by this he does not cast any hindrance or impediment in our way

14. Comm. on Heb. 11:3, *OE* 19:184.4–6; *CNTC* 12:160.
15. Comm. on Heb. 11:3, *OE* 19:184.6–10; *CNTC* 12:160.
16. Comm. on Rom. 1:19, *Romanos* 29; *CNTC* 8:31.
17. Comm. on 1 Tim. 4:8, *CO* 52:300A; *CNTC* 10:244.

to keep us from elevating our minds to heaven, but ladders are by this means rather erected to enable us to mount up thither step by step."[18] When we confine our attention to the benefits of this life and seek our sole enjoyment in them alone, we turn the ladders into obstacles and pervert the purpose of the image of God in the universe. God descends to us in the living image of God in this world so that we might ascend to God by means of that same image.

The Beautiful Garment of God

The third metaphor Calvin uses to describe the universe is that of a garment. According to Calvin, the invisible God clothes Godself with the garment of the universe in order thereby to become somewhat visible. Calvin derives this metaphor from Ps. 104:1–2: "For thou hast clothed thyself with praise and glory, being arrayed with light as with a garment, and spreading out the heavens as a curtain." The advantage of this metaphor is that it allows Calvin to describe the way God remains hidden even as God manifests Godself. Calvin comments on this verse: "In respect of his essence, God undoubtedly dwells in light that is inaccessible; but as he irradiates the whole world by his splendor, this is the garment in which he, who is hidden in himself, appears in a manner visible to us."[19] Calvin adopts this metaphor in particular when he wishes to celebrate the great beauty of the universe. "That we may enjoy the sight of God, he must come forth to view with his clothing; that is to say, we must first cast our eyes upon the very beautiful fabric of the world in which he wishes to be seen by us."[20]

According to Calvin, when we rightly contemplate the beauty of the richly ornamented garment of the world, our minds and hearts should be ravished with admiration, so that our hearts might be incited to praise and thank God, even as we become aware of our inability to do justice to the beauty of the world that we behold. "Accordingly, breaking off his description, he exclaims with admiration—How greatly to be praised are thy works! Even as we then only ascribe to God due honor when seized with astonishment, we acknowledge that our tongues and all our senses fail in doing justice to so great a subject."[21] Our experience of being ravished with admiration and astonishment facilitates our ascent from the beautiful garment of the universe to the invisible God who is appearing therein, even as it awakens within us true praise for the glory

18. Comm. on Ps. 128:3, *CO* 32:328B; CTS 12:117.
19. Comm. on Ps. 104:1, *CO* 32:85A; CTS 11:145.
20. *CO* 32:85A; CTS 11:145.
21. Comm. on Ps. 104:24, *CO* 32:93C; CTS 11:164.

of God. "We only praise God aright when we are filled and overwhelmed with an ecstatic admiration of the immensity of his power. This admiration will form the fountain from which our praises of him will proceed, according to the measure of our capacity."[22]

The metaphor of the world as the garment of God allows Calvin to speak of the intimate care of God for all living creatures in the world, over and above human beings. Certainly no part of the world seems more hostile to human interests and well-being than the desert wilderness, yet even here Calvin would have us contemplate the beauty and goodness of God. "Rivers run through the great and desolate wildernesses, where the wild beasts enjoy some blessings of God; and no country is so barren as not to have trees growing here and there, on which birds make the air to resound with the melody of their singing."[23] Calvin draws two consequences from the tender care that God clearly exhibits toward all creatures, even in the wilderness. On the one hand, as we might expect, we are to follow the analogy and anagoge between God's care for other creatures and God's care for humanity. "It is not to be wondered at, if God so bountifully nourishes humans who are created after his image, since he does not grudge to extend his care even to trees, . . . which are high and of surpassing beauty."[24] On the other hand, we ourselves are to care for all the creatures of God, in imitation of the care that God has for them. Thus, in his comment on the prohibition of killing a mother bird on her nest, Calvin says, "For if there is one drop of compassion in us, it will never enter our minds to kill an unhappy little bird, which so burns either with the desire of offspring, or with love towards its little ones, as to be heedless of life, and to prefer endangering itself to the destruction of its eggs, or its brood."[25] Nor should we denude the earth of trees during warfare, not only because their fruit manifests the blessing of God toward us, but also because such an act would deprive the earth of its beautiful ornamentation created by God.

It is impossible to harmonize Calvin's teaching with Lynn White's claim that "Christianity made it possible to exploit nature in a mood of indifference to the feelings of natural objects," or his claim that, "to a Christian, a tree can be no more than a physical fact."[26] According to Calvin, God excludes no creature from God's care, and neither should we. Moreover, God is somewhat visible in the beautifully ornamented garment of the world. We should not, therefore, despoil such a garment, but should instead seek to preserve and enhance its beauty, so that we

22. Comm. on Ps. 145:1, *CO* 32:413B; CTS 12:273.
23. Comm. on Ps. 104:10, *CO* 32:89B; CTS 11:154.
24. Comm. on Ps. 104:16, *CO* 32:91–92; CTS 11:160.
25. Comm. on Deut. 22:6, *CO* 24:634B; CTS 5:56.
26. White, "Historical Roots," 25, 28.

might be ravished with admiration and inflamed to praise God from the depths of our hearts.

The godly are also to imitate God by contemplating the goodness and beauty of the universe. "I do not, however, doubt but that God created the world in six days and rested on the seventh, that he might give a manifestation of the perfect excellency of his works, and thus, proposing himself as the model for our imitation, he signifies that he calls his own people to the true goal of felicity."[27] Calvin thinks that such contemplation ought to occupy every waking moment in the lives of Christians. "There is indeed no moment which should be allowed to pass in which we are not attentive to the consideration of the wisdom, power, goodness, and justice of God in his admirable creation and government of the world."[28] However, God rested on the Sabbath to leave us an example to imitate, that we might take at least one day a week to rest from our works in order to contemplate the beauty of the works of God in the world. "And certainly God took the seventh day for his own and hallowed it, when the creation of the world was finished, that he might keep his servants free from every care, for the consideration of the beauty, excellence, and fitness of his works."[29]

Calvin advises his readers that the best way to undertake the contemplation of the beauty of God's works in the universe is to begin with the heavens, for they are a more clear and distinct image of God than the earth. "There is certainly nothing so obscure or contemptible, even in the smallest corners of the earth, in which some marks of the power and wisdom of God may not be seen; but as a more distinct image of him is engraven on the heavens, David has particularly selected them for contemplation, that their splendor might lead us to contemplate all parts of the world."[30] Once our eyes have been trained to see the image of God in the heavens, we ought to direct our gaze to the earth, so that we see below the same powers that were so conspicuously portrayed in the heavens. "When a person, from beholding and contemplating the heavens, has been brought to acknowledge God, he will learn also to reflect upon and admire his wisdom and power displayed on the face of the earth, not only in general, but even in the minutest plants."[31]

Our admiration of the goodness, wisdom, and power of God should increase in us the more we come to understand the universe by scientific observation, even when such observation reveals that the universe is in fact different from the way it is described in Scripture. "For astronomy

27. Comm. on Exod. 20:8, *CO* 24:578C; CTS 4:436.
28. Comm. on Exod. 20:8, *CO* 24:579A; CTS 4:437.
29. Comm. on Exod. 20:8, *CO* 24:579A; CTS 4:437.
30. Comm. on Ps. 19:1, *CO* 31:194C; CTS 8:808.
31. Comm. on Ps. 19:1, *CO* 31:194C; CTS 8:808–9.

is not only pleasant, but also very useful to be known; it cannot be denied that this art unfolds the admirable wisdom of God."[32] Hence, the contemplation of the powers of God in God's works includes scientific observation, so long as we do not confine ourselves to secondary causes, but lift our minds from the fabric of the world to the God being represented therein. "As soon as we acknowledge God to be the supreme architect, who has erected the beauteous fabric of the universe, our minds must necessarily be ravished with wonder at his infinite goodness, wisdom, and power."[33]

The Proper Use of Creation

Calvin was well aware of the temptations presented to humanity by the way that God reveals Godself to us in the world. The world, which is the theater of God's glory, might be abused by us in trying to make it the stage on which we attain our own glory. The image of God in the universe might be mistaken for the God that it represents, so that we seek only the good things offered to us in this world, and not the God who wishes to be sought through this image. The beautiful fabric of this world might allure us by its sweetness to enjoy it alone, and not seek our happiness in the goodness of the God who is clothed with this garment. Our scientific exploration of the works of God might stop with the mediate causes we observe, so that we obscure the powers of God shining forth in all of God's works and confine our attention only to this life. In sum, we might be tempted to think that when God created the whole world for our benefit, the whole of our good is to be sought in this world, not in its Creator.

According to Calvin, all of the ungodly succumb to these forms of temptation. They seek only the good things of this life, not the God who is inviting us to Godself by means of these benefits. They are captivated by the sweetness and beauty of the universe, so that they are not invited and allured to God, but rather seek their happiness solely in temporal blessings. As a consequence, no matter how much the ungodly may enjoy worldly abundance, they always desire more, and yet their desire is never satisfied, even after they plunder the whole world. "However great the abundance of the ungodly, yet their covetousness is so insatiable, that, like robbers, they plunder right and left, and yet are never satisfied."[34] The ungodly hoard the good things of this earth and never think of using their abundance to care for those in need. The ungodly are blind to the

32. Comm. on Gen. 1:16, *CO* 23:22B; CTS 1:86.
33. Comm. on Ps. 19:1, *CO* 31:195B; CTS 8:309.
34. Comm. on Ps. 37:21, *CO* 31:376C; CTS 9:36.

powers of God shining forth in the universe and are ungrateful to God for any of the blessings they enjoy. They feed on the good things of this world like beasts with their snouts in a trough, never once lifting their eyes, minds, or hearts to seek the God who feeds them.

The godly, on the other hand, have been given the eyes of faith by the Holy Spirit, and the spectacles of the Word of God in Scripture, so that they can clearly discern the image of God represented in the universe, and lift up their minds and hearts to the God manifested therein. Since the godly ascend from the benefits they enjoy to the love and favor of God revealed therein, they are content with that love alone and do not seek their happiness or satisfaction in the good things of this life. Like David, the godly use the benefits they enjoy in this life as steps of a ladder by which they might ascend from earth to heaven.

> For this reason, we ought the more carefully to mark the example which is here set before us by David, who, elevated to the dignity of sovereign power, surrounded with the splendor of riches and honors, possessed of the greatest abundance of temporal good things, and in the midst of princely pleasures, not only testifies that he is mindful of God, but calling to remembrance the benefits which God had conferred on him, makes them ladders by which he may ascend nearer to him.[35]

Because the pious rest in the love and care of God, and not in the good things that reveal that care, they will be able to discern the blessing of God even in extreme poverty, and will use the good things that they receive with moderation, tempered by their gratitude toward God and their care for the needs of others. "And although the faithful also desire and seek after worldly comforts, yet they do not pursue them with immoderate and irregular ardor; but they can patiently bear to be deprived of them, provided they know themselves to be the objects of divine care."[36] Most important for our purposes, the contemplation of the beauty of the universe will lead the godly to care for the beautiful garment of the world the way that God cares for it, so that they might leave it even more beautiful than they first found it.

How, then, did Calvin teach us to regard the world in which we live? We should be attentive spectators in the theater of God's glory, seeking to recognize the actor on the stage by means of the powers revealed in God's actions. We should contemplate and meditate on the world as the living image of God, in which the invisible God becomes somewhat visible, so that the powers of God that we behold, feel, and enjoy might lead us to the God represented in this image. We should be ravished with

35. Comm. on Ps. 23:1, *CO* 31:238A; CTS 8:391.
36. Comm. on Ps. 4:7, *CO* 31:64B; CTS 8:49.

amazement and astonishment by the beautiful fabric of the universe in which the invisible God is clothed, which reveals the goodness of God to us and sweetly allures us to seek God from the depths of our hearts.

> For God—by other means invisible—clothes himself, so to speak, with the image of the world, in which he would present himself to our contemplation. . . . Therefore, as soon as the name of God sounds in our ears, or the thought of him occurs to our minds, let us also clothe him with this most beautiful ornament; finally, let the world become our school if we rightly desire to know God.[37]

Moreover, because the world is the theater of God's glory, the living image of the invisible God, and the beautiful garment that God wears, we have the responsibility to care for this universe and all of the creatures in it, the way that God already cares for everything that God has made.

> The custody of the garden was given in charge to Adam, to show that we possess the things which God has committed to our hands, on the condition, that being content with a frugal and moderate use of them, we should take care of what shall remain. Let him who possesses a field, so partake of its yearly fruits, that he may not suffer the ground to be injured by his negligence; but let him endeavor to hand it down to posterity as he received it, or even better cultivated. Let him so feed on its fruits, that he neither dissipates it by luxury, nor permits it to be marred or ruined by neglect. Moreover, that this economy and this diligence, with respect to those good things which God has given us to enjoy, may flourish among us; let every one regard himself as the steward of God in all things which he possesses. Then he will neither conduct himself dissolutely, nor corrupt by abuse those things which God requires to be preserved.[38]

If we had followed the teaching of Calvin about creation, would we really have been led to exploit and defile the earth with a good conscience, or even with indifference? If we had heeded Calvin's teaching of our responsibilities toward the created world, would we really have been encouraged to gorge ourselves on the good things of this world as though we would never have to render an account of our behavior to God? If we had listened to his teaching about the beauty of the world, would we have been led to leave the world more depleted, defiled, and ugly than it was before we came along? Is the ecological crisis, at least in the Western world, due to the fact that too many people followed Calvin's teaching about creation, or is it due to the fact that his teaching was apparently ignored?

37. Comm. on Genesis, argumentum, *CO* 23:7–8; CTS 1:60.
38. Comm. on Gen. 2:15, *CO* 23:44B; CTS 1:125.

12

Jesus Christ as the Living Image of God

According to Calvin, the living image of God in the universe would not be enough to lead us to eternal life with God. Since the fall of Adam into sin, the universe not only manifests the blessings of God; it also manifests the curse of God against sinful humanity. Once we see this curse in the fabric of the world, our consciences are awakened to the sin within us as being the reason God has disowned us as God's children. We therefore need another image of God to manifest God to us, one that takes away our sin and curse, and also restores to us all that we lost in Adam. "It is evident from this that we cannot believe in God except through Christ, in whom God in a manner makes himself little, in order to accommodate himself to our comprehension, and it is Christ alone who can make our consciences at peace, so that we may dare come in confidence to God."[1] The invisible God must appear to us in the flesh of

1. Comm. on 1 Pet. 1:20, *CO* 55:227A; *CNTC* 12:250.

This essay was originally published in a slightly different form under the title "Jesus Christ as the Image of God in Calvin's Theology," *Calvin Theological Journal* 25, no. 1 (1990): 45–62. Reprinted by permission.

Jesus Christ, the living image of God, if we are to be reconciled to God and united with God in eternal life.[2]

However, Calvin's understanding of the person of Christ has been the subject of intense interest and debate, both in the Reformation era and in the twentieth century. Calvin's rejection of the Lutheran use of the communication of properties, which was developed to undergird a Lutheran understanding of the real presence of Christ in the Lord's Supper, led to the charge that he had a Nestorian Christology that did not sufficiently address the unity of God and humanity in Jesus Christ and the subsequent glorification of his humanity in its hypostatic union with the eternal Son of God. In the twentieth century, the debate between Brunner and Barth regarding the relationship between the natural and revealed knowledge of God has polarized scholarship on Calvin between those who emphasize the revelation of God in creation and those who emphasize the revelation of God in Christ.[3] Also, theologians like Tillich have claimed that the theological tradition has emphasized incarnational Christology at the expense of Spirit Christology.[4] Finally, there is little or no consensus among Calvin scholars on the central christological motif of Calvin's theology: van Buren claims that it is "Christ in our place," while Peterson claims that there is no central motif.[5]

This chapter will address these conflicts of Calvin interpretation by focusing on the theme of Jesus Christ as the image of the invisible God, who reveals in his person, office, and work God the Father as the fountain of every good offered freely to sinful humanity. In light of this theme, it will be seen, first, that Calvin does in fact address the glorification of humanity in the incarnation, anointing, and ascension of Jesus Christ, and that it is precisely in light of this that he rejects the Lutheran understanding of the communication of properties. Second, Calvin has the

2. Stephen Edmondson claims that for Calvin, Christ is the image of God as a result of Christ's saving work as Mediator, which he takes to be the heart of Christ's work. I highlight Christ as the image of the invisible God because of its relationship to the self-revelation of God as the author and fountain of every good thing in creation. But Edmondson is certainly correct to note that Christ would not be the living image of God were he not also the Mediator. See Stephen Edmondson, *Calvin's Christology* (Cambridge: Cambridge University Press, 2004), 3, 176.

3. *Natural Theology: Comprising "Nature and Grace" by Emil Brunner and the Reply "No!" by Karl Barth*, trans. Peter Fraenkel (London: G. Bles, Centenary, 1946); Edward A. Dowey Jr., *The Knowledge of God in Calvin's Theology*, 2nd ed. (New York: Columbia University Press, 1952); T. H. L. Parker, *Calvin's Doctrine of the Knowledge of God* (Edinburgh: Oliver & Boyd, 1969).

4. Paul Tillich, *Systematic Theology*, vol. 2 (Chicago: University of Chicago Press, 1957), 145–50.

5. Paul van Buren, *Christ in Our Place: The Substitutionary Character of Calvin's Doctrine of Reconciliation* (Grand Rapids: Eerdmans, 1957); Robert A. Peterson, *Calvin's Doctrine of the Atonement* (Phillipsburg, NJ: Presbyterian & Reformed, 1983).

same theological epistemology in his understanding of the revelation of God in creation and in Jesus Christ. Third, Calvin combines a traditional incarnational Christology with a Spirit Christology. Finally, Jesus Christ as the image of the Father is the central theme of Calvin's Christology, unifying his discussion of the person, office, and work of Christ.

The Image of God as "God Manifested in the Flesh"

Calvin's understanding of Jesus Christ is rooted in the description of Christ found in the confession of faith in 1 Timothy: "God was manifested in the flesh" (1 Tim. 3:16 as in some MSS). This confession lies behind Calvin's understanding of Jesus Christ both as the self-revelation of God the Father (Christ as the image of the invisible God) and as the Mediator between God and humanity (Christ as prophet, king, and priest). Thus, Calvin begins his discussion of the person and work of Christ in the 1559 *Institutes* with a statement that is in accord with the Definition of Chalcedon, but which Calvin interprets in light of 1 Tim. 3:16: "Now it has been of the greatest importance for us that he who was to be our Mediator be both true God and true [hu]man."[6] Calvin does not, like Anselm, argue for the necessity of Christ as true God and true human apart from Christ—on the basis of what must obtain if there is to be reconciliation between God and sinful humanity—but rather on the basis of the free decision of God the Father. "If someone asks why this was necessary, there has been no simple (to use the common expression) or absolute necessity. Rather, it stemmed from a heavenly decree, on which men's salvation depended. Our most merciful Father decreed what was

6. *Inst.* 2.12.1, *OS* 3:437.3–4; LCC 1:464. It should be noted that both E. David Willis and Wilhelm Niesel emphasize the centrality of the theme of "God manifested in the flesh" in Calvin's Christology. However, neither of them associates this theme with that of Christ as "the image of the invisible God" (Col. 1:15), as this chapter will do; and so they miss the relationship between Calvin's Christology and the epistemology he develops in book 1 of the *Institutes* regarding how we come to a true knowledge of God, along with the way in which Calvin understands Christ as the fountain of every good thing [*fons omnium bonorum*], who reveals the Father to us in his humanity. See E. David Willis, *Calvin's Catholic Christology* (Leiden: Brill, 1966), 60–100; Wilhelm Niesel, *The Theology of Calvin*, trans. Harold Knight (Grand Rapids: Baker, 1980), 110–19. The same problem emerges in the discussion of the knowledge of God in Dowey and Parker. Dowey completely skips any discussion of Jesus Christ in his discussion of the knowledge of God and therefore misses the object of faith in Calvin's theology. By speaking repeatedly of Christ as the image of the Father [*imago patris*], Parker comes the closest to the position set forth here, but he does not understand that image in light of the Father as the fountain of every good thing in Jesus Christ and so fails to link the knowledge of God in Jesus Christ with the knowledge of God the Creator. See Dowey, *Knowledge of God in Calvin's Theology*, esp. chap. 4; and Parker, *Calvin's Doctrine of the Knowledge of God*, esp. chap. 5.

best for us."[7] The decree of the Father has as its goal the adoption of sinners as children of God, and it is in light of this decree that the Son of God became human in Jesus Christ.[8]

Even though it is impossible to establish an external necessity for the fact that the Mediator must be both true God and true human, or God manifested in the flesh, apart from the decree of the Father, it is still possible to understand why God willed that our Mediator be the incarnate Son of God. On the one hand, we can understand the incarnation in light of the way in which human beings as creatures of God—even apart from their sinfulness—come to know God. According to Calvin, we cannot know God the Creator in his essence, but must instead come to know him through the manifestation of his powers. "For the Lord manifests himself by his powers, the force of which we feel within ourselves and the benefits of which we enjoy."[9] God depicts these powers of God—wisdom, righteousness, life, power, goodness, mercy, etc.—in the works of creation. "We must therefore admit that in God's individual works—but especially in them as a whole—that God's powers are depicted as in a painting."[10] This is true not only in terms of God's works of creation as a whole, but also in terms of humanity as a microcosm of creation and as the highest of God's works of creation.[11] True knowledge of God, which gives birth to piety and religion, is rooted in the awareness of the powers of God depicted in his works in creation. "For this sense of the powers of God is for us a fit teacher of piety, from which religion is born."[12] The testimony of Scripture and the Holy Spirit to God the Creator do not circumvent this way of knowing God, but instead correct our corrupted judgment of God's works so that we might become aware of the powers already depicted in those works, just as spectacles help those with poor eyesight to see more clearly and distinctly.[13] Thus, if the Father is to make himself known to the children of Adam, then he must do so by setting forth and depicting his powers in his works in the creaturely sphere (in the humanity of Jesus Christ). This is especially necessary after the fall, because our minds are even more bounded by carnality than they were at creation. "Otherwise, God's majesty is too lofty to be attained by mortal men, who are like grubs crawling upon the earth."[14]

7. *Inst.* 2.12.1, *OS* 3:437.4–8; LCC 1:464.

8. "Here, surely, the fall of Adam is not presupposed as preceding God's decree in time; but it is what God determined before all ages that is shown, when he willed to heal the misery of mankind" (*Inst.* 2.12.5, *OS* 3:442.37–39; LCC 1:469).

9. *Inst.* 1.5.9, *OS* 3:53.14–16; LCC 1:62.

10. *Inst.* 1.5.10, *OS* 3:54.19–21; LCC 1:63.

11. *Inst.* 1.5.3, *OS* 3:46–47; LCC 1:54.

12. *Inst.* 1.2.1, *OS* 3:35.2–3; LCC 1:41.

13. *Inst.* 1.6.1, *OS* 3:60–61; LCC 1:70.

14. *Inst.* 2.6.4, *OS* 3:325.20–22; LCC 1:346.

On the other hand, it is precisely because we are children of *Adam* that God must reveal himself as our Father not only in the creaturely sphere in general, but also in the life of a child of Adam in particular; for humanity, in the person of Adam, both received and lost all of the good spiritual things that the Father freely bestowed on us.

> Therefore, after the heavenly image was obliterated in him, he was not the only one to suffer this punishment—that, in place of wisdom, virtue, holiness, truth, and justice, with which adornments he had been clad, there came forth the most filthy plagues, blindness, impotence, impurity, vanity, and injustice—but he also entangled and immersed his offspring in the same miseries.[15]

Because we as human creatures have lost every good spiritual thing which God had bestowed upon us in Adam, and have subjected ourselves and creation to the curse of God because of our sin, the powers of God by which we might come to know God as Father again cannot be set forth in the works of creation in general, but must in particular be set forth in the life of a human being, in whom we are freed from all the evil things to which we have subjected ourselves, and in whom we find every good thing which we lost in Adam. Commenting on the description of Christ as "the heir of all things" (Heb. 1:1–2), Calvin says:

> The name "heir" is attributed to Christ as manifested in the flesh; for in being made man and putting on the same nature as us, He took on Himself this heirship, in order to restore to us what we had lost in Adam. In the beginning God had established man as His son to be the heir of all good things; but the first man by his sin alienated from God both himself and his posterity and deprived them both of the blessing of God and of all good things. We begin to enjoy the good things of God by right only when Christ, who is the heir of all things, admits us to His fellowship. He is heir so that He might make us wealthy by His riches.[16]

The Son of God becomes the Son of Adam, and therefore the Second Adam, in order to manifest God in the creaturely sphere by being the fountain of every good set forth by God the Father for sinful creatures, to restore to sinful humanity every good thing that it lost in Adam, and to free sinful humanity from every evil thing that it acquired in Adam.

Jesus Christ as God manifested in the flesh means Jesus Christ as the fountain of every good thing who reveals the invisible Father in his

15. *Inst*. 2.1.5, *OS* 3:232–33; LCC 1:246.
16. Comm. on Heb. 1:1–2, *CO* 55:10–11; *CNTC* 12:7.

humanity. It is in this sense that Calvin calls Jesus Christ "the image of the invisible God" (cf. Heb. 1:3; Col. 1:15). "For God would have remained hidden afar off if Christ's splendor had not beamed upon us. For this reason the Father laid up with his only-begotten Son all that he had to reveal himself in Christ so that Christ, by communicating his Father's benefits, might express the true image of his glory (cf. Heb. 1:3)."[17] God manifested in the flesh means that God the Father reveals himself to sinners in Jesus Christ by bestowing upon Christ every good thing which we lack, so that Christ might reveal the Father by himself being the fountain of every good thing to the children of Adam. "Moreover, if apart from God there is no salvation, no righteousness, no life, yet Christ contains all these in himself, God is certainly revealed."[18] To put this another way, by not only setting forth the good things which we lack, but by himself also revealing the *source* of every good thing, Jesus Christ not only sets forth the powers of God, but also sets forth God himself in his humanity, thereby truly being "God manifested in the flesh."

> The sum is, that God in Himself, that is, in His naked majesty, is invisible; and that not only to the physical eyes, but also to the human understanding; and that He is revealed to us in Christ alone, where we may behold Him as in a mirror. For in Christ He shows us His righteousness, goodness, wisdom, power, in short, His entire self. We must, therefore, take care not to seek Him elsewhere; for outside Christ, everything that claims to represent God will be an idol.[19]

God reveals himself as the Father of the children of Adam and Eve by sending his only-begotten Son to be the Second Adam, in order to manifest the fountain of every good in his humanity. In this way, Jesus Christ, as God manifested in the flesh, is the image of the invisible God, apart from whom it is impossible to know God as Father (as the fountain of every good).[20]

17. *Inst*. 3.2.1, *OS* 4:8.11–15; LCC 1:544.

18. *Inst*. 1.13.13, *OS* 3:125.34–36; LCC 1:137.

19. Comm. on Col. 1:15, *CO* 52:85–86; *CNTC* 11:308.

20. Calvin's rejection of images in the worship of God is based not only on God's infinite and spiritual essence (*Inst*. 1.13.1, *OS* 3:108–9; LCC 1:120–21), as it was for Zwingli, but also primarily on the fact that Jesus Christ *alone* is the image of the invisible God. All other images, and all other ways of imaging God, are idolatrous because God has set forth his image in Christ alone. "For Paul is not concerned here with those things which by communication belong also to creatures, but with the perfect wisdom, goodness, righteousness and power of God, for the representing of which no creature would suffice" (Comm. on Col. 1:15, *CO* 52:85; *CNTC* 11:308). Only God can represent God. Therefore, only *God incarnate* can give us the true image of the invisible God. Jesus Christ is therefore the one true *self-representation* of God.

The Image of God in the Wonderful Exchange

God not only must set forth every good thing that we lack in Jesus Christ but also must remove from us every evil thing to which we have subjected ourselves. Christ not only must bestow upon us the blessing of God but also must remove from us the curse of God; he not only must restore life, but also he must remove death; he not only must restore strength to us, but also he must take away our weakness; he not only must restore righteousness, but also he must remove our iniquity. Calvin calls the event in which evil is removed and good is restored in Jesus Christ the wonderful exchange, and it is central to his understanding of Christ as the Mediator between God and humanity.

> This is the wonderful exchange which, out of his measureless benevolence, he has made with us; that, becoming Son of man with us, he has made us sons of God with him; that, by his descent to earth, he has prepared an ascent to heaven for us; that, by taking on our mortality, he has conferred his immortality upon us; that, accepting our weakness, he has strengthened us by his power; that, receiving our poverty upon himself, he has transferred his wealth to us; that, taking the weight of our iniquity upon himself (which oppressed us), he has clothed us with his righteousness.[21]

The wonderful exchange means that the Son of God became human in order to bestow upon us every good thing that we lack by first removing from us every evil thing that we have. Only in this way could Christ reveal the invisible Father to sinners.

Calvin depicts Christ as the image of the invisible God, and as the fountain of every good, in three distinct but inseparable ways: in the event of the incarnation (the Son of God becoming the Son of humanity); in the event of his being anointed by the Holy Spirit (the threefold office of Christ); and in the events of his death, resurrection, ascension, and coming in judgment. All three ways depict Christ as the fountain of every good to sinners by means of the wonderful exchange: Christ takes away all the evil things that we have and gives us all the good things that we lack.

The Incarnation of the Son of God

In the event of the incarnation, the only-begotten Son of God becomes a child of Adam in order to bestow on us the benefit of being children of God, and to remove from us our sin, which makes us subject to

21. *Inst*. 4.17.2, *OS* 5:343–44; LCC 2:1362.

God's curse and condemned to eternal death. The only-begotten Son of God, who is the eternal king and head of the kingdom of God, took upon himself our mortal humanity in order to make the children of Adam into children of God, thereby bestowing on them the good that they lack. "His task was so to restore us to God's grace as to make of the children of men, children of God; the heirs of Gehenna, heirs of the heavenly kingdom. Who could have done this had not the self-same Son of God become the Son of man, and had not taken what was ours as to impart what was his to us, and to make what was his by nature ours by grace?"[22] By taking what is ours—our human nature—upon himself, the only-begotten Son of God freely bestows upon us by grace what is his alone by nature, to be a child of God.

Yet if this is the case, then Jesus Christ must be the only-begotten Son of God not only according to his divinity, but also according to his humanity: for he could not make us, who are only human, into children of God by grace if he were not the Son of God by nature even according to his humanity. "We therefore hold that Christ, as he is God and man, consisting of two natures united but not mingled, is our Lord and true Son of God even according to, but not by reason of, his humanity."[23] In this way, the humanity of Jesus Christ is distinguished from all other humanity, for he alone is Son of God by nature, while all others are adopted as children of God in him by grace. "We admit Christ is indeed called 'son' in human flesh; not as we believers are sons, by adoption and grace only, but the true and natural, and therefore the only, Son in order that by this mark he may be distinguished from all others."[24] The pledge that we human beings have been adopted as children of God in Jesus Christ lies in the fact that he is the only-begotten Son of God not only according to his divinity, but also according to his humanity.[25]

22. *Inst*. 2.12.2, *OS* 3:438.22–27; LCC 1:465.

23. *Inst*. 2.14.4, *OS* 3:463.14–18; LCC 1:486.

24. *Inst*. 2.14.6, *OS* 3:466.15–20; LCC 1:489.

25. It is important to emphasize this point in light of Calvin's disagreement with the Lutherans about the ubiquity of the humanity of Christ and the presence of Christ in the Supper. As this line of reasoning makes clear, Calvin has a very strong sense of the unity of the Son of God and the Son of humanity in Jesus Christ; for only on the basis of such a unity could Christ be the Son of God by nature even according to his humanity (*secundum humanitatem*). However, it is *precisely* because the humanity of Christ is the pledge of our adoption as children of God that the humanity of Christ must be of the same essence as ours and cannot be distinguished from ours by participating in and thereby taking on the properties of divinity—especially omnipresence—by the communication of properties (*communication idiomatum*), as the Lutherans contended. If Christ's *humanity* is not the same as ours, even though it alone can be called the Son of God by nature, then the incarnate Son of God cannot bestow the good of adoption on those who are *only* human.

However, Jesus Christ cannot be the Son of God by reason of his humanity, for that would be to annihilate his genuine humanity by divinizing it and would also deny the sheer grace of the Son of God assuming our human nature into hypostatic union with himself.[26] The human nature of Jesus receives a good that it can never claim as its possession, but can only receive as sheer grace, to be the only-begotten Son of God. For this reason Calvin agrees with Augustine that the assumption of the humanity of Jesus Christ into hypostatic union with the eternal Son of God is the best mirror of God's grace. "Now we confess that the Mediator, who was born of the virgin, is properly the Son of God. And the man Christ would not be mirror of God's inestimable grace unless this dignity had been conferred upon him, that he should both be the only-begotten Son of God and be so called."[27] On the one hand, therefore, the humanity of Jesus Christ is the *source* of our adoption, for our union with the one who is Son of God by nature according to his humanity is the pledge that we are children of God by grace. On the other hand, the humanity of Jesus Christ is the *mirror* of the free grace of adoption, for the dignity that the eternal Son of God bestows upon it, to be the Son of God by nature, is something that it can only receive as grace, and can never claim as its proper possession.

The incarnate Son of God can only bestow the grace of adoption on sinners if he also takes away the sin, guilt, and wrath of God which they inherit in Adam, through rendering the obedience to God that Adam refused to give, and by making satisfaction for his sin. "The second requirement of our reconciliation with God was this: that man, who by his disobedience had become lost, should by way of remedy counter it with obedience, satisfy God's judgment, and pay the penalties for sin."[28] It was necessary for Jesus Christ to be true human, for otherwise he could not have taken the place of Adam in obeying the Father and in subjecting our flesh to death in order to satisfy God's wrath; and yet it was also necessary that he be true God, for otherwise he could not triumph over the sin and death which he took upon himself. "In short, since neither as God alone could he feel death, nor as man alone could he overcome it, he coupled human nature with divine that to atone for sin he might submit the weakness of the one to death; and that, wrestling with death by the power of the other nature, he might win victory for us."[29] The Son of God in the humanity of Jesus Christ subjects himself to the curse and

26. Again, Calvin disagreed with the ontological way in which the Lutherans understood the communication of properties because it would deny both the genuine humanity of the incarnate Son of God, and the grace of the hypostatic union.

27. *Inst.* 2.14.5, *OS* 3:464–65; LCC 1:487–88.

28. *Inst.* 2.12.3, *OS* 3:439.21–24; LCC 1:466.

29. *Inst.* 2.12.3, *OS* 3:439–40; LCC 1:466.

wrath of God by taking our place as guilty sinners before the judgment seat of God, and he overcomes the power of sin, guilt, death, and the wrath of God by rising from the dead.

The event of the incarnation therefore sets forth Jesus Christ as the fountain of every good by means of the wonderful exchange. The Son of God became the Son of humanity in order to bestow on us the good of being children of God through our adoption in the one who is Son of God by nature even according to his humanity; and as the Son of humanity the Son of God takes the place of Adam in obeying the will of the Father, and in taking upon himself our sin, guilt, curse, and death, so that his victory over these evils might be ours. In the event of the incarnation, Jesus Christ represents the fountain of every good and is therefore the image of the invisible God, for in him alone do we find freedom from sin and death and the power to become children of God and heirs of the kingdom of God.

The Anointing of Jesus as the Christ

Jesus is further known as the image of the Father in the event of his anointing by the Holy Spirit into the threefold office of Christ (prophet, king, and priest). Calvin makes it clear that the anointing by the Spirit sets forth Christ as the fountain of every good. "Christ was filled with the Holy Spirit and loaded with a perfect abundance of gifts, that he might impart them to us. . . . So from him as the only source we draw whatever spiritual blessings we possess."[30] To call Jesus the Christ is the same as to call him the fountain of every spiritual blessing that the Father wills to give us, according to Calvin.[31]

Calvin claims that the term "Messiah" especially refers to the office of Christ as king, but it also refers to Christ as prophet and priest. As the one anointed by the Spirit to be prophet, Jesus Christ is the last of the prophets to bear witness to the Father; he is also the consummation of all prophecy. The prophetic office of Christ not only refers to the actual preaching and witness of Jesus himself, but also refers to the preaching of the gospel through the power of the Holy Spirit from Pentecost to the last day. Christ as prophet bears witness to the Father not by pointing us directly to the Father—for the Father is hidden in majesty and cannot be directly known—but rather by pointing to himself as the one in whom the Father has deposited every good thing. Thus, Christ as prophet bears witness to himself as the image of the invisible God, so

30. *Geneva Catechism, CO* 6:22; *Calvin: Theological Treatises*, 95.

31. Thus Calvin shows, contrary to Tillich (*Systematic Theology*, 2:149), that a traditional Chalcedonian Christology can be combined with an "adoptionist" Spirit Christology.

that we might have faith in Christ as the fountain of every good through the preaching of the gospel and the illumination of the Holy Spirit.[32] Far from playing a tangential role in his theology, it is more accurate to say that without the prophetic office of Christ, Christ as the fountain of every good would profit no one.[33]

The central element of Christ's threefold office is that of king. Christ is not a king who rules us by giving us temporal blessings and peace; rather, he gives us spiritual blessing and peace while we labor under temporal hardship and the cross, just as Christ did not ascend to the right hand of the Father before he had first been crucified. Christ gives us the power to endure the cross in this life so that we might inherit the kingdom of God, by sharing with us the Spirit that he has abundantly received from the Father. "For the Spirit has chosen Christ as his seat, that from him might abundantly flow the heavenly riches of which we are in such need. Thus, believers stand unconquered through the strength of their king, and his spiritual riches abound in them. Hence, they are justly called Christians."[34]

Christ as king is therefore both the fountain from which flows to us the Holy Spirit, and the Lord who rules over both heaven and earth, especially the godly, whom he governs by his Spirit. It is clear that Calvin considers Christ as Lord primarily in terms of his humanity. "Further, we must note that He has been appointed Lord and supreme King so that He may be the Father's Vice-regent, so to speak, in the governing of the world. . . . Of course we acknowledge that God is the Ruler, but His rule is actualized in the man Christ."[35] The exaltation of Jesus Christ to the right hand of the Father not only means that Christ is the king who bestows on us the Holy Spirit, but it also means that he is the one who exercises lordship in the place of the Father, and who will punish every

---

32. Barth raises the question of whether Calvin understands Jesus Christ not only as prophet but also as the *subject matter* of the prophecy: "What was supposed to be the theme and content of the prophetic or revelatory action in Jesus Christ?" As this chapter makes clear, the content of Jesus's testimony as prophet is Jesus Christ himself as the image of the invisible God, in material agreement with Barth. See Karl Barth, *Church Dogmatics* IV/3, first half, trans. G. W. Bromiley (Edinburgh: Clark, 1961), 13–18.

33. J. F. Jansen makes the claim that the prophetic office of Christ is tangential at best and not integrated into the fabric of Calvin's thought. Jansen fails to see that Christ as prophet sets forth Christ as the fountain of every good thing in the preaching of the gospel, and it is Christ as fountain who is the object of faith, through whom alone we know God as Father and from whom flows the twofold grace of justification and sanctification. Without the prophetic office of Christ, in other words, there would be no preaching of the gospel and, hence, no faith. Far from being tangential to Calvin's thought, the prophetic office of Christ is foundational to books 3 and 4 of the 1559 *Institutes*. See J. F. Jansen, *Calvin's Doctrine of the Work of Christ* (London: Clarke, 1956).

34. *Inst*. 2.15.5, *OS* 3:478.6–8; LCC 1:500.

35. Comm. on 1 Cor. 15:27, *CO* 49:549; *CNTC* 9:327.

disobedience, not only now, but also at the last judgment.[36] Christ as king thus corresponds with the incarnation of the Son of God. Christ the king is not only the fountain from which the Holy Spirit flows to us, but he is also the human who has been exalted to a dignity that could only be bestowed upon him by the grace of God, to be the Lord at the right hand of the Father.

The third office that Christ received from the Father is that of priest. If the office of king has to do with the actual bestowal of every spiritual good, the office of priest has to do with the removal of every spiritual evil. Christ as priest makes the expiation for our sins that is necessary if God is to regard sinners as his children, and if they are to know him as their Father. Calvin bases his understanding of Christ as priest almost entirely on Heb. 7–10, where Christ is set forth as having made the once-for-all expiatory sacrifice for our sins by his death on the cross. "To sum up his argument: the priestly office belongs to Christ alone because by the sacrifice of his death he blotted out our guilt and made satisfaction for our sins."[37] Even though Calvin discusses this office of Christ last, this is not done to diminish its importance, for it is the "principal point on which . . . our whole salvation turns," for without Christ as priest atoning for our sins with his sacrifice, we would not be able to know or call upon God as Father.[38]

Christ as priest thus corresponds to the incarnate Son of God, who takes the place of Adam in obeying the Father and in taking our sins upon himself in order to remove them from us. Christ as priest also represents the other half of the wonderful exchange: for as priest Christ removes from us every evil thing that we have (sin, guilt, eternal death, and wrath) in order as king to bestow on us every good thing that we lack (the grace of the Holy Spirit and the inheritance of the kingdom of God).[39]

The Saving Work of Jesus Christ

Calvin's discussion of the incarnation and anointing of Christ have as their object the setting forth of Christ as the fountain of every good offered to sinners by the Father in the wonderful exchange. "What we

36. *Inst.* 2.15.5, *OS* 3:479; LCC 1:501.
37. *Inst.* 2.15.6, *OS* 3:480.12–15; LCC 1:502.
38. *Inst.* 2.15.6, *OS* 3:480.18–21; LCC 1:502.
39. "In the praise of Christ is comprehended His eternal Kingdom and Priesthood, that He reconciles God to us and wins perfect righteousness, expiating our sins by His sacrifice, that He keeps His own, whom He has received into His trust and care, and adorns and enriches us with every kind of blessing" (Comm. on Matt. 16:16, *CO* 45:472–73; *CNTC* 2:185).

have said so far concerning Christ must be referred to this one objective: condemned, dead, and lost in ourselves, we should seek righteousness, liberation, life, and salvation in him, as we are taught in that well-known saying of Peter: 'There is no other name under heaven given to men in which we must be saved' (Acts 4:12)."[40] However, thus far Calvin has primarily discussed the *person* of the Mediator, both as the incarnate Son of God and as the anointed Christ. In order to make it clear that the totality of what we as sinners lack in ourselves is found in Jesus Christ alone, it is necessary to discuss the saving *work* of Christ, especially his death, resurrection, ascension, and coming in judgment. "But here we must earnestly ponder how he accomplishes salvation for us. This we must do not only to be persuaded that he is its author, but also to gain a sufficient and stable support for our faith, rejecting whatever could draw us away in one direction or another."[41] We do not fully know Jesus Christ as the image of the invisible God until we know how he won salvation for us.

On the basis of Rom. 5:19—"For as by one man's disobedience many were made sinners, so by one man's obedience many will be made righteous" (RSV)—Calvin states that the way in which Christ has accomplished the wonderful exchange is "by the whole course of his obedience."[42] Although the whole of Christ's life was one of willing obedience to the will of the Father, Calvin nonetheless sees the heart of that obedience in his free sacrifice of himself for our sins on the cross. "And we must hold fast to this: that no proper sacrifice to God could have been offered unless Christ, disregarding his own feelings, subjected and yielded himself wholly to his Father's will."[43] By obeying the will of the Father to take the place of condemned sinners, Christ not only takes away all of our sin and guilt, but also renders the obedience by which we might be reckoned as righteous before God.[44]

The sacrifice that expiates our sins takes place when the incarnate Son of God takes our sin, guilt, and condemnation upon himself, and in this way he makes satisfaction for our sins.[45] This is graphically de-

---

40. *Inst.* 2.16.1, *OS* 3:481–82; LCC 1:503.

41. *Inst.* 2.16.1, *OS* 3:483.1–5; LCC 1:504.

42. *Inst.* 2.16.5, *OS* 3:486.1–2; LCC 1:507.

43. *Inst.* 2.16.5, *OS* 3:487.7–9; LCC 1:508.

44. *Inst.* 2.17.5, *OS* 3:512–14; LCC 1:532–34.

45. In this I am in agreement with van Buren: "Satisfaction was accomplished by substitution" (*Christ in Our Place*, 78). "God indeed wishes to remit our sins of His free goodness, but yet the price of our redemption was paid in the person of His only Son. Now we here have to observe that it is because our Lord Jesus suffered condemnation that we are delivered and absolved and that our faults are so buried as not to be taken into account by God. When we speak of the forgiveness of sins, it is not that God clears us because we have paid and satisfied Him. He acts from pure liberality" (sermon on Isa.

picted in the New Testament accounts of Jesus's trial and condemnation before Pilate. On the one hand, Jesus's arraignment and condemnation testify that he took the place of guilty sinners; yet Pilate's testimony to his innocence attests that he was condemned for our sin and guilt, not his own. "Thus we shall behold the person of a sinner and evildoer represented in Christ, yet from his shining innocence it will at the same time be obvious that he was burdened with another's sin rather than his own."[46] Thus, the condemnation of Jesus Christ before the judgment seat of Pilate testifies that in him the Son of God has himself taken our place as sinners condemned before the judgment seat of God, and has forgiven our sins by taking our guilt upon himself. "This is our acquittal: the guilt that held us liable for punishment has been transferred to the head of the Son of God (Isa. 53:12)."[47] If Christ has taken our sin and guilt upon himself, then it necessarily follows that he has subjected himself to the curse of God, which would otherwise lie upon us due to our sins. That Christ did take upon himself the curse of God is openly attested by his death on the cross, for the cross is accursed by both human and divine judgment. "Hence, when Christ is hanged upon the cross, he makes himself subject to the curse. It had to happen in this way in order that the whole curse—which on account of our sins awaited us, or rather lay upon us—might be lifted from us, while it was transferred to him."[48] To say that the death of Christ satisfies the wrath of God does not mean that it changes God's will from wrath to mercy by paying satisfaction to the justice of God, but rather means that the wrath and curse of God have been transferred from us to the incarnate Son of God.[49]

Christ's death on the cross also indicates that Christ took upon himself the death to which we subjected ourselves by our sin and guilt. "Death held us captive under its yoke; Christ, in our stead, gave himself over to

53:4–6, *CO* 35:626; *Sermons on Isaiah's Prophecy of the Death and Passion of Christ*, trans. T. H. L. Parker [London: Clarke, 1956], 72–73). Contrast this statement of Calvin's with the principle of satisfaction in Anselm: "Nothing is less tolerable in the order of things, than for the creature to take away the honor due to the Creator and not repay what he takes away" (*Cur Deus homo* 1.13; *A Scholastic Miscellany: Anselm to Ockham*, trans. Eugene Fairweather [New York: Macmillan, 1970], 122).

46. *Inst.* 2.16.5, *OS* 3:489.10–13; LCC 1:509.

47. *Inst.* 2.16.5, *OS* 3:489.16–18; LCC 1:509–10.

48. *Inst.* 2.16.6, *OS* 3:489.23–27; LCC 1:510.

49. Calvin has a full discussion of the relation of the death of Christ to the love of God. On the one hand, the death of Christ is the manifestation of the love of the Father for sinners, in that he sends the Son to take the place of sinners on the cross. On the other hand, the love of God is grounded in the death of Christ on the cross, for only in light of that death can God fully accept sinners into fellowship with himself, and only in light of that death can sinners be assured that God is their Father, since it is there that their sins have been forgiven. See *Inst.* 2.16.1–4, *OS* 3:481–85; LCC 1:503–7.

its power to deliver us from it."[50] However, it is not primarily physical death that afflicts us, but eternal death under the rejection and damnation of God. If Christ genuinely took our place, then he must have subjected himself to our eternal rejection and damnation by God. This is attested by the cry of dereliction on the cross: "My God, my God, why have you forsaken me?" (Matt. 27:46). "This is what we are saying. He bore the weight of divine severity, since he was 'stricken and afflicted' (Isa. 53:5) by God's hand, and experienced all the signs of a wrathful and avenging God."[51] If we do not maintain this, then we do not know how much it cost the Son of God to obtain our salvation. We cannot take our place in heaven unless the Son of God takes our place in hell.

The obedience of Jesus Christ unto death on the cross fulfills the first half of the wonderful exchange, whereby all the evils that separate us from God are transferred from us to the incarnate Son of God. However, the victory of the Son of God over all of those evils is accomplished in his resurrection from the dead. "Therefore, we divide the substance of our salvation between Christ's death and resurrection as follows: through his death, sin was wiped out and death extinguished; through his resurrection, righteousness was restored and life raised up, so that—thanks to his resurrection—his death manifested its power and efficacy in us."[52] If the death of Jesus Christ represents the fulfillment of the removal of all evil from us, then the resurrection represents the beginning of the bestowal of every good thing upon us. Just as Christ by his death takes our sin on himself, so by rising he bestows his righteousness upon us; as his death means the putting to death of the old person of sin, so his resurrection means the bestowal of newness of life upon us; and as his death means that we no longer need to fear death, so his resurrection is the pledge of our resurrection from the dead.

However, it is especially Christ's ascension to and session at the right hand of the Father that truly begins the bestowal of all good things upon us; for it is in his ascension that he inaugurates his kingdom. "Now having laid aside the mean and lowly state of mortal life and the shame of the cross, Christ by rising again began to show forth his glory and power more fully. Yet he truly inaugurated his Kingdom only at his ascension into heaven."[53] In particular, it is only in his ascension into heaven that Jesus Christ exercises his office as king, not only by governing heaven and earth as the vice-regent of the Father but also primarily by bestowing the Holy Spirit, which he himself received from the Father, upon the elect. "For the chief glory of Christ's Kingdom is that He governs the church

50. *Inst.* 2.16.7, *OS* 3:491.12–14; LCC 1:511.
51. *Inst.* 2.16.11, *OS* 3:496.21–23; LCC 1:517.
52. *Inst.* 2.16.13, *OS* 3:500.12–16; LCC 1:521.
53. *Inst.* 2.16.14, *OS* 3:501.22–25; LCC 1:522.

by His Spirit. But he entered into lawful and, as it were, ceremonial possession of His Kingdom when he was exalted to the right hand of the Father."[54] The exalted humanity of Jesus Christ is the pledge that we also will inherit the kingdom of God, of which he is the king even according to his humanity; and the exalted humanity of Jesus is also the fountain from which we receive the Holy Spirit, which both protects us from our enemies—sin, the world, and Satan—and brings us to the inheritance of the kingdom by newness of life. However, as the lifelong obedience of Christ is fulfilled in his death on the cross, so the bestowal of every good thing by our king will only be fulfilled on the last day. On that day all of the good things that we are promised in Christ, and that we know to be in him as the fountain of every good, will actually be bestowed on us. "Moreover, he who now promises eternal blessedness through the gospel will then fulfill the promise in judgment."[55] Until that day, faith must always be buttressed by hope. "Although, therefore, Christ offers us in the gospel a present fullness of spiritual benefits, the enjoyment thereof ever lies hidden under the guardianship of hope, until, having put off corruptible flesh, we be transfigured in the glory of him who goes before us."[56]

The Image of the Father Illumined by the Spirit

The whole of Calvin's Christology—the incarnation, the anointing, and the death, resurrection, ascension, and coming in judgment—has as its purpose and goal the depiction of Christ as the fountain of every good offered to sinners by the Father in the wonderful exchange. In Christ we find deliverance from all that oppresses us, reconciliation with God, and the bestowal of every good thing that we need to inherit the kingdom of God as children of God. "In short, since rich store of every good abounds in him, let us drink our fill from this fountain, and from no other."[57] Jesus Christ is therefore the image of the invisible God, who reveals the Father to sinners, especially in his office and work as king and priest. However, this does not mean that Calvin downplays Christ in his office as prophet. For even though the fountain of every good is in fact found in Jesus Christ alone, that fountain benefits no one to whom it is not offered, or who does not accept it by faith; and it is precisely Christ as prophet who offers himself to us as the image of the Father, the fountain of every good, in the preaching of the gospel. "That is, outside Christ

54. Comm. on John 7:38, *CO* 47:182; *CNTC* 4:199.
55. *Inst.* 2.16.18, *OS* 3:506.5–7; LCC 1:526.
56. *Inst.* 2.9.3, *OS* 3:400–401; LCC 1:426.
57. *Inst.* 2.16.19, *OS* 3:508.15–17; LCC 1:528.

there is nothing worth knowing, and all who by faith perceive what he is like have grasped the whole immensity of heavenly benefits. For this reason, Paul writes in another passage: 'I decided to know nothing precious . . . except Jesus Christ and him crucified' (1 Cor. 2:2)."[58]

The revelation of the Father in Christ as the image of God should not, however, be taken to mean that human beings can come to know God as Father in Christ alone and his gospel, apart from the illumination of the Holy Spirit. This is true not only because of the blindness of our minds due to sin, but also because the fountain of every good is set forth in Jesus Christ *crucified*.[59] The revelation of the Father in the Son is incomplete without the revelation of the Son by the illumination of the Holy Spirit.

> It all comes back to this: It is the Father's gift that the Son is known, for by his Spirit He opens the eyes of our minds and we perceive the glory of Christ which would otherwise be hidden from us. But the Father, who dwells in light inaccessible and is in Himself incomprehensible, is revealed to us by the Son, His lively image, and in vain do we seek Him elsewhere.[60]

Although we have argued throughout that the heart of Calvin's Christology centers on Jesus Christ as the image of God the Father, in whom alone the Father is represented and made known to sinners, we conclude by being reminded that the self-revelation of God is trinitarian, according to Calvin, and cannot leave out of account the illumination of the Holy Spirit. The self-representation of the Father in Jesus Christ, his image, is itself revealed only by the illumination of the Spirit, which the Father only bestows upon those whom he has chosen. The God who represents himself as the Father of all sinners in Jesus Christ is only truly known as Father by the elect, for they alone seek to know him in Christ his living image. "It has been said that we must be drawn by the Spirit to be aroused to seek Christ; so, in turn, we must be warned that the invisible Father is to be sought solely in this image."[61] Only the Holy Spirit brings about the knowledge of, and participation in, the fountain of every good set forth in Jesus Christ through the wonderful exchange. For those lacking the illumination of the Spirit, the fountain of every good found in Christ is of no profit.[62] The ultimate source of every good thing that the Father

58. *Inst.* 2.15.2, *OS* 3:474.10–14; LCC 1:496.
59. For our inability to know Christ as the image of God because of our sin, see *Inst.* 2.2.20, *OS* 3:262–63; LCC 1:278–80; for our inability due to the image being Christ crucified, see *Inst.* 2.6.1; *De scandalis*, *OS* 2:172–73; LCC 1:340–42.
60. Comm. on Matt. 11:27, *CO* 45:320; *CNTC* 2:24.
61. *Inst.* 3.2.1, *OS* 4:8–9; LCC 1:544.
62. *Inst.* 3.1.1, *OS* 4:1–2; LCC 1:537–38.

offers to sinners in Jesus Christ, his image, through the illumination of the Holy Spirit is therefore the eternal election of the Father.[63]

Conclusion

According to Calvin, Jesus Christ is the image of the invisible God, the one true representation of God the Father as the fountain of every good to sinners. As such, Jesus Christ both takes from us every evil thing that we have, and bestows upon us every good thing that we lack, through the wonderful exchange. By focusing on Jesus Christ as the image of God in the wonderful exchange, Calvin can unite several aspects of the person and work of Christ—the incarnation of the Son of God, his anointing by the Spirit as the Christ, and his obedience to the Father—into a unified presentation of Christ and his significance for us. In the process, Calvin can demonstrate, against the Lutheran criticism of his Christology, that he does emphasize the unity of the person of Jesus as the basis of the wonderful exchange, and the glorification of his humanity as its result, and yet precisely on that basis rejects the Lutheran conception of the communication of properties. Calvin can also use the theme of Jesus Christ as the image of God to unite the way we come to know God the Creator with the way we know God the Redeemer—through the awareness of the powers of God depicted in the works of God in the world—thereby freeing the interpretation of Calvin's theology from a false dichotomy. Finally, Calvin can unite the Christology of Chalcedon with a Spirit Christology in a way apparently unknown to Tillich. In sum, by seeing Jesus Christ as the image of the Father as the center of Calvin's Christology, over against the claim that there is no such center, we can free ourselves from three false dichotomies that have plagued the interpretation of the theology of Calvin; thereby we can come to a better assessment of the kind of influence that his Christology might have on our own.

63. *Inst.* 3.21.1, *OS* 4:369.10–14; LCC 2:921: "We shall never be clearly persuaded, as we ought to be, that our salvation flows from the wellspring [*ex fonte*] of God's free mercy until we come to know his eternal election, which illumines God's grace by this contrast: that he does not indiscriminately adopt all into the hope of salvation but gives to some what he denies to others."

Conclusion

John Calvin began his writing career as a highly learned person who accommodated his commentary on Seneca's treatise *On Clemency* to those he termed "the best," meaning the most learned members of European society. However, after his "sudden conversion to teachableness," this learned person dedicated the rest of his considerable literary endeavors to teaching those whom he considered to be the most unlearned members of European society, those he termed "ordinary Christians." Calvin set in place both teachers and pastors and wrote works guiding each of them, so that ordinary Christians might be guided in their reading of Scripture. The production of several editions of the *Institutes*, the commentaries on most of the books of the Bible, the three editions of his *Catechism*, and the hundreds of sermons that he preached—all were meant to restore the reading of Scripture, "the book of the unlearned," to every member of the Christian community. Calvin sought to transform the church into "the school of Christ" in which students would eventually be able to instruct their teachers, and teachers would be willing to learn from their students, as all sought to be instructed by Christ.

However, for all his interest in teaching, preaching, and reading, Calvin also sought to direct his fellow believers to the pious contemplation of the many "living images of God," in which the invisible God becomes somewhat visible to us, so that we might come to know God according to our own creaturely capacities. For all of his interest in allowing all Christians to inquire into the truth of the Word of God, Calvin was also aware that God manifests Godself in the beauty and glory of God's works, in which the powers of God are portrayed as in a painting. Teachers and students in the school of Christ not only need to inquire into the meaning of Scripture; they also need to behold, feel, and enjoy the powers of God portrayed in the universe, in themselves, and especially in Christ, the visible image of the invisible God. We only truly know God when we behold with our eyes the images of God's goodness about which we also hear with our ears, so that we might move by analogy and anagoge from the earthly symbols of God's goodness and love to the invisible reality of that love. Calvin cleared the church of all images created by human imagination so that the godly might directly contemplate the living images of God in creation and Christ, including the sermon, the sacraments, the rites and ceremonies of worship, and even one another. We concluded by looking at the most prominent of these images, the universe and Jesus Christ, leaving a fuller examination of this theme to another work.[1]

This work has examined Calvin's method as a teacher and a pastor, seeking to understand the intended audience for each genre of instruction and recognize the objectives Calvin sought to accomplish in each work. However, a fuller examination of Calvin's work as a teacher would have to include his polemical writings and his correspondence with the teachers of his day other than Philip Melanchthon, such as Heinrich Bullinger, Martin Bucer, Peter Vermigli, and his own successor, Théodore de Bèze. Finally, such a treatment would have to include a discussion of the creation of the Geneva Academy in 1559.[2] Moreover, we have examined Calvin's work as a pastor primarily insofar as a pastor is a teacher of his congregation. A fuller understanding of Calvin as pastor would have to look at his involvement in the Congregation and the Company of Pastors, as well as his work with the Consistory.[3] Calvin was also directly involved in the reform of the worship life of Geneva, which could be the subject of a study unto

1. Randall C. Zachman, *Image and Word in the Theology of John Calvin* (Notre Dame: University of Notre Dame Press, forthcoming).

2. Karin Maag, *Seminary or University? The Genevan Academy and Reformed Higher Education, 1560–1620*, St. Andrews Studies in Reformation History (Aldershot, UK: Scolar; Brookfield, VT: Ashgate, 1995).

3. Robert Kingdon, "Catechesis in Calvin's Geneva," in *Educating People of Faith: Exploring the History of Jewish and Christian Communities*, ed. John van Engen (Grand Rapids: Eerdmans, 2004), 294–313; Thomas A. Lambert, "Preaching, Praying, and Policing the Reform in Sixteenth-Century Geneva" (Ph.D. diss., University of Wisconsin–Madison, 1998); *Registers of the Consistory of Geneva in the Time of Calvin*, vol. 1, *1542–1544*, ed. Robert Kingdon, Thomas Lambert, and Isabella Watt, trans. M. Wallace McDonald (Grand Rapids: Eerdmans, 1996); John Witte Jr. and Robert M. Kingdon, *Sex, Marriage, and Family in John Calvin's Geneva*, vol. 1, *Courtship, Engagement, and Marriage* (Grand Rapids: Eerdmans, 2005); Eric de Boer, "The Congregation: An In-Service Training Center for Preachers to the People of Geneva," in *Calvin and the Company of Pastors*, ed. David Foxgrover (Grand Rapids: CRC Product Services, 2004).

itself.[4] However, this study has attempted primarily to be a guide to the best-known Calvin writings, most of which are available in English—the *Institutes*, commentaries, catechisms, and sermons—in order to understand their place in the curriculum Calvin tirelessly created for the school of Christ.

4. Elsie McKee, *John Calvin: Writings on Pastoral Piety*, Classics of Western Spirituality (New York: Paulist Press, 2001).

SCRIPTURE INDEX

Genesis

1:16   123
1:26   232, 233
17:9   64, 108
28:12   223

Exodus

25:40   221, 222
34:6–7   214

Deuteronomy

10:16   144

2 Samuel

12:25   110n16

Psalms

24:1   233
45   109n16
51:4   184
77:7   214
77:9   215
77:14   215n28
79   118n50
84:2   221
104:1   179, 180
104:1–2   237

Isaiah

14:2   110

14:12   110
14:22   110
40:18   217n38
53   55, 71–75, 223
53:2   195
53:4   74, 144
53:4–5   71
53:4–7   71
53:5   72, 257
53:5–6   71
53:6   72
53:9   112
53:12   256
54:13   80n12
65:7   109

Jeremiah

4:4   144
17:11   123
23:22   109
23:28   110
24:6   111
30:4–6   111
31:9   217

Ezekiel

21–48   12
34:2–4   61n27

Daniel

2   120

Hosea

14:9   127

Joel

2:28   56–57

Amos

5:8   123

Zephaniah

1:12   215n31

Zechariah

9:16   119n55

Malachi

1:6   217

Matthew

7:11   218
8:17   223
11:27   182
16:16   254n39
27:46   257

Luke

1:37   184

John

1:1   215

Subject Index